Botanic Garden and The Domain

Kings Cross and Darlinghurst

Paddington

OTANIC GARDEN
ND THE DOMAIN

KINGS CROSS
AND
DARLINGHURST

PADDINGTON

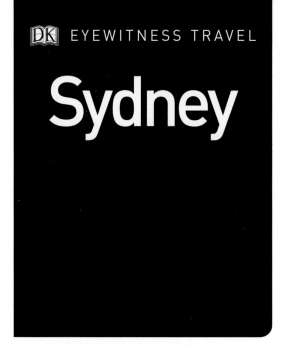

DK EYEWITNESS TRAVEL

Sydney

DK EYEWITNESS TRAVEL

Sydney

Main Contributors **Ken Brass, Kirsty McKenzie &
Deborah Soden**

Penguin
Random
House

Produced by The Watermark Press, Sydney,
Australia
Project Editor Siobhán O'Connor
Art Editor Claire Edwards
Editors Robert Coupe, Leith Hillard,
Jane Sheard
Designers Katie Peacock, Claire Ricketts,
Noel Wendtman

Dorling Kindersley Limited
Senior Editor Fay Franklin
Senior Art Editor Jane Ewart
Senior Revisions Editor Esther Labi

Contributors
Anna Bruechert, John Dengate,
Carrie Hutchinson, Graham Jahn,
Kim Saville, Susan Skelly, Deborah Soden

Photographers
Max Alexander, Simon Blackall, Michael
Nicholson, Rob Reichenfeld, Alan Williams

Illustrators
Richard Draper, Stephen Gyapay, Alex Lavroff
Associates, The Overall Picture, Robbie Polley

Printed and bound in China

First American edition 1996
17 18 19 20 10 9 8 7 6 5 4 3 2 1

Published in the United States by
DK Publishing, 345 Hudson Street, New York,
New York 10014

**Reprinted with revisions 1997, 1999,
2000, 2001, 2002 (twice), 2003, 2005,
2006, 2008, 2009, 2010, 2015, 2017**
Copyright 1996, 2017 © Dorling Kindersley
Limited, London
A Penguin Random House Company

Published in the UK by Dorling
Kindersley Limited.

A catalog record for this book is available
from the Library of Congress.
ISSN 1542-1554
ISBN 978-1-46546-132-2

Floors are referred to throughout in
accordance with European usage, i.e., the
"first floor" is the floor above ground level.

Introducing
Sydney

Sydney Area by
Area

Sydney Harbour Bridge

**The information in this
DK Eyewitness Travel Guide is checked regularly.**
Every effort has been made to ensure that this book is as up-to-date as possible
at the time of going to press. Some details, however, such as telephone numbers,
opening hours, prices, gallery hanging arrangements and travel information are
liable to change. The publishers cannot accept responsibility for any consequences
arising from the use of this book, nor for any material on third party websites, and
cannot guarantee that any website address in this book will be a suitable source of
travel information. We value the views and suggestions of our readers very highly.
Please write to: Publisher, DK Eyewitness Travel Guides, Dorling Kindersley,
80 Strand, London, WC2R 0RL, UK, or email: travelguides@dk.com.

◀ **Title page** Sydney Opera House, photographed from the east, shortly after sunrise **Front cover image** Sydney Opera House with
Sydney Harbour Bridge in the background **Back cover image** Sydney panorama from Mosman Bay

Contents

Detail of bench mosaic at Bondi Beach

Three Sisters rock formation, Blue Mountains

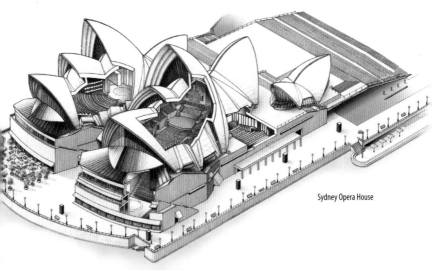

Sydney Opera House

HOW TO USE THIS GUIDE

This guide helps you to get the most from your visit to Sydney. It provides both expert recommendations and detailed practical information. *Introducing Sydney* locates the city geographically, sets modern Sydney in its historical and cultural context and describes events through the entire year. *Sydney at a Glance* is an overview of the city's main attractions, including a feature on the city shoreline and Sydney's best beaches. *Sydney Area by Area* is the main

sightseeing section, covering all the sights, with photographs, maps and drawings. *Further Afield* looks at sights just outside the city centre while *Beyond Sydney* explores other places close to Sydney. Carefully researched tips on hotels, restaurants, pubs and entertainment venues are found in *Travellers' Needs*. The *Survival Guide* contains useful practical advice on everything from banking and local currency to public transport.

Finding your way around the sightseeing section

The centre of Sydney has been divided into six sightseeing areas. Each area has its own chapter and is colour-coded

for easy reference. Every chapter opens with a list of the sights described. All sights are numbered and plotted on an

Area Map. Detailed information for each sight is presented in numerical order, making it easy to locate within the chapter.

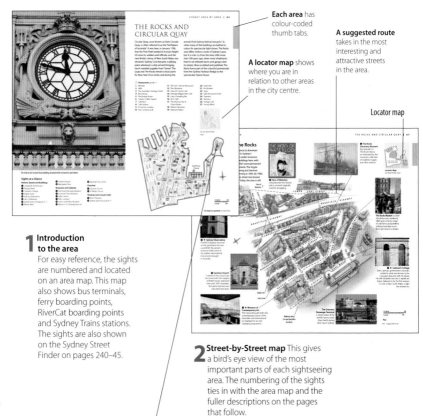

Each area has colour-coded thumb tabs.

A suggested route takes in the most interesting and attractive streets in the area.

A locator map shows where you are in relation to other areas in the city centre.

Locator map

1 Introduction to the area

For easy reference, the sights are numbered and located on an area map. This map also shows bus terminals, ferry boarding points, RiverCat boarding points and Sydney Trains stations. The sights are also shown on the Sydney Street Finder on pages 240–45.

The area shaded pink is shown in greater detail on the Street-by-Street map on the following pages.

2 Street-by-Street map This gives a bird's eye view of the most important parts of each sightseeing area. The numbering of the sights ties in with the area map and the fuller descriptions on the pages that follow.

Sydney Area Map

The coloured areas shown on this map (see pp18–19) are the six main sightseeing areas – each covered by a full chapter in *Sydney Area by Area* (pp62–151). The six areas are also highlighted on other maps throughout the book. In *Sydney at a Glance* (pp34–49), for example, they help locate the top sights, including art galleries and museums, significant architecture and the best parks and reserves. They are also used to show some of the top shopping areas (pp200–1).

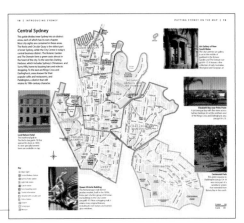

Façades of important buildings are often pictured to help you recognize them quickly.

Numbers refer to each sight's position on the area map and its place in the chapter.

Practical information lists all the information you need to visit every sight, including a map reference to the Street Finder (pp240–45).

The visitors' checklist provides all the practical information needed to plan your visit.

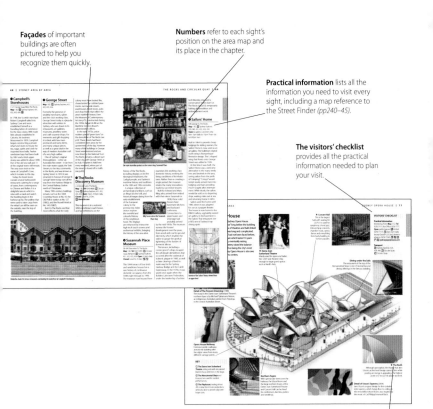

3 Detailed information on each sight

All the important sights in Sydney are described individually. They are listed in order, following the numbering on the area map. Addresses and practical information are provided. The key to the symbols used is on the back flap.

Stars indicate the features no visitor should miss.

4 Sydney's top sights Museums and galleries have colour-coded floorplans to help you locate the most interesting exhibits; historic buildings are dissected to reveal their interiors.

INTRODUCING SYDNEY

GREAT DAYS IN SYDNEY

Planning a one-day itinerary to take in the best that Sydney has to offer need not be a challenge. The magnificent harbour or beaches, as well as cultural and architectural highlights, would ideally be included. These four itineraries offer a mix of activities in different parts of Sydney, all accessible by public transport. They are designed to be flexible – you might choose to leave out some stops or include other attractions that are nearby. Prices show the cost for two adults or for a family of two adults and two children, including food and drinks.

Sydney Opera House and Harbour Bridge by night

Around the Harbour

Two adults allow at least A$110

- **The view from Sydney Harbour Bridge**
- **A tour of The Rocks**
- **Ferry ride to Manly**
- **Sunset over the harbour**

Morning
Start early at an Australian icon, the **Sydney Harbour Bridge** *(see pp72–3)*, built in 1932. Cross on the pedestrian walkway or, from $288 per person, let **BridgeClimb** guide you to the top of the steel arch bridge (bookings are essential). Climbs depart every ten minutes, and take 3½ hours including orientation. The view at the top is well worth it. Recharge with a pit stop at one of the cafés in the vicinity *(see pp186–7)*; there's everything from pastries and sandwiches to pizza, pasta and ice cream. Explore the historic

Rocks area where you'll find the convict-carved Argyle Cut and the military **Garrison Church** *(see pp70–71)*. Cobblestoned alleys lead to the original docks of Old Sydney Town at **Campbell's Storehouses** *(see p68)* and **Cadman's Cottage** *(see p70)*, Sydney's oldest surviving residential dwelling. Finish your stroll at Circular Quay.

Afternoon
Enjoy a classic ferry trip to **Manly** *(see p135)*. Once there, stroll down The Corso to the ocean beach or walk around the headland *(see pp148–9)*. Buy fish and chips and eat them on the beach, or try some parasailing, boating or kayaking, activities that are on offer at the jetty. Treat yourself to a beer at the Manly Wharf Hotel *(see p197)* where you can find a window seat and watch the sunset over the harbour. End the day with the return ferry back to Circular Quay.

Take in the lights of the city by the harbour as night falls.

Art and Opera

Two adults allow at least A$160

- **Colonial buildings on Macquarie Street**
- **Aboriginal art at the Yiribana Gallery**
- **The Royal Botanic Garden**
- **Sydney Opera House**

Morning
Stroll down **Macquarie Street** *(see pp114–17)*, named after Governor Lachlan Macquarie. You can still see several of the buildings he commissioned here. Other architectural gems include the **Hyde Park Barracks** *(see pp116–17)* and **St James' Church** *(see p117)*, both designed by convict James Greenway. The old Rum Hospital now houses the **Sydney Mint** *(see p116)* and **Parliament House** *(see pp114–15)*, where free tours run every half hour. At the **State Library of NSW** *(see p114)*, admire the mosaic replica of the Tasman Map, illustrating 17th-century voyages to Australia, and the majesty of the reading room.

Henry Moore sculpture outside the Art Gallery of New South Wales

◄ Australian Aboriginal mural, by Danny and Jamie Eastwood

Afternoon

Across **The Domain** (see p109), the **Art Gallery of New South Wales** (see pp110–13) houses both traditional and modern Aboriginal art in the Yiribana Gallery, the largest space in the world devoted to the art of Indigenous Australians. Rest weary legs and enjoy lunch in the gallery's café (see p191), then stroll along to the scenic **Mrs Macquaries Chair** (see p108) for a fine view across the harbour before taking the Fleet Steps down the hill into the **Royal Botanic Garden** (see pp106–7). On the other side of Farm Cove is **Sydney Opera House** (see pp76–9). Stop in at the Opera Bar (see pp187), then take a tour of the world-famous building (booking is recommended). If you want to make an evening of it, last-minute tickets are sometimes available for an opera, play or concert.

Giraffe at Taronga Zoo, on the foreshore of Sydney Harbour

do laps. Then stretch your legs with the Bondi-to-Bronte section of the famous cliff walk (see pp146–7). When you reach Bronte, sit on the grass or sand with a refreshing drink, then head to Oxford Street, Paddington, to begin browsing the glamorous boutiques. The renowned **Paddington Markets** (see p128) are open every Saturday.

Afternoon

Take lunch in the leafy surrounds of beautiful **Queen Street** at Crème Café (see p194), then, if you wish, visit the store of prominent designer Akira Isogawa (see p205). Stop by the London Tavern (see p126), the area's oldest pub, before exploring the streets of terraced houses near **Five Ways**. Admire the art at Olsen Irwin Gallery (No. 63 Jersey Road), Australian Galleries (No. 15 Roylston Street) and Martin Browne Contemporary (No. 15 Hampden Street). Later, have a drink at the Tilbury Hotel (see p194) in **Woolloomooloo** and cap off the day with a pie from Harry's Café de Wheels (see p193) on the **Finger Wharf**.

Beaches and Browsing

Two adults allow at least A$170

- **Breakfast at Bondi Beach**
- **A clifftop walk**
- **Fashion, terraces and galleries in Paddington**
- **Cocktails on the Finger Wharf**

Morning

Have breakfast at **Bondi Beach**'s Icebergs Bistro (see p197), at the legendary Bondi Icebergs (on weekends) or at the Crabbe Hole (see p196). Admire the view and watch the die-hard swimmers

Family Fun

Family of 4 allow at least A$365

- **A spin through the city's main streets**
- **Ferry and Sky Safari**
- **Koalas, kangaroos and platypuses at Taronga Zoo**
- **Up high in Sydney Tower**

Morning

Start with a stroll along Circular Quay, then head to Wharf 2 where you can save time by buying your zoo ticket before boarding a ferry to **Taronga Zoo** (see pp136–7). Take the included Sky Safari cable car ride to the main entrance for a bird's eye view of the animals from above the tree canopy. At the entrance you'll find information on daily events such as keeper talks, feeding times and seal and bird shows. As you explore the zoo, make sure you stop by all of the native Australian animals, including monotremes, echidnas and platypuses.

Afternoon

Have lunch at the Taronga Food Market or picnic on the concert lawns, before heading back to the wharf for the return ferry. Finish the day at **Sydney Tower** (see p85). Ride the lift to the Sydney Tower Eye Observation Deck and take in a virtual tour of Sydney in the 4-D cinema. Use a telescope to spot the zoo and other landmarks as far away as the Blue Mountains on a clear day, or enjoy the sunset.

Bathers enjoying the golden sand and surf at Bronte Beach

2 Days in Sydney

- Take centre stage on an Opera House tour
- See one of the world's biggest collections of Aboriginal art
- Journey across the harbour to Manly Beach

Day 1

Morning Start your day with a behind-the-scenes tour at the **Sydney Opera House** (pp76–9). Stand on the Concert Hall stage and admire the stunning interior of this landmark before having breakfast in the "green room". Afterwards, take the harbour foreshore walk to the **Royal Botanic Garden** (pp106–7), established as Australia's first European farm, and join a guided tour of the exotic plants and historic monuments. Buy a snack from the kiosk, and picnic in the park.

Afternoon Exit the gardens near the **Art Gallery of New South Wales** (pp110–13), and visit its famous Yiribana Gallery, which features one of the world's largest collections of Aboriginal and Torres Strait Islander art. Stroll along Macquarie Street to **The Mint** (p116), a former coining factory and the oldest public building in the city centre. Then head to Darling Harbour to watch the dugongs and sharks at **SEA LIFE Sydney Aquarium** (p98).

Day 2

Morning Catch a ferry from Circular Quay to **Manly** (p135). Stroll the shop-lined Corso to the surf beach, and walk the track to Shelly Beach marine preserve. Have lunch overlooking the water before your return ferry trip.

Afternoon Walk to the **Museum of Contemporary Art** (p75), home to more than 4,000 modern artworks. Meander through The Rocks' historic streets to the BridgeClimb head-quarters for a three-and-a-half hour adventure to the top of the **Harbour Bridge** (pp72–3).

The stunning interior of the beautifully restored Queen Victoria Building

3 Days in Sydney

- Step aboard a replica of the *Endeavour* at Darling Harbour
- Admire the splendour of the Queen Victoria Building
- Follow in convicts' footsteps at Hyde Park Barracks

Day 1

Morning Starting at Darling Harbour, walk across the **Pyrmont Bridge** (p100) to the **Australian National Maritime Museum** (pp96–7). Roam the wharves and explore historic vessels, including a replica of Captain Cook's *Endeavour*, then meet native Australian animals at **WILD LIFE Sydney Zoo** (p99).

Afternoon Catch a ferry to Circular Quay. Visit **The Rocks Discovery Museum** (pp68–9) to learn about the area's history. Walk through The Rocks to the pedestrian deck of the Harbour

Bridge. Go up the sandstone **Pylon Lookout** (p70) for an overview of the bridge's creation and great views.

Day 2

Morning Combine shopping, history and architecture at the immaculately restored **Queen Victoria Building** (p84), with its stained-glass windows and clocks. Head to Circular Quay, enjoying entertainment from waterfront street buskers.

Afternoon Take a ferry ride to Manly, passing small harbour island Fort Denison and **North Head** (p135), where the harbour starts. Wander along Manly Cove to dive with sharks at **Manly SEA LIFE Sanctuary** (p135). Have a sunset drink on Manly Wharf before returning.

Day 3

Morning Stroll through **Hyde Park** (pp88–9). Walk along tree-lined pathways and past the Archibald Fountain's grand sculptures. Sink into a convict hammock at **Hyde Park Barracks** (pp116–17), formerly home to 50,000 convicts. Later, peek inside the stately reading room in the Mitchell Wing of the **State Library of NSW** (p114).

Afternoon Walk through **The Domain** (p109) to the **Art Gallery of New South Wales**, and take a free tour of the gallery highlights. Wind through the **Royal Botanic Garden** to the **Sydney Opera House**. Admire the beauty of its famous white sails with evening drinks by the water's edge.

Manly Cove, as viewed from Sydney Harbour National Park

5 Days in Sydney

- Watch the sun set from the top of the Harbour Bridge
- Feel the sand between your toes at iconic Bondi Beach
- Take in the rugged beauty of the Blue Mountains

A bench decorated with a mosaic of lifeguards at Bondi Beach

Day 1
Morning Start your day watching harbour life at **Circular Quay**, or get the adrenaline flowing with a spin in a jet boat. Walk to the **Museum of Contemporary Art** *(see p75)* and admire the stunning works on display there. Enjoy lunch at one of the area's historic pubs.

Afternoon Step back in time with a stroll through The Rocks and the dramatic **Argyle Cut** *(p66)*, a passage cut through sandstone by convicts. Then join BridgeClimb for a twilight ascent of the **Harbour Bridge**, and watch the sun set over the city.

The lake at the peaceful Chinese Garden of Friendship, in Darling Harbour

Day 2
Morning Head to Hyde Park for a game of chess on the giant outdoor board near St James Station, stroll to the grand **Archibald Fountain** *(p88)*, featuring Apollo, then visit the **Anzac Memorial** reflection pool *(p88)* and museum commemorating those who served in war.

Afternoon Take advantage of the park's proximity to Oxford Street and travel to **Paddington** *(pp126–7)*. Stroll down beautiful Queen Street with its antiques stores, galleries and cafés, and continue on to **Bondi Beach** *(p139)*. Take the stunning Bondi-to-Bronte coastal walk and return for a drink overlooking the ocean at one of the seaside cafés.

Day 3
Morning Shop till you drop in the world's most expensive retail floor space, **Pitt St Mall** *(pp 198 & 201)*. Window shop in the Victorian-style **Strand Arcade** *(p86)*, which was completely rebuilt after a fire in 1976. Afterwards, take in some culture with a tour of the majestic **State Theatre** *(p84)*, with its exquisite architectural features, important artworks and the world's second-biggest chandelier.

Afternoon Escape the hustle and bustle of the city, entering the Royal Botanic Garden from Macquarie Street to admire the **Conservatorium of Music** *(p108)*, a striking Neo-Gothic building housing one of the nation's most prestigious music colleges. Afterwards, head to stately **Government House** *(p108)*, the former residence of the Governor of New South Wales. En route, look out for noisy flying foxes (large bats) and cockatoos. Exit near the **Art Gallery of New South Wales**, and enjoy free entry to its impressive collections. Make your way to the **Opera House** for an evening show.

Day 4
Morning Take a ferry to Sydney's zoo with a view, **Taronga Zoo** *(pp136–7)*. Get the Sky Safari cable car to the top, and visit some of the many fascinating animal enclosures on your way back down. Be sure to stop by the Australian Walkabout for a close-up encounter with kangaroos and koalas. Other highlights include elephants and Sumatran tigers. Don't miss the QBE Free Flight Bird Show and the Seal Show *(see p137)*.

Afternoon Catch the ferry to Darling Harbour. Enjoy the quiet solitude of the **Chinese Garden of Friendship** *(p100)*. Children will enjoy the Darling Quarter playground, with water games, rope climbing nets and slides. Head back to **Chinatown** *(pp100–101)* for a great-value dinner and souvenir shopping.

Day 5
Morning to afternoon Venture from the city with a day trip to Katoomba, in the Greater **Blue Mountains** World Heritage Area *(pp162–3)*. Hire a car, take a train or join a bus tour to experience the rugged beauty of the vast Australian bush. Visit Echo Point lookout for spectacular views of the iconic **Three Sisters** rock formation *(p162)* and learn its Aboriginal dreamtime legend. Take the **Giant Stairway** down to the valley floor, and glide between clifftops on the glass-floored **Scenic Skyway cablecar** (www.scenicworld.com.au) before returning to Sydney.

Putting Sydney on the Map

Situated on Australia's eastern coastline within the state of New South Wales, Sydney spreads with the rare luxury of space – 3,700 sq km (1,430 sq miles) in all – around what is considered one of the world's finest harbours, and west to the natural barrier of the mountainous Great Dividing Range. Greater Sydney is home to more than 5 million people and, while it is not the nation's capital, it is Australia's oldest and largest city, as well as its media and financial centre. Sydney is also the main gateway to Australia and it enjoys good air, road and rail links to other major centres.

Southeast Asia and the Pacific Rim

Key

✈	International airport
✈	Domestic airport
⛴	Passenger ship terminal
═	Freeway or motorway
═	Highway
—	Railway
▪▪▪	State boundary

Greater Sydney and Environs

Palm Beach

Hornsby

Mona Vale

Penrith

Blacktown

Glenbrook

Parramatta

Chatswood

See next page

Manly

Burwood

Bankstown

Bondi

Sydney Airport

Maroubra

Campbelltown

Sutherland

Cronulla

afura Sea

Torres *Strait*

Cape York

Gulf of Carpentaria

Groote Eylandt

Mornington Island

Cooktown

Cairns

ERN ORY

Mount Isa

QUEENSLAND

Townsville

Proserpine

Great Barrier Reef

Mackay

Pacific Ocean

Longreach

Blackall

Rockhampton

Hervey Bay

Fraser Island

Charleville

Maroochydore

Toowoomba

Brisbane

Coolangatta

Moree

Bourke

Coffs Harbour

USTRALIA

Lake Eyre

NEW SOUTH WALES

Broken Hill

Dubbo

Maitland

Newcastle

Lake Torrens

Whyalla

Sydney

Wollongong

Adelaide

Mildura

Wagga Wagga

Canberra

Kangaroo Island

VICTORIA

STRALIAN CAPITAL TERRITORY

Melbourne

Geelong

King Island

Bass Strait

Flinders Island

Tasman Sea

Devonport

Launceston

TASMA

Hobart

Flinders

Diamantina

Darling

Murray

Lake ardner na

ber y

54

71

39

15

34

93

31

76

32

66

66

66

78

1

1

1

1

1

8

79

31

1

66

1

Central Sydney and Suburbs

Sydney has gradually expanded to fill both sides of the harbour.
Parramatta to the west was once a separate settlement, but is
now the geographic centre of Greater Sydney. To the east are the
beaches and seaside suburbs that have come to typify coastal
living. The area as a whole is served by rail links and roads.

Key

- Central Sydney
- Parks and reserves
- Sydney Olympic Park
- Airport
- Central Railway Station
- Ferry boarding point
- RiverCat boarding point
- ③ Metroad route
- Freeway or motorway
- Major road
- Minor road
- Railway
- Tunnel

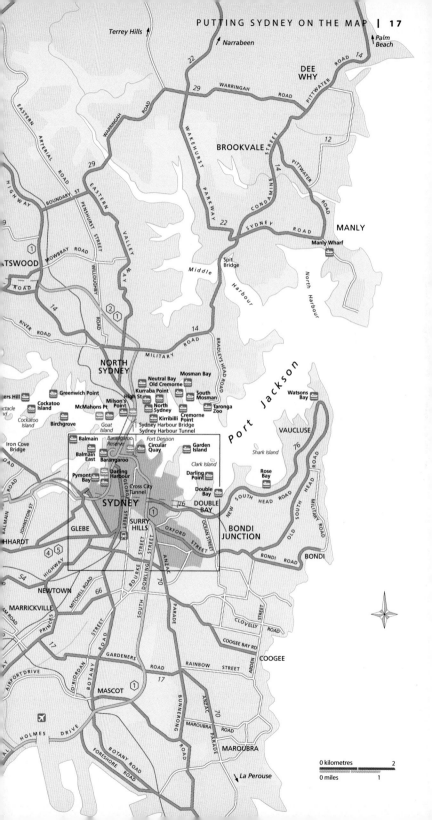

Terrey Hills

Narrabeen

Palm Beach

DEE WHY

WARRINGAH ROAD

BROOKVALE

PITTWATER ROAD

MANLY

Manly Wharf

Spit Bridge

Middle Harbour

North Harbour

WAKEHURST PARKWAY

SYDNEY ROAD

CONDAMINE STREET

EASTERN ARTERIAL ROAD

HIGHWAY

BOUNDARY ST

MOWBRAY ROAD

PENSHURST STREET

WILLOUGHBY ROAD

EASTERN VALLEY WAY

BRADLEYS HEAD ROAD

TSWOOD

RIVER ROAD

MILITARY ROAD

NORTH SYDNEY

Neutral Bay
Old Cremorne
Kurraba Point
Mosman Bay
South Mosman
Taronga Zoo
Cremorne Point
Kirribilli
High St
Milson's Point
North Sydney
McMahons Pt

Greenwich Point

rs Hill
Cockatoo Island
Cockatoo Island
Birchgrove
Goat Island

Watsons Bay

VAUCLUSE

Port Jackson

Shark Island

Iron Cove Bridge

Balmain
Balmain East
Barangaroo
Barangaroo Reserve
Pymont Bay
Darling Harbour

Sydney Harbour Bridge
Sydney Harbour Tunnel

Fort Denison
Circular Quay
Garden Island
Clark Island
Darling Point
Double Bay
Rose Bay

Cross City Tunnel

SYDNEY

GLEBE

SURRY HILLS

DOUBLE BAY

BONDI JUNCTION

BONDI

HHARDT

JOHNSTON ST

BALMAIN

GEORGE STREET

CROWN STREET

OXFORD STREET

OCEAN STREET

NEW SOUTH HEAD ROAD

OLD SOUTH HEAD ROAD

MILITARY ROAD

BONDI ROAD

ANZAC PDE

NEWTOWN

MARRICKVILLE

MITCHELL ROAD

PRINCES HIGHWAY

KING STREET

SOUTH DOWLING STREET

BOURKE STREET

GARDENERS ROAD

CLOVELLY ROAD

COOGEE BAY RD

RAINBOW STREET

ARDEN STREET

COOGEE

AIRPORT DRIVE

O'RIORDAN STREET

BOTANY ROAD

MASCOT

BUNNERONG ROAD

ANZAC PARADE

MAROUBRA ROAD

MAROUBRA

HOLMES DRIVE

FORESHORE ROAD

BOTANY ROAD

La Perouse

0 kilometres 2
0 miles 1

Central Sydney

This guide divides inner Sydney into six distinct areas, each of which has its own chapter. Most city sights are contained in these areas. The Rocks and Circular Quay is the oldest part of inner Sydney, while the City Centre is today's central business district. The Botanic Garden and The Domain form a green oasis almost in the heart of the city. To the west lies Darling Harbour, which includes Sydney's Chinatown, and Surry Hills, home to buzzing bars and eclectic shopping. To the east are Kings Cross and Darlinghurst, areas known for their popular cafés and restaurants, and Paddington, a district that still retains its 19th-century character.

Lord Nelson Hotel
This traditional pub in The Rocks *(see pp64–79)* first opened its doors in 1834. Its own specially brewed beers are available on tap.

Key

- 🏛 Major sight
- 🚉 Central Railway Station
- 🚆 Sydney Trains station
- 🚊 Light Rail station
- 🚌 Coach station
- ⛴ Ferry boarding point
- ℹ Tourist information
- ➕ Hospital with casualty unit
- 🚔 Police Station
- ⛪ Church
- ✡ Synagogue
- ☪ Mosque

Queen Victoria Building
This Romanesque-style former produce market, built in the 1890s, forms part of a fine group of Victorian-era buildings in the City Centre *(see pp80–91)*. Now a shopping mall, it retains many original features, including its roof statues and stained-glass windows.

Map labels:
Sydney Harbour Bridge
Sydney Opera House
THE ROCKS AND CIRCULAR QUAY
ARGYLE ST
Sydney Cove
OBSERVATORY PARK
Museum of Contemporary Art
TOLL POINT
CAHILL EXPRESSWAY
CIRCULAR QUAY
Circular Quay
GROSVENOR PLACE
GROSVENOR ST
BRIDGE STREET
Museum of Sydney
Wynyard
MARTIN PLACE
CITY CENTRE
Martin Place
DOM
Australian National Maritime Museum
WILD LIFE Sydney Zoo
Pyrmont Bay
Sydney Tower
St James
SEA LIFE Sydney Aquarium
Cockle Bay
Convention
Sydney Aquarium
HYDE
Town Hall
PARK
BATHURST STREET
PARK
Australian Museum
Exhibition Centre
LIVERPOOL STREET
Museum
Powerhouse Museum
DARLING HARBOUR
GOULBURN STREET
Paddy's Markets
HAY STREET
Capitol Square
ULTIMO ROAD
CAMPBELL STREET
Central
ALBION STREET
RAILWAY SQUARE
EDDY AVE
Central Railway Station
FOVEAUX STREET
SURRY HILLS
DEVONSHIRE STREET

Art Gallery of New South Wales
The city's premier art gallery is set in the middle of parkland in the Botanic Garden and The Domain (see pp104–17). It houses a fine collection of early Australian, Aboriginal and European art.

Elizabeth Bay near Potts Point
A picturesque bay with fine views across Sydney Harbour, it is at the northern end of the Kings Cross and Darlinghurst area (see pp118–23).

Centennial Park
This green expanse in Paddington (see pp124–9) was once part of a sanddune system that extended from Botany Bay in the south.

0 metres   250
0 yards   250

THE HISTORY OF SYDNEY

The first inhabitants of Australia were the Aboriginal peoples. Their history began in a time called the Dreaming when the Ancestor Spirits emerged from the earth and gave form to the landscape. Anthropologists believe the Aboriginal peoples arrived from Asia more than 50,000 years ago. Clans lived in the area now known as Sydney, until the arrival of Europeans caused violent disruption to this world.

In 1768, Captain James Cook began a search for the fabled "great south land". Travelling in the wake of other European explorers, he was the first to set foot on the east coast of the land the Dutch had named New Holland, and claimed it for King and country. He landed at Botany Bay in 1770, naming the coast New South Wales.

At the suggestion of Sir Joseph Banks, Cook's botanist on HMS *Endeavour*, a penal colony was established here to relieve Britain's overflowing prisons. The First Fleet of 11 ships reached Botany Bay in 1788, commanded by Captain Arthur Phillip. He felt the land there was too swampy and the bay windswept. Just to the north, however, he found "one of the finest harbours in the world," naming it Sydney Cove, after the Home Department's Secretary of State. Here, 1,485 convicts,

guards, officers, officials, wives and children landed on 26 January, now commemorated as Australia Day. This marked the beginning of the rapid devastation of the Aboriginal peoples, as they fell to introduced diseases and the overwhelming invasion of the heavily armed new settlers. Full citizenship rights were finally granted to the Aboriginal peoples in 1973, and their traditions are now accorded respect.

The city of Sydney soon flourished, with the construction of impressive public buildings befitting an emerging maritime power. In 1901, amid a burgeoning nationalism, the Federation drew the country's six colonies together and New South Wales became a state of Australia.

In its two centuries of European settlement, Sydney has experienced alternating periods of growth and decline. It has weathered the effects of gold rush and trade booms, depressions and world wars, to establish a distinctive character marked by a vibrant eclecticism. The underlying British culture, married with Aboriginal influences and successive waves of Asian and European migration, has produced today's modern cosmopolitan city.

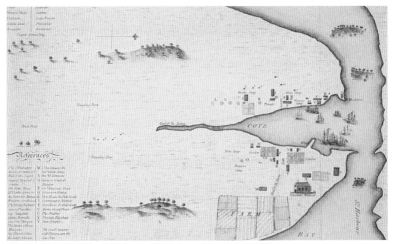

Sketch & Description of the Settlement at Sydney Cove (1788), by transported convict Francis Fowkes

◄ *Desmond, a New South Wales Chief* (about 1825), by Augustus Earle

Sydney's Original Inhabitants

Anthropologists believe that Aboriginal peoples reached Sydney Harbour at least 50,000 years ago. One of the clans of coastal Sydney was the Eora people. Their campsites were usually close to the shore, particularly in the summer when fish were plentiful. Plant and animal foods supplemented their seafood diet. Artistic expression was a way of life, with their shields decorated with ochre, designs carved on their implements, and their bodies adorned with scars, animal teeth and feathers. Sacred and social ceremonies are still vital today. Oral traditions recount stories of the Dreaming *(see p21)* and describe the Eora's strong attachment to the land.

Aborigines Fishing (1819) Sixty-seven Eora canoes were counted in the harbour on a single day. Spears were used as tools and weapons.

Berow Wate

Glenbrook Crossing The Red Hand Caves near Glenbrook in the lower Blue Mountains contain stencils where ochre was blown over outstretched hands.

The name Parramatta means "place where eels lie down or sleep", or "the head of the river".

Glenbrook •

Parramatta •

Cabramatta •

Cabramatta means "land where the cobra grub is found".

Red Ochre and Shell Paint Holder Ochre was a commonly used material in rock painting. Finely ground, then mixed with water and a binding agent, it would be applied by brush or hand.

Aboriginal Rock Art

There are approximately 5,500 known rock art sites in the Sydney basin alone. Early colonists such as Watkin Tench said that paintings and engravings were on every kind of surface. The history of colonization was also recorded in rock engravings, with depictions of the arrival of ships and fighting.

43,000–38,000BC Tools found in a gravel pit beside Nepean River are among the oldest firmly dated signs of human occupation in Australia	**20,000** Humans lived in the Blue Mountains despite extreme conditions. Remains found of the largest mammal, *Diprotodon*, date back to this period	**11,000** Burial s excavated Victoria of mo than 40 individu of this peri
Diprotodon		
50,000 BC	**20,000 BC**	
28,000 Funerary rites at Lake Mungo, NSW. Complete skeleton has been found of man buried at this time	**18,000** People now inhabit the entire continent, from the deserts to the mountains	
23,000 One of the world's earliest known cremations carried out in Western NSW		**13,000** Final stages of Ice Age, with small glaciers in the Snowy Mountains

Ku-ring-gai
is named after
clans who lived
in this coastal
district. It is rich in
rock engravings.

Hunting and Fishing Implements
Multi-pronged Eora spears were used for fishing,
while canoes were shaped from a single piece of
bark. Boomerangs, with their angled shape and
asymmetrical curves, made for highly effective
hunting weapons.

Where to See Aboriginal Rock Art and Artifacts

The soft sandstone of Sydney
was a natural canvas. Much of the
rock art of the original inhabitants
remains and can be found on
walking trails in Ku-ring-gai Chase
National Park (see pp156–7) and
in the Royal National Park (p167).
The NSW Office of Environment
and Heritage has information on
a number of Aboriginal sites
(www.environment.nsw.gov.au/
nswcultureheritage/RockArt.htm).

Fish Carving at West Head
This area in Ku-ring-gai Chase has
51 figures and is acknowledged
as one of the richest sites in
the greater Sydney region.

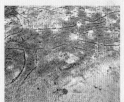

Gumbooya Reserve in suburban Allambie Heights has a
collection of 68 rock carvings.
This human figure appears to
be inside or on top of a whale.

The name Bondi
comes from the
word *boondi*,
meaning "the
sound of water
crashing".

**Allambie
Heights**

Bondi

Coogee

Maroubra

Coogee means
"bad smell of
rotten seaweed
washed ashore".

Maroubra comes either
from the *merooberah* tribe,
or means "place where shells
are found".

Bundeena

Shell Fish-Hooks
Introduced from the
Torres Strait, these
hooks were ground-
down mollusc shells.

This python skeleton is on
view at the Australian Museum
(see pp90–91), along with a large
collection of Aboriginal artifacts.

Water Carrier
These bags were
usually made of
kangaroo skin. The
skin was removed in
one piece and either
turned inside out or
tanned with the sap
from a gum tree.

8,000 BC The
oldest returning
boomerangs
are in use in
South Australia

5,000 BC Dingo
reaches Australia,
thought to have
been brought
by seafarers

Captain James Cook

AD 1606 Dutch ship, *Duyfken*, records first
European sighting of the continent. Lands on
the eastern coast of Gulf of Carpentaria

10,000 BC

AD 1

10,000–8,500 BC
Tasmania is separated
from mainland Australia
by rising seas

*Copperplate print
of a dingo*

AD 1700 Macassans search for trepang
or sea slugs off Australia's north coast

AD 1770 James Cook
lands at Botany Bay

The Early Colony

The colony's beginnings were rugged and hungry, imbued with a spirit that would give Sydney its unique character. Convicts were put to work establishing roads and constructing buildings out of mud, reeds, unseasoned wood and mortar made from a crushed shell mixture. From these simple beginnings, a town grew. Officers of the New South Wales Corps became farmers, encouraged to work their land alongside convict labour. Because the soldiers paid for work and goods in rum, they soon became known as the Rum Corps, in 1808 overthrowing Governor Bligh (of *Bounty* fame) when he threatened their privileges. By the early 1800s farms were producing crops, with supplies arriving more regularly – as were convicts and settlers with more appropriate skills and trades.

Growth of the City
☐ Today ▨ 1810

Boat building at the Government dockyard

Pitts Row

First Fleet Ship (c.1787)
This painting by Francis Holman shows three angles of the *Borrowdale*, one of the fleet's three commercial storeships.

Government House

Scrimshaw
Engraving bone or shell was a skilful way to pass time during long months spent at sea.

A View of Sydney Cove

This idyllic image, drawn by Edward Dayes and engraved by F Jukes in 1804, shows the Aboriginal peoples living peacefully within the infant colony alongside the flourishing maritime and agricultural industries. In fact, they had been entirely ostracized from the life and prosperity of the town by this time.

1787 The First Fleet leaves Portsmouth, bound for Botany Bay

1788 The First Fleet arrives, the first white child is born in the colony, and the first man is hanged

Barrington, the convict and thespian star of The Revenge

1796 *The Revenge* opens Sydney's first, but short-lived, playhouse, simply named The Theatre

1785

1790

1795

Bennelong pictured in European finery

1789 The Aboriginal Bennelong is held captive and ordered to act as an intermediary between the whites and blacks

1790 First detachment of the New South Wales Corps arrives in the colony. Fears of starvation are lessened with the arrival of the supply ship *Lady Juliana*

1793 Arrival of the first free settlers

1797 Merino sheep are from Cape of Good H

The Arrest of Bligh
This shameful, and invented, scene shows the hated Governor William Bligh, in full regalia, hiding under a servant's bed to avoid arrest by the NSW Rum Corps in 1808.

The buildings may look impressive, but most were poorly built with inferior materials.

Male and female convicts were housed separately

Waratah (1803)
John Lewin, naturalist and engraver, drew delicate and faithful representations of the local flora and fauna.

Barracks housing NSW Rum Corps

Kangaroo (1813)
Naturalists were amazed at Sydney's vast array of strange plant and animal species. The first pictures sent back to England caused a sensation.

Where to See Early Colonial Sydney

The Rocks was the hub of early Sydney. Wharves, warehouses, hotels, rough houses and even rougher characters gave it its colour. Dramatic cuts were made in the rocky point to provide building materials and filling for the construction of Circular Quay, and allow for streets. The houses are gone, except for Cadman's Cottage (see p70), but the irregular, labyrinthine lanes still give a flavour of this early history.

Elizabeth Farm (pp140–41) at Parramatta is the oldest surviving building in Australia. It was built by convicts using lime mortar from the penal colony of Norfolk Island.

Experiment Farm Cottage, an early dwelling (see p141), displays marked convict-made bricks. Masons also marked each brick, as they were paid according to the number laid.

1799 Explorers Bass and Flinders complete their circumnavigation of Van Diemen's Land (now Tasmania), before returning to Port Jackson

1803 The first issue of the weekly *Sydney Gazette*, Australia's first newspaper, is published

1808 Rum Rebellion brings social upheaval. Estimated population of New South Wales stands at 9,100

1800 **1805** **1810**

1801 Ticket-of-leave system introduced, enabling the convicts to work for wages and to choose their own master

1804 Irish convict uprising at Castle Hill

1802 Aboriginal leader Pemulwy is shot and killed following the killing of four white men by Aboriginal men

Love token

1810 New convict arrivals craft such items as love tokens

The Georgian Era

Sydney's early decades were times of turbulence and growth. Lachlan Macquarie, governor from 1810 to 1821, was one of the most significant figures. He took over a town-cum-jail and left behind a fully fledged city with a sense of civic pride. Noted for his sympathetic attitude to convicts and freed women and men, he commissioned many fine buildings, including work by convict Francis Greenway (see p116). When Macquarie left in 1822, Sydney boasted main roads, regular streets and an organized police system. By the 1830s, trade had expanded, and labour and land were plentiful. In 1840, transportation of convicts was abolished. A decade of lively debate followed: on immigration, religion and education.

Growth of the City
🞑 Today   🞖 1825

The domed saloon is elliptical, and has a cantilevered staircase.

Bedroom

The breakfast room was used for informal dining.

View from the Summit
Blaxland, Lawson and Wentworth were the first Europeans to cross the Blue Mountains in 1813. Augustus Earle's painting shows convicts working on a road into this fertile area.

The kitchen was originally in a separate block to avoid the danger of fire.

The Macquaries
Governor Macquarie and his wife Elizabeth arrived in the city with a brief to "improve the morals of the Colonists".

Elizabeth Bay House

This extravagant Regency villa was built in 1835–9 for Colonial Secretary Alexander Macleay (see p122). After only six years' occupancy, lavish building and household expenses forced him into bankruptcy.

1814 Holey dollar eases coin shortage

Holey dollar and dump, made from Spanish coins

1820 Macquarie Chair crafted of she-oak and wallaby skin

Macquarie Chair

1830 Sir Thomas Mitchell discovers megafauna fossils in New South Wales

| 1810 | 1815 | 1820 | 1825 | 1 |

1816 Convict architect Francis Greenway designs his first building, Macquarie Lighthouse

1817 The Bank of NSW opens. Macquarie recommends adoption of the name Australia for the continent, as suggested by explorer Matthew Flinders

1831 First Austral novel, *Quintus Servint* is printed and publish

1824 Hume and Hovell are the first Europeans to see the Snowy Mountains

Lyrebird (1813)
As the colony continued to expand, more exotic birds and animals were found. The male of this species has an impressive tail that spreads into the shape of a lyre.

Servants' quarters

Aboriginal Explorer
Bungaree took part in the first circumnavigation of the continent, sailing with Matthew Flinders.

Drawing room

The Classical design was to be complemented by a colonnade, but money ran out.

The dining room was furnished in a florid style out of keeping with the Neo-Classical architecture.

Where to See Georgian Sydney

Governor Macquarie designated the street now bearing his name (see pp114–17) as the ceremonial centre of the city. It has an elegant collection of buildings: the Hyde Park Barracks, St James' Church, the Sydney Mint, Parliament House and Sydney Hospital. Other fine examples are the Victoria Barracks (p129), Vaucluse House (p138) and Macquarie Lighthouse (p139).

Old Government House, the oldest surviving public building in Australia (see p141), was erected in 1799. Additions ordered by Governor Macquarie were completed in 1816.

High Fashion, 1838
Stylish ladies would promenade through Hyde Park (see pp88–9) in the very latest London fashions, which were available from the David Jones department store.

Naturalist and author, Charles Darwin

1842 Sydney town becomes a city

1838 Myall Creek massacre of Aboriginal peoples

1844 Edward Geoghegan's Australian musical comedy, *The Currency Lass*, first performed

1850 Work begins on NSW's first railway line, from Sydney to Parramatta

1835	1840	1845	1850

1836 Charles Darwin visits Sydney on HMS *Beagle*

1837 Victoria is crowned Queen of England

1841 Female Immigrants' Home established in Sydney by Caroline Chisholm. Gas lights illuminate Sydney

1840 Transportation of convicts to NSW is abolished

1848 Parramatta's Female Factory, a notorious women's prison, closes down

Caroline Chisholm, philanthropist

Victorian Sydney

In the 1850s, gold was discovered in New South Wales and Sydney came alive with gold seekers, big spenders and a new wave of settlers. It was the start of a peaceful period of solid growth. Education became compulsory, an art gallery was opened and the Australian Academy of Arts held its first exhibition. The city skyline became more complex, with spires and "tall" buildings. Terrace houses proliferated. Victorian decorum and social behaviour borrowed from the mother country flourished, with much social visiting and sporting enthusiasm. It was an age of pleasure gardens and regattas, but also a time of unruliness and political agitation. In the 1890s, fervent nationalism and an Australian identity began to take shape as the country moved towards Federation.

Growth of the City

☐ Today   ▨ 1881

The structure was built of hollow pine.

The dome was 30 m (98 ft) in diameter.

Mrs Macquaries Chair (1855)
This prime harbour viewing spot *(see p108)*, with the seat carved from rock for the governor's wife, was "the daily resort of all the fashionable people in Sydney".

Boer War
The 1st Australian Horse division was praised for its bushcraft, horsemanship and accurate shooting.

The Garden Palace

Built in the Botanic Garden especially for the occasion, in 1879–80, the Garden Palace hosted the first international exhibition held in the southern hemisphere. Twenty nations took part. Sadly, the predominantly timber building and most of its contents were destroyed by fire in 1882.

Henry Parkes

1851 The discovery of gold near Bathurst, west of the Blue Mountains, sparks a gold rush

1868 The Duke of Edinburgh visits and survives an assassination attempt. The Prince Alfred Hospital is later named in his honour

1872 Henry Parkes elected NSW Premier

1850

1860

1870

1867 Henry Lawson born

1857 *Dunbar* wrecked at The Gap with the loss of 121 lives and only one survivor

Henry Lawson, notable poet and author of short stories

1869 Trend in the colony towards the segregation of Aboriginal peoples on reserves and settlements

1870 The last British troops withdraw from the colony

The Waverly
This clipper brig, with its extra sails and tall masts, enabled the fast transport of wool exports and fortune seekers hastening to newly discovered Colonial gold fields.

Where to See Victorian Sydney

Sydney's buildings reflect the spirit of the age. The Queen Victoria Building (see p84), Sydney Town Hall (p89) and Martin Place (p86) mark grand civic spaces. In stark contrast, the Argyle Terraces and Susannah Place (p69) in The Rocks give some idea of the cramped living conditions endured by the working class.

The "Strasburg" Clock
In 1887, Sydney clockmaker Richard Smith began work on this astronomical model now in the Powerhouse Museum (see pp102–3).

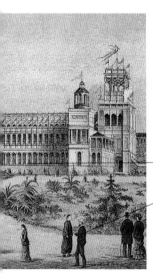

The Macquarie Street entrance to the Garden is home to the Palace's surviving carved Sydney sandstone gateposts and wrought iron gates.

St Mary's Cathedral (see p88), built in Gothic Revival style, is thought to be the largest Christian church in the former "Empire", outside Britain.

The exhibition attracted over one million people.

Arthur Streeton
In 1891, Streeton and Tom Roberts, both Australian Impressionist painters, set up an artists' camp overlooking Sydney Harbour in Mosman.

Victorian terrace houses, decorated with iron lace, began to fill the streets of Paddington (see pp124–9) and Glebe (p133) from the 1870s onwards.

Sydney Between the Wars

Federation took place on 1 January 1901 and New South Wales became a state of the Australian nation. In Sydney, new wharves were built, roads widened and slums cleared. The 1920s were colourful and optimistic in "the city of pleasure". The skyline bristled with cranes as modern structures replaced their ornate predecessors. The country was hit hard by the Great Depression in 1931, but economic salvation came in the form of rising wool prices and growth in manufacturing. The opening of the Sydney Harbour Bridge in 1932 was a consolidation of all the changes brought by Federation and urbanization.

Growth of the City
☐ Today ▨ 1945

The poster depicts the youthful vigour of the nation.

Home in the Suburbs
The Federation bungalow became a unique architectural style *(see p43)*. Verandas, gables and chimneys featured amid much red brick.

Surf lifesaver

"Making Do"
This chair, made in 1910, used packing case timber, cotton reels, fencing wire and the mouldings of picture frames.

SYDNEY CELEBI

MARCH 19th 1932

Bronzed Lifesavers
No surf beach was complete without these supervisors forever looking to sea.

Sydney Harbour Bridge
After nine years of construction, the largest crowd ever seen in Sydney greeted the bridge's opening. Considered a wonder of engineering at the time, it linked the harbour's north and south shores.

Miles Franklin

1901 Miles Franklin's *My Brilliant Career* is published

1912 High-rise era begins in Sydney with the erection of the 14-storey Culwulla Chambers in Macquarie Street. First surfboard arrives in Sydney from Hawaii

1920 Prince Edward, the Prince of Wales, visits

1918 Sydneysiders greet the Armistice riotously

1900 **1910** **1920**

1902 Women win the right to vote in New South Wales

1907 Trunk line between Melbourne and Sydney opens

Poster for telephone trunk line

1919 The Archibald Prize for portraiture is first awarded. Influenza epidemic hits Sydney

1901 Proclamation of the Commonwealth of Australia. Edmund Barton elected as first prime minister

1915 Anzacs land at Gallipoli

Luna Park
This harbourside amusement park opened in 1935 (see p134). A maniacally grinning face looms at the entranceway. Millions of Australians recall the terrifying thrill of running the gauntlet through the gaping mouth as children.

Where to See Early 20th-Century Sydney

The years after Federation yielded stylish and sensible buildings like Central Railway Station, the Commonwealth Savings Bank in Martin Place (see p42) and the State Library of New South Wales. The suburbs of Haberfield and Strathfield best exemplify the Federation style of gentrified residential housing.

One million people crossed the bridge on its opening day.

Donald Bradman
The 1932 English team used "dirty" tactics to outsmart this brilliant cricketer, almost causing a diplomatic rift with Great Britain.

The Anzac Memorial (1934) is in Hyde Park (see pp88–9). The Art Deco memorial, with its reflecting pool, commemorates all Australians killed in wars.

The wireless became a popular fixture in most sitting rooms in the 1930s. This 1935 AWA Radiolette is held at the Powerhouse Museum (see pp102–103).

Australian Women's Weekly
This magazine, first published in 1933, became a family institution full of homespun wisdom, recipes, stories and handy hints.

1924 Sydney swimmer Andrew "Boy" Charlton wins a gold medal at the Paris Olympics

Painted glass pub sign

1937 Heyday of painted glass pub art depicting local heroes

1938 Sydney celebrates her 150th anniversary

1942 Japanese midget submarines enter Sydney Harbour

1930

1940

1928 Kingsford Smith and Ulm make first flight across Pacific in the *Southern Cross*

Kingsford Smith, Ulm

1935 Luna Park opens

1932 Sydney Harbour Bridge opens

1939 Australia declares war on Germany

1941 Australia declares war on Japan

1945 Street celebrations mark the end of World War II

Modern Sydney

The postwar baby boom and mass immigration, initially from Britain and Europe, created a suburban sprawl. The 1970s saw rapid social transformation, with political unrest around the Vietnam War, increased migration from Asia, the start of the skyscraper boom and the opening of the Sydney Opera House *(see pp76–9)*. In the 1980s, Darling Harbour was redeveloped as a cultural and entertainment hub for Australia's bicentenary. Sydney came of age as a global city after hosting the 2000 Olympics. As the population continues to grow, major high-rise residential, commercial and parkland developments, such as Barangaroo *(see p134)*, are transforming the city.

Growth of the City
☐ Today ▨ 1966

Nighttime light projections transfom major landmarks into an outdoor canvas of art during the Vivid Sydney festival.

Green Bans
In the 1970s, the Builders' Labourers Federation placed work bans on developments in the inner city in order to preserve the environment or cultural heritage and protect low-cost housing from destruction and redevelopment.

Sydney Gay and Lesbian Mardi Gras
This parade lasts for one night *(see p51)*, but the surrounding international festival offers a month of art, sporting and community events.

Vivid Sydney
From its humble beginnings in 2009 with just 25 light installations around Circular Quay, Vivid Sydney has grown into the world's biggest festival of outdoor lights, music and ideas. More than 80 installations across the city and 1,500 hours of talks and music events take place over three weeks from May to June (see p52).

1950 Petrol, butter and tea rationing ends

1958 Qantas Airlines embarks on its first round-the-world flights

Johnny O'Keefe

1965 Conscription re-introduced; first regular army battalion sent to Vietnam

1973 Official opening of the Sydney Opera House

1979 Sydney's Eastern Suburbs Railway opens

1950	1960	1970	1980

1954 Elizabeth II is the first reigning monarch to visit Australia

1959 Population of Australia reaches 10 million

1964 Rocker Johnny O'Keefe, "The Wild One", continues to top the music charts

1973 Patrick White wins the Nobel Prize for Literature

1978 Brett Whiteley wins Archibald Prize, Wynne Prize and Sulman Prize for three works of art

Patrick White

Sydney Olympic Park
The facilities built west of the city centre for the 2000 Olympic Games are a lasting legacy for a booming population that lives and works in this precinct. The ANZ Stadium hosts matches of the rugby union, rugby league, Australian Football League and the Australian national soccer team.

Mr Eternity

Arthur Stace (1885–1967), a reformed alcoholic, was inspired by an evangelist who said that he wanted to "shout eternity through the streets of Sydney". "I felt a powerful call from the Lord to write 'Eternity'." At least 50 times a day, for over 30 years, he chalked this word in perfect copperplate on the footpaths and walls of the city. A plaque in Sydney Square pays tribute to Mr Eternity's endeavours.

Arthur Stace and "Eternity", 1963

Bicentenary
The re-enactment of the First Fleet's journey ended in Sydney Harbour on Australia Day, 1988. A chaotic flotilla greeted the "tall ships".

Oz Magazine, 1963–73
This satirical magazine was the mouthpiece of an irreverent generation inspired by a left-wing subculture of intellectuals known as the Sydney Push, who challenged the status quo from the 1940s to the 1970s.

Aboriginal Land Rights
In 1975, the first handover of land was made to Vincent Lingiari, representative of the Gurindji people, by Prime Minister Gough Whitlam.

1990 Population of Australia reaches 17 million

1997 INXS singer Michael Hutchence commits suicide in a Sydney hotel

2003 England beats Australia as Sydney hosts the Rugby World Cup final

2007 Sydney stages first Earth Hour and Live Earth concert for climate change awareness

2015 Malcolm Turnbull becomes Australia's fourth Prime Minister in 5 years following a leadership challenge

2016 Australia's population reaches 23 million; Sydney's tops 5 million

| 1990 | 2000 | 2010 | 2020 |

1992 Sydney Harbour Tunnel opens

1989 Earthquake strikes Newcastle causing extensive damage

2010 Julia Gillard named as country's first female Prime Minister

2000 Sydney hosts the first Olympic Games of the new millennium

2013 Kevin Rudd becomes Prime Minister for a second time, only to lose to Tony Abbott three months later

2015 Barangaroo Reserve opens, transforming the Sydney Harbour headland foreshore

SYDNEY AT A GLANCE

There are more than 100 places of interest described in the *Area by Area* section of this book. A broad range of sights is covered: from the Colonial simplicity of Hyde Park Barracks *(see pp116–17)* to the ornate Victorian terraces of Paddington; from the tranquillity of Centennial Park *(see p129)* to the bustle of the cafés and shops of Oxford Street. To help you make the most of your stay, the following 14 pages are a time-saving guide to the best Sydney has to offer. Museums and galleries, architecture and parks and reserves all have sections of their own. There is also a guide to the diverse cultures that have helped to shape the city into what it is today. Below is a selection of attractions that no visitor should miss.

Sydney's Top Ten Attractions

The Rocks
See pp64–79

Sydney Opera House
See pp76–9

Art Gallery of New South Wales
See pp110–13

Royal Botanic Garden
See pp106–7

Sydney Tower
See p85

Oxford Street and Paddington
See pp118–29

Darling Harbour and Chinatown
See pp92–103

Taronga Zoo
See pp136–7

Harbour ferries
See pp234–5

Sydney's beaches
See pp56–7

◄ Sydney Harbour Bridge *(see pp72–3)* and city skyline, from Lavender Bay

Sydney's Best: Museums and Galleries

Sydney is well endowed with museums and galleries, and much emphasis is placed on social history, examining the lifestyles of past and present Sydneysiders. Most of the major collections are housed in architecturally significant buildings – the Classical façade of the Art Gallery of NSW makes it a city landmark, while the Museum of Contemporary Art adds a modern twist to a 1950s Art Deco-style building at Circular Quay. Small museums are also a feature of the Sydney scene, with a number of historic houses recalling the Colonial days. These are covered in greater depth on pages 38–9.

Museum of Sydney
The *Edge of the Trees* is an interactive installation by the entrance.

THE ROCKS AND CIRCULAR QUAY

CITY CENTRE

Museum of Contemporary Art
This waterfront space is Australia's only museum dedicated to exhibiting national and international contemporary art.

The National Maritime Museum
The museum is the home port for HMS *Endeavour*, a replica of the vessel that charted Australia's east coast in 1770, with Captain Cook in command.

DARLING HARBOUR AND SURRY HILLS

0 metres   500
0 yards   500

Powerhouse Museum
This museum, set in a former power station, uses both traditional and interactive displays to explore Australian innovations in science and technology.

Art Gallery of New South Wales
The Australian collection includes Colonial watercolours which, to avoid deterioration, are only shown for a few weeks each year, such as Charles Meere's *Australian Beach Pattern* (1940).

Elizabeth Bay House
The dining room is elegantly furnished to the 1840s period, when the Colonial Secretary Alexander Macleay briefly lived in the house that ultimately caused his bankruptcy.

BOTANIC GARDEN AND THE DOMAIN

Hyde Park Barracks Museum
Originally built by convicts for their own incarceration, these barracks were later home to poor female immigrants. Exhibits recall the daily life of these occupants.

KINGS CROSS AND DARLINGHURST

PADDINGTON

Australian Museum
Discover the Earth's age, find out about meteorites, volcanic activity and dinosaurs at Australia's largest natural history museum.

Sydney Jewish Museum
The history of the city's Jewish community is documented here. Included is a reconstruction of George Street in 1848, a major location for Jewish businesses.

Exploring Sydney's Museums and Galleries

Sydney is home to a flourishing arts scene and the country's largest cultural institutions, which welcome more than 10 million visitors each year. Among its most popular attractions are a rich variety of museums and galleries. As well as examining the cultural, artistic and historical heritage and future of Australia's biggest city – and of the country as a whole – the range of museums covers natural history, science and antiquities, as well as other areas. From the traditional to the cutting edge, there is a museum or gallery to suit every taste.

Detail from *Window of Dreams* at the Australian National Maritime Museum

Collage on one of the internal doors of the Brett Whiteley Studio

Visual Arts

The **Art Gallery of NSW** has one of the finest existing collections of modern Australian and Aboriginal art. It also boasts an outstanding collection of late 19th- and early 20th-century English and Australian works as well as a gallery devoted to Asian art and a collection of contemporary and photographic works. Thematic temporary exhibitions are also a regular feature here.

The newer **Museum of Contemporary Art** (MCA) is best known for its impressive blockbuster exhibitions. Many of these take advantage of its prime harbour site to create a fine sense of spectacle. It also has a considerable permanent collection, and hosts literary readings and talks.

The **Brett Whiteley Studio**, housed in the studio of the late artist, commemorates the life and works of perhaps the most celebrated and controversial Sydney painter of the late 20th century.

The substantial collection of Australian painting and sculpture held by the **S H Ervin Gallery** is supplemented by frequent thematic and other specialized exhibitions.

Technology and Natural History

The undisputed leader in this area is the **Powerhouse**, with traditional and interactive displays covering fields as diverse as space travel, silent films and solar energy. The **Australian National Maritime Museum** has the world's fastest boat, *Spirit of Australia*, as part of its indoor/outdoor display. Also part of their fleet are the destroyer HMAS *Vampire*, the *Onslow* (a submarine), and the *James Craig* (1874), a three-masted barque.

The **Australian Museum**, in contrast, emphasizes natural history with its displays of the exotic and extinct: from birds, insects and rock samples to giant Australian megafauna.

Aboriginal Culture

With more than 200 works, both traditional and contemporary, on display, the **Art Gallery of NSW**'s Yiribana Gallery has the best and most comprehensive

Jabarrgwa Wurrabadalumba's
Dugong Hunt (1948), Art Gallery of NSW

collection of Aboriginal art in the country. The **Australian Museum** has displays ranging from rocks and minerals, birds and insects to the permanent indigenous exhibition. In its community access space, it also presents performances that celebrate Aboriginal culture.

The First Australians exhibit at the **Australian National Maritime Museum** includes audio and video material, with traditional tools made by Aboriginal communities.

The **Museum of Sydney** uses images, artifacts and oral histories to evoke the life of the Eora, the indigenous people of the Sydney region, up to the years of first contact with the European colonists.

Colonial History

Elizabeth Bay House's superb interior is furnished to show early Colonial life at its most elegant, but while at first the house may appear to celebrate a success story, the enormous cost of its construction brought bankruptcy to its owner. Also built in grand style, **Vaucluse House** celebrates the life and times of W C Wentworth, explorer and politician.

Experiment Farm Cottage, **Hambledon Cottage** and **Elizabeth Farm** in and around Parramatta are testament to the crucial role of agriculture in the survival of a colony that was brought to the brink of starvation. The former has been restored as a gentleman's cottage of the mid-19th century, while the latter two have been furnished to the period of 1820–50. Parramatta's **Old Government House** was once the vice-regal "inland" residence. The Colonial furniture on display predates 1855.

The **Museum of Sydney** is built on the site of the first Government House, close to Sydney Cove. On display are unearthed relics from that building, some of which are

The Georgian-style front bedroom in the cottage at Elizabeth Farm

Water dip at Experiment Farm Cottage

visible under windows at the entrance to the museum.

Susannah Place Museum looks at working-class life in the 19th century. **Cadman's Cottage**, also in The Rocks, is a simple stone dwelling dating from 1816 and the city's oldest extant building. Adjacent is the **Sailors' Home**, built in 1864 as lodgings for visiting sailors. It now houses the Billich Gallery, home to works by the prominent Australian Surrealist painter, Charles Billich (see p69). The important role of gold in the history of Australia and how it determined patterns of migration and expansion are shown at the **Powerhouse Museum**. **Hyde Park Barracks Museum** evokes the often brutal lives and times of the convicts who were housed there in the early 19th century, while not neglecting its other place in history as an immigration depot.

Side view of the veranda at Elizabeth Farm, near Parramatta

Specialist Museums

The **Nicholson Museum** at the University of Sydney houses the southern hemisphere's largest collection of antiquities. The **Justice and Police Museum** examines a far less comfortable history, investigating Australian crime and punishment, while the Caroline Simpson Library & Research Collection at **The Mint** covers the history of Australian homes and gardens. Experiences of Jewish migrants to Australia and the story of the Holocaust are examined at the **Sydney Jewish Museum**.

Finding the Museums and Galleries

Sydney's Best: Architecture

Sydney possesses a large diversity of architectural styles, from the simplicity of Francis Greenway's Georgian buildings *(see p116)* to Jørn Utzon's Expressionist Sydney Opera House *(see pp76–9)* and Frank Gehry's Postmodern Dr Chau Chak Wing Building *(see p132)*. Practical Colonial structures gave way to elaborate Victorian edifices such as Sydney Town Hall, and the same passion for detail is seen in Paddington's terraces. Federation buildings brought in a uniquely Australian style.

Colonial Convict
The first structures were very simple yet formal English-style cottages with shingled roofs and no verandas. Cadman's Cottage is a fine representative of this style.

Contemporary
Governor Phillip Tower is a modern commercial building incorporating a historical site *(see p87)*.

THE ROCKS AND CIRCULAR QUAY

Colonial Georgian
Francis Greenway's courthouse design was ordered to be adapted to suit the purposes of a church. St James' Church is the result.

CITY CENTRE

American Revivalism
Shopping arcades connecting streets, such as the Queen Victoria Building, were 1890s vogue.

DARLING HARBOUR AND SURRY HILLS

Contemporary Expressionism
Innovations in sports stadiums and museum architecture, such as the National Maritime Museum, emphasize roof design and the silhouette.

Victorian
The Town Hall interior includes Australia's first pressed metal ceiling, installed for fear that the organ would vibrate a plaster one loose.

0 metres 500
0 yards 500

Interwar Architecture
Bruce Dellit's Anzac Memorial in Hyde Park, with sculptures by Raynor Hoff, encapsulates the spirit, form and detail of Art Deco.

Modern Expressionism
One of the world's greatest examples of 20th-century architecture, Jørn Utzon's Sydney Opera House beat 234 entries in a design competition. Work commenced in 1959 and, despite the architect's resignation in 1966, it was opened in 1973.

Australian Regency
During the 1830s, the best-designed villas were the work of John Verge. Elizabeth Bay House was his masterpiece.

Early Colonial
The first buildings of character and quality, such as Hyde Park Barracks, were for the government.

BOTANIC GARDEN AND THE DOMAIN

Colonial Grecian
Greek Revival was the major style for public buildings, such as the Darlinghurst Court House, designed by the Colonial Architect in the 1820–50 period.

KINGS CROSS AND DARLINGHURST

Victorian Iron Lace
Festooned with a filigree of cast-iron lace in a wide range of prefabricated patterns, Paddington verandas demonstrate 1880s workmanship.

PADDINGTON

Colonial Military
Victoria Barracks, designed by engineers, is an impressive example of a well-preserved Georgian military compound.

Exploring Sydney's Architecture

While European settlement in Sydney has a relatively short history, architectural styles have rapidly evolved from provincial British buildings and the simplicity of convict structures, many of which used local sandstone. From the mid-19th century until the present day, architectural innovations have borrowed from a range of international trends to create vernacular styles more suited to local materials and conditions. The signs of affluence and austerity, from gold rush to depression, are also manifested in bricks and mortar.

Entrance detail from the Victorian
St Patrick's Seminary in Manly

Façade of the Colonial Susannah Place,
with corner shop window

Colonial Architecture

Little remains of the Colonial buildings from 1790–1830. The few structures still standing have a simple robustness and unassuming dignity. They rely more on form, proportion and mass than on detail.

The Rocks area has one of the best collections of early Colonial buildings: **Cadman's Cottage** (1816), the **Argyle Stores** (1826) and **Susannah Place Museum** (1844). The Georgian **Hyde Park Barracks** (1819) and **St James' Church** (1820), by Francis Greenway *(see p116)*, as well as the Greek Revival **Darlinghurst Court House** (1835) and **Victoria Barracks** (1841–8) are excellent examples of this period.

Australian Regency

Just as the Colonial style was reaching its zenith, the city's increasingly moneyed society abandoned it as undignified and unfashionable. London's residential architecture, exemplified by John Soane under the Prince Regent's patronage, was in favour from the 1830s to the 1850s. Fine examples of this shift towards Regency are John Verge's stylish town houses at **39–41 Lower Fort Street** (1834–6), The Rocks, and the adjoining **Bligh House** built for a wealthy merchant in 1833 in High Colonial style complete with Greek Classical Doric veranda columns.

Regency-style homes often had Grecian, French and Italian details. **Elizabeth Bay House** (1835–8), internally the finest of all John Verge's works, is particularly noted for its cantilevered staircase rising to the arcaded gallery. The cast-iron Ionic-columned **Tusculum Villa** (1831) by the same architect at Potts Point *(see p120)* is unusual in that it is encircled by a double-storeyed veranda, now partially enclosed.

Victorian

This prosperous era featured confident business people and merchants who designed their own premises. Tracts of the city west of York Street and south of Bathurst Street are testimony to these self-assured projects. The cast-iron and glass **Strand Arcade** (1891) by J B Spencer originally included a gas and electricity system, and hydraulic lifts.

Government architect James Barnet's best work includes the "Venetian Renaissance" style **General Post Office**, Martin Place (1864–87), and the extravagant **Lands Department Building** (1877–90) with its four iron staircases and, originally, patent lifts operated by water power. The **Great Synagogue** (1878), **St Mary's Cathedral** (1882), **St Patrick's Seminary** (1885), **Sydney Town Hall** and **Paddington Street** are also of this period.

American Revivalism

After federation in 1901, architects looked to styles such as Edwardian, American Romanesque and Beaux Arts from overseas for commercial buildings. The former **National Mutual Building** (1892) by Edward Raht set the change of direction, followed by warehouse buildings in Sussex and Kent Streets. The Romanesque **Queen Victoria Building**

The Australian Regency-style Bligh House in Dawes Point

(1893–98) was a grand council project by George McRae. The distinctive Beaux Arts **Commonwealth Savings Bank** (1928) features an elaborate chamber in Neo-Classical style.

Interwar Architecture

Architecture between World Wars I and II produced skyscrapers such as the **City Mutual Life Assurance Building** (1936), by Emil Sodersten. This building exhibits German Expressionist influences such as pleated or zigzag windows.

Two important structures are the **ANZAC Memorial** (1929–34) in Hyde Park and **Delfin House** (1938–40), by the Art Deco architect Bruce Dellit. The latter, a skyscraper, features a vaulted ceiling and a granite arch decorated with an allegory of modern life.

The 67-storey MLC Centre in Martin Place, by architect Harry Seidler

Modern Architecture

From the mid-1950s, modern architecture was introduced to the city through glass-clad curtain-walled office blocks, proportioned like matchboxes on their ends. The contrasting expressed frame approach of **Australia Square** (1961–7) gives structural stability to one of the world's tallest lightweight concrete office towers. This city block was formed by amalgamating 30 properties. Harry Seidler's **MLC Centre** (1975–8)

Federation Architecture

This distinctly urban style of architecture developed to meet the demands of the prosperous, newly emerging middle classes at the time of Federation in 1901. Particular features are high-pitched roofs, which form a picturesque composition or architectural tableau, incorporating intricate gables, wide verandas and chimneys. The decorative timber fretwork the verandas and archways and the leadlight windows reveal the influence of the Art Nouveau period, as do the vibrant red roof tiles. Patriotic references are seen throughout, and Australian flora and fauna are recurring decorative motifs.

"Verona" in The Appian Way, Burwood

is a 67-storey office tower comprising a reinforced concrete tube structure with column-free floors.

Jørn Utzon's **Sydney Opera House** (1959–73) is widely regarded as one of the architectural wonders of the world.

Contemporary Architecture

The elliptical **Allianz Stadium** (1985–8) and the **Australian National Maritime Museum** (1986–9), both by Philip Cox, make use of advanced steel engineering systems. Detailed masonry has made a return to commercial buildings such as the highly regarded **Governor Phillip Tower** (1989–94). The dictates of office design do not detract from the historical Museum of Sydney, ingeniously sited on the lower floors.

The **ABN-AMRO Tower** at Aurora Place (2000) was designed by Renzo Piano and was awarded the Sulman Prize for Architecture in 2004. Challenging conventional design, the 41-storey, 200-m- (656-ft-) tall building fans wider as it rises. Frank Gehry's striking **Dr Chau Chak Wing Building** (2015) divides opinion with its warped façade of undulating brickwork. The interior is equally striking, with the building designed from the inside out. It won the 2016 Australia Engineering Excellence Bradfield Award, among many other accolades.

Where to Find the Buildings

Sydney's Many Cultures

Sydney has one of the world's most cosmopolitan societies, reflected in the extraordinary variety of restaurants, religions, community centres and cultural activities to be found throughout the city and its environs. Over 235 birthplaces outside Australia were named in the last census. Indeed, the Sydney telephone directory lists interpreting services for 22 languages, including Greek, Italian, Spanish, Chinese, Vietnamese, Turkish, Korean and Arabic, and many of these groups have their own newspapers. While immigrants have settled all over the city, there are still pockets of Sydney that retain a distinctive ethnic flavour.

Thai Community
Thai culinary traditions have caused a revolution in Sydney eating houses. The Loy Krathong Festival in Parramatta celebrates the transplanted Thai culture.

Auburn Mosque
This lavish mosque rises above the thriving Turkish businesses nearby.

Thailand

Turkey

Cambodian
Cabramatta is the hub of the Cambodian community. Songkran, the three-day new year celebration is held at Bonnyrigg.

Cambodia

Vietnam

Philippines

Lebanon

Filipinos
Over 60 per cent of this rapidly expanding migrant group arrive as the brides of Australian men.

Vietnamese
This sculpture of a cow stands in Cabramatta's Freedom Plaza, an area offering all the sights, smells and street life of Southeast Asia.

Lakemba
Once known as "potato hill" for its potato farms in the early colony, today Lakemba is home to a large Lebanese community.

0 kilometres   4

0 miles   2

St Patrick's Day
Sydney's first settlers, many of them Irish, made their home in The Rocks. With its proliferation of pubs, it is the focal point for jubilant St Patrick's Day celebrations on 17 March each year.

Little Italy
Long home to the Italian community, Leichhardt evokes the flavour of Europe with its bars, cafés, restaurants and a sprawling annual street fair.

Jewish Delicatessen
The sizeable Jewish community in the city's eastern suburbs, about half of whom were born in Australia, is well served by kosher supermarkets and butchers' shops.

Ireland

Italy   China

Israel

Greece

Indigenous Australia

Aboriginal Peoples
The annual Yabun Festival is held on 26 January in Victoria Park, Camperdown on the traditional land of the Cadigal people (see p51).

St Nicholas Church
Marrickville's Greek Orthodox church is the home of worship for the community, mostly based in the southern suburbs.

Chinese New Year
Each year, revellers pack Dixon Street, at the heart of Chinatown, to celebrate with fireworks and Chinese dragons.

Sydney's Best: Parks and Reserves

Sydney is almost completely surrounded by national parks and intact bushland. There are also a number of national parks and reserves within Greater Sydney itself. Here, the visitor can gain some idea of how the landscape looked before the arrival of European settlers. The city parks, too, are filled with plant and animal life. The more formal plantings of both native and exotic species are countered by the indigenous birds and animals that have adapted and made the urban environment their home. One of the highlights of a trip to Sydney is the huge variety of birds to be seen, from large birds of prey such as sea eagles and kites, to the shyer species such as wrens and tiny finches.

Garigal National Park
Rainforest and moist gullies provide shelter for superb lyrebirds and sugar gliders.

Lane Cove National Park
The open eucalypt forest is dotted with grass trees, as well as fine stands of red and blue gums. The rosella, a type of parrot, is common.

North Arm Walk
In spring, grevilleas and flannel flowers bloom profusely on this foreshore walk.

Barangaroo Reserve
This former industrial site has been transformed into a six-hectare (15-acre) park on the Sydney Harbour headland foreshore.

Bicentennial Park
Situated at Homebush Bay on the Parramatta River, the park features a mangrove habitat. It attracts many water birds, including pelicans.

Hyde Park
Situated on the edge of the city centre, the park provides a peaceful respite from the hectic streets. The native iris is just one of the plants found in the lush gardens. The sacred ibis, a water bird, is often seen.

Middle Head and Obelisk Bay
Gun emplacements, tunnels and bunkers built in the 1870s to protect Sydney from invasion by sea dot the area. The superb fairy wren lives here and water dragons can at times be seen basking on rocks.

North Head
Coastal heathland, with banksias, tea trees and casuarinas, dominates the cliff tops. On the leeward side, moist forest surrounds tiny harbour beaches.

Grotto Point
Bottlebrushes, grevilleas and flannel flowers line paths winding through the bush to the lighthouse.

South Head
Unique plant species such as the sundew cover this heathland.

Bradleys Head
The headland is a nesting place for the ringtail possum. Noisy flocks of rainbow lorikeets are also often in residence.

0 kilometres 4
0 miles 2

Nielsen Park
The kookaburra is easily identified by its call, which sounds like laughter.

The Domain
Palms and Moreton Bay figs are a feature of this former common. The Australian magpie, with its black and white plumage, is a frequent visitor.

Centennial Park
Lakes, ponds and groves of paperbark and eucalypt trees are home to a variety of birds, such as black swans and sulphur-crested cockatoos. The bushtail possum is a shy creature that comes out at night.

Moore Park
Huge Moreton Bay figs provide an urban habitat for the flying fox.

Exploring the Parks and Reserves

Despite 200 years of European settlement, Sydney's parks and reserves contain a surprising variety of native wildlife. Approximately 2,000 species of native plants, 1,000 cultivated and weed species and 300 bird species have managed to adapt favourably to the changes.

Several quite distinct vegetation types are protected in the bushland around Sydney, and these in turn provide shelter for a wide range of birds and animals. Even the more formal parks such as Hyde Park and the Royal Botanic Garden are home to many indigenous species, allowing the visitor a glimpse of the city's diverse wildlife.

Colourful and noisy rainbow lorikeets at Manly's Collins Beach

Coastal Hinterland

One reason Sydney has so many heathland parks, such as those found at South Head and North Head, is that the soil along the city's coastline is deficient in almost every known nutrient. What these areas lack in fertility, they make up for in species diversity.

Heathland contains literally hundreds of species of plants, including some unique flora that have adapted to the poor soil. The most surprising ones are the carnivorous plants, which rely on passing insects for their food. The tiny sundew (*Drosera spatulata*), so called because of its sparkling foliage, is the commonest of the carnivorous species. This low-growing plant snares insects on its sticky, reddish leaves, which lie flat on the ground. Two other distinctive plants

Red bottlebrush (*Callistemon sp.*)

are casuarinas (*Allocasuarina* species) and banksias (*Banksia* species), both of which attract smaller birds such as honey-eaters and blue wrens.

Rainforest and Moist Forest

Rainforest remnants do exist in a few parts of Sydney, especially in the Royal National Park to the south of the city (*see pp166–7*). Small pockets can also be found in Garigal National Park, Ku-ring-gai Chase (*see pp156–7*) and some gullies running down to Middle Harbour. The superb lyrebird (*Menura novaehollandiae*) is a feature of these forest areas. The sugar glider (*Petaurus breviceps*), a small species of possum, can sometimes be heard calling to its mate during the night.

One of the deadliest spiders in the world, the Sydney funnel-web (*Atrax robustus, see p91*), also lives here. You are unlikely to see

one unless you poke under rocks and logs. A common plant in this habitat is the cabbage tree palm (*Livistona australis*). Its heart was used as a vegetable by the early European settlers.

The soft tree fern (*Dicksonia antarctica*) decorates the gullies and creeks of moist forest. You may see a ringtail possum (*Pseudocheirus peregrinus*) nest at the top of one of these ferns at Bradleys Head. The nest looks rather like a hairy football and is found in hollow trees or ferns and shrubs.

Rainbow lorikeets (*Trichoglossus haematodus*) also inhabit Bradleys Head, as well as Clifton Gardens and Collins Beach. Early in the morning, they shoot through the forest canopy like iridescent bullets.

Open Eucalypt Forest

Some of Sydney's finest smooth-barked apple gums (*Angophora costata*) are in the Lane Cove National Park. These ancient trees, with their gnarled pinkish trunks, lend an almost "lost world" feeling.

Tall and straight blue gums (*Eucalyptus saligna*) stand in the lower reaches of the park, where the soil is better, while the smaller grey-white scribbly gum (*Eucalyptus rossii*), with its distinctive gum veins, lives on higher slopes. If you examine the markings on a scribbly gum closely, you will see they start out thin, gradually become thicker, then take a U-turn and stop. This is the track made by an *ogmograptis* caterpillar the

Coastal heathland lining the cliff tops at Manly's North Head

previous year. The grubs that made the track become small, brownish-grey moths and are commonly seen in eucalypt or gum forests.

Grass trees (*Xanthorrhoea* species), also common in open eucalypt forest, are an ancient plant species with a tall spike that bears white flowers in spring. Lyrebirds, echidnas, currawongs and black snakes are predominant wildlife.

A smooth-barked apple gum in Lane Cove National Park

Wetlands

More than 60 per cent of New South Wales' coastal wetlands have been lost. This makes the remaining areas of wetland especially important. Most of Sydney's wetlands are mangrove swamps, with some of the best-preserved examples at Bicentennial Park and the North Arm Walking Track. Mangrove swamps are one of the most hostile places for a

A grey mangrove swamp near the Lane Cove National Park

plant or animal to live. There is no fresh water and, unlike soil, the mud has no oxygen whatsoever below the very surface level. Mangroves have developed some fascinating ways around these problems.

First, excess salt is excreted from their leaves. Secondly, they get oxygen to the roots by pushing special peg-like roots, called pneumatophores, into the air. At low tide, these can be clearly seen around the base of most mangroves. They allow air to diffuse down into the roots so that they can survive the stifling conditions under the mud. The Sydney rock oyster (*Saccostrea commercialis*), a popular local delicacy, is found in mangrove areas, particularly around the Hawkesbury and Botany Bay.

City Parks

A large number of birds and animals make the city parks their home. Silver gulls (*Larus novae-hollandiae*) and sulphur-crested cockatoos (*Cacatua galerita*) are frequent daytime visitors to Hyde Park, Centennial Park, The Domain and the Botanic Garden.

After dark, brush-tailed possums (*Trichosurus vulpecula*) go in search of food and may be seen scavenging in rubbish bins. Also a night creature, the fruit-eating grey-headed flying fox (*Pteropus poliocephalus*) can be seen swooping through the trees. There is sometimes a

The nocturnal grey-headed flying fox, at rest during the daytime

temporary colony of these in the Botanic Garden, where they hang upside down from trees.

Moore Park and The Domain are good places to spot flying foxes and they also have wonderful specimens of Moreton Bay and other fig species.

While paperbarks (*Melaleuca* species) are a feature of Centennial Park, a range of palms can be seen in the Botanic Garden. The superb fairy-wren (*Malurus cyaneus*) can also be seen here, flitting between shrubs, while overhead honeyeaters dart after each other in the tree canopy.

With more than 75,000 native shrubs and trees, Barangaroo Reserve is a harbour park on re-created naturalistic headland and is frequented by many birds.

Strangler Figs

The majestic figs in the city parks hide a dark secret. While most of the Moreton Bay figs (*Ficus macrophylla*) you see have been grown by gardeners long past, in the wild these trees have a different origin. They start as a tiny seedling, sprouted from a seed dropped by a bird in the fork of a tree. Over decades, the pencil-thin roots grow downwards. Once they reach the ground, new roots are sent down, forming a lacy network around the trunk of the host tree. They eventually become an iron-hard cage around the host tree's trunk so that it dies and rots away, leaving the fig with a hollow trunk.

The Moreton Bay fig, with its massive spreading canopy

SYDNEY THROUGH THE YEAR

Sydney's temperate climate allows for the enjoyment of outdoor activities throughout the year. Seasons in Sydney are the opposite of those in the northern hemisphere. September ushers in the three months of spring; summer stretches from December to February; March, April and May are the autumn months; while the shorter days and falling temperatures of June announce the onset of winter. In reality, however, Sydney seasons often merge into one another with little to mark their changeover. Balmy nights, the sweet, pervasive scent of jasmine blossom and the colourful blooming of shrubs and flowers are typical of spring. Summer caters for sun- and surf-lovers as well as being Sydney's festival season. Autumn, with warm days and cooler nights, is often perfect for bushwalks and picnics. And the crisp days of winter are ideal for historic walks and exploring art galleries and museums.

Spring

With the warmer weather, the profusion of spring flowers brings the city's parks and gardens excitingly to life. Food, art and music festivals abound. Footballers finish their seasons with action-packed grand finals, professional and backyard cricketers warm up for their summer competitions and the horse-racing fraternity gets ready to place its bets.

Spring display of tulip beds at the Leura Garden Festival

September
David Jones Spring Flower Show *(first two weeks)*, Elizabeth Street department store. Breathtaking floral artwork on the ground floor.
Festival of Dangerous Ideas *(first weekend)*, Sydney Opera House. Talks and debates featuring leading thinkers and culture creators from around the world.
Blackmores Sydney Running Festival *(3rd Sun)*. Four running events catering to all ages and fitness levels.
Primavera *(Sep–mid-Nov)*. Highly regarded talent-spotting show at the Museum of Contemporary Art *(see p75)*.
Tulip Time Bowral *(late Sep–early Oct)*, Bowral *(see p164)*. A two-

week festival of open gardens, talks and 100,000 tulips in bloom.
Spring Racing Carnival *(Sep–Oct)*. The horse-racing action is shared between Rosehill racecourse and the Royal Randwick racecourse.
Festival of the Winds *(dates vary)*, Bondi Beach *(see p139)*. Multi-cultural kite-flying festival.

October
Good Food Month *(all month)*. Food events across the city, highlighted by Night Noodle Markets in Hyde Park.
Australian Rugby League Grand Final *(first Sun)*, ANZ Stadium, Homebush.
Manly International Jazz Festival *(Labour Day weekend)*. World-class jazz at a variety of venues *(see p135)*.
Kidtopia *(early Oct)*, Parramatta Park. Three days of family fun, music and food.
Leura Garden Festival *(early Oct)*, Blue Mountains *(see pp162–3)*.

A village fair launches the festival, when magnificent private gardens featuring flower displays may be viewed.
Bathurst 1000 *(second Sun)*, Mount Panorama Circuit, Bathurst. The premier endurance event on Australia's motor-sport calendar.
Sculpture by the Sea *(late Oct–early Nov)*, Bondi Beach. Amazing sculptures line the sand and path between Bondi and Tamarama beaches.

November
Melbourne Cup Day *(first Tue)*. Sydney tunes in to Australia's most popular horse race, held mid-afternoon in Melbourne. Restaurants and hotels offer special luncheons on the day.
Sydney to the Gong Bicycle Ride *(first Sun)*. From Moore Park to Wollongong. Over 10,000 cyclists of all standards do this 92-km (57-mile) ride.

Kite-flying on Bondi Beach at the Festival of the Winds

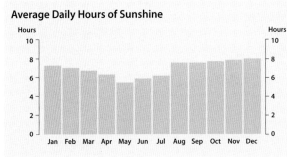

Average Daily Hours of Sunshine

Hours (left axis) / Hours (right axis): 10, 8, 6, 4, 2, 0

Jan Feb Mar Apr May Jun Jul Aug Sep Oct Nov Dec

Sunshine Hours
A sunny climate is one of Sydney's main attractions. There are very few days with no sunshine at all, even in the middle of winter. An up-to-date weather forecast is available by telephoning 1196. Coastal weather conditions can be obtained by dialling 11541.

Summer

Sydney turns festive in the summer. Christmas pageants and open-air carol singing in The Domain mark the start of the season. Then there is the Sydney Festival, three weeks of cultural events and other popular entertainment, culminating in Australia Day and the Yabun Festival celebrations on 26 January. Summer, too, brings a feast for sport lovers, with surfing and life-saving events, yacht races and both domestic and international cricket matches.

Surfing "Santa Claus": Christmas Day celebrations on Bondi Beach

December

Carols in The Domain *(second Sat before Christmas)*. Carols by candlelight in the parkland of the city's favourite outdoor gathering spot *(see p109)*.
Sydney to Hobart Yacht Race *(26 Dec)*. The harbour teems with small craft as they escort racing yachts out to sea for the start of their journey.
New Year's Eve *(31 Dec)*. Street parties in The Rocks and Circular Quay and fireworks displays in Sydney Harbour.

January

Opera in The Domain *(one Sat)*, The Domain *(see p109)*. A free

performance of opera highlights by Opera Australia.
Symphony in The Domain *(one Sat)*, The Domain *(see p109)*. Free concert by the Sydney Symphony Orchestra.
Cricket Test matches and one-day internationals at Sydney Cricket Ground *(see p54)*.
Flickerfest *(early–mid-Jan)*, Bondi Pavilion *(see pp146)*. Festival of Australian and international short films and animation.
Sydney Festival *(three weeks)*. Fantastic music, theatre and art events are staged.
Apia Sydney International *(mid-Jan)*, Olympic Park Tennis Centre. Week-long tennis tournament attracting some of the top players in the world.

Chinese New Year lion

Yabun Festival *(26 Jan)*, Victoria Park. Australia's largest celebration of indigenous cultures features traditional performances, music and talks.
Ferrython *(26 Jan)*, Sydney Harbour. Ferries compete for line honours, as do rigged

competitors in the Tall Ships Race held on the same day.
Australia Day Concert *(26 Jan)*. Music concerts take place all over the city to celebrate this national holiday.
Chinese New Year *(late Jan or early Feb)*. Lion dancing, fireworks and other festivities in Chinatown *(see pp100–101)*, Darling Harbour and Cabramatta *(p44)*.

February

Sydney Gay and Lesbian Mardi Gras, various inner-city venues *(see p32)*. A month of events culminating in a street parade, mainly on Oxford Street, usually running from late Feb or early March.
North Bondi Classic Ocean Swim *(one Sun in early Feb)*, North Bondi *(see p139)*. A popular 2-km (1½-mile) race that any swimmer is eligible to enter.
Coogee Surf Carnival *(first weekend)*, Coogee *(see p57)*.
Tropfest *(second Sun)*, Parramatta Park. Outdoor screenings of the competition finalists in this popular short-film festival.

Australia Day Tall Ships Race in Sydney Harbour

Average Monthly Rainfall

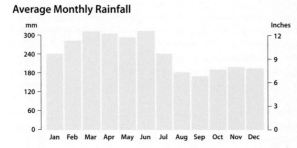

Rainfall Chart

Autumn is Sydney's rainiest season, with March being the wettest month, while spring is the driest time of year. Rainfall, however, can often be unpredictable. Long stretches of sunny weather are common, but so, too, are periods of unrelenting rain.

Autumn

After the humidity of the summer, autumn brings fresh mornings and cooler days that are tailor-made for outdoor pursuits. There are many sporting and cultural events – some of them colourful and eccentric – to tempt the visitor. For many, the Royal Easter Show is the highlight of the season. Anzac Day (25 April) is a national holiday on which Australians commemorate their war dead.

March

Dragon Boat Races Festival (late Feb–early Mar), Darling Harbour (see pp94–5). Brilliantly decorated Chinese dragon boats race across Cockle Bay.
ArtExpress (all month), Art Gallery of NSW (pp110–13). Exhibition of major artworks by the pick of the state's best graduating high school students.

St Patrick's Day beer

Seniors Week (mid-Mar), statewide. Activities and events, many of them free, including talks, exhibitions and concerts for the state's older citizens.
St Patrick's Day (17 Mar, or closest Sun). The city's Irish pubs mark the day with celebrations and music, serving Irish food and, sometimes, green beer (see p45).
Sydney Regatta (early Mar). One of the largest competitive keelboat regattas in Australia.
Autumn Racing Carnival (six weeks during Mar and Apr). Sydney's premier horseracing event, held at Randwick racecourse, with millions of dollars in prize money up for grabs.

Easter

Sydney Royal Easter Show (opens for two weeks over Easter period), Olympic Park, Homebush. Country meets city for around 14 days of ring events, livestock and produce judging, woodchopping competitions,

Entrant in a woodchopping competition at the Easter Show

sheepdog trials, craft displays and sideshow alley attractions.

April

National Trust Heritage Festival (dates vary). Celebration of the natural and cultural heritage of Sydney (see www.nsw.nationaltrust.org.au).
Anzac Day (25 Apr). Dawn remembrance service held at the Cenotaph, Martin Place (see p86), with a parade by war veterans along George Street.
Sydney Comedy Festival (late Apr–late May). Sketches, satire, improv, magic and more by the world's best and top emerging talent at venues across Sydney.

May

Sydney Writers' Festival (dates vary, one week mid-May), Pier 4/5, Hickson Road, Walsh Bay. Australia's finest literary celebration, with more than 300 events featuring Australian and international writers and publishers.
Vivid Sydney (late May–early Jun). Sydney is transformed into a canvas of lights, music and creative forums (see pp32–3).

Traditional decorative dragon boats on Darling Harbour's Cockle Bay

Average Monthly Temperature

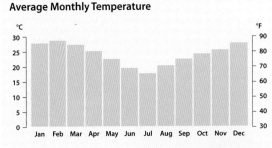

Temperature Chart
This chart gives the average minimum and maximum temperatures for Sydney. Spring and autumn are generally free of extremes, but be prepared for sudden cold snaps in winter and occasional bursts of oppressive humid heat in summer.

Winter

Winter in Sydney can be cold enough to require warm jackets; temperatures at night may drop dramatically away from the coast. The days are often clear and sometimes surprisingly mild. Arts are a major feature of winter. There are lots of exhibitions and the Sydney Film Festival, which no film buff will want to miss.

June

Manly Food and Wine Festival (first weekend), Manly Beach (see p135). Annual food and wine festival plus train rides, bouncy castles and more for children.

The familiar logo of the Film Festival

Queen's Birthday Weekend (early Jun), Darling Harbour (see pp94–5). This long weekend of celebrations also marks the official opening of the Australian ski season.

Sydney Film Festival (two weeks mid-Jun), State Theatre (see p84). The latest short and feature films, as well as retrospectives and showcases.

Winter Magic Festival (weekend closest to winter solstice), Katoomba. Celebrate the winter solstice with elves and fairies in a street parade.

July

Biennale of Sydney (two months, mid-year), various venues. International festival, held in even-numbered years, encompassing and showcasing many forms of visual art, from painting and installations to photography and performance art.

Yulefest (throughout winter), Blue Mountains (see pp162–3). Hotels, guesthouses and some restaurants celebrate a midwinter "Christmas" with log fires and all the Yuletide trimmings.

NAIDOC (National Aboriginal and Torres Strait Islander) Week (dates vary). Week-long celebrations to build awareness and understanding of Aboriginal culture and history.

The Rocks Aroma Festival (late Jul), The Rocks (see pp66–7). A festival celebrating ground coffee, spices and teas.

Splendour in the Grass (late Jul), Byron Bay. A weekend of alternative music and arts.

Archibald, Wynne and Sulman exhibitions (Jul–Sep), Art Gallery of NSW (pp110–13). Annual exhibition of competition entries for prestigious prizes in portrait, landscape and genre painting.

Australian soldiers or "Diggers" at an Anzac Day ceremony

Public Holidays

New Year's Day (1 Jan)
Australia Day (26 Jan)
Good Friday (variable)
Easter Monday (variable)
Anzac Day (25 Apr)
Queen's Birthday (second Mon in Jun)
Bank Holiday (first Mon in Aug: only banks and some financial institutions are closed)
Labour Day (first Mon in Oct)
Christmas Day (25 Dec)
Boxing Day (26 Dec)

August

Sydney International Boat Show (early Aug), ICC Sydney and Cockle Bay Marina, Darling Harbour (see pp94–5; www.sydneyboatshow.com.au).

City to Surf Race (second Sun). From the city to Bondi Beach (see p139). A 14-km (9-mile) community event that attracts all types, from amateurs to leading marathon runners.

Runners in the City to Surf Race, surging down William Street

SPORTING SYDNEY

Throughout Australia sport is a way of life and Sydney is no exception. On any day you'll see locals on golf courses at dawn, running around the streets keeping fit, or having a quick set of tennis after work. At weekends, during summer and winter, there is no end to the variety of sports you can watch. Thousands gather at Allianz Stadium and Sydney Cricket Ground whenever a big game is on, while, for those who cannot make it, sport reigns supreme on weekend television.

Cricket

During the summer months, Test cricket, one-day internationals and the entertainment-fuelled domestic Big Bash series Twenty20 games are played at the Sydney Cricket Ground (SCG). Tickets for weekday sessions of the Tests can often be bought at the gate (check online for availability of tickets on the day), although it is advisable to book well in advance (through **Ticketek**) for weekend sessions of Test matches and for all the one-day international matches.

Rugby League and Rugby Union

The popularity of Rugby League knows no bounds here. This is what people are referring to when they talk about "the footy". There are three major competition levels: national, State of Origin – which matches Queensland against New South Wales – and international Tests. The National Rugby League (NRL) competition fields teams from all over Sydney as well as Newcastle, Canberra, Melbourne, Brisbane, the Gold Coast, Far

Australia's Wallabies playing the All Blacks in a Rugby Test

North Queensland and Auckland, New Zealand. Many of these matches are held in different areas of Sydney, although the ANZ Stadium at Sydney Olympic Park is by far the biggest venue. Tickets for State of Origin and Test matches often sell out quickly.

Rugby Union Test matches and provincial Super Rugby games are also very popular. For premium trans-Tasman rivalry, watch Australia's "Wallabies" and the New Zealand All Blacks battle it out for the Bledisloe Cup.

Golf and Tennis

Golf enthusiasts need not do without their round of golf.

There are many courses throughout Sydney where visitors are welcome. These include **Moore Park**, **St Michael's** and **Warringah** golf courses. It is sensible to phone beforehand for a booking, especially at weekends.

Tennis is another favoured sport. Courts available for hire can be found all over Sydney. Many centres also have flood-lit courts available for night time. Try **Cooper Park** or **Parkland Sports** Centre.

Playing golf at Moore Park, one of Sydney's public courses

Australian Rules Football

Although not as popular as in Melbourne, "Aussie Rules" has a strong following in Sydney. The original local team, the Sydney Swans, plays its home games at the Sydney Cricket Ground. A second Sydney-based team, the Greater Western Sydney Giants, plays at Homebush.

Rivalry between the Sydney supporters and their Melbourne counterparts is always strong. Tickets can usually be bought at the ground on match day.

Basketball

Basketball is a popular spectator and recreational sport in the city. Sydney has male and female teams competing in the National Basketball League. The men's games, held at the Sydney Olympic Park's

Aerial view showing both Allianz Stadium and Sydney Cricket Ground

The Allianz Stadium at Moore Park

Qudos Bank Arena, have much of the pizzazz, colour and excitement of American basketball. Tickets can be purchased from Ticketek, on the phone or on the Internet.

Cycling and Inline Skating

Sydney has excellent, safe locations for the whole family to go cycling. One of the most frequented is Centennial Park (see p129). You can hire bicycles and safety helmets from **Centennial Park Cycles**.

Another popular pastime in summer is inline skating, and skaters can often be seen on the paths of the city's parks as well as on the streets. **Rollerblading.com.au** runs tours starting at Milsons Point to all parts of Sydney. If you're unsteady, they also do group and private lessons.

For those who like to keep both feet firmly on the ground, you can watch skateboarders and inline skaters practising their moves at the ramps at Bondi Beach (see p139).

Inline skaters enjoying a summer evening on the city's streets

Horse Riding

For a leisurely ride, head to Centennial Park or contact the **Centennial Parklands Equestrian Centre**. They will give details of the five riding schools that operate in the park. **Shelby Equestrian Centre** conducts trail rides through Ku-ring-gai Chase National Park (see pp156–7).

Further afield, you can enjoy the scenery of the Blue Mountains (see pp162–3) on horseback. The **Megalong Australian Heritage Centre** has rides lasting from one hour to overnight. All levels of experience are catered for.

Horse riding in one of the parks surrounding the city centre

Adventure Sports

You can participate in guided bushwalking, mountain biking, canyoning, rock climbing and abseiling expeditions in the nearby Blue Mountains National Park. The **Blue Mountains Adventure Company** runs one-day or multi-day courses and trips for all standards of adventurer.

In the city, **BridgeClimb** offers 2½- and 3½-hour guided climbs to the summit of Sydney Harbour Bridge (see p73).

DIRECTORY

Blue Mountains Adventure Company
84a Bathurst Rd, Katoomba.
Tel 4782 1271. w bmac.com.au

BridgeClimb
3 Cumberland St, The Rocks, Sydney. **Map** 1 A3. **Tel** 8274 7777.
w bridgeclimb.com.

Centennial Park Cycles
50 Clovelly Rd, Randwick.
Tel 9398 5027.
w cyclehire.com.au

Centennial Parklands Equestrian Centre
Cnr Lang & Cook Rds, Moore Park.
Map 6 D5. **Tel** 9332 2809.
w cpequestrian.com.au

Cooper Park Tennis Courts
Off Suttie Rd, Double Bay.
Tel 9389 3100.
w cptennis.com.au

Megalong Australian Heritage Centre
Megalong Valley Rd, Megalong Valley. **Tel** 4787 8188.
w megalongcc.com.au

Moore Park Golf Club
Cnr Cleveland St & Anzac Parade, Moore Park. **Map** 5 B5.
Tel 9663 1064.
w mooreparkgolf.com.au

Parkland Sports
Cnr Anzac Parade & Lang Rd, Moore Park. **Tel** 9662 7033.
w centennialparklands.com. au/sports

Rollerblading.com.au
Tel 0411 872 022.

St Michael's Golf Club
Jennifer St, Little Bay.
Tel 9326 8009.
w stmichaelsgolf.com.au

Shelby Equestrian Centre
90 Booralie Rd, Terrey Hills.
Tel 9450 1745.
w shelbyec.com.au

Ticketek
Tel 132849. w ticketek.com.au

Warringah Golf Club
397 Condamine St, North Manly.
Tel 9905 1326.

Sydney's Beaches

As Sydney is a city built around the water, it is no wonder that many of its recreational activities involve the sand, sea and sun. There are many harbour and surf beaches in Sydney, most of them accessible by bus *(see p236)*. Even if you're not a swimmer, the beaches offer a chance to just relax and enjoy the fresh air and coastal way of life.

A group of scuba divers preparing to enter the water at Gordons Bay

Swimming

Harbour beaches such as Camp Cove, Shark Bay and Balmoral Beach are generally smaller and more sheltered than the ocean beaches. The latter have surf lifesavers in distinctive red and yellow caps. Surf lifesaving carnivals are held throughout summer. Check **Surf Life Saving NSW** for a calendar of events. The **Beachsafe** website has information on facilities, weather conditions and lifesaving services. District councils also provide their own lifeguards, who wear blue uniforms. Rules about swimming are rigorously enforced, so try to familiarize yourself with beach signage.

The beaches can sometimes become polluted, especially after heavy rain. Find up-to-date details at **Beach Watch and Harbour Watch Information**.

Surfing

Surfing is more a way of life than a leisure activity for some Sydney-siders. Beginners can try Bondi, Bronte, Palm Beach or Collaroy.

Two of the best surf beaches are Maroubra and Narrabeen. Bear in mind that local surfers do not take kindly to "intruders" who drop in on their waves or leave litter on their beaches. To hire a surfboard, try Bondi Surf Co on Campbell Parade, Bondi Beach, or Aloha Surf on Pittwater Road, Manly. If you would like to learn, try surf schools such as **Manly Surf School** and **Lets Go Surfing** at Bondi Beach. They also hire out boards and wetsuits.

Windsurfing and Sailing

Sydney has locations suitable for every level of windsurfer. Boards can be hired from **Balmoral Sailing School** at Balmoral Beach. Good spots include Palm Beach, Narrabeen Lakes, La Perouse, Brighton-Le-Sands and Kurnell Point (for beginner and intermediate boarders) and Long Reef Beach, Palm Beach and Collaroy (for the more experienced windsurfer).

One of the best (though expensive) ways to see the harbour is while sailing. A sailing boat, including a skipper, can be hired for the afternoon from the **East Sail** sailing club. If you'd like to learn how to sail, the sailing club has two-day courses and also hires out sailing boats and motor cruisers to experienced sailors.

Scuba Diving

There are some excellent dive spots around Sydney. More favoured spots are Gordons Bay, Shelly Beach, and Camp Cove.

Pro Dive Coogee offers a complete range of courses, escorted dives, introductory dives for beginners, and hire equipment. **Dive Centre Manly** also runs courses and introductory dives, hires out equipment and conducts boat dives seven days a week.

DIRECTORY

Balmoral Sailing School
Balmoral Park, The Esplanade, Mosman. **Tel** 9960 5344.
W sailingschool.com.au

Beach Watch and Harbour Watch Information
W environment.nsw.gov.au/beach

Beachsafe
W beachsafe.org.au

Dive Centre Manly
10 Belgrave St, Manly.
Tel 9977 4355.
W divesydney.com.au

East Sail
d'Albora Marinas, New Beach Rd, Rushcutters Bay. **Tel** 9327 1166.
W eastsail.com.au

Lets Go Surfing
128 Ramsgate Ave, North Bondi.
Tel 9365 1800.
W letsgosurfing.com.au

Manly Surf School
North Steyne Rd, Manly.
Tel 9932 7000.
W manlysurfschool.com.au

Pro Dive Coogee
27 Alfreda St, Coogee. **Tel** 9665 6333. W prodivesydney.com

Surf Life Saving NSW
Tel 9471 8000.
W surflifesaving.com.au

Rock baths and surf lifesaving club at Coogee Beach

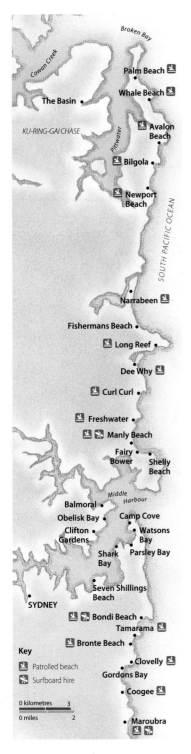

Top 30 beaches

These beaches have been selected for their safe swimming, water sports, facilities available or their picturesque setting.

	Swimming Pool	Surfing	Windsurfing	Fishing	Scuba Diving	Picnic/Barbecue	Restaurant/Café
Avalon	●	●	●	●		●	
Balmoral	●		●	●	●	●	●
The Basin	●					●	
Bilgola							
Bondi Beach	●	●		●	●	●	●
Bronte	●	●		●	●	●	●
Camp Cove					●		
Clifton Gardens	●		●	●	●	●	
Clovelly	●			●	●	●	●
Coogee	●		●	●	●	●	●
Curl Curl	●	●		●			
Dee Why	●	●		●	●	●	●
Fairy Bower					●		
Fishermans Beach		●	●	●	●		
Freshwater	●	●		●		●	
Gordons Bay				●	●		
Long Reef		●	●		●		
Manly Beach	●	●		●			●
Maroubra		●		●		●	●
Narrabeen	●	●		●			
Newport Beach	●	●	●	●		●	
Obelisk Bay							
Palm Beach	●	●	●	●		●	●
Parsley Bay	●					●	
Seven Shillings Beach	●					●	
Shark Bay	●					●	●
Shelly Beach					●	●	●
Tamarama		●		●	●	●	●
Watsons Bay	●		●	●			●
Whale Beach	●	●	●	●		●	●

The Types of Waves

Cresting waves can be identified by the foam that is created as they break from the top. These waves are ideal for board riding and body surfing.

Plunging waves curl into a tube before breaking close to the shore. Fondly known as "dumpers", these waves should only be tackled by experienced surfers.

Surging waves are those that don't appear to break. They often travel way into the beach before breaking and can easily sweep a young child off its feet.

Garden Island to Farm Cove

Sydney's vast harbour, also named Port Jackson after a Secretary in the British Admiralty (who promptly changed his name), is a drowned river valley which was transformed over millions of years. Its intricate coastal geography of headlands and secluded bays can sometimes confound even lifelong residents. This waterway was the lifeblood of the early colony, with the maritime industry a vital source of wealth and supply. The legacies of alternate recessions and booms can be viewed along the shoreline: a representative story in a nation where an estimated 70 per cent of the population cling to the coastal cities, especially along the eastern seaboard.

The city skyline developed at random. The careless destruction of architectural history in the 1960s–70s was halted, and towers now stand amid preserved Victorian buildings.

Two harbour beacons, known as "wedding cakes" because of their three tiers, are solar powered and equipped with a fail-safe back-up. There are around 350 buoys and beacons now in operation.

KEY

① **Garden Island** marks a 1940s construction project with 12 ha (30 acres) reclaimed from the harbour.

② **The barracks** for the naval garrison date from 1888.

③ **Woolloomooloo Finger Wharf** has been developed as a dynamic dining and residential complex.

0 metres		250
0 yards		250

Sailing on the harbour is a pastime not exclusively reserved for the rich and elite. Of the several hundred thousand pleasure boats registered, some are available for hire while others take out groups of inexperienced sailors.

Mrs Macquaries Chair is a carved rock seat (see p108) by Mrs Macquaries Road. In the early days of the colony this was the site of a fruit and vegetable garden, which was farmed until 1805.

The Andrew (Boy) Charlton Pool is a favourite bathing spot for inner-city residents, and is named after the Sydneysider who, at the age of 16, won an Olympic gold medal in 1924. It was erected in 1963 on the Domain Baths' site, which had a grandstand for 1,700 spectators.

Locator Map
See Street Finder, map 2

Harry's Café de Wheels, a snack van, is a Sydney culinary institution, and has been operating continuously since 1945. Photographs of celebrity customers are pinned to the van.

The Royal Botanic Garden displays both flowering and non-flowering plants. Here the first trees were planted by the new European colonists; some of these trees survive today.

Farm Cove has long been a mooring place for visiting naval vessels. The land opposite, now the Royal Botanic Garden, has been continuously cultivated for over 200 years.

Sydney Cove to Walsh Bay

It is estimated that over 70 km (43 miles) of harbour foreshore have been lost as a result of the massive land reclamation projects carried out since the 1840s. That the 13 islands existing when the First Fleet arrived in 1788 have now been reduced to just eight is a startling indication of rapid and profound geographical transformation. Redevelopments around Circular Quay and the Walsh Bay area from the 1980s have opened up the waterfront for public use and enjoyment, as has the opening in 2015 of Barangaroo Reserve, a reclaimed six-hectare (15-acre) foreshore park adjacent to Walsh Bay.

Conservatorium of Music

1857 Man O'War Steps

The Sydney Opera House was designed to take advantage of its spectacular setting. The roofs shine during the day and seem to glow at night. The building can appear as a visionary landscape to the pedestrian onlooker.

Government House, a Gothic Revival building, was home to the state's governors until 1996

Harbour cruises regularly depart from Circular Quay, taking visitors out and about both during the day and in the evening. Along with the public ferries, they are a great way to see the city and its waterways.

| 0 metres | 250 |
| 0 yards | 250 |

The Sydney Harbour Bridge was also known as the "Iron Lung" at the time of its construction. During the Great Depression it provided on-site work for approximately 1,400, while many more were employed in the specialist workshops.

The Rocks, settled by convicts and troops in 1788, is one of Sydney's oldest neighbourhoods. Rich in heritage, many of its old sandstone buildings have been restored and house speciality and craft shops.

Locator Map
See Street Finder, maps 1 & 2

The Tank Stream, the colony's first water supply, now runs underground and spills into the quay.

Cahill Expressway

Circular Quay, originally and more accurately known as Semi-Circular Quay, was the last and arguably greatest convict-built structure. Tank Stream mudflats were filled in to shape the quay, and sandstone from The Rocks formed the sea wall.

The Wharf Theatres reside on a pier that took six years to build, mostly due to the diversion of labour and materials during World War I. The theatres opened in 1984.

The wharves were completed in 1922.

Imports and exports to and from the city were stored in these wharves until 1977.

The wharves' design included a rat-proof sea wall around the port. This was an urgent response to the 1900 bubonic plague outbreak, attributed to rats on the wharves.

View across Sydney Cove to Circular Quay ▶

SYDNEY AREA BY AREA

The clock on the Customs House building, decorated with sea monsters and tridents

Sights at a Glance

Historic Streets and Buildings

THE ROCKS AND CIRCULAR QUAY

Circular Quay, once known as Semi-Circular Quay, is often referred to as the "birthplace of Australia". It was here, in January 1788, that the First Fleet landed its human freight of convicts, soldiers and officials, and the new British colony of New South Wales was declared. Sydney Cove became a rallying point whenever a ship arrived bringing much-needed supplies from "home". The Quay and The Rocks remain a focal point for New Year's Eve revels, and during the annual Vivid Sydney festival (see pp32–3), when many of the buildings are bathed in colour for spectacular light shows. The Rocks area offers visitors a taste of Sydney's past, but it is a far cry from the time, little more than 100 years ago, when most inhabitants lived in rat-infested slums and gangs ruled its streets. Now scrubbed and polished, The Rocks forms part of the colourful promenade from the Sydney Harbour Bridge to the spectacular Opera House.

☐ **Restaurants** *pp186–7*

1 Altitude	**11** The East Chinese Restaurant	**20** Opera Bar
2 ARIA	**12** The Glenmore	**21** Pei Modern
3 The Australian Heritage Hotel	**13** Ground Control Café	**22** Quay
4 Bennelong	**14** Heritage Belgian Beer Café	**23** Saké Restaurant & Bar
5 The Bridge Room	**15** Lotus Dumpling Bar	**24** Tapavino
6 Cabrito Coffee Traders	**16** MCA Café	**25** Ventuno
7 Café Nice	**17** The Morrison Bar &	**26** Vintage Café
8 Café Sydney	Oyster Room	**27** Young Alfred
9 El Camino Cantina	**18** Nelson's Brasserie	
10 The Cut Bar & Grill	**19** Neptune Palace	

See also Street Finder, map 1

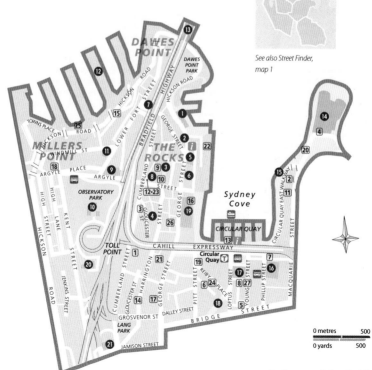

0 metres 500
0 yards 500

For keys to symbols *see back flap*

Street-by-Street: The Rocks

Named for the rugged cliffs that were once its dominant feature, this area has played a vital role in Sydney's development. In 1788, the First Fleeters under Governor Phillip's command erected makeshift buildings here, with the convicts' hard labour used to establish more permanent structures in the form of rough-hewn streets. The Argyle Cut, a road carved through solid rock using just hammer and chisel, took 18 years to build, beginning in 1843. By 1900, The Rocks was overrun with disease; the street now known as Suez Canal was once Sewer's Canal. Today, the area is still rich in Colonial history and colour.

⑪ Hero of Waterloo
Lying beneath this historic pub is a tunnel originally used for smuggling.

⑩ ★ Sydney Observatory
The first European structure on this prominent site was a windmill. The present museum holds some of the earliest astronomical instruments that were brought to Australia.

⑨ Garrison Church
Columns in this church are decorated with the insignia of British troops stationed here until 1870. Australia's first prime minister was educated next door, at Fort Street Public School.

Argyle Cut

Suez Canal

⑫ ★ Museum of Contemporary Art
The Classical façade belies the contemporary nature of the Australian and international art displayed in an ever-changing programme.

Walkway along Circular Quay West foreshore

❸ The Rocks Discovery Museum
Key episodes in The Rocks' history are illustrated by this museum's collection of maritime images and other artifacts.

Locator Map
See Street Finder, map 1

The Rocks Market is a hive of activity every weekend, offering an eclectic range of craft items and jewellery utilizing Australian icons from gum leaves to koalas.

❻ ★ Cadman's Cottage
John Cadman, government coxswain, resided in what was known as the Coxswain's Barracks with his family. His wife Elizabeth was also a significant figure, believed to be the first woman to vote in New South Wales, a right that she insisted on.

The Overseas Passenger Terminal is where some of the world's luxury cruise liners berth during their stay in Sydney.

| 0 metres | | 100 |
| 0 yards | | 100 |

Key
— Suggested route

❶ Campbell's Storehouses

7–27 Circular Quay West; The Rocks.
Map 1 B2. 🚌 Sydney Explorer,
Circular Quay routes from Elizabeth St.
🚉 Circular Quay. ♿

In 1798, the Scottish merchant Robert Campbell sailed into Sydney Cove and soon established himself as a founding father of commerce for the new colony. With trade links already established in Calcutta, his business blossomed. In 1839, Campbell began constructing a private wharf and stores to house the tea, sugar, spirits and cloth that he imported from India. Twelve sandstone bays had been built by 1861 and a brick upper storey was added in about 1890. Part of the old sea wall and 11 of the original stores still remain. The area soon took on the name of Campbell's Cove, which it retains to this day.

Today, the bond stores contain several harbourside restaurants catering for a range of tastes, from contemporary to Chinese and Italian. It is a delightful area in which to relax with a meal and watch the bustling boats in the harbour go by. The pulleys that were used to raise cargo from the wharf can still be seen on the outside, near the top of the building.

❷ George Street

Map 1 B2. 🚌 Sydney Explorer.
🚉 Circular Quay.

Formerly the preserve of wealthy merchants, sailors and the city's working class, George Street today is a popular attraction with visitors to Sydney, who are drawn to its restaurants, art galleries, museums, jewellery stores and craft souvenir shops.

One of Sydney's original thoroughfares – some say Australia's first street – it ran from the main water supply, the Tank Stream, to the tiny community in the Rocks, and was known as Spring Street. In 1810, it was renamed in honour of George III. George Street today runs from the Harbour Bridge to the Central Railway Station north of Chinatown.

Many 19th-century buildings remain, such as the 1844 Counting House at No. 43, the Old Police station at No. 127 (1882), and the Russell Hotel at No. 143 (1887).

But it is The Rocks end that most reflects what the early colony must have looked like, characterized by cobbled pavements, narrow side streets, warehouses, bond stores, pubs and shop fronts that reflect the area's maritime history. Even the Museum of Contemporary Art (see p75), constructed during the 1950s, began its life as the Maritime Services Board's administration offices.

In the early 1970s, union workers placed "green bans" on the demolition of The Rocks (see p32). These streets had been considered slum areas by the government of the day. However, many of the buildings in George Street were restored and are now listed by the National Trust. The Rocks remains a vibrant part of the city, with George Street at its hub. A market is held here every weekend, when part of the street is closed off to traffic (see p203).

A new Light Rail line running the length of George Street is due to open in 2019, aimed at reducing traffic and returning the street to its glory days as a grand pedestrian thoroughfare.

❸ The Rocks Discovery Museum

2–6 Kendall Lane, The Rocks.
Map 1 B2. **Tel** 9240 8680. 🚌 Sydney Explorer, Circular Quay routes from Elizabeth St. 🚉 Circular Quay. **Open** 10am–5pm daily. **Closed** Good Fri, 25 Dec. 🇼 **therocks.com**

This museum is in a restored 1850s sandstone coach house, and has exhibitions on the history of The Rocks, including displays on its first Aboriginal inhabitants, the Cadigal people,

Umbrellas shade the terrace restaurants overlooking the waterfront at Campbell's Storehouses

Old-style Australian products at the corner shop, Susannah Place

and Sydney's maritime history and traditions in the 18th and 19th centuries.

A unique collection of archaeological artifacts, such as an illegal alcohol still, and historical images dating from the early establishment of the European colony to the postwar era, helps visitors explore the eventful and colourful history of this neighbourhood. The displays are enhanced by interactive high-tech touch screens and audiovisual exhibits, bringing the history of the area alive.

❹ Susannah Place Museum

58–64 Gloucester St, The Rocks.
Map 1 B2. **Tel** 9241 1893.
🚌 Sydney Explorer, Circular Quay routes from Elizabeth St. 🚉 Circular Quay, Wynyard. **Open** 2–5pm daily. **Closed** Good Fri, 25 Dec. ♿ 📷
🌐 sydneylivingmuseums.com.au

This 1844 terrace of four brick and sandstone houses has a rare history of continuous domestic occupancy from the 1840s right through to 1990. The museum now housed here examines this working-class

Billy Tea on sale at the Susannah Place shop

domestic history, evoking the living conditions of its inhabitants. Rather than re-creating a single period, the museum retains the many renovations made by successive tenants.

Built for Edward and Mary Riley, who arrived from Ireland with their niece Susannah in 1838, these solid houses have basement kitchens and backyard outhouses. Connections to piped water and sewerage had probably arrived by the mid-1850s. The museum surveys the houses' development over the years, from wood and coal to gas and electricity, which enables the visitor to gauge the gradual lightening of the burden of domestic labour.

The terrace, including a corner grocer's shop, escaped the wholesale demolitions that occurred after the outbreak of bubonic plague in 1900, as well as later clearings of land to make way for the Sydney Harbour Bridge and the Cahill Expressway. In the 1970s, it was saved once again when the Builders Labourers' Federation, under the leadership of activist Jack Mundey, imposed a conservation "green ban" on

The Rocks *(see p32)*, temporarily halting all demolition and redevelopment work.

❺ Sailors' Home

106 George St, The Rocks.
Map 1 B2. 🚌 Sydney Explorer, Circular Quay routes from Elizabeth St. 🚉 Circular Quay. **Open** to gallery customers only: 9am–7pm daily (to 10pm Thu–Sat; to 8.30pm Sun).

Built in 1864 to provide cheap lodgings for visiting seamen, the Sailors' Home is now used as an art gallery. The building's original north wing is Romanesque Revival in design. The L-shaped wing that fronts onto George Street was added in 1926.

At the time it was built, the Sailors' Home was a welcome alternative to the many seedy inns and brothels in the area, saving sailors from the perils of "crimping". "Crimps" would tempt newly arrived men into lodgings and bars providing much-sought-after entertainment. While drunk, the sailors would be sold on to departing ships, waking miles out at sea and returning home in debt.

Sailors used the home until 1980, when it was adapted for use as a puppet theatre. The house is now home to the Billich Gallery, a privately owned art gallery exhibiting the art of controversial Sydney-based Surrealist painter Charles Billich, whose work also hangs in the Vatican and the United Nations.

Interior of the Sailors' Home, viewed from an upper level

Façade of Cadman's Cottage, the oldest extant building in the city

❻ Cadman's Cottage

110 George St, The Rocks. **Map** 1 B2.
Tel 9247 5033. 🚌 Sydney Explorer,
Circular Quay routes from Elizabeth St.
🚆 Circular Quay. **Closed** to the
public.

Dwarfed by the adjacent Sailors'
Home, of which it was once
part, this small historic site is
no longer open to the public,
though it is possible to walk
around the outside of it. Built in
1816 to house the crews of the
governor's boats, it is Sydney's
oldest surviving dwelling.
    The cottage is named after
John Cadman, a convict who
was transported in 1798 for
stealing horses. By 1813, he was
coxswain of a timber boat and
the following year received an
unconditional pardon. In 1821,
he was granted a full pardon. Six
years later, he was made boat
superintendent of government
craft and took up residence
in the four-room cottage
that now bears his name.
    Cadman married Elizabeth
Mortimer in 1830. She had
also arrived in Sydney as a
convict, sentenced to seven
years' transportation for the
theft of one hairbrush. The
couple, along with Elizabeth's
two daughters, lived in the
cottage until 1846.
    When Cadman's Cottage was
built it stood on the foreshore
of Sydney Harbour. At high
tide, the water used to lap
just 2.5 m (8 ft) from the door.

Now, as a result of successive
land reclamations such as the
filling in of Circular Quay in the
1870s, it is set well back from
the waterfront.

❼ Pylon Lookout

South-east pylon, Sydney Harbour
Bridge. **Map** 1 B1. **Tel** 9240 1100.
🚌 Sydney Explorer, Circular Quay
routes from Elizabeth St, 311.
🚆 Circular Quay. **Open** 10am–
5pm daily. **Closed** 25 Dec. 🅿️
🌐 pylonlookout.com.au

This site not only offers visitors
one of the best views of Sydney
from the top, but it also houses
a series of exhibitions about
the building and history of the
Sydney Harbour Bridge. Take
the time to absorb the stories
and gaze upon the artifacts
and stained-glass memorial
feature windows as you walk
the 200 steps from the bridge's
pedestrian deck to the upper
reaches of the sandstone pylon.

❽ Argyle Stores

12–20 Argyle St, The Rocks. **Map** 1 B2.
🚌 Sydney Explorer, Circular Quay
routes from Elizabeth St. 🚆 Circular
Quay. **Open** 10am–6pm daily.
Closed Good Fri, 25 Dec. ♿

The Argyle Stores consists of
a number of warehouses set
around a cobbled courtyard.
They have been converted
into a retail complex of mostly
accessories and fashion shops
that retains its period character.
    Built between 1826 and the
1880s, the stores held imported
goods such as spirits. All goods
forfeited for the non-payment
of duties were auctioned in the
courtyard. The oldest store was
built for Captain John Piper, but
it was confiscated and sold after
his arrest for embezzlement.

The Argyle Centre, as seen from the
cobbled courtyard

❾ Garrison Church

Cnr Argyle and Lower Fort Sts, Millers
Point. **Map** 1 A2. **Tel** 9247 1071.
🚌 311. **Open** 9am–6pm daily.
🕆 9:30am & 4pm Sun. ♿
🌐 churchhillanglican.com

The Holy Trinity Church is known
as the Garrison Church because
it was the colony's first military
church. Officers and men from
various British regiments, stationed at Dawes Point fort, came

Sandstone pylon of Sydney Harbour Bridge, housing historic exhibits

for morning prayers until 1870. Henry Ginn designed the church and, in 1840, the foundation stone was laid. In 1855, the architect Edmund Blacket was engaged to enlarge the church to accommodate up to 600 people. These extensions, minus the spire that Blacket proposed, were completed in 1878. Regimental plaques, hung along interior walls, recall the church's military associations.

Other features to look out for are the brilliantly coloured east window and the carved red cedar pulpit. The window was donated by a devout parishioner, Dr James Mitchell, scion of a leading Sydney family. Display cabinets at the back of the church house a few early Australian military and historical items.

East window, Garrison Church

❿ Sydney Observatory

Watson Rd, Observatory Hill, The Rocks. **Map** 1 A2. **Tel** 9921 3485. Sydney Explorer, 311. **Open** 10am–5pm daily. Night viewings Mon–Sat: phone to book. **Closed** Good Fri, 25 & 26 Dec. **maas. museum/sydney-observatory**

In 1982, this domed building, which had been a centre for astronomical observation and research for almost 125 years, became the city's astronomy museum. It has interactive equipment and games, along with night-sky viewings; it is essential to book for these.

The building began life in the 1850s as a time-ball tower. At 1pm daily, the ball on top of the tower dropped to signal the correct time. A cannon was fired simultaneously at Fort Denison. This custom continues today *(see p109)*.

In the 1880s, some of the first astronomical photographs of the southern sky were taken here. From 1890 to 1962, the observatory mapped 750,000 stars as part of an international project that produced an atlas of the entire night sky.

⓫ Hero of Waterloo

81 Lower Fort St, The Rocks. **Map** 1 A2. **Tel** 9252 4553. 311. **Open** 10am–11pm Mon & Tue, 10am–11:30pm Wed–Sat, 10am–10pm Sun. **Closed** Good Fri, 25 Dec. ground floor only.

This picturesque old inn is welcoming in the winter, when its log fires and cosy ambience offer respite from the chill outside. Built in 1844 from sandstone excavated from the Argyle Cut, this was a favourite drinking place for the nearby garrison's soldiers. Unscrupulous sea captains were said to use the hotel to recruit. Patrons who drank themselves into a stupor were pushed into the cellars through a trapdoor. From here they were carried along underground tunnels to the wharves nearby and onto waiting ships.

⓬ Wharf Theatres

Pier 4, Hickson Rd, Walsh Bay. **Map** 1 A1. **Tel** 9250 1700. 324, 325. Box office: **Tel** 9250 1777. **Open** 9am–7pm Mon, 9am–8:30pm Tue–Fri, 11am–8:30pm Sat. phone in advance. **sydneytheatre.com.au** *See Entertainment: p210.*

In 1984, the then recently formed Sydney Theatre Company took possession of this early 20th-century finger wharf at Walsh Bay. Pier 4/5 is one of four finger wharves

The corner façade of the Hero of Waterloo hotel in Millers Point

at Walsh Bay, reminders of the time when this was a busy part of the city's maritime industry.

The site fulfilled the Sydney Theatre Company's need for a base large enough to hold two theatres, rehearsal rooms and administration offices. The ingenious conversion of the once-derelict heritage building into a modern theatre complex is recognized as an outstanding architectural achievement.

Since then, the main theatre (Wharf 1) and the smaller second theatre (Wharf 2) have hosted many of the company's productions. They have seen premieres of plays from leading Australian playwrights such as Michael Gow and David Williamson, as well as international productions.

At the tip of the wharf, the bright and breezy bar area commands superb harbour views across to the Harbour Bridge *(see pp72–3)*.

The Wharf Theatres, on a former finger wharf, jutting onto Walsh Bay

⓭ Sydney Harbour Bridge

Completed in 1932, the construction of the Sydney Harbour Bridge was an economic feat, given the depressed times, as well as an engineering triumph. Prior to this, the only links between the city centre on the south side of the harbour and the residential north side were by ferry or via a circuitous 20-km (12½-mile) road route with five bridge crossings. Known as the "Coathanger", the single-span arch bridge was manufactured in sections and took eight years to build, including the railway line. Loans for the total cost of approximately 6.25 million Australian pounds were paid off in 1988. Intrepid visitors can make the vertiginous climb to its summit, with spectacular views as reward.

The 1932 Opening
The ceremony was disrupted when zealous royalist Francis de Groot rode forward and cut the ribbon in honour, he claimed, of King and Empire.

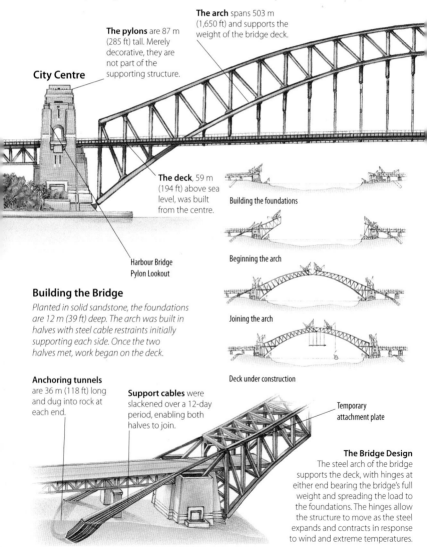

The arch spans 503 m (1,650 ft) and supports the weight of the bridge deck.

The pylons are 87 m (285 ft) tall. Merely decorative, they are not part of the supporting structure.

City Centre

The deck, 59 m (194 ft) above sea level, was built from the centre.

Harbour Bridge Pylon Lookout

Building the foundations

Beginning the arch

Joining the arch

Deck under construction

Building the Bridge

Planted in solid sandstone, the foundations are 12 m (39 ft) deep. The arch was built in halves with steel cable restraints initially supporting each side. Once the two halves met, work began on the deck.

Anchoring tunnels are 36 m (118 ft) long and dug into rock at each end.

Support cables were slackened over a 12-day period, enabling both halves to join.

Temporary attachment plate

The Bridge Design
The steel arch of the bridge supports the deck, with hinges at either end bearing the bridge's full weight and spreading the load to the foundations. The hinges allow the structure to move as the steel expands and contracts in response to wind and extreme temperatures.

BridgeClimb

Thousands of people have enjoyed the spectacular bridge-top views after a $2^1/_2$- or $3^1/_2$-hour guided tour up ladders, cat-walks and finally the upper arch of the bridge (see p55).

VISITORS' CHECKLIST

Practical Information
Map 1 B1. Pylon Lookout and Museum: **Tel** 9240 1100. **Open** 10am–5pm daily. **Closed** 25 Dec.
🅿 🆆 **pylonlookout.com.au**
🆆 **bridgeclimb.com**

Transport
🚌 all routes to Circular Quay, 311. ⛴ Circular Quay.
🚉 Circular Quay (City Centre), Milsons Point (North Shore).

Over 150,000 vehicles cross the bridge each day, about 15 times as many as in 1932.

Bridge Workers

The bridge was built by 1,400 workers, 16 of whom were killed in accidents during construction.

North Shore

Maintenance

Painting the bridge has become a metaphor for an endless task. Approximately 30,000 litres (6,593 gal) of paint are required for each coat, enough to cover an area equivalent to 60 soccer pitches.

The vertical hangers support the slanting crossbeams which, in turn, carry the deck.

Father of the Bridge

Chief engineer Dr John Bradfield shakes the hand of the driver of the first train to cross the bridge. Over a 20-year period, Bradfield supervised all aspects of the bridge's design and construction. At the opening ceremony, the highway linking the harbour's south side and northern suburbs was named in his honour.

Paying the Toll

The initial toll of sixpence helped pay off the construction loan. The toll is now used for maintenance and to pay for the 1992 Sydney Harbour Tunnel.

Strolling along a section of the Writers' Walk at Circular Quay

⑭ Sydney Opera House

See pp76–9.

⑮ Writers' Walk

Circular Quay. **Map** 1 C2. 🚌 Sydney Explorer, Circular Quay routes from Elizabeth St. 🚆 Circular Quay.

This series of plaques set in the pavement at regular intervals between East and West Circular Quay gives visitors the chance to ponder the observations of famous Australian writers, both past and present, on their home country, as well as the musings of some noted literary visitors.

Each plaque is dedicated to a particular writer, with a quotation and a brief biographical note. Australian writers include novelists Miles Franklin, Peter Carey, and Thomas Keneally, poets Oodgeroo Noonuccal and Judith Wright, humorists Clive James and Barry Humphries, and feminist Germaine Greer. Among visiting writers are Charles Darwin, D H Lawrence and Mark Twain.

⑯ Justice and Police Museum

Cnr Albert & Phillip Sts. **Map** 1 C3. **Tel** 9252 1144. 🚌 Sydney Explorer, Circular Quay routes from Elizabeth St. 🚆 Circular Quay, Martin Place. **Open** 10am–5pm Sat & Sun (daily Jan & NSW school hols). **Closed** Good Fri, 25 Dec. 🚗 📷 ♿ restricted. 🌐 sydneylivingmuseums.com.au

The museum's buildings were originally the Water Police Court, designed by Edmund Blacket

in 1856; Water Police Station, designed by Alexander Dawson in 1858; and Police Court designed by James Barnet in 1885. Here the rough-and-tumble underworld of quayside crime, from the petty to the violent, was dealt swift and, at times, harsh justice. The museum exhibits bear vivid testimony to that turbulent period, as they document and re-create legal and criminal history. Late Victorian legal proceedings can be easily imagined in the fully restored courtroom.

Menacing implements from knuckledusters to bludgeons are displayed as the macabre relics of violent and notorious crimes. The bushranger exhibit, prison artifacts, and forensic display powerfully evoke the realities of the justice system in Australia. There are also regularly changing exhibitions.

Montage of criminal "mug shots", Justice and Police Museum

⑰ Customs House

31 Alfred St, Circular Quay. **Map** 1 B3. **Tel** 9242 8551. 🚌 Sydney Explorer, Circular Quay routes from Elizabeth St. 🚆 Circular Quay. **Open** 8am–midnight Mon–Sat (from 10am Sat), 11am–5pm Sun & pub hols. **Closed** Good Fri, 25 Dec. 🚗 📷 ♿ 🌐 sydney customshouse.com.au

Colonial architect James Barnet designed this 1885 sandstone Classical Revival building on the site of an earlier Customs House. It recalls the days when trading ships loaded and unloaded their goods at the quay. Features include columns in polished granite, a sculpted coat of arms and a clock face, added in 1897, bearing a pair of tridents and dolphins. It contains a City Library with a reading room and exhibition space, and an open lounge area with an international newspaper and magazine salon, Internet access and bar. On the roof, Café Sydney offers great views.

Detail from Customs House

⑱ Macquarie Place

Map 1 B3. 🚌 Sydney Explorer, Circular Quay routes from Elizabeth St. 🚆 Circular Quay.

In 1810, Governor Lachlan Macquarie created this park on what was once part of the vegetable garden of the first Government House. The sandstone obelisk, designed by Francis Greenway *(see p116)*, was erected in 1818 to mark the starting point for all roads in the colony. The gas lamps recall the fact that this was also the site of Sydney's first street lamp, installed in 1826.

Also in this little triangle of history are the remains of the bow anchor and cannon from HMS *Sirius*, flagship of the First Fleet. There is also a statue of Thomas Mort, a 19th-century industrialist whose vast business interests embraced gold, coal and copper mining, dairy and cotton farming, wool auctioning and ship repair. These days his statue is a marshalling place for the city's somewhat kamikaze bicycle couriers.

Façade of the Museum of Contemporary Art

⓲ Museum of Contemporary Art

Circular Quay West, The Rocks. **Map** 1 B2. **Tel** 9245 2400. 🚌 Sydney Explorer, Circular Quay routes from Elizabeth St. 🚊 Circular Quay. **Open** 10am–5pm daily (to 9pm Thu). **Closed** 25 Dec. ♿ 🅿 🌐 **mca.com.au**

Sydney's substantial collection of contemporary art has grown steadily, but largely out of public view, since 1943. This was the year John Power died, leaving his art collection and a financial bequest to the University of Sydney.

In 1991, the permanent collection, including works by Hockney, Warhol, Lichtenstein and Christo, was transferred to this 1950s Art Deco-style former Maritime Services Board Building. The museum also hosts temporary exhibitions of works by both Australian and international artists.

The grassed area at the front of the building is an ideal location for a harbour-front picnic. The MCA Store sells distinctive gifts by Australian designers, as well as books on contemporary art and design.

⓴ National Trust Centre

Observatory Hill, Watson Rd, The Rocks. **Map** 1 A3. **Tel** 9258 0123. 🚌 Sydney Explorer, 311. 🚊 Circular Quay, Wynyard. **Open** 9am–5pm Mon–Fri. Gallery: **Open** 11am–5pm Tue–Sun. **Closed** public hols. 🅿 ♿ 🌐 🌐 **nationaltrust.org.au/places/national-trust-centre**

The buildings that form the headquarters of the conservation organization, the National Trust of Australia (NSW), date from 1815, when Macquarie chose the site on Observatory Hill for a military hospital.

Today they house the S H Ervin Gallery, with changing exhibitions throughout the year, designed to explore the richness and diversity of Australian art.

㉑ St Philip's Church

3 York St (enter from Jamison St). **Map** 1 A3. **Tel** 9247 1071. 🚌 311. **Open** 9am–5pm Mon–Fri. **Closed** 26 Jan. ♿ 🕐 8:30am, 10:15am (for children), 6pm Sun. 🌐 **churchhillanglican.com**

Despite its elevated site, this Victorian Gothic church seems overshadowed in its modern setting. Yet, when it was first built, the tall square tower with its decorative pinnacles was a local landmark.

Begun in 1848, St Philip's is by Edmund Blacket, dubbed "the Christopher Wren of Australia" for the 58 churches he designed. In 1851, work was disrupted when its stonemasons left for the gold fields, but was completed by 1856.

A peal of bells was donated in 1858, with another added in 1888 to mark Sydney's centenary. These bells are still in use.

The interior and pipe organ of St Philip's Anglican church

The Founding of Australia, by Algernon Talmage, which hangs in Parliament House (see pp114–15)

A Flagpole on the Mudflats

It is easy to miss the modest flagpole in Loftus Street near Customs House. It flies a flag, the Union Jack, on the spot where Australia's first ceremonial flag-raising took place. On 26 January 1788, Captain Arthur Phillip came ashore to hoist the flag and declare the foundation of the colony. A toast to the King was drunk and a musket volley fired. On the same day, the rest of the First Fleet arrived from Botany Bay to join Phillip and his men. (On this date each year, the country marks Australia Day with a national holiday.) In 1788, the flagpole was on the edge of mudflats on Sydney Cove. Today, because of the large amount of land reclaimed to build Circular Quay, it is some distance from the water's edge.

⑭ Sydney Opera House

No other building on earth looks like the Sydney Opera House. Popularly known as the "Opera House", it is, in fact, a complex of theatres, performance spaces and concert halls linked beneath its famous shells. Its birth was long and complicated. Many of the construction problems had not been faced before, resulting in an architectural adventure which lasted 14 years (see p79). As well as being Australia's most popular tourist destination, the Sydney Opera House is also one of the world's busiest performing arts centres, hosting nearly 2,000 performances for more than 1.4 million audience members every year.

★ **Joan Sutherland Theatre**
With a seating capacity of up to 1,507, the venue's second-largest theatre is home to Opera Australia and The Australian Ballet.

Detail of Possum Dreaming (1988)
The mural in the Joan Sutherland Theatre's northern foyer is by Michael Tjakamarra Nelson, an indigenous Australian painter from Papunga, in the central Australian desert.

Opera House Walkway
Extensive public walkways around the building offer the visitor views from many different vantage points.

KEY

① **The Joan Sutherland Theatre** ceiling and walls are painted black to focus attention on the stage.

② **The Monumental Steps** and forecourt are used for outdoor performances.

③ **The Playhouse**, seating almost 400, is ideal for intimate productions while also able to present plays with larger casts.

Northern Foyers
With spectacular views over the harbour, the Utzon Room and the large northern foyers of the Joan Sutherland Theatre on the eastern side of the building, as well as the Concert Hall on the western side, can be hired for conferences, lunches, parties and weddings.

★ Concert Hall
This is the largest hall, with seating for 2,679. With a high-vaulted ceiling and white birch and brush box finish, it makes for a splendid setting for classical and contemporary music, talks, comedy shows and many other events.

VISITORS' CHECKLIST

Practical Information
Bennelong Point. **Map** 1 C2. **Tel** 9250 7111. Box Office: 9250 7777. **Open** performances. ♿ limited (9250 7777). 🕐 9am–5pm daily (except Good Fri, 25 Dec); phone in advance (9250 7250). ♿ 🚻 💻 📷 🌐 **sydneyoperahouse.com**

Transport
🚌 Sydney Explorer, Circular Quay routes from Elizabeth St. 🚢 Circular Quay. 🚆 Circular Quay.

Bennelong
At the top of the Monumental Steps is the fine-dining Bennelong Restaurant *(see p187)*, one of several bars and eateries in the Opera House.

② ③

★ The Roofs
Although apocryphal, the theory that Jørn Utzon's arched roof design came to him while peeling an orange is appealing. The highest point is 67 m (221 ft) above sea level.

Detail of Utzon's Tapestry (2004)
Jørn Utzon's original design for this Gobelin-style tapestry, which hangs floor to ceiling in the remodelled Utzon Room, was inspired by the music of Carl Philipp Emanuel Bach.

Exploring Sydney Opera House

The Sydney Opera House covers almost 2 ha (4.5 acres), and is the fourth building to stand on this prominent site. Underneath the ten spectacular roofs of varying planes and textures lies a complex maze of more than 1,000 rooms of all shapes and sizes. One of the world's busiest performing arts centres, the Opera House hosts more than 2,000 events every year.

Sydney Dance Company poster advertising a production of *Poppy*

A scene from *La Bohème*, being performed in the Joan Sutherland Theatre

Joan Sutherland Theatre

The relatively compact size of this venue makes for an intimate experience, and stage designers show off the theatre's great versatility for both opera and dance. The proscenium opening is 12 m (39 ft) wide, and the stage extends back 25 m (82 ft), while the orchestra pit accommodates up to 70–80 musicians. It is rumoured that Box C plays host to a resident ghost.

Concert Hall

The rich concert acoustics under the vaulted ceiling of this venue are much admired. Sumptuous Australian wood panelling and the 18 acoustic rings above the stage clearly reflect back the sound. The 10,500 pipe Grand Organ was designed and built by Ronald Sharp in 1969–79.

Drama Theatre, Studio and Playhouse

The Drama Theatre was not included in the original building plan, so jackhammers were brought in to hack it out of the concrete. Refrigerated aluminium panels in the ceiling control the temperature.

The Playhouse is used for small-cast plays and is also a fully equipped cinema. The Sydney Theatre Company (*see p71*) stages at least one performance here every year.

The Studio hosts innovative, contemporary music and performances in an intimate space that seats just 350 people.

Backstage

Artists performing at the Opera House have the use of five rehearsal studios, 60 dressing rooms and suites and a green room, where visitors can enjoy a breakfast at the end of the Backstage Tour.

The scene-changing machinery works on very well-oiled wheels – most crucial in the Joan Sutherland Theatre where there is regularly a change of performance, with an average of 14 productions being staged in repertoire each year.

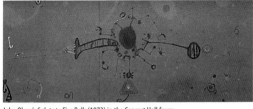

John Olsen's *Salute to Five Bells* (1973) in the Concert Hall foyer

1955 International design competition announced

Old tram shed at Bennelong Point

1948 Sir Eugene Goossens lobbies government and Bennelong Point is chosen as opera house site

1959 Construction begins

1957 Utzon's design wins and a lottery is established to finance the building

1963 Building of roof shells begins

1963 Utzon opens Sydney office

1966 Utzon resigns. Australian architects appointed to complete interior design

Roof in mid-construction

1973 Opera House officially opened by Queen Elizabeth II

1973 Prokofiev's opera *War and Peace* is the first public performance in Opera House

2009 A State memorial serv held in the Co Hall following Utzon's death

2007 Opera Hous becomes the youn building to achieve UNESCO World He status as a site of n cultural significanc

| 1945 | 1950 | 1955 | 1960 | 1965 | 1970 | 2010 |

The Design of the Opera House

In 1957, Jørn Utzon won the international competition to design the Sydney Opera House. He envisaged a living sculpture that could be viewed from any angle – land, air or sea – with the roofs as a "fifth façade". It was boldly conceived, posing architectural and engineering problems that Utzon's initial compendium of sketches did not begin to solve. When construction began in 1959, the intricate design proved impossible to execute and had to be greatly modified. The project remained so controversial that Utzon resigned in 1966 and an Australian design team completed the building's interior. In 1999, Utzon agreed to be involved in guiding future changes to the building. Since Utzon's death in 2008, his son Jan has taken on this role.

The Red Book, as submitted for the 1957 design competition, contains Utzon's original concept sketches for the Sydney Opera House.

Segmented globe

Segments separated

Roof comes into view

Several pieces cut out of a globe were used in an ingenious manner by architect Jørn Utzon to make up the now familiar shell roof structure.

Utzon's Opera House Model

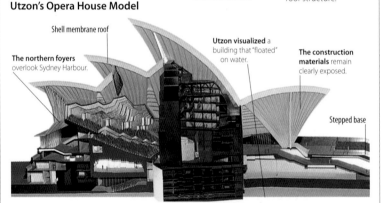

Shell membrane roof

The northern foyers overlook Sydney Harbour.

Utzon visualized a building that "floated" on water.

The construction materials remain clearly exposed.

Stepped base

Utzon's original interiors and many of his design features now exist only in model form. The architect donated his models and plans to the State Library of NSW (see p114).

The pre-cast roof has its inspiration in nature. The basic idea for the formwork of the roof was taken from the fanlike ribs of a palm. Realizing this deceptively simple idea took Utzon six years of design work.

The roof tiles were not fixed in place individually, but installed in panels to create the smooth and continuous roof surface.

The mythological figure of Apollo atop the Archibald Fountain, Hyde Park

Sights at a Glance

0 metres   500

0 yards   500

CITY CENTRE

Australia's first thoroughfare, George Street, was originally lined with clusters of mud-and-wattle huts. The gold rushes brought bustling prosperity, and by the 1880s shops and the architecturally majestic edifices of banks dominated the area. The city's first sky-scraper – Culwulla Chambers in Castlereagh Street – was completed in 1913, before the city council imposed a 46-m (150-ft) height restriction which remained in place until 1956. Hyde Park, on the edge of the city centre, was first used as a racecourse, later

becoming a popular venue for informal games of cricket. Slated for housing in the 1830s, it was saved by Governor Bourke, who reaffirmed its status as a park. Today it remains a peaceful oasis, with Sydney's legal, financial and commerical centre located to its north, full of glamorous boutiques, discount stores, offices, arcades and malls. Major transport, infrastructure, public art and open space projects are under way to revitalize this core area, spearheaded by the widening and pedestrianization of George Street.

Restaurants pp187–9

1 Bambini Trust
2 Barrafina
3 Bistrode CBD
4 Bodhi in the Park
5 Chophouse
6 Danjee
7 Diethnes
8 Double Barrel Coffee Merchants
9 Eleven Bridge
10 est.
11 Felix
12 Fix Wine Bar + Restaurant
13 Glass Brasserie
14 Gowings Bar & Grill
15 GPO Pizza by Wood
16 Machiavelli
17 Madame Nhu
18 Mother Chu's Vegetarian Kitchen
19 Mr Wong
20 No. 1 Bent St
21 Pablo and Rusty's
22 Rockpool Bar & Grill
23 Spice Temple
24 Sushi e
25 Sushi Hotara
26 Tetsuya's
27 Workshop Expresso
28 York Lane

See also Street Finder, maps 1, 4 & 5

For keys to symbols see back flap

Street-by-Street: City Centre

Encompassing the commercial and business district of Sydney, the comparatively small city centre of this sprawling metropolis is squeezed within just a few blocks. Because Sydney grew in a haphazard fashion, with many of today's streets following tracks originally made by bullocks, there was no allowance for the expansion of the burgeoning city into what has become a major international centre. The streets used to empty at night after workers and shoppers retreated to the suburbs. However, a booming population and the growing appeal of living in the city centre is driving a renaissance, with an emerging vibrant night scene of cafés, bars, restaurants and cultural venues. Rapid development of high-rise apartments has been accompanied by plans to pedestrianize the major boulevard, George Street, by 2019.

❷ ★ Queen Victoria Building
Taking up an entire city block, this 1898 former produce market has been lovingly restored and is now a shopping mall.

❸ State Theatre
A gem from the era when the movies reigned, this glittering and richly decorated 1929 cinema was once hailed as "the Empire's greatest theatre".

```
0 metres        100
0 yards         100
```

The Queen Victoria Statue was found after a worldwide search in 1983 ended in a small Irish village. It had lain forgotten and neglected since being removed from the front of the Irish Parliament in 1947.

YORK STREET

STREET

GEORGE

To Sydney
Town Hall

PITT STREET

MA

Key

— Suggested route

CASTLEREAGH

PARK

STREET

ELIZABE

❶ Marble Bar
Once a landmark bar in the 1893 Tattersalls Hotel, it was dismantled and re-erected in the Sydney Hilton in 1973.

5 Strand Arcade
A reminder of the late 19th-century Victorian era when Sydney was famed as a city of elegant shopping arcades, this faithfully restored example is said to have been the finest of them all.

Locator Map
See Street Finder, maps 1 & 4

MLC Centre

6 ★ Martin Place
Martin Place's 1929 Art Deco Cenotaph is the site of annual Anzac Day war remembrance services.

Theatre Royal

Westfield Sydney is an upscale shopping mall housing a wide range of both local and international designer labels.

Hyde Park's northern end

4 ★ Sydney Tower
The tower tops the city skyline, giving a bird's eye view of the whole of Sydney. It rises 305 m (1,000 ft) above the ground and can be seen from as far away as the Blue Mountains.

Entrance to the Marble Bar, in the basement level of the Hilton Sydney

❶ Marble Bar

488 George St. **Map** 1 B5.
Tel 9266 2000. Ⓣ Town Hall.
Open 4pm to late Mon–Thu,
5pm–2am Fri & Sat, 5–11pm Sun.
Closed public hols.

The Marble Bar, originally part of George Adams' Tattersalls Hotel built in 1893, is an inspired link with the Sydney of an earlier era. The bar, whose rich and decadent Italian Renaissance style had made it a local institution, was dismantled before the demolition of the hotel in 1969. Its colonnade entrance, fireplaces and counters were re-erected in the Sydney Hilton basement and reopened in 1973.

During the week, the bar attracts a broad range of city workers for after-work drinks. On Fridays and at weekends if a band is playing, the bar bustles with a younger crowd who come to hear mostly jazz and rhythm and blues music.

❷ Queen Victoria Building

455 George St. **Map** 1 B5. **Tel** 9264 9209. Ⓣ Town Hall. **Open** 9am–6pm Mon–Sat (to 9pm Thu), 11am–5pm Sun. Ⓖ Ⓒ *See Shops and Markets: p198 and p200.* Ⓦ **qvb.com.au**

French Designer Pierre Cardin called the Queen Victoria Building "the most beautiful shopping centre in the world". Yet this spacious, ornate Romanesque building, better known as the QVB, began life as the Sydney produce market. The dust, flies, grime and shouts as horses struggled with heavy loads on the slippery ramps are now difficult to imagine. Completed to the design of City Architect George McRae in 1898, the dominant features are the central dome, sheathed in copper, as are the 20 smaller domes, and the glass barrel-vault roof which lets in a flood of natural light.

The market closed at the end of World War I and the building fell into disrepair. It had various roles during this time, including that of City Library. By the 1950s, after extensive remodelling and neglect, it was threatened with demolition.

Refurbished at a cost of over A$75 million, the QVB reopened in 1986 as a grand shopping gallery, with over 190 shops and boutiques on four levels. At the Town Hall end a wishing well incorporates a stone from Blarney Castle, Ireland, and a sculpture of Islay, beloved dog of Queen Victoria. In 1983, a worldwide search began for a statue of the queen herself. One was finally found in the village of Daingean, Republic of Ireland, where it had lain forgotten since its removal from the front of the Irish Parliament in 1947.

Fully restored, the Queen Victoria Statue stands near the wishing well. Inside the QVB, suspended from the ceiling, is the Royal Clock. Weighing more than 1 tonne and over 5 m (17 ft) tall, the clock was designed by Neil Glasser in 1982. The upper structure features part of Balmoral Castle above a copy of the four dials of Big Ben. At one minute to every hour, a fanfare is played and there follows a parade depicting six scenes from the lives of various kings and queens of England.

Roof detail, Queen Victoria Building

❸ State Theatre

49 Market St. **Map** 1 B5. **Tel** 9373 6655. Ⓣ Town Hall, Martin Place. Box office: **Open** 9am–5:30pm Mon–Fri. **Closed** Good Fri, 25 Dec. Ⓖ Ⓒ 10am & 1pm Mon–Wed; bookings essential. Ⓦ **statetheatre.com.au.**

When it opened in 1929, this picture palace was hailed as the finest that local craftsmanship could achieve. The State Theatre is one of the best examples in Australia of the architectural fantasies used to entice people to the movies.

Its Cinema Baroque style is evident right from the Gothic foyer, with its vaulted ceiling, mosaic floor, richly decorated marble columns and statues. Inside the brass and bronze doors, the auditorium, which seats over 2,000 people, is lit by a 20,000-piece chandelier. The Wurlitzer organ (currently under repair) rises from below stage just before performances. Now one of Sydney's premier concert and theatre venues, it is also the main base for the Sydney Film Festival, held in June each year (*see p53*).

The ornately decorated Gothic foyer of the State Theatre

❹ Sydney Tower

The highest observation deck in the southern hemisphere, the Sydney Tower was conceived as part of a 1970s shopping centre, but was not completed until 1981. About one million visitors a year admire the stunning views, often stretching for over 85 km (53 miles), as far as the Blue Mountains. A landmark in itself, it can be seen from almost anywhere in the city. Visitors can also take a Skywalk tour on a platform around the turret's exterior.

Sydney Tower Eye Observation Deck
Views stretch to Pittwater in the north, Botany Bay to the south, westwards to the Blue Mountains, and out to the sea.

The 30-m (98-ft) spire completes the total 309 m (1,014 ft) of the tower's height.

The water tank holds 162,000 litres (35,500 gallons) and acts as an enormous stabilizer on very windy days.

Skywalk

Level 4: Observation deck

Level 3: Private event space

Level 2: Buffet restaurant

Level 1: A la carte restaurant

The turret's nine levels include two restaurants, a café and the Observation Level.

The windows comprise three layers. The outer has a gold dust coating. The frame design prevents panes falling outwards.

The shaft is designed to withstand wind speeds expected only once in 500 years.

The 56 cables weigh seven tonnes each. If laid end to end, they would reach from New Zealand to Sydney.

The stairs are two separate, fireproofed emergency escape routes.

Double-decker lifts can carry up to 2,000 people per hour. At full speed, a lift takes only 40 seconds to ascend the 76 floors to the Observation Level.

The 4-D cinema experience takes you on a journey around Sydney.

Construction of the Turret
The nine turret levels were erected on the roof of the base building, then hoisted up the shaft using hydraulic jacks.

Skywalk
Visitors can step out with a guide onto an open-air walkway around the outside of the Sydney Tower. The glass-floor viewing platform provides spectacular views of the city below.

❺ Strand Arcade

412–414 George St. **Map** 1 B5.
Tel 9265 6800. Ⓣ Martin Place,
Wynyard. **Open** 9am–5:30pm Mon–
Wed & Fri, 9am–9pm Thu, 9am–8pm
Sat, 11am–4pm Sun. **Closed** some
public hols, 25 & 26 Dec. ⓖ *See Shops
and Markets: pp198–201.*

Victorian Sydney was a city of
grand shopping arcades. The
Strand, joining George and Pitt
Streets and designed by English
architect John Spencer, was the
finest jewel in the city's crown.
The blaze of publicity surrounding
its opening in April 1892 was
equalled only by the natural
light pouring through the glass
roof and the artificial glare from
the chandeliers, each carrying
50 jets of gas as well as 50 lamps.
   The boutiques and shops in
the galleries make window
shopping a delight in this airy
building which, after a fire in
1976, was restored to its original
splendour. Be sure to stop,
as shoppers have done since
opening day, for refreshments
at one of the beautiful coffee
shops in the arcade.

The Pitt Street entrance to the majestic
Strand Arcade

❻ Martin Place

Map 1 B4. 🚌 Elizabeth St routes.
Ⓣ Martin Place.

Running from George Street
across Pitt, Castlereagh and
Elizabeth Streets to Macquarie
Street, this plaza was opened
in 1891 and made a traffic-free
precinct in 1971. It is busiest at
lunchtime when city workers
enjoy their sandwiches while
watching free entertainment,
sponsored by the Sydney City

Interior of National Australia Bank, George Street end of Martin Place

Council, in a performance space
near Castlereagh Street.
   Every Anzac Day, a national
day of war remembrance on
25 April, the focus moves to
the Cenotaph at the George
Street end. Thousands of past
and present servicemen and
women attend a dawn service
and wreath-laying ceremony,
followed by a march-past. The
shrine, with bronze statues of a
soldier and a sailor on a granite
base, by Bertram MacKennal,
was unveiled in 1929.
   On the southern side of the
Cenotaph is the symmetrical
façade of the Renaissance-
style General Post Office,
considered to be the finest
building by James Barnet,
Colonial Architect. Con-
struction of the GPO, as
Sydneysiders call it, took
place between 1866 and
1874, with additions in Pitt
Street between 1881 and
1885. Most controversial
were the relief figures
executed by Tomaso
Sani. Although Barnet
declared that the figures
represented Australians
in realistic form, they were
labelled "grotesque".
   The Commonwealth Savings
Bank is further north, just after
the intersection with Pitt Street.
Built in 1928, this Beaux-Arts

building has a pink granite façade
with four huge Ionic columns.
   The next building along
is the MLC Centre, a famous
skyscraper designed by Harry
Seidler *(see p43)*.

❼ Lands Department Building

23 Bridge St. **Map** 1 B3. 🚌 325,
George St routes. **Open** only one
day of the year, date varies. ⓖ
Ⓦ **sydneylivingmuseums.com.au**

Designed by the Colonial
Architect James Barnet, this
three-storey Classical Revival
sandstone edifice was built
between 1877 and 1890.
   As with the GPO building,
Pyrmont sandstone was
used for the exterior.
Decisions about the
subdivision of much of rural
eastern Australia were made
in offices within. Statues of
explorers and legislators
who "promoted settle-
ment" fill 23 of the
façade's 48 niches;
the remainder are still
empty. The luminaries
include the explorers Hovell
and Hume, Sir Thomas Mitchell,
Blaxland, Lawson and Wentworth
(see p138), Ludwig Leichhardt,
Bass and Matthew Flinders and
the botanist Sir Joseph Banks.

Statue of explorer
Gregory Blaxland

⑧ Museum of Sydney

Cnr Bridge & Phillip Sts. **Map** 1 B3.
Tel 9251 5988. Ⓣ Circular Quay,
Martin Place. **Open** 10am–5pm daily.
Closed Good Fri, 25 Dec. 🖼 🅿 🚫
🅰 ♿ Ⓦ **sydneylivingmuseums.
com.au/museum-of-sydney**

Situated at the base of Governor
Phillip Tower, the Museum of
Sydney is on the site of the first
Government House, the home,
office and seat of authority for
the first nine governors of NSW
from 1788 until its demolition
in 1846. The design assimilates
a valuable archaeological site
into a modern office block.
The museum itself traces the
city's turbulent history, from
the 1788 arrival of the British
colonists until the present day.

Indigenous Peoples

The museum sits on Cadigal
land. A gallery explores the
culture, history, continuity
and place of Sydney's original
Aboriginal inhabitants, and the
"turning point" of colonization/
invasion. Collectors' chests
hold items of daily use such
as flint and ochre, each piece
painstakingly catalogued and
evocatively interpreted.

There are two audiovisual
exhibits which explore the
history of indigenous peoples

The Viewing Cube, Level 2, overlooking the
piazza to Circular Quay

from a contemporary perspec-
tive. In the square at the front
of the complex, the acclaimed
Edge of the Trees sculpture, a
collection of 29 sandstone, steel
and wooden pillars, symbolizes
the first contact
between the
Aboriginal peoples
and Europeans.
Haunting voices
in the Eora tongue
fill the space.
Inscribed in the
wood are signa-
tures of the First
Fleeters and names
of botanical species
in both the indigenous language
and Latin. Incisions made in the
pillars are filled with organic
materials such as ash, feathers,
bone, shells and human hair.

The Trade Wall display
on Level 1

History of Sydney

Outside the museum, a paving
pattern outlines the site of
the first Government House.
Original foundations, lost under
street level for many years,
can be seen here through a
window. Inside the entrance
a viewing floor reveals more
foundations. A segment of wall
has been reconstructed using
sandstone excavated during
archaeological exploration of
the site.

The Colony display on Level 1
focuses on Sydney during the
critical decade of the 1840s when
convict transportation ended,
the town officially became a
city and suffered an economic
depression. There is also a set of
scale models of the 11 First Fleet
ships. The museum
presents stories
of the Fleet's
journey, arrival,
first contacts
with indigenous
people and the
survival challenges
faced by those on
board. On Level 2,
20th-century Sydney
is explored, with
panoramic images of the
developing city providing a
vivid backdrop. The Museum of
Sydney has a regular changing
exhibition programme.

Edge of the Trees sculptural installation, by Janet Laurence and Fiona Foley (1995)

Gothic Revival-style façade of St Mary's Cathedral

❾ St Mary's Cathedral

St. Mary's Rd. **Map** 1 C5. **Tel** 9220 0400. Elizabeth St routes. St James, Martin Place. Cathedral: **Open** 6:30am–6pm Mon–Fri (to 7pm Sat & Sun). Crypt: **Open** 10am–4pm Mon–Fri. with advance notice. by prior arrangement. **stmaryscathedral.org.au**

Although Catholics arrived with the First Fleet, the celebration of Mass was at first prohibited in case the priests provoked civil strife among the colony's large Irish Catholic population. The first priests were appointed in 1820 and services allowed. In 1821, Governor Macquarie laid the foundation stone for St Mary's Chapel on the site of today's cathedral, the first land granted to the Catholic Church in Australia.

The initial section of the Gothic Revival-style cathedral was opened in 1882. In 1928, the building was completed, but without the twin southern spires proposed by the architect, William Wardell. By the entrance steps are statues of Australia's first cardinal, Moran, and Archbishop Kelly who laid the stone for the final stage in 1913. They were sculpted by Bertram MacKennal, also responsible for the Martin Place Cenotaph (see p86) and the Shakespeare group outside the State Library (see p114). The crypt houses a historical exhibition of the early Sydney church. The terrazzo mosaic floor here took 15 years to complete.

⓫ Great Synagogue

187 Elizabeth St, entrance on 166 Castlereagh St. **Map** 1 B5. **Tel** 9267 2477. Elizabeth St routes. St James. **Open** for services and tours. **Closed** public & Jewish hols. with advance notice. **greatsynagogue.org.au**

Candelabra from the Great Synagogue

The longest-established Jewish Orthodox congregation in Australia assembles in this synagogue, consecrated in 1878. Although Jews had arrived with the First Fleet, worship did not begin until the 1820s. With its carved entrance columns and stained-glass windows, the synagogue is perhaps the finest work of Thomas Rowe, the architect of Sydney Hospital (see p115). The panelled ceiling is decorated with hundreds of tiny gold-leaf stars.

❿ Hyde Park

Map 1 B5. Elizabeth St routes. St James, Museum.

Fenced and named after its London equivalent by Governor Macquarie in 1810, Hyde Park marked the outskirts of the township. It was a popular exercise field for garrison troops and was later used as a racecourse.

Tomb of the Unknown Soldier in the Art Deco Anzac Memorial

Though much smaller today, it still provides a peaceful haven.

Anzac Memorial
The 30-m- (98-ft-) high Art Deco memorial, reflected in the poplar-lined Pool of Remembrance, commemorates those Australians who were killed at war in the service of their country. Opened in 1934, it now includes a photographic and military artifact exhibition downstairs. Nearby, the Yininmadyemi artwork, depicting standing bullets and fallen shells, honours the Aborigines who have served in Australia's military.

Sandringham Gardens
In spring, the pergola here is a cascade of mauve-flowering wisteria. The gardens, a memorial to the English kings George V and George VI, were opened by Queen Elizabeth II in 1954.

Diana, goddess of purity and the chase, Archibald Fountain

Archibald Fountain
This bronze and granite fountain commemorates the French and Australian World War I alliance. It was completed by François Sicard in 1932 and donated by J F Archibald, one of the founders of the *Bulletin*, a popular literary magazine which encouraged the work of Henry Lawson and "Banjo" Paterson, among many others. It was Archibald's bequest that established the Archibald Prize for portraiture (see p53).

The Grand Organ in Sydney Town Hall's Centennial Hall

⑫ Sydney Town Hall

483 George St. **Map** 4 E2. **Tel** 9265 9333. 🚇 Town Hall. **Open** 8:30am–6pm Mon–Fri. **Closed** public hols. 🚹 ⭕ 🅆 sydneytownhall.com.au

The steps of this sandstone building, central to George Street's Victorian architecture, have been a favourite Sydney meeting place since it opened in 1869. Walled burial grounds had originally covered the site.

It is a fine example of high Victorian architecture. The original architect, J H Wilson, died during its construction, as did several of the architects who followed. The vestibule – an elegant salon with intricate plasterwork, lavish stained glass and a crystal chandelier – is the work of Albert Bond. The Bradbridge brothers completed the clock tower in 1884. From 1888–9, other architects were used for the Centennial Hall, with its coffered zinc ceiling and the imposing 19th-century Grand Organ with over 8,500 pipes.

On the façade, you will see numerous carved lion heads. Just to the north of the main entrance, facing George Street, a lion has been carved with one eye shut. This oddity appeared because of the head stonemason's habit of checking the line of the stonework by closing one eye. The sly joke was not found until work was finished.

Some people have concluded that Sydney Town Hall became the city's most elaborate building by accident, as each architect strove to outdo similar buildings in Manchester and Liverpool. Today, it makes a magnificent event venue.

⑬ St Andrew's Cathedral

Sydney Square, cnr George & Bathurst Sts. **Map** 4 E3. **Tel** 9265 1661. 🚇 Town Hall. **Open** contact the cathedral for opening hours and tour times. 🚹 ⭕ 🅆 sydneycathedral.com

While the foundation stone for the country's oldest cathedral was laid in 1819, almost 50 years elapsed before the building was consecrated in 1868. The Gothic Revival design is by Edmund Blacket, whose ashes are interred here. Inspired by York Minster in England, the twin towers were completed in 1874. In 1949, the main entrance was moved to the eastern end near George Street.

The Great Bible, St Andrew's Cathedral

Inside are memorials to Sydney pioneers, including Thomas Mort (*see p74*), as well as a collection of religious memorabilia.

The southern wall incorporates stones from London's St Paul's Cathedral, Westminster Abbey and the House of Lords.

Obelisk
This monument was dubbed "Thornton's Scent Bottle" after the mayor of Sydney who had it erected in 1857. The mock-Egyptian edifice is in fact a ventilator for a sewer.

Emden Gun
Standing at the corner of College and Liverpool Streets, this monument commemorates a World War I naval action. HMAS *Sydney* destroyed the German raider *Emden* off the Cocos Islands on 9 November 1914, and 180 crew members were taken prisoner.

City Circle Railway
The park we see today bears very little resemblance to the Hyde Park of old. In fact, the dictates of city railway tunnels have largely created its present landscape. Tunnels were excavated through an open cut that ran through the park, and after the rail system was opened in 1926 the entire area had to be remodelled and replanted.

Busby's Bore Fountain
This is a reminder of Busby's Bore, the city's first piped water supply opened in 1837. John Busby, a civil engineer, conceived and supervised the construction of the 4.4-km (2¾-mile) tunnel. It carried water from bores on Lachlan Swamp, now within Centennial Park (*see p129*), to horse-drawn water carriers on the corner of Elizabeth Street and Park Street.

Game in progress on the giant chessboard, near Busby's Bore Fountain

⓮ Australian Museum

The Australian Museum, the nation's leading natural science museum, founded in 1827, was the first museum established and remains the premier showcase of Australian natural history. The main building, an impressive sandstone structure with a marble staircase, faces Hyde Park. Architect Mortimer Lewis was forced to resign his position when building costs began to far exceed the budget. Construction was completed in the 1860s by James Barnet. The collection provides a journey across Australia and the near Pacific, covering biology and both natural and cultural history. The museum runs a changing programme of special events, including talks, workshops, demonstrations and kids' activities.

Crystal Hall Main Entrance
As originally intended by the architect in the 19th century, the main entrance is now on William Street. Opened in 2015, the glass walkway features a façade of diamond-shaped glass pleats.

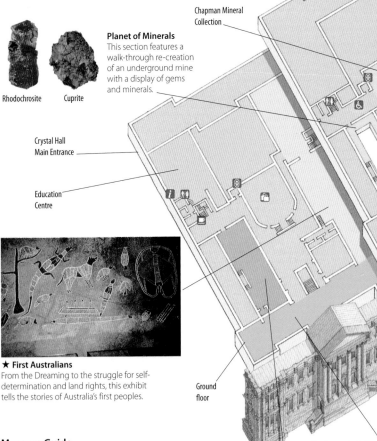

Chapman Mineral Collection

Planet of Minerals
This section features a walk-through re-creation of an underground mine with a display of gems and minerals.

Rhodochrosite Cuprite

Crystal Hall Main Entrance

Education Centre

★ **First Australians**
From the Dreaming to the struggle for self-determination and land rights, this exhibit tells the stories of Australia's first peoples.

Ground floor

Museum Guide

The First Australians Gallery is on the ground floor, as are the Long Gallery and Wild Planet. Mineral and rock exhibits are in two galleries on level 1. Birds and Insects are found on level 2, along with Kidspace, Surviving Australia and Dinosaurs.

The Long Gallery, on the ground floor, provides insights into 100 famous Australians.

The historic College Street entrance has been converted into an exhibition space – Wild Planet – with over 400 animal specimens.

★ Search & Discover
Sydneysiders bring bugs, rocks and bones to this hands-on area for identification. The public can also access an online research facility.

VISITORS' CHECKLIST

Practical Information
1 William St. **Map** 4 F3.
Tel 9320 6000. **Open** 9:30am–5pm daily (till 9pm Wed Dec–Feb). **Closed** 25 Dec. 🅿️ ♿

🇼 australianmuseum.net.au

Transport
🚌 Sydney Explorer, 323, 324, 325, 389. 🚇 Museum, Town Hall.

Level 2

Surviving Australia
This exhibit explores wild Australia, including this venomous Speckled Brown Snake, as well as sharks, crocodiles and other dangerous animals.

Dinosaurs
Discover the 200-million-year-old story of dinosaurs in this exhibition.

Level 1

Birds and Insects
Australia's most poisonous spider, the male of the Sydney funnel-web species, dwells exclusively in the Greater Sydney region.

★ Kidspace
This mini museum is designed especially for children aged five and under to investigate the natural world.

Key to Floorplan

- Dinosaurs
- Kidspace
- Surviving Australia
- First Australians
- Temporary exhibition space
- Non-exhibition space
- Plants and Minerals
- Birds and Insects
- Search & Discover
- Long Gallery
- Wild Planet

"Welcome Stranger" Gold Nugget Cast

In 1869, the largest gold nugget ever found in Australia was discovered in Victoria. It weighed 71.06 kg (156 lb). The museum holds a cast of the original in a display examining the impact of the gold rush, when the Australian population doubled in ten years.

← 67.5 cm (26½ in) wide →

Darling Harbour, seen from the waterside

Sights at a Glance

0 metres 250
0 yards 250

DARLING HARBOUR AND SURRY HILLS

Darling Harbour is named after the seventh governor of New South Wales, Ralph Darling. It was an unsavoury place in the late 19th century, known for its thieves' dens and bawdy houses. The docks were an embarkation point for wool and other exports. As Sydney Harbour industry declined, Darling Harbour became rundown, only to be revived as a focal point of the 1988 Bicentenary. Several decades on, Darling Harbour is being transformed, through world-class entertainment venues,

high-rise residential, hotel and commercial developments, a pedestrian boulevard and walkways, and increased public green space.

Until the 1940s, Surry Hills was a depressed, inner city slum area, vividly described in Ruth Park's *The Harp in the South*. In the postwar years, it became home to mostly European migrants and the garment and fashion trade. More recently, young professionals have moved in, lured by a thriving café and restaurant scene and proximity to the city.

☐ **Restaurants** *pp189–191*

1 BBQ King	**6** Caysorn Thai	**14** King Street Brewhouse
2 Berta	**7** Chat Thai	**15** Kobe Jones
3 Bodega	**8** Devon	**16** El Loco at Slip Inn
4 Boon	**9** Din Tai Fung	**17** Longrain
5 Cafe Rumah	**10** The Dolphin Hotel Dining Room	**18** LuMi Bar & Dining
	11 Encasa	**19** Mahjong Room
	12 Golden Century	**20** The Malaya
	13 Home Café & Thai Restaurant	**21** Mamak
		22 Marigold
		23 Mohr Fish
		24 Momofuku Seiobo
		25 Nick's Bar & Grill
		26 Paramount Coffee Project
		27 Pasteur
		28 Reuben Hills
		29 Sepia
		30 Steerson's Steakhouse
		31 Taste Baguette on Sussex Lane
		32 Zaafran

See also Street Finder, maps 1, 3 & 4

Street-by-Street: Darling Harbour

Darling Harbour was New South Wales' bicentennial gift to itself, turning a former busy industrial centre and international shipping terminal catering for the local wool, grain, timber and coal trades, into a tourism and entertainment destination that opened in 1988, complete with the Australian National Maritime Museum and SEA LIFE Sydney Aquarium. In 2013, a major reinvention of the precinct commenced, combining stunning high-rise architecture with pedestrian walkways, open spaces and many restaurants, cafés and shops. The landmark, striking ICC Sydney opened in 2016, and the area continues to develop, with more luxury hotels, residential towers and shopping facilities.

Harbourside Complex offers restaurants and cafés with superb views over the water to the city skyline. There is also a wide range of speciality shops, selling unusual gifts and other items.

❺ ICC Sydney
The International Convention Centre includes a theatre, a large ballroom and convention space.

The Goods Line

DARLI

The Tidal Cascades sunken fountain was designed by Robert Woodward, also responsible for the El Alamein Fountain *(see p122)*. The double spiral of water and paths replicate the patterns of the cockleshells that were once plentiful on the rocks at the water's edge, and after which Cockle Bay was named.

WESTERN DISTRIBUTOR

WESTERN DISTRIBUTOR

IMAX Darling Harbour, featuring the world's largest screen, is being rebuilt and will reopen in 2019.

Chinese Garden of Friendship

❻ The Chinese Garden of Friendship is a haven of peace and tranquillity in the heart of Sydney. Its landscaping, with winding pathways, waterfalls, lakes and pavilions, offers an insight into the rich culture of China.

Key

— Suggested route

Locator Map
See Street Finder, maps 3 & 4

❹ Pyrmont Bridge
The swingspan bridge opens for vessels up to 14 m (46 ft) tall.

A historic fleet of 14 vessels is docked at the museum's wharves, making it one of the world's largest collections held at a museum.

The Star casino

❶ ★ Australian National Maritime Museum
Compelling exhibits detail the nation's seafaring history before and after European settlement.

The HMAS *Vampire* (1959), a destroyer built for the Royal Australian Navy, is the largest vessel in the fleet moored outside the museum.

WILD LIFE Sydney Zoo

King Street Wharf →

Wharf for harbour cruise departures

❷ ★ SEA LIFE Sydney Aquarium
The aquatic life of Sydney Harbour, the open ocean and the Great Barrier Reef is displayed in massive tanks, which can be seen from underwater walkways.

Cockle Bay Wharf is vibrant and colourful, and an exciting food and entertainment precinct.

0 metres	100
0 yards	100

● Australian National Maritime Museum

Bounded as it is by the sea, Australia's history is inextricably linked to maritime traditions. The museum displays material in a broad range of permanent and temporary thematic exhibits. As well as artifacts relating to the enduring Aboriginal maritime cultures, the exhibits survey the history of European exploratory voyages in the Pacific, the arrival of convict ships, successive waves of migration and naval life.

Historic vessels on show at the wharf include a flimsy Vietnamese refugee boat, sailing, fishing and pearling boats, a navy patrol boat and a World War II commando raider. Visitors can board a submarine and a replica tall ship as part of the many interactive exhibits.

Museum Façade
The billowing steel roof design by Philip Cox suggests both the surging sea and the sails of a ship.

Passengers has a model of the Orcades, which reflects the grace of 1950s liners. This display also charts harrowing sea voyages made by migrants and refugees.

The Tasman Light was used in a Tasmanian lighthouse.

Eora Indigenous Gallery – First People traces the seafaring traditions of Aboriginal peoples and Torres Strait Islanders.

★ Navigators
This 1754 engraving of an East Indian sea creature is a European vision of the uncharted, exotic "great south".

The *Sirius* anchor is from a 1790 wreck off Norfolk Island.

Main entrance (sea level)

Mini Mariners is a dedicated maritime-themed play area for children under 5 years.

The Navy exhibit examines naval life in war and peace, as well as the history of Colonial navies.

The USA Gallery honours enduring maritime links between the US and Australia through trade, migration and defence. American traders stopped off in Australia on their way to China.

Key to Floorplan

- ☐ Navigators and Eora Indigenous Gallery – First People
- ☐ Passengers
- ☐ Mini Mariners
- ☐ Navy
- ☐ USA Gallery
- ☐ Temporary exhibitions
- ☐ Non-exhibition space

Action Stations
Experience the compelling history of the Royal Australian Navy by exploring the drama and danger of navy life in this interactive exhibition, housed in the striking Waterfront Pavilion.

VISITORS' CHECKLIST

Practical Information
2 Murray St, Darling Harbour. **Map** 3 C2. **Tel** 9298 3777. **Open** 9:30am–5pm daily (Jan: 6pm). **Closed** 25 Dec. 🖼 (special exhibitions, submarine, *Endeavour* & destroyer). ♿ 🖼 🖥 📷 🅦 anmm.gov.au

Transport
🚌 Sydney Explorer. 🚉 Town Hall. ⛴ Pyrmont Bay.

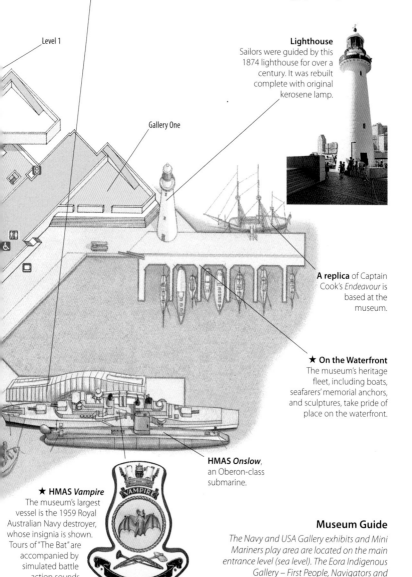

Level 1

Lighthouse
Sailors were guided by this 1874 lighthouse for over a century. It was rebuilt complete with original kerosene lamp.

Gallery One

A replica of Captain Cook's *Endeavour* is based at the museum.

★ On the Waterfront
The museum's heritage fleet, including boats, seafarers' memorial anchors, and sculptures, take pride of place on the waterfront.

HMAS *Onslow*, an Oberon-class submarine.

★ HMAS *Vampire*
The museum's largest vessel is the 1959 Royal Australian Navy destroyer, whose insignia is shown. Tours of "The Bat" are accompanied by simulated battle action sounds.

Museum Guide
The Navy and USA Gallery exhibits and Mini Mariners play area are located on the main entrance level (sea level). The Eora Indigenous Gallery – First People, Navigators and Passengers sections are on the first level.

❷ SEA LIFE Sydney Aquarium

SEA LIFE Sydney Aquarium's themed zones bring visitors close to more than 13,000 animals from 700 species in both marine and freshwater aquatic environments, including the world's largest Great Barrier Reef display. The highlight is a walk "on the ocean floor" through 100 m (328 feet) of underwater tunnels. These allow close observation of sharks, stingrays and schools of fish, as well as two rare dugongs. The conservation-focused aquarium also includes penguin breeding and animal rescue programmes.

VISITORS' CHECKLIST

Practical Information
Aquarium Wharf, Darling Harbour.
Map 4 D2. **Tel** 1800 199 657.
Open 9am–7pm daily (last adm 6pm). 🐾🦽🖥️📷
🌐 sydneyaquarium.com.au

Transport
🚌 Sydney Explorer. 🚢 Darling Harbour. Ⓣ Town Hall.
🚉 Paddy's Markets.

Dugongs viewed from the underwater tunnel

Exploring the Aquarium
Built on a pier in Darling Harbour, SEA LIFE Sydney Aquarium comprises over 4,000 sq m (43,000 sq ft) of exhibition space and is one of the largest aquariums in the world. Exhibits are organised by theme and take the visitor on a journey through the different marine habitats of the Australian continent. Habitat zones include South Coast Shipwreck, Sydney Harbour, Dugong Island, Shark Valley and Jurassic Seas.

It is worth checking the website or asking on arrival about feeding times and talks throughout the day. For an added cost, visitors can ride out on a glass-bottom boat to watch and feed the sharks first hand; take a 20-minute snorkel in a transparent enclosure; or ride in a raft through the Penguin Expedition exhibit, which simulates a rugged sub-Antarctic environment, albeit at a more comfortable – though still chilly – 6 degrees centigrade (43 degrees Fahrenheit).

Attractions
SEA LIFE Sydney Aquarium offers a great variety of exhibits and animal encounters.

Platypuses
Endemic to the rivers, streams, billabongs and lakes of the east coast and Tasmania, the platypus is an iconic symbol of Australia. When discovered by Europeans, the animal's strange collection of physical attributes, including a duck-like bill and otter's tail, was once thought to be some kind of elaborate hoax.

Claws
This exhibit features the world's largest crab species – the Japanese Spider Crab. It can grow to a claw-to-claw span of almost 4 m (13 ft).

Dugong Island
An exciting attraction are the two dugongs (sea cows) – only five are currently held in captivity. Related to elephants, these docile, herbivorous mammals can reach up to 3 m (9.8 ft) in length and live for more than 70 years. Named "Pig" and "Wuru" (an Aboriginal word meaning "young child"), the dugongs were originally rescued

as orphaned calves. Visitors can see them from above the water in the open-air ocean pool and swimming down to feed in the underwater tunnel.

Discovery Rockpool
Visitors get the opportunity to gently touch the spiral eggs of a Port Jackson shark and feel the spongy texture of a sea cucumber and the bumpy skin of a starfish while learning about the conservation and careful handling of sea animals.

Shark Walk and Shark Valley
Through an underwater tunnel, visitors can encounter huge stingrays, shoals of fish as well as the largest sharks on display in the aquarium – the critically endangered grey nurse shark.

Great Barrier Reef Oceanarium
The world's largest coral reef extends along 2,300 km (1,430 miles) of Australia's coast. Vibrant blue tangs, clownfish and ornate lionfish are on display as well as tropical sharks and rays. At the end of the oceanarium, the floor-to-ceiling Reef Theatre glass panel offers an unparalleled spectacle of the exotic creatures.

Sharks and hundreds of other fish on view from the Reef Theatre

❸ WILD LIFE Sydney Zoo

WILD LIFE Sydney Zoo contains over 100 Australian land-dwelling species, including insects, birds, reptiles and mammals. Together with the nearby aquarium, the complex comprises the world's largest collection of native Australian animal species to be housed in one location. In the heart of Darling Harbour, the undulating see-through mesh roof is a sight to behold in itself. Although compact in size, the zoo contains ten different temperature- and humidity-controlled habitats, and the experience is enhanced by soundscapes, graphics and interactive models.

Visitors can get close to kangaroos at WILD LIFE Sydney Zoo

VISITORS' CHECKLIST

Practical Information
Aquarium Wharf, Darling Harbour.
Map 4 D2. **Tel** 1800 614 069.
Open 9:30am–5pm daily (last adm 4pm) (Dec–Mar: to 6pm; last adm 5pm). 🚗♿🍴📷🎁
W wildlifesydney.com.au
Transport
🚌 Sydney Explorer. 🚢 Darling Harbour. 🚉 Town Hall.
🚈 Paddy's Markets.

Exploring the Zoo
There are multi-attraction passes available for WILD LIFE Sydney Zoo and SEA LIFE Sydney Aquarium and both sites can be visited in one day; another pass also includes Sydney Tower Eye (see p85).

Exhibits are laid out over three floors with one kilometre (0.6 miles) of enclosed walkways. The habitats are climate controlled and visitors largely view the animals through vast viewing panels.

Throughout the day, feeds and talks are given by the keepers, and visitors get the chance to get closer to the animals. Another good option is to book a group or "VIP" guided tour.

Attractions
WILD LIFE Sydney Zoo groups the animals by their natural habitats and houses a variety of intriguing, often unique, species that are native to the Australian continent.

Butterfly Tropics
The butterfly tropics zone contains such spectacular species as the Zebra, Blue Triangle and Ulysses butterflies, the latter with its huge 14-cm (5.5-in) wingspan. There are also frogs, turtles and a green tree python.

Frilled-Neck Lizard
Native to the dry landscape of the Kimberley in north Western Australia, this bizarre-looking lizard flares the folds of skin around its neck when feeling threatened or scared. It will also hiss and lunge to ward off predators. It used to feature on the Australian 2c coin.

Nocturnal Animals
The Nightfall exhibit features animals that venture out in the dark, such as possums, bilbies, bats, quolls, geckos, betongs and gliders, including the "false vampire bat" of Australia's north.

Invertebrates
The Outback Adventurers Café is home to all kinds of creepy crawlies such as the carnivorous praying mantis, the giant rhinoceros cockroach and the world's most dangerous spider – the Sydney funnel-web.

Koalas
A raised walkway under the open-air mesh roof winds through the koala and wallaby habitats and allows visitors to get closer to these cuddly, iconic animals and even have a photo taken with them. The koala's diet of eucalyptus leaves is so low in nutrients it has to conserve energy by moving slowly and sleeping a lot.

Yellow-Footed Rock Wallaby
Bounding about on rocks in the Wallaby Cliff habitat, this stripy-tailed wallaby is perhaps the most attractive of the kangaroo species, so much so it used to be hunted for its beautiful fur. Its huge feet have strong muscles and a brush of stiff hairs to help it get around over rocky terrain.

Koala

Southern Cassowary
This distinctive blue-necked bird, a close relation of the emu, is considered the most dangerous bird in the world. It has powerful talons and one spear-like inner claw which can reach up to 12 cm (4.7 in) in length. This heavy, flightless bird is capable of killing dogs and even humans if provoked. Around half of the bird species in Australia are found nowhere else in the world.

➍ Pyrmont Bridge

Darling Harbour. **Map** 1 A5. 🚉 Town Hall. 🚌 Paddy's Markets, Pyrmont Bay. ♿ ✉

Pyrmont Bridge opened in 1902. The world's oldest electrically operated swingspan bridge, it was fully functional before Sydney's streets were lit by electricity. It provided access to what, at the time, was a busy international shipping terminal with warehouses and wool stores. Electricity for the new bridge came from the Ultimo power station, the building that now houses the Powerhouse Museum (see pp102–3).

Percy Allan, the bridge's designer, went on to design 583 more bridges. J J Bradfield, the designer of the Sydney Harbour Bridge (see pp72–3), was also involved in construction of this bridge.

The 369-m- (1,200-ft-) long Pyrmont Bridge has 14 spans, with only the two central swingspans being made of steel. The remaining spans are made of ironbark, an Australian hardwood timber. The bridge was permanently closed to road traffic in 1981, but reopened to pedestrians when the Darling Harbour complex opened in 1988. It is also popular with cyclists riding to work. The central steel swingspans are still driven by their original motor. The bridge is opened regularly to allow boats access to and from Cockle Bay.

The view from Pyrmont Bridge looking up towards the city centre

Pavillions in the peaceful Chinese Garden of Friendship, a traditional Chinese garden

➎ ICC Sydney

Darling Harbour. **Map** 4 D3. 🚌 Paddy's Markets, Convention, Exhibition Centre, Pyrmont Bay. **Tel** 9215 7100. **Open** daily. 🖥 ♿ 🅆 **iccsydney.com.au**

A sprawling modern complex with a crystalline glass façade, ICC Sydney comprises a convention centre, the largest exhibition space in Australia and the 8,000-seat ICC theatre, all connected by internal walkways. It also boasts a huge ballroom and the biggest kitchen in the southern hemisphere. The multi-purpose venue hosts a variety of events, including international concerts, festivals, conventions and sporting fixtures. Adjacent to the megacomplex, one of Sydney's largest hotels, the luxury Sofitel, is due to open at the end of 2017.

➏ Chinese Garden of Friendship

Darling Harbour. **Map** 4 D3. **Tel** 9240 8788. 🚉 Town Hall. 🚌 Paddy's Markets. **Open** 9:30am–5pm daily. **Closed** Good Fri, 25 Dec. 🎧 🖥 ♿ limited. 🅆 **darlingharbour.com**

The Chinese Garden of Friendship was built in 1988. It is a tranquil refuge from the city streets. The garden's design was a gift to Sydney from its Chinese sister city of Guangdong. The Dragon Wall is in the lower section beside the lake. It has glazed carvings of two dragons, one representing Guangdong province and the

other the state of New South Wales. In the centre of the wall, a carved pearl, symbolizing prosperity, is lifted by the waves. The lake is covered with lotus and water lilies for much of the year and a rock monster guards against evil. On the other side of the lake is the Twin Pavilion. Waratahs (New South Wales's floral symbol) and flowering apricots are carved into its woodwork, and also grow at its base.

A tea house, found at the top of the stairs in the Tea House Courtyard, serves traditional Chinese tea and cakes.

➐ Chinatown

Dixon St Plaza, Sydney. **Map** 4 E–D4. 🚉 Central. 🚌 Paddy's Markets.

Originally concentrated around Dixon and Hay Streets, Chinatown is expanding to fill Sydney's Haymarket area, stretching west to Harris Street, south to Broadway and east to Castlereagh Street. Visitors will notice Chinese eateries, shops and signage in nearby areas, as Chinese businesses grow and multiply in line with Chinatown's local population.

While it today rubs shoulders with the eastern and western edges of the increasingly slick Darling Harbour, for years, Chinatown was a run-down district at the edge of the city's produce markets. Today Dixon Street, its main thoroughfare, has been spruced up, with street lanterns, archways and public spaces featuring trees and artworks, while still retaining its unique character and heritage.

The streets of Chinatown are distinctive, with greengrocers, traditional herbalists, butchers' shops with wind-dried ducks hanging in their windows and a Friday night market . Jewellers, clothing shops, food courts and confectioners fill the arcades.

Towering over the corner of George Street and Hay Street is a sculpture by artist Lin Li, *Golden Water Mouth* (1999). Made from the trunk of a eucalyptus tree covered in gold-leaf, it is said to bring good fortune to the area.

❽ Capitol Theatre

13 Campbell St, Haymarket. **Map** 4 E4. **Tel** 9320 5000. ⓣ Central. 🚊 Capitol. **Open** performances only. Box office: **Open** 9am–5pm Mon–Fri & 2 hrs before shows. ♿ 🕸 **capitoltheatre. com.au**

In the mid-1800s a cattle and corn market was situated here. It became Paddy's Market Bazaar with sideshows and an outdoor theatre, in turn replaced by a circus with a floodable ring. The present building was erected in the 1920s as a luxurious picture palace. In the mid-1990s, the cinema was restored, in keeping with the original theme of a Florentine Garden.

The Capitol reopened as a lyric theatre with productions staged beneath a Mediterranean-blue ceiling studded with stars reflecting the southern sky.

❾ Paddy's Markets

Cnr Thomas & Hay Sts, Haymarket. **Map** 4 D4. **Tel** 1300 361 589. ⓣ Central. 🚊 Paddy's Markets. **Open** 10am–6pm Wed–Sun. **Closed** 25 Apr, 25 Dec. ♿ *See also Shops and Markets: p203.* 🕸 **paddysmarkets.com.au**

Haymarket, in Chinatown, is home to Paddy's Markets, Sydney's oldest market. It has been in this area, on a number of sites, since 1869 (with only one five-year absence). The name's origin is uncertain, but is believed to have come from either the Chinese, who originally supplied much of its produce, or the Irish, their main customers.

Once the shopping centre for the inner-city poor, Paddy's Markets is now an integral part of an ambitious development including residential apartments and the Market City Shopping Centre. However, the familiar clamour and chaotic bargain-hunting atmosphere of the original marketplace remain. Every weekend the market has up to 800 stalls selling everything from fresh produce to chickens, T-shirts, towels, trinkets and souvenirs.

❿ The Goods Line

Between Devonshire St tunnel (Central Station) and Powerhouse Museum. **Map** 4 D4. 🚌 Railway Square. ⓣ Central. 🚊 Paddy's Markets, Exhibition Centre. 🚻 ♿ 📷 🕸 **darlingharbour.com**

Built along a former freight rail track originating in 1855, this partly elevated, 500-m- (1640-ft) long shared pedestrian and cycle path is a triumph of urban design. It connects Darling Harbour to Central Station and Ultimo district's cultural, media and educational institutions, including the Powerhouse Museum, University of Technology, Sydney, the Dr Chau Chak Wing Building *(see p132)* and the Australian Broadcasting Corporation.

There are various facilities to enjoy along the way, including communal tables, open grassy spaces, table tennis tables, study pods set among the trees, an outdoor gym and a children's water play area with a sandpit shaded by trees.

⓫ Powerhouse Museum

See pp102–3.

⓬ Surry Hills

Map 5 A2–5. 🚌 301, 302, 303, 304, 339. *See Shops and Markets pp200–207.*

A curious mixture of funky fashion, foodie havens and shabby seediness can be found on the streets of Surry Hills. Newly renovated houses stand alongside dilapidated dwellings, while streets of elegant Victorian terraces abut modern high-rise flats and former warehouses converted into cool cafés.

For the visitor, the suburb offers a wide range of ethnic cuisines, often at bargain prices. It is famed for its Lebanese and Turkish restaurants on Cleveland Street, but you will also find Indian, Chinese, Thai, French and numerous Italian eateries scattered around the suburb, along with stylish pubs.

Once the centre of Sydney's garment and fashion trade, Surry Hills is still home to a number of factory outlets where clothing, haberdashery, linens and lingerie can be bought at below retail prices. A range of alternative fashion and retro clothing shops can also be found at the Oxford Street end of Crown Street.

The Goods Line, an urban walkway following the route of a historic railway line

⓫ Powerhouse Museum

This former power station, completed in 1902 to provide power for Sydney's tramway system, was redesigned to cater for the needs of an interactive, hands-on museum. The revamped Powerhouse opened in 1988. The early collection was housed in the Garden Palace where the 1879 international exhibition of invention and industry from around the world was held. Few exhibits survived the devastating 1882 fire, and today's huge and ever-expanding collection was gathered after this disaster. The building's monumental scale provides an ideal context for the epic sweep of ideas encompassed within: everything from the realm of space and technology to the decorative and domestic arts. The museum emphasizes Australian innovations and achievements, celebrating both the extraordinary and the everyday.

What's It Like to Live in Space?
Find out how astronauts live and work in space, and experience weightlessness in the zero gravity space lab.

Level 2

Transport
Discover the air, land and sea vehicles that helped shape our way of life.

★ **Experimentations**
Investigate the principles of temperature, pressure, electricity, magnetism, light, gravity, motion and chemistry in this exciting interactive exhibit.

Level 1

Nuclear Matters
This is a great space in which to explore the complex worlds of nuclear science, medicine and power.

Ecologic shows the science behind global warming and what can be done to prevent it.

Museum Guide

The museum is housed in two buildings: the former Powerhouse and the Neville Wran building. There are over 20 exhibitions on four levels, descending from Level 4. The shop, entrance and temporary exhibits are on Level 3. Level 2 has thematic exhibits. Level 1 has experiments and displays on space, transport and computers.

Level 4

Level 3

VISITORS' CHECKLIST

Practical Information
500 Harris St, Ultimo. **Map** 4 D4.
Tel 9217 0111. **Open** 10am–5pm daily. **Closed** 25 Dec.

🅿 ♿ 📷 🖥 📷
w maas.museum

Transport
🚌 501. ⛴ Darling Harbour.
🚉 Central. 🚕 Paddy's Markets.

★ **Boulton and Watt Engine**
The oldest surviving rotative steam engine in the world, it powered a London brewery for 102 years from 1875. It is regularly put into operation in the museum.

Icons
Explore what makes an object iconic through more than 70 items, such as this Regency settee and matching armchairs, designed by Thomas Hope in London in about 1802.

Main entrance

The Neville Wran Building, a 1980s addition, is based on the design of grand exhibition halls and railway stations of the 19th century.

★ **Locomotive No. 1**
Robert Stephenson built this locomotive in England in 1854. It hauled the first train in New South Wales in 1855. Using models and voices, the display re-creates a 19th-century day trip for a group of Sydneysiders.

Key to Floorplan

⬜ Temporary exhibitions
⬜ Social History and Design
⬜ Science and Technology
⬜ Non-exhibition space

BOTANIC GARDEN AND THE DOMAIN

The Royal Botanic Garden Sydney, the site of the city's first European farm, and the adjoining Domain, with its open grassy space, provide respite from the bustle of the busy city. Tranquil in spite of the regularly congested traffic nearby, they make an ideal spot for a picnic or to simply relax. The Royal Botanic Garden has an extensive collection of native and exotic flora. One of Sydney's most loved locations for open-air events, The Domain attracts up to 100,000 people to free community concerts such as Carols, Opera and Symphony in The Domain (see p51). The Botanic Garden and The Domain are flanked by some of the city's most historic buildings, including the Art Gallery of New South Wales and the Mitchell Wing of the State Library. Nearby, Macquarie Street is rich in convict and Colonial history, with the barracks, hospital, church and mint among the country's oldest surviving public buildings, while political power brokers can often be seen at Parliament House.

Sights at a Glance

Historic Streets and Buildings
2 Conservatorium of Music
3 Government House
6 Woolloomooloo Finger Wharf
9 State Library of NSW
10 Parliament House
11 Sydney Hospital
12 The Mint
13 Hyde Park Barracks Museum

Museums and Galleries
7 Art Gallery of New South Wales pp110–13

Churches
14 St James' Church

Islands
5 Fort Denison

Monuments
4 Mrs Macquaries Chair

Parks and Gardens
1 Royal Botanic Garden pp106–7
8 The Domain

0 metres 250
0 yards 250

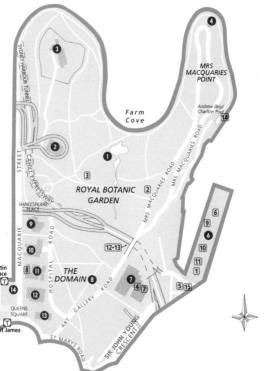

See also Street Finder, maps 1 & 2

◀ The lush surroundings of the Royal Botanic Garden

For keys to symbols see back flap

● Royal Botanic Garden

The Royal Botanic Garden Sydney, an oasis of 30 ha (74 acres) in the heart of the city, occupies a superb position, wrapped around Farm Cove at the harbour's edge. Established in 1816 as a series of pathways through shrubbery, it is the oldest living scientific institution in the country and houses an outstanding collection of plants from Australia and overseas. A living museum, the garden is also the site of the first European farm in the fledgling colony. Fountains, statues and monuments are today scattered throughout. Plant specimens collected by Joseph Banks on Captain James Cook's epic voyage along the east coast of Australia in 1770 are displayed in the National Herbarium of New South Wales, an important centre for research on Australian plants.

Locator Map
See Street Finder, maps 1 & 2

★ **Palm Grove**
Begun in 1862, this cool summer haven is one of the world's finest outdoor collections of palms. There are about 180 species. Borders planted with kaffir lilies make a colourful display in springtime.

★ **Herb Garden**
Herbs used worldwide for various purposes – culinary, medicinal and aromatic – are on display here, along with a sensory fountain and a sundial modelled on the celestial sphere.

KEY

① **Government House (1897)**

② **The Calyx**, a glasshouse constructed for the garden's 200th birthday in 2016, is a magnificent structure, integrating indoor and outdoor areas. It hosts changing horticultural exhibitions and events.

③ **Cadi Jam Ora**, a bush tucker display, features native plants that would have grown on the site prior to Colonial settlement.

④ **Wollemi Pine**

★ **Sydney Fernery**
Opened in 1993, on the site where earlier ferneries had previously stood, this feature garden is a tribute to some of the most ancient plants on earth.

Macquarie Wall
In 1810, work began on this 290-m- (950-ft-) long wall intended to separate the convict domain from the town's "respectable Class of Inhabitants". Only a small section remains standing today.

Choragic Monument (1870)
This replica of the marble monument of Lysicrates in Athens was sculpted in sandstone by Walter McGill.

★ **Australia's First European Farm**
It is claimed that some Middle Garden oblong beds follow the direction of the first furrows ploughed in the colony in 1788.

National Herbarium of New South Wales
More than 1.2 million of the dried plant specimens stored here document biological diversity. The charting of new plants provides essential information for conservation decision making.

0 metres   200
0 yards   200

❷ Conservatorium of Music

Macquarie St. **Map** 1 C3. **Tel** 9351 1222.
🚌 Sydney Explorer, Elizabeth St routes.
Ⓣ Martin Place. **Open** 8am–6pm
Mon–Sat (public areas only). **Closed**
pub hols, Easter Sat, 24 Dec–2 Jan. ♿
📷 Wed, Thu & Sat by appt (call 0404
256 256). Free concerts: 1:10pm Wed
(donation). 🌐 music.sydney.edu.au

When it was finished in 1821,
this striking castellated Colonial
Gothic building was meant to
be stables and servants' quarters
for Government House, but
construction of the latter was
delayed for almost 25 years. That
stables should be built in so grand
a style, and at such great cost,
brought forth cries of outrage
and led to bitter arguments
between the architect, Francis
Greenway *(see p116)*, and
Governor Macquarie – and a
decree that all future building
plans be submitted to London.

Between 1908 and 1915,
"Greenway's folly" underwent
a dramatic transformation. A
concert hall, roofed in grey slate,
was built on the central courtyard
and the entire building was
converted for the use of the new
Sydney Conservatorium of Music.

The Conservatorium's
facilities include a café which
holds lunchtime concerts
during the school term and
an upper level with harbour
views. "The Con" continues to
be a training ground for future
musicians as well as being
a great place to visit.

HMS *Orlando* in dry dock at Cockatoo
Island in the 1890s

❸ Government House

Macquarie St. **Map** 1 C2. **Tel** 9228 4111.
🚌 Sydney Explorer, Elizabeth St
routes. Ⓣ Martin Place. House:
Open 10:30am–3pm Fri–Sun
(guided tour only; ID required).
Closed Good Fri, 25 Dec. Garden:
Open 10am–4pm daily. ♿ 📷 every
30 mins. 🌐 governor.nsw.gov.au

What used to be the official
residence of the governor of
New South Wales overlooks
the harbour from within the
Royal Botanic Garden, but the
grandiose, somewhat sombre,
turreted Gothic Revival edifice
seems curiously out of place
in its beautiful park setting.

It was built of local sandstone
and cedar between 1837
and 1845. A fine collection of
19th- and early 20th-century
furnishings is housed within.

The History of Cockatoo Island

Now deserted, the largest of the 12
Sydney Harbour islands was used
to store grain from the 1830s. It was
a penal establishment from the
1840s to 1908, with prisoners being
put to work constructing dock
facilities. The infamous bushranger
"Captain Thunderbolt" made his
escape from Cockatoo in 1863 by
swimming across to the mainland.
From the 1870s to the 1960s,
Cockatoo Island was a thriving
naval dockyard and shipyard, the
hub of Australian industry.

Resting on the carved stone seat of
Mrs Macquaries Chair

❹ Mrs Macquaries Chair

Mrs Macquaries Rd. **Map** 2 E2.
🚌 Sydney Explorer, 441. ♿

The scenic Mrs Macquaries
Road winds alongside much
of what is now the city's
Royal Botanic Garden, from
Farm Cove to Woolloomooloo
Bay and back again. The road
was built in 1816 at the
instigation of Elizabeth
Macquarie, wife of the
Governor. In the same year,
a stone bench, inscribed with
details of the new road, was
carved into the rock at the point
where Mrs Macquarie would
stop to admire the view on
her daily constitutional.

Although today the outlook
from this famous landmark
is much changed, it is just as
arresting, taking in the broad
sweep of the harbour and
foreshore with all its landmarks.

The Conservatorium of Music, at the edge of the Royal Botanic Garden

Historic Woolloomooloo Finger Wharf redevelopment, including stylish apartments, restaurants and a hotel

❺ Fort Denison

Sydney Harbour. **Map** 2 E1. **Tel** 9361 5208. 🚢 from Circular Quay and Darling Harbour. **Closed** 25 Dec. 🏛 💻 🚻 phone to book.
Ⓦ fortdenison.com.au
Ⓦ nationalparks.nsw.gov.au
Ⓦ captaincook.com.au

First named Rock Island, this prominent, rocky outcrop in Sydney Harbour was very quickly dubbed "Pinchgut". This was probably because of the meagre rations given to convicts who were confined there as punishment. It had a grim history of incarceration in the early years of the colony.

In 1796, convicted murderer Francis Morgan was hanged on the island in chains. His body was left to rot on the gallows for three years as a grisly warning to the other convicts.

Between 1855 and 1857, the Martello tower (the only one in Australia), gun battery and barracks were built as part of Sydney's defences and the site was renamed after the governor of the time. The gun, still fired at 1pm each day, was an important aid for navigation, allowing mariners to set their ships' chronometers.

Today, Fort Denison is a popular tourist spot with a restaurant and museum. It can be reached by Captain Cook Cruises ferries from Wharf 2, Circular Quay or Darling Harbour.

❻ Woolloomooloo Finger Wharf

Cowper Wharf Roadway, Woolloomooloo. **Map** 2 E4. 🚌 Sydney Explorer, 311.

The largest of several finger wharves that jut out into the harbour, this timber wharf, completed in 1914, was an embarkation point for soldiers bound for both world wars. Following World War II, it was a landing place for many of the thousands of immigrants who came to make a new life in Australia.

Fort Denison in 1907

The wharf was the subject of public controversy in the late 1980s and early 1990s, when demolition plans were thwarted by conservation groups. Since then, this National Trust-listed maritime site has been redeveloped to include prime residential apartments, the Ovolo Woolloomooloo luxury hotel (see p179), and fashionable bars and restaurants whose patios offer fantastic views of Sydney Harbour and the city skyline.

❼ Art Gallery of New South Wales

See pp110–13.

❽ The Domain

Art Gallery Rd. **Map** 1 C4. 🚌 Sydney Explorer, Elizabeth St routes, 441. ♿

Free open-air concerts featuring some of the country's top artists at The Domain's shell-like covered amphitheatre is something of a summer tradition in Sydney. More than 100,000 people are drawn to the events here, from Carols in The Domain on the Saturday before Christmas to Symphony and Opera under the stars in January (see p51). By day, the vast green space is a magnet for active city workers, who can be found jogging or playing touch football during their lunch breaks.

This extensive public space has long been a rallying point for crowds of Sydneysiders whenever emotive issues of public importance have arisen, such as the attempt in 1916 to introduce military conscription or the dismissal of the elected federal government by the then governor-general in 1975.

Since the 1890s, The Domain has been the setting for speakers to get on their soapbox and make their point on Sunday afternoons at "Speakers' Corner".

❼ Art Gallery of New South Wales

Established in 1871, the art gallery has occupied its present imposing building since 1897. Designed by the Colonial Architect WL Vernon, the gallery doubled in size following 1988 building extensions. Two equestrian bronzes by Gilbert Bayes (1872–1953) – *The Offerings of Peace* and *The Offerings of War* – greet the visitor on entry. The gallery itself houses some of the finest works of art in Australia, with permanent collections of Australian, Aboriginal, European, Asian and contemporary art. The Yiribana Gallery is one of the largest in the world to exclusively exhibit Aboriginal and Torres Strait Islander art and culture. Free guided tours take place daily, covering Aboriginal art, highlights of the collection or major exhibitions.

Lower Level 3

Mars and the Vestal Virgin (1638)
This oil on canvas by Parisian painter Jacques Blanchard (1600–38) depicts Mars's encounter with a Vestal Virgin, who subsequently gave birth to Romulus and Remus, founders of Rome.

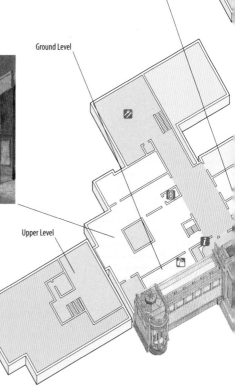

Ground Level

Sofala (1947) Russell Drysdale's visions of Australia show "ghost" towns laid waste by devastating natural forces such as drought.

Upper Level

Gallery Guide

There are five levels. The Upper Level, Ground Level and Lower Level 1 host temporary exhibitions. The Ground Level also showcases European and Australian works. The Contemporary Galleries on Lower Level 2 have the most comprehensive collection of contemporary art in the country. On Lower Level 3 is the Yiribana Aboriginal Gallery.

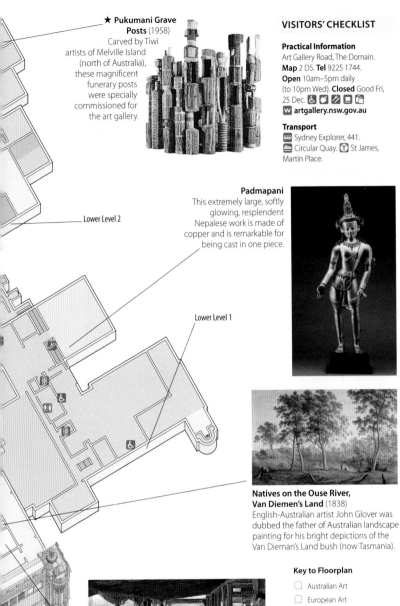

★ Pukumani Grave Posts (1958)
Carved by Tiwi artists of Melville Island (north of Australia), these magnificent funerary posts were specially commissioned for the art gallery.

Padmapani
This extremely large, softly glowing, resplendent Nepalese work is made of copper and is remarkable for being cast in one piece.

Lower Level 2

Lower Level 1

Natives on the Ouse River, Van Diemen's Land (1838)
English-Australian artist John Glover was dubbed the father of Australian landscape painting for his bright depictions of the Van Dieman's Land bush (now Tasmania).

Key to Floorplan

- ☐ Australian Art
- ☐ European Art
- ☐ Asian Art
- ☐ Modern Gallery (20th-Century European Art)
- ▥ Contemporary Art
- ☐ Domain Theatre
- ☐ Yiribana Aboriginal Gallery
- ▥ Temporary exhibition space
- ▨ Photography Gallery
- ▥ Study Room/Prints and Drawings
- ▥ Non-exhibition Space

★ The Golden Fleece (1894)
Also known as *Shearing at Newstead*, this work by Tom Roberts marks the coming of age of Australian Impressionist art.

The sandstone entrance was added in 1909.

Exploring the Art Gallery's Collection

Although local works had been collected since 1875, the gallery did not seriously begin seeking Australian and non-British art until the 1920s, and not until the 1940s did it begin acquiring Aboriginal and Torres Strait Islander paintings. These contrasting collections are now its great strength. Major temporary exhibitions are also regularly staged, with the annual Archibald, Wynne and Sulman prizes being most controversial and highly entertaining.

Chaucer at the Court of Edward III (1847–51), by Ford Madox Brown

Australian Art

Among the most important Colonial works is John Glover's *Natives on the Ouse River, Van Diemen's Land* (1838), an idealised image of Aboriginal people in a landscape unsullied by European contact.

The old wing holds paintings from the Heidelberg School of Australian Impressionism. Charles Conder's *Departure of the Orient – Circular Quay* (1888) and Tom Robert's *The Golden Fleece – Shearing at Newstead* (1894) hang alongside fine works by Frederick McCubbin and Arthur Streeton. Rupert Bunny's sensuous *Summer Time* (c.1907) and *A Summer Morning* (c.1908), and George Lambert's heroic *Across the Black Soil Plains* (1899), impress with their huge size and complex compositions.

There is also a significant collection of Australian Modernist works, including the iconic *Implement Blue* (1927) by Margaret Preston and *The Curve of the Bridge* (1928–9) by Grace Cossington Smith. The Gallery's paintings by Sidney Nolan exploit

myths of early Australian history, and range from *Boy in Township* (1943) to *Burke* (c.1962). There are fine holdings by Thea Proctor, William Dobell and Russell Drysdale, as well as important works of Arthur Boyd, Fred Williams, Robert Klippel, Ian Fairweather and Brett Whiteley *(see p132)*.

European Art

The scope of the scattered European collection ranges from Medieval to modern art. British art from the late 19th to the early 20th centuries forms an outstanding component.

Among the Old Masters are some significant Italian works that reflect Caravaggio's influence. There are also several notable works from the Renaissance in Sienese and Florentine styles. Hogarth, Turner and Joshua Reynolds are represented, as are Neo-Classical works. *The Visit of the Queen of Sheba to King Solomon* (1884–90) by Edward Poynter has been on display since 1892. Ford Madox Brown's *Chaucer at the Court of*

Edward III (1847–51) is the most commanding work in the Pre-Raphaelite collection.

The Impressionists and Post-Impressionists are represented by late 1880s Pissarro and Monet, Kandinsky, Braque and many other well-known European artists. *Mother and Daughter* (1946) by Max Beckmann and *Three Bathers* (1913) by Ernst Ludwig Kirchner are examples of German Expressionism. The gallery's first Picasso, *Nude in a Rocking Chair* (1956), was purchased in 1981. Among the distinguished sculptures on show is Henry Moore's *Reclining Figure: Angles* (1980), which is displayed by the side of the entrance.

Photography

Australian photography, represented in all its various forms, is a major part of the collection. There are over 5,000 prints, from 19th-century works by the likes of Charles Kerry and Charles Bayliss to fine examples of 20th-century Pictorialism by Harold Cazneaux, Norman C Deck and many others. The collection further traces the development of Modernist photography through the works of Olive Cotton, Max Dupain and their peers, while also showcasing the innovative approaches to the medium of contemporary practitioners like Tracey Moffatt, Anne Ferran, Rosemary Laing and Pat Brassington. Major international figures such as Eadweard Muybridge, Robert Mapplethorpe, Dorothea Lange,

Brett Whiteley's vivid *The balcony 2* from 1975

Man Ray, Cindy Sherman and Yasumasa Morimura are also represented.

Asian Art

The Gallery houses a remarkable collection of both historical and contemporary Asian art, particularly works of East Asia from the pre-Shang dynasty (c.1600–1027 BC) to the 20th century. It is recognized for its fine Chinese ceramics and Japanese paintings. There are also excellent holdings of South and Southeast Asian art, especially sculptures and paintings. Dynamic exhibitions, held across two dedicated Asian galleries, change regularly. The upper gallery is housed within a glass pavilion, with the design inspired by floating lanterns.

Prints and Drawings

Drawings and prints are on display throughout the Gallery in the various collections, as well as in the Study Room. They represent the European tradition from the Renaissance to the 19th and 20th centuries, with works by Rembrandt, Constable, William Blake and Edvard Munch. A strong bias towards Sydney artists has resulted in a fine gathering of works by Thea Proctor, Norman and Lionel Lindsay, and Lloyd Rees.

Spearing the Kangaroo (c.1880s–90s) by renowned Aboriginal artist Tommy McRae

Contemporary Art

The contemporary galleries encompass works in all media by artists from Australia and across the globe, including Fiona Hall, Bill Henson, Tracey Moffatt, Simryn Gill, Anish Kapoor, Cy Twombly, Louise Bourgeois and Ai Weiwei. Following the addition of the John Kaldor Family Collection, which includes works by Sol LeWitt, Nam June Paik and Robert Rauschenberg, the Gallery now holds Australia's most comprehensive representation of art from the 1960s to the present day. A series of rotating exhibitions reflect the range and richness of this collection, while offering fresh perspectives on both classic pieces and new acquisitions.

Yiribana Gallery

Yiribana means "this way" in the language of the Eora people, an acknowledgment of the gallery's location on Cadigal Land. Home of the Aboriginal and Torres Strait Islander collection, the Yiribana Gallery showcases Australia's enduring Indigenous cultural heritage, from Tommy McRae's late 19th-century drawings to works by contemporary artists. Traditional bark paintings hang alongside innovative works from both desert and urban areas. The application by contemporary artists of traditional ceremonial body and sand painting styles to new media forms, and the endurance of "Aboriginality", are repeatedly demonstrated. Topographical, geographical and cultural mapping of the land is displayed in a number of intricate landscapes. The qualities and forms of the natural world, and the actions and tracks of Ancestral Beings, are coded within the images.

Tutini (Pukumani grave posts) (1958) is a solemn ceremonial work dealing with death, while Emily Kame Kngwarreye honours the land from which she comes: the canvases of her intricate dot paintings, created using new tools and technology, appear to move and shimmer, telling stories of the animals and food to be found there.

Margaret Preston's *Wheelflower* (c.1929)

Mosaic replica of the Tasman Map in the State Library of NSW

❾ State Library of NSW

Macquarie St. **Map** 1 C4. **Tel** 9273 1414. 🚌 Sydney Explorer, Elizabeth St routes. **Open** 9am–8pm Mon–Thu, 9am–5pm Fri, 10am–5pm Sat & Sun. **Closed** pub hols; Mitchell Library closed Sun. 📷 🚻 🎫 📷 🌐 sl.nsw.gov.au

The State Library is housed in two separate buildings connected by a passageway and a glass bridge. The older building, the Mitchell Library wing (1910), is a majestic sandstone edifice facing the Royal Botanic Garden. Huge stone columns supporting a vaulted ceiling frame the impressive vestibule. On the vestibule floor is a mosaic replica of an old map illustrating the two voyages made to Australia by Dutch navigator Abel Tasman in the 1640s. The original Tasman Map is held in the Mitchell Library as part of its large collection of historic Australian paintings, books, documents and pictorial records.

The Mitchell wing's vast reading room, with its huge skylight and oak panelling, is just beyond the main vestibule. The newest section, a modern structure facing Macquarie Street, houses the State Reference Library and a gourmet café.

Outside the library, also facing Macquarie Street, is a statue of explorer Matthew Flinders. Behind him on the windowsill is a statue of his co-voyager and faithful cat, Trim.

❿ Parliament House

Macquarie St. **Map** 1 C4. **Tel** 9230 2111. 🚌 Sydney Explorer, Elizabeth routes. 🚇 Martin Place. 🎫 book in advance 9230 3444. **Open** 9am–5pm Mon–Fri. **Closed** most public hols. 🚻 🌐 parliament.nsw.gov.au

Malby's celestial globe, Parliament House

The central section of this building, which houses the State Parliament, is part of the original Sydney Hospital built in 1811–16. It has been a seat of government since 1829, when the newly appointed Legislative Council first held meetings here. The building was extended twice during the 19th century and again in the 1970s and 1980s. The current building contains the chambers for both houses of state parliament and parliamentary

---

Macquarie Street

🚌 Sydney Explorer, Elizabeth St routes. 🚇 Circular Quay, Martin Pl, St James.

Named after Governor Lachlan Macquarie, the street was designed as a ceremonial thoroughfare from the harbour to Hyde Park. It houses some of Australia's most important architectural and historical treasures, the consulting rooms of the city's top medical specialists and the home of the state government.

The Legislative Assembly, the lower house of state parliament, is furnished in the traditional green of the British House of Commons.

The new wing of the library was built in 1988 and connected to the old section by a glass walkway.

The Mitchell Library wing's portico (1906) has Ionic columns.

Parliament House was once the convict-built Rum Hospital's northern wing.

State Library of NSW *(1906–41)*　　　　**Parliament House** *(1811–*

offices. Parliamentary memorabilia is on view in the Jubilee Room, as are displays showing Parliament House's development and the legislative history of New South Wales.

The corrugated-iron building, with a cast-iron façade tacked on at the southern end, was a pre-fabricated kit from England. It was originally intended as a chapel for the gold fields, but was diverted from this purpose and sent to Sydney. In 1856, this dismantled kit became the chamber for the new Legislative Council. Its packing cases were used to line this chamber; the rough timber is still on view inside.

⓫ Sydney Hospital

Macquarie St. **Map** 1 C4. **Tel** 9382 7111. 🚌 Sydney Explorer, Elizabeth St routes. 🚇 Martin Place. **Open** daily. 📷 for tours. ♿ 🎧 must be pre-booked by phone. 🌐 **seslhd.health. nsw.gov.au**

This imposing collection of Victorian sandstone buildings stands on the site of what was once the central section of the

Stained glass at Sydney Hospital

original convict-built Sydney Hospital – known as the Rum Hospital because the builders were paid by being allowed to import rum for resale. Both the north and south wings of the Rum Hospital survive as Parliament House and the Sydney Mint. The central wing, which was in danger of collapsing, was demolished in 1879 and the new hospital, which still functions today, was completed in 1894. The Classical Revival building boasts a Baroque staircase and elegant floral stained-glass windows in its entrance hall.

Florence Nightingale approved the design of the 1867 nurses' wing. In the inner courtyard, there is a brightly coloured Art Deco fountain (1907).

At the front of the hospital sits *Il Porcellino*, a brass boar. It is a copy of a 17th-century fountain in Florence's Mercato Nuovo. Donated in 1968 by an Italian woman whose relatives had worked at the hospital, the statue is an enduring symbol of the close friendship between Italy and Australia.

Like his Florentine counter-part, *Il Porcellino* is supposed to bring good luck to all those who rub his snout. All coins tossed in the shallow pool at his feet for luck and fortune are collected for the hospital.

Il Porcellino, the brass boar in front of Sydney Hospital

The lamps hanging over the gateways of Parliament House are reproductions of the 19th-century gas lamps that used to stand here.

The Little Shop, a tiny corner store, currently resides in one of two domed former gatehouses.

The entrance stairs of Pyrmont sandstone have set the tone for all renovations. The stone, quarried in Colonial times, must be matched exactly.

Arched sandstone bridges

Arcaded stone verandas with ornate balustrading

Corrugated iron and cast-iron façade

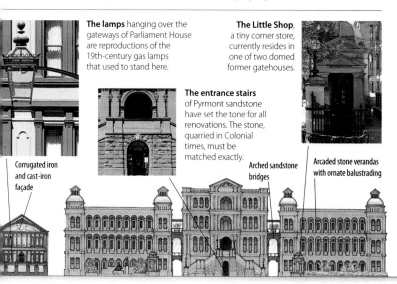

Sydney Hospital *(1868–94)*

⑫ The Mint

10 Macquarie St. **Map** 1 C5. **Tel** 8239 2288. 🚌 Sydney Explorer, Elizabeth St routes. 🚆 St James, Martin Place. **Open** 9am–5pm Mon–Fri. **Closed** Good Fri, 25 Dec. 🖥 ♿ ground floor only. 🌐 sydneylivingmuseums.com.au/the-mint

The gold rushes of the mid-19th century transformed Colonial Australia. The Sydney Mint opened in the 1816 Rum Hospital's south wing in 1854 to turn recently discovered gold into bullion and currency.

It was the first branch of the Royal Mint to be established outside London. The Mint was closed in 1927 as it was no longer competitive with the Melbourne and Perth Mints. The Georgian building went into its own decline after it was converted into government offices. In the 1950s, the front courtyard was even used as a car park. In 1982, it opened as a branch of the Powerhouse Museum (see pp102–3), but the collection moved to the main museum in Harris Street.

This building is now the head office of the Historic Houses Trust of NSW and you can wander through the front of the building, or view the small historical display near the entrance.

Replica convict hammocks on the third floor of Hyde Park Barracks

⑬ Hyde Park Barracks Museum

Queens Square, Macquarie St. **Map** 1 C5. **Tel** 8239 2311. 🚌 Sydney Explorer, Elizabeth St routes. 🚆 St James, Martin Place. **Open** 10am–5pm daily. **Closed** Good Fri, 25 Dec. 🖥 🖥 ♿ level one only. 📷 on request. 🌐 sydneyliving museums.com.au/hyde-park-barracks-museum

Described by Governor Macquarie as "spacious" and "well aired", the beautifully proportioned barracks are the work of Francis Greenway and are considered his

Francis Greenway, Convict Architect

Until the 1990s, Australian A$10 notes bore the portrait of the early Colonial architect Francis Greenway, the only currency in the world to pay tribute to a convicted forger. Greenway was transported to Sydney in 1814 to serve 14 years for his crime. Under the patronage of Governor Macquarie, who appointed him Civil Architect in 1816, Greenway designed more than 40 buildings, of which only 11 remain today. He received a full pardon in 1819, but soon fell out of favour as he persisted in charging large fees while still on a government salary. Greenway died in poverty in 1837.

Francis Greenway (1777–1837)

Macquarie Street

Fine examples of Francis Greenway's Georgian style are within an easy walk of one another at the Hyde Park end of Macquarie Street. The brick and sandstone of Hyde Park Barracks, St James Church and the Old Supreme Court Building form a harmonious group on the site the governor envisaged as the city's civic centre.

The Mint, like its twin, Parliament House, has an unusual double-colonnaded two-storeyed veranda.

The roof of The Mint has now been completely restored to replicate the original wooden shingles in casuarina (she-oak).

The stone wall, of Hyde Park Barracks' northwest pavilion still bears the marks of the convicts' chisels.

The Mint (1816)

masterpiece. They were completed in 1819 by convict labour and designed to house 600 convicts who had previously been forced to find their own lodgings after their day's work. The building later housed Irish orphans and then single female immigrants, before becoming courts and legal offices. Refurbished in 1990, it reopened as a museum with exhibits about the site and its occupants over the years.

The displays include a room reconstructed as convict quarters of the 1820s, as well as pictures, models and artifacts relating to this period of Australian history. Many of the objects now on display, recovered during archaeological digs at the site, had previously been dragged away by rats to their nests; the scavenging rodents are acknowledged as valuable agents of preservation.

The Greenway Gallery on the first floor holds temporary exhibitions on history, ideas and culture.

Hyde Park Barracks is one of 11 Australian convict sites included on the UNESCO World Heritage List for their universal significance.

Detail from the Children's Chapel mural in the St James' Church crypt

⓯ St James' Church

173 King St. **Map** 1 B5. **Tel** 8227 1300. Sydney Explorer, Elizabeth St routes. T St James, Martin Place. **Open** 10am–4pm Mon–Fri, 9am–1pm Sat, 7:30am– 4pm Sun. Free concerts: Mar–Dec: Wed 1:15pm. W **sjks.org.au**

This fine Georgian building, constructed with convict-made bricks, was designed as a courthouse in 1819. The architect, Francis Greenway, was forced to convert it into a church in 1820, when plans to build a grand cathedral on George Street were abandoned.

Greenway, unhappy about the change, designed a simple yet elegant church. Consecrated in 1824 by Samuel Marsden, the infamous "flogging parson", it is Sydney's oldest church. Many additions have been carried out, including designs by John Verge in which the pulpit faced towards high-rent pews, while convicts and the military sat behind the preacher where the service would have been inaudible. A Children's Chapel was added in 1930.

Prominent members of early 19th-century society, many of whom died violently, are commemorated in marble tablets. These tell the full and bloody stories of luckless explorers and shipwreck victims, among other untimely demises.

L. MACQUARIE ESQ GOVERNOR. 1817

This clock, dating from 1817 and one of Sydney's oldest, is on the Hyde Park Barracks façade.

The Land Titles Office, a WL Vernon building from 1908, has a Classical form with some fine Tudor Gothic detailing.

The stained-glass windows in the Chapel of the Holy Spirit of St James' Church are mostly 20th century.

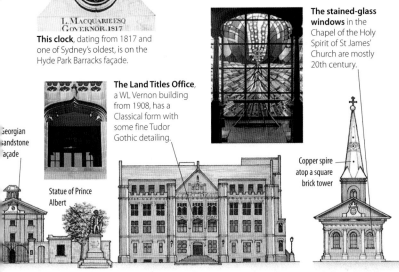

Georgian sandstone façade

Statue of Prince Albert

Copper spire atop a square brick tower

Hyde Park Barracks (1817–19)   **Land Titles Office** (1908–13)   **St James'** (1820)

Waterfront view of the Elizabeth Bay skyline

Sights at a Glance

Historic Streets and Buildings

2 Victoria Street
3 Elizabeth Bay House
6 Old Gaol, Darlinghurst
7 Darlinghurst Court House

Museums and Galleries

5 Sydney Jewish Museum

Parks and Gardens

4 Beare Park

Monuments

1 El Alamein Fountain

See also Street Finder,
maps 2, 3 & 5

KINGS CROSS AND DARLINGHURST

On the eastern side of the city, Kings Cross ("The Cross") and Darlinghurst ("Darlo") are a couple of Sydney celebrities. With a reputation as a gangland hotbed of criminal ativity and raucous red-light district, Kings Cross is undergoing rapid transformation into a gentrified residential enclave. While the late-night seedy bar scene remains, albeit on a smaller scale, the impact of high rents and the introduction in 2014 of controversial "lockout laws" forcing earlier closing times, has seen developers snap up former nightspots and convert them into apartments. A thriving daytime economy has emerged, with hospitality and lifestyle businesses serving a growing local community. By evening, restaurants and wine bars have added a touch of sophistication to the area's traditional bohemian roots. Still scruffy around the edges, Darlinghurst is also making a mark as a go-to dining destination, while retaining its reputation as a social hub for the gay and lesbian community, including the flamboyant annual Gay and Lesbian Mardi Gras Parade.

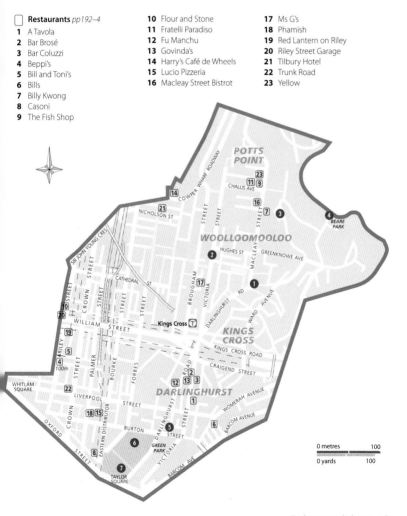

Street-by-Street: Potts Point

The substantial Victorian houses filling the streets of this old suburb are excellent examples of the 19th-century concern with architectural harmony. New building projects were designed to enhance rather than contradict the surrounding buildings and general streetscape. Monumental structures and fine details of moulded stuccoed parapets, cornices and friezes, even the spandrels in herringbone pattern, are all integral parts of a grand suburban plan. (This plan included an 1831 order that all houses cost at least £1,000.) The gentrification of this part of the suburb, with its pretty, tree-lined streets and air of sophistication, earned it the enduring moniker, "The Paris End of Potts Point".

The McElhone Stairs were preceded by a wooden ladder that linked Woolloomooloo Hill, as Kings Cross was known, to the estate far below.

Horderns Stairs

These villas, from the Georgian and Victorian eras, can be broadly labelled as Classical Revival and are fronted by leafy gardens.

②★ Victoria Street
From 1972 to 1974, residents of this historic street fought a sometimes violent battle against developers wanting to build high-rise towers, motels and blocks of flats.

Kings Cross Station

Werrington, a mostly serious and streamlined building, also has flamboyant Art Deco detailing, which is now hidden under brown paint.

Tusculum Villa was just one of a number of 1830s houses subject to "villa conditions". All had to face Government House, be of a high monetary value and be built within three years.

Challis Avenue is a fine and shady complement to nearby Victoria Street. This Romanesque group of terrace houses has an unusual façade, with arches fronting deep verandas and a grand ground-floor colonnade.

Locator Map
See Street Finder, map 2

Rockwall, a symmetrical and compact Regency villa, was built to the designs of the architect John Verge *(see p122)* in 1830–37.

Del Rio is a finely detailed high-rise apartment block. It clearly exhibits the Spanish Mission influence that filtered through from California in the first quarter of the 20th century.

Landmark Hotel

The Arthur McElhone Reserve

❸ ★ Elizabeth Bay House
A contemporary exclaimed over the beauty of the 1830s garden: "Trees from Rio, the West Indies, the East Indies, China…the bulbs from the Cape are splendid."

Art Deco Birtley Towers

Elizabeth Bay was part of the original land grant to Alexander Macleay *(see p122)*. He created a botanist's paradise with ornamental ponds, quaint grottoes and promenades winding all the way down to the harbour.

0 metres   50
0 yards   50

Key

— Suggested route

El Alamein Fountain, commemorating the World War II battle

❶ El Alamein Fountain

Fitzroy Gardens, Macleay St, Potts Point. **Map** 2 E5. 🚌 311.

This dandelion-shaped fountain in the heart of the Kings Cross district has a reputation for working so spasmodically that passers-by often murmur facetiously, "He loves me, he loves me not." Built in 1961, it commemorates the Australian army's role in the siege of Tobruk, Libya, and the battle of El Alamein in Egypt during World War II. At night, when it is brilliantly lit, the fountain looks surprisingly ethereal.

❷ Victoria Street

Potts Point. **Map** 2 E5. 🚌 311, 324, 325.

At the Potts Point end, this street of 19th-century terrace houses, interspersed with a few incongruous-looking high-rise blocks, is, by inner-city standards, almost a boulevard. This gracious street was once at the centre of a bitter conservation struggle, one which almost certainly cost a prominent heritage campaigner's life.
In the early 1970s, many residents, buoyed by the "green bans" *(see p33)* put in place by the Builders' Labourers' Federation of New South Wales, fought to prevent demolition of old buildings for high-rise development. Heiress

Juanita Nielsen, publisher of a local newspaper, vigorously took up the conservation battle. On 4 July 1975, she disappeared without trace. An inquest into her disappearance returned an open verdict, and the case that captivated Sydney and dominated the front pages of newspapers remains unsolved to this day.
As a result of the actions of the union and residents, most of Victoria Street's superb 19th-century buildings still stand.

❸ Elizabeth Bay House

7 Onslow Ave, Elizabeth Bay. **Map** 2 F5. **Tel** 9356 3022. 🚌 Sydney Explorer, 311. **Open** 10am–4pm Fri–Sun. **Closed** Good Fri, 25 Dec. 🅿️ 🆆 sydneylivingmuseums.com.au/ elizabeth-bay-house

Elizabeth Bay House *(see pp26–7)* has the finest Colonial interior on display in Australia. It is a potent expression of how the 1840s depression cut short the 1830s prosperous optimism. Designed in the fashionable Greek Revival style by John Verge, it was built for Colonial Secretary Alexander Macleay, in 1835–9. The domed oval saloon with its cantilevered staircase is recognized as Verge's masterpiece. The exterior is less satisfactory, as the intended colonnade and portico were not finished owing to a crisis in Macleay's financial affairs.

Juanita Nielsen

The present portico dates from 1893. The interior is furnished to reflect Macleay's occupancy from 1839 to 1845, based on inventories drawn up in 1845 for the transfer of the house to Macleay's son, William Sharp. He took the house in return for payment of his father's debts, leading to a rift never to be resolved.
Macleay's original 22-hectare (54-acre) land grant was subdivided for flats and villas from the 1880s to 1927. In the 1940s, the house itself was divided into 15 flats. In 1942, the artist Donald Friend, while standing on the balcony of his flat – the former morning room – saw the ferry *Kuttabul* hit by a torpedo from a Japanese midget submarine.
The house was restored and opened as a museum in 1977.

The sweeping staircase under the oval dome, Elizabeth Bay House

❹ Beare Park

Ithaca Rd, Elizabeth Bay. **Map** 2 F5. 🚌 311.

Originally a part of the Macleay Estate, Beare Park is now encircled by a jumble of apartment blocks. A refuge from hectic Kings Cross, it is one of only a handful of parks serving a densely populated area. In the shape of a natural amphitheatre, the park puts Elizabeth Bay on glorious view.
The family home of J C Williamson, a famous theatrical entrepreneur who came to Australia from America in the 1870s, formerly stood at the eastern extremity of the park.

Star of David in the lobby of the Sydney Jewish Museum

❺ Sydney Jewish Museum

148 Darlinghurst Rd, Darlinghurst.
Map 5 B2. **Tel** 9360 7999. 🚌 Sydney
Explorer, Bondi & Bay Explorer, 311,
389. **Open** 10am–4pm Mon–Thu &
Sun, 10am–2:30pm Fri. **Closed** Sat,
Jewish hols. 🐾 ♿ 📷 📷
🅦 sydneyjewishmuseum.com.au

Sixteen Jewish convicts were on the First Fleet and many more were to be transported before the end of the convict era. As with other convicts, most would endure and some would thrive, seizing all the opportunities the colony had to offer for those wishing to make something of themselves.

The Sydney Jewish Museum relates stories of Australian Jewry within the context of the Holocaust. The ground floor display explores present-day Jewish traditions and culture within Australia. Ascending the stairs to mezzanine levels 1–6, the visitor passes through chronological and thematic exhibitions which unravel the history of the Holocaust.

From Hitler's rise to power and *Kristallnacht*, through the evacuation of the ghettos and the Final Solution, to the ultimate liberation of the infamous death camps and Nuremberg Trials, the harrowing events are graphically documented. This horrific period is recalled using photographs and relics, some exhumed from mass graves, as well as audiovisual exhibits and oral testimonies.

Holocaust survivors act as volunteer guides. Their presence, bearing witness to the recorded events, lends considerable power and moving authenticity to the exhibits.

❻ Old Gaol, Darlinghurst

Cnr Burton & Forbes Sts, Darlinghurst.
Map 5 A2. **Tel** 9339 8744. 🚌 333, 378,
380, 389. **Open** 10:30am–5pm Mon–
Fri. **Closed** public hols. ♿ 📷 11am,
1pm, 2pm, 3pm.

Originally known as the Woolloomooloo Stockade and later as Darlinghurst Gaol, this site has been home to the National Art School since 1922. It was constructed over a 20-year period from 1822.

Surrounded by walls almost 7 m (23 ft) high, the cell blocks radiate from a central round-house. The former jail is built of stone quarried on the site by convicts, which was then chiselled by them into blocks.

No fewer than 67 people were executed here between 1841 and 1908. Perhaps the most notorious hangman was Alexander "The Strangler" Green, after whom Green Park, outside the jail, is thought to have been named. Green lived near the park until public hostility forced him to live in relative safety inside the jail.

Some of Australia's most noted artists, including Frank Hodgkinson, Jon Molvig and William Dobell, trained or taught at the art school which was established here in 1921.

The former Governor's house, Old Gaol, Darlinghurst

❼ Darlinghurst Court House

Taylor Square, Darlinghurst. **Map** 5 A2.
Tel 1300 679 272. 🚌 333, 378, 380.
Open Feb–mid-Dec: 10am–4pm
Mon–Fri & Sun. **Closed** mid-Dec–Jan,
public hols. ♿ 📷

Abutting the grim old jail, to which it is connected by under-ground passages, and facing Taylor Square, this unlikely gem of Greek Revival architecture was begun in 1835 by Mortimer Lewis, the Colonial Architect of New South Wales from 1835 to 1843. He was only responsible for the central block of the main building with its splendid six-columned Doric portico. The balancing side wings were added in the 1880s.

The court house is still used by the state's Supreme Court mainly for criminal cases, and these are open to the public.

Beare Park, a quiet inner-city park with harbour views

A row of Victorian terrace houses in the suburb of Paddington

Sights at a Glance

Historic Streets and Buildings

1. Paddington Street
2. The Entertainment Quarter
4. Five Ways
5. Juniper Hall
6. Paddington Town Hall
7. Paddington Village
8. Victoria Barracks

Parks and Gardens

9. Centennial Park

Markets

3. Paddington Markets

0 metres   500
0 yards   500

PADDINGTON

The genteel area of Paddington, home to an array of fashionable boutiques, prestigious galleries, fine cafés, restaurants and historic pubs, is a leafy residential suburb of finely restored early Victorian houses. Most of its famed terrace homes, with their distinctive wrought-iron "lace" balconies, were built in the late 19th century and evolved from 1830s Georgian and Regency homes, which were knocked down, rebuilt and subdivided. Large parts of Paddington are recognized as heritage conservation areas for the aesthetic value of their highly consistent streetscape of handsome terraces in the winding backstreets. With its elegant "village" feel,

"Paddo" is a shopping haven for those who favour small independent stores over mass-market shopping malls. Oxford Street is home to emerging and established fashion designers, Queen Street is the place to head for fine antiques, while Sydney's longest-running community market, the famous Saturday's Paddington Markets, brims with local designers showcasing their wares. Centennial Park provides a peaceful oasis, while the leisure and sporting precinct, including the Entertainment Quarter, Sydney Cricket Ground and Allianz Stadium, gets the adrenalin pumping.

See also Street Finder, maps 5 & 6

Street-by-Street: Paddington

Paddington began to flourish in the 1840s following the construction of Victoria Barracks. A village emerged around the workers' cottages and rapid development followed with the building of rows of narrow Victorian terrace houses. Hard hit by the Great Depression, the area became rundown and slum-like. A 1947 plan proposing mass demolition to build blocks of flats was thwarted by an influx of postwar European migrants, who found the area convenient and affordable. The 1960s saw the restoration of homes and gentrification of the bohemian suburb.

❹ ★ Five Ways
This shopping hub was established in the late 19th century on the busy Glenmore roadway trodden out by bullocks.

Duxford Street's terrace houses in toning pale shades constitute an ideal of town planning: the Victorians preferred houses in a row to have a pleasingly uniform aspect.

"Gingerbread" houses can be seen in Broughton and Union streets. With their steeply pitched gables and fretwork barge-boards, they are typical of the rustic Gothic Picturesque architectural style.

The London Tavern opened for business in 1875, making it the suburb's oldest pub. Like many of the pubs and delicatessens in this well-serviced suburb, it stands at the end of a row of terraces.

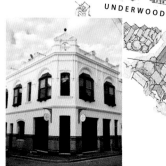

Key

— Suggested route

The Korban/Flaubert design and sculpture studio is housed in this strikingly modern building. The former home of the Sherman Galleries, it was designed to hold contemporary sculpture and paintings. Suitable access gates and a special in-house crane enable the movement of large-scale artworks.

Paddington's streets are a treasure trove of galleries, bars and restaurants. A wander through the area should prove an enjoyable experience.

Locator Map
See Street Finder, maps 5 & 6

Warwick, built in the 1860s, is a minor castle lying at the end of a row of humble terraces. Its turrets, battlements and assorted decorations, in a style somewhat fancifully described as "King Arthur", even adorn the garages at the rear.

Windsor Street's terrace houses are, in some cases, a mere 4.5 m (15 ft) wide.

Street-making in Paddington's early days was often an expensive and complicated business. A cascade of water was dammed to build Cascade Street.

0 metres 50
0 yards 50

❶ ★ **Paddington Street**
Under the established plane trees, some of Paddington's finest Victorian terraces exemplify the building boom of 1860–90. Over 30 years, 3,800 houses were built in the suburb.

A typical pretty terrace house on Paddington Street

❶ Paddington Street

Map 6 D3. 🚌 333, 378, 380.

With its huge plane trees shading the road and fine two-, three- and four-storey terrace houses on each side, Paddington Street is one of the oldest, loveliest, and at the same time most typical of the suburb's streets.

Paddington grew rapidly as a commuter suburb in the late 19th century and most of the terraces were built for renting to the city's artisans. They were cheaply decorated with iron lace (some of which had arrived in ships as ballast), as well as Grecian-style friezes, worked parapets, swagged urns, lions rampant, cornices, pilasters, scrolls and other fancy plastering. By the 1900s, these terraces had become unfashionable, but in the 1960s, tastes changed again and Paddington experienced a renaissance.

Paddington Street now has a chic atmosphere, and small art galleries operate out of quaint and grand shopfronts.

❷ The Entertainment Quarter

Lang Rd, Moore Park. **Tel** 8117 6700. **Map** 5 C5. 🚌 339, 355. **Open** most retail shops are open 10am–10pm. 🖥 eqmoorepark.com.au

There's a vibrant atmosphere at the Entertainment Quarter, located next door to Sydney Cricket Ground, Allianz Stadium and Fox Studios, which produced such well-known films as *The Matrix* and *Moulin Rouge*.

There are 16 cinema screens where you can watch the latest movies, and at the La Premiere cinema you can enjoy your movie with wine and cheese, sitting on comfortable sofas. There are four live-entertainment venues which regularly feature the latest local and international acts. You can also enjoy bungy trampolining, bowling or seasonal ice-skating, and children will love the three well-designed playgrounds.

In addition to shops there are plenty of restaurants, cafés and bars offering a range of meals, drinks and snacks.

Every Wednesday and Saturday you can sample fresh produce at the EQ Village Markets or try a gourmet delicacy from one of the dozens of stallholders. Sunday's market focuses on merchandise rather than food.

Shops are open until late, offering a good selection of fashion, books and homewares. There is plenty of undercover parking and the complex is a pleasant stroll from Oxford Street.

❸ Paddington Markets

395 Oxford St. **Map** 6 D4. **Tel** 9331 2923. 🚌 333, 378, 380. **Open** 10am–4pm Sat. **Closed** 25 Dec. ♿ *See Shops and Markets: p203.* 🖥 paddingtonmarkets.com.au

This market, which began in 1973, takes place every Saturday, come rain or shine, in the grounds of Paddington Village Uniting Church and its neighbouring school. It is a place to meet and be seen as much as it is to shop. Stallholders come from all over the world, and many young designers hoping to launch their careers display their wares. Among the offerings are jewellery, pottery, new and secondhand clothing, and an array of other arts and crafts. Whatever you are looking for, you are likely to find it here, from designer bags to tarot reading, and from Oriental massages to handmade soaps.

❹ Five Ways

Cnr Glenmore Rd & Heeley St. **Map** 5 C3. 🚌 389.

There is a busy shopping hub at this picturesque junction by the tramline that once ran to Bondi Beach. On the five corners stand Victorian and early 20th-century shops, one now a restaurant.

On another corner is the impressive Royal Hotel, built in 1888. This mixed Victorian and Classical Revival building has a characteristic intricate cast-iron "lace"-screen balcony offering stunning harbour views.

Balcony of the Royal Hotel in the heart of Paddington

❺ Juniper Hall

250 Oxford St. **Map** 5 C3. **Tel** 9357 5222. 🚌 333, 378, 380. **Open** see website for exhibition details and dates. 🖥 juniperhall.com.au

The emancipist gin distiller Robert Cooper built this superb example of Colonial Georgian architecture for his third wife, Sarah. He named it after the main ingredient of the gin that made his fortune.

Completed in 1824, it is the oldest building in Paddington still standing. It is probably also the largest and most extravagant. It had to be: he already had 14 children when he declared that Sarah would have the finest house in Sydney.

Juniper Hall was saved from demolition in the mid-1980s and fully restored. It is now home to the annual Moran Art Prize (www.moranprizes.com.au).

❻ Paddington Town Hall

249 Oxford St (cnr Oatley Rd). **Map** 5 C3. **Tel** 9265 9189. 🚌 333, 378, 380. Library: **Open** 9:30am–6pm Mon, Tue, Thu & Fri, noon–8pm Wed, 10am–4pm Sat. 🅦 **palacecinemas.com.au**

The Paddington Town Hall was completed in 1891. An international competition which, in a spirit of Victorian self-confidence, was intended to produce the state's finest town hall, was won by local architect J E Kemp. His Classical Revival building, to which a clock tower was later added, still dominates the surrounding area, although it is no longer a centre of local government.

The building now houses Chauvel Cinema in the former ballroom, which is managed by the Australian Film Institute, as well as the Paddington Library.

Paddington Town Hall, at the highest point in the Oxford Street ridge

❼ Paddington Village

Cnr Gipps & Shadforth Sts. **Map** 5 C3. 🚌 333, 378, 380.

Paddington began its life as a working-class suburb. The community comprised the carpenters, quarrymen and stonemasons who supervised the convict gangs that built Victoria Barracks in the 1840s.

The artisans and their families occupied a tight huddle of spartan houses, a few of which still remain, crowded into the narrow streets nearby. Like the barracks, these dwellings and surrounding shops and hotels were built mainly of locally quarried stone.

The lush green expanse of Centennial Park

❽ Victoria Barracks

Oxford St. **Map** 5 B4. **Tel** 8335 5330. 🚌 333, 378, 380. Museum: **Open** 10am–1pm Thu (last adm noon), 10am–4pm first Sun of month. **Closed** Dec & Jan. ♿ 📷 Parade & tour: 10am Thu. 🅦 **armymuseum nsw.com.au**

The Regency-style Victoria Barracks, covering almost 12 ha (29 acres), is one of the best-known examples of military architecture, not only in Australia but also in the world.

Designed by the Colonial Engineer, Lieutenant Colonel George Barney, the barracks were built between 1841 and 1848 using local sandstone quarried by mainly convict labour. Originally intended to house 800 men, it has been in continuous military use ever since, and still operates as a centre of military planning, administration and command.

The main block is 225 m (740 ft) long and has symmetrical two-storey wings with cast-iron verandas flanking a central archway. The perimeter walls, which are designed to repel surprise attacks, have

The archway at the Oxford Street entrance to Victoria Barracks

foundations 10 m (40 ft) deep in places. In a former jail block, a museum traces New South Wales' military heritage.

❾ Centennial Park

Map 6 E5. **Tel** 9339 6699. 🚌 Clovelly, Coogee, Maroubra, Randwick, Bronte, City, Bondi Beach & Bondi Junction routes, Bondi Explorer Bus. **Open** the park is open permanently; cars are permitted from sunrise. 🚻 📷 ♿ 📷 on request. 🅦 **centennialparklands.com.au**

Entering this large park through one of its sandstone and wrought-iron gates, the visitor may wonder how such an extensive and idyllic space has survived so close to the centre of the city.

Formerly a common, it was dedicated "to the enjoyment of the people of New South Wales forever" on 26 January 1888, the centenary of the foundation of the colony. On 1 January 1901, more than 100,000 people gathered here to witness the birth of the Commonwealth of Australia with the proclamation of the Federation of Australia. The striking Federation Pavilion marks the site of this event.

Today picnickers, painters, runners, horse riders, cyclists and inline skaters enjoy this vast recreation area.

Once the source of Sydney's water supply, the swamps are now home to many waterbirds. Within the park are ornamental ponds, cultivated gardens, an Avenue of Palms, a sports ground and a café.

FURTHER AFIELD

Around the harbour foreshores are secluded beaches, cultural and historic sights and scenic outlooks, including those afforded by Taronga Zoo's stunning setting. The spectacular Barangaroo precinct brings a beautiful headland park, Barangaroo Reserve, and a buzzing dining and shopping area to the northwestern edge of the city centre. Among Sydney's beachside playgrounds are the famed Manly to the north and Bondi to the south of the harbour. In Balmain, Glebe and Surry Hills, visitors can experience the vibrant character of the inner suburbs, with each area home to a thriving foodie scene and lively markets. Imaginative urban planning and architecture has revitalized the inner west suburb of Ultimo as a creative and education hub, home to the city's first Gehry-designed building. Further west at Parramatta, Sydney's "second city", sights recall early European settlement.

Sights at a Glance

Historic Districts and Buildings
2 Dr Chau Chak Wing Building
3 University of Sydney
6 Balmain
9 Kirribilli Point
13 North Head
14 Vaucluse House
16 Watsons Bay
17 Macquarie Lighthouse
19 Captain Cook's Landing Place
21 Elizabeth Farm
22 Hambledon Cottage
23 Experiment Farm Cottage
25 Old Government House

Museums and Galleries
1 Brett Whiteley Studio
10 Nutcote

Parks and Gardens
7 Barangaroo
15 Nielsen Park

Entertainment
8 Luna Park
11 *Taronga Zoo pp136–7*
20 Sydney Olympic Park

Beaches
12 Manly
18 Bondi Beach

Restaurants and Pubs
4 Glebe

Markets
5 Sydney Fish Market

Cemeteries
24 St John's Cemetery

KEY

▓ Main sightseeing area

▢ Park or reserve

③ Metrod route

═ Freeway or motorway

━ Major road

═ Minor road

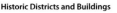

0 km   6
0 miles   3

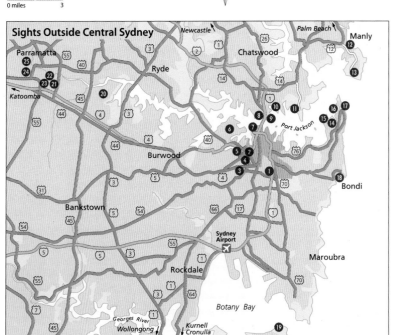

Sights Outside Central Sydney

◄ The Ferris wheel at Luna Park

Brett Whiteley Studio: former artist's studio, now a museum

❶ Brett Whiteley Studio

2 Raper St, Surry Hills. **Map** 5 A4.
Tel 9225 1881. 🚌 343, 372, 393.
Open 10am–4pm Fri–Sun, or by appointment on Wed & Thu.
Closed Easter Sun, 25 Dec.
♿ partial access.

In June 1992, Brett Whiteley, *enfant terrible* of Australian contemporary art, died unexpectedly at the age of 53. An internationally acclaimed and prolific artist, he produced some of the most sumptuous images of Sydney and its distinctive harbour ever painted.

In 1985, Whiteley bought a former factory and converted it into a studio and residence. The studio is now a public museum and art gallery.

Very few changes have been made to the building since Whiteley was in residence. The furniture, lighting, collections of memorabilia, postcards, photographs and other objects are all as he arranged them.

The upstairs studio includes his unfinished paintings, art equipment, collections of reference books, and a graffiti wall covered with his quotes and images. Even the music that is played is from Whiteley's own collection.

The studio is under the administration of the Art Gallery of New South Wales *(see pp110–13)*, and displays changing exhibitions of the artist's works borrowed from the Whiteley Estate, the Art Gallery of New South Wales and private collections.

❷ Dr Chau Chak Wing Building

14–28 Ultimo Rd, University of Technology, Sydney, Ultimo. **Map** 4 D4.
Tel 9514 2000. Ⓣ Central Station.
🚌 Parramatta Rd & City Rd routes.
Ⓦ **uts.edu.au**

Named after the philanthropist who funded its construction, the Dr Chau Chak Wing Building is the first building in Australia designed by the renowned and influential architect, Frank Gehry.

Affectionately dubbed the "crumpled brown paper bag" building, this 2015 masterpiece of design and engineering is home to the Business School at the University of Technology (UTS).

Gehry described the design as a metaphorical tree house, a "growing, learning organism with many branches of thought".

The design is striking, both on the outside and the inside. The exterior features an east-facing, sandstone-coloured brick façade that undulates like fabric, and a western façade of angular glass shards that reflects the city back to itself. The "fluid" brickwork was a technical feat, with custom-made brick shapes laid by hand.

Statue of Hermes, Nicholson Museum

The building is on the route of The Goods Line pedestrian walkway *(see p101)*.

❸ University of Sydney

Parramatta Rd, Camperdown.
Map 3 A5. **Tel** 9351 2222. 🚌 343, Parramatta Rd & City Rd routes.
Open daily. ♿ 📞 phone 9351 2274 (book one week in advance).

Inaugurated in 1850, this is Australia's oldest university. The campus is a sprawling mix of buildings from different eras, often of dubious architectural merit. However, the original Victorian Gothic main building still stands on its elevated site, dominating its surroundings. The work of the Colonial Architect Edmund Blacket, it is scrupulously modelled on the architecture of Cambridge and Oxford. It features intricate stone tracery, a clock tower with carved pinnacles and gargoyles, and a cloistered main quadrangle.

The gem of the campus is the Great Hall at the main building's northern end. This sombre building, with its carved cedar ceiling and stained-glass windows depicting famous philosophers and scientists, is used for public concerts and university ceremonies.

The Nicholson Museum of antiquities *(see p39)*, the Macleay Museum and the War Memorial Art Gallery are all within the grounds. They are open to the public on most weekdays.

The east-facing façade of the unusual Dr Chau Chak Wing Building

Badde Manors Café on Glebe Point Road, Glebe

❹ Glebe

Map 3 A4. 🚌 431, 433.
See Shops and Markets: p203.

The word "Glebe" means land assigned to a clergyman as part of his benefice. In 1789, Governor Phillip granted 162 ha (400 acres) to Richard Johnson, the First Fleet chaplain, and his wife Mary. Almost all of the present suburb was once part of that Glebe Estate. Many of its streets wind down to the working harbour and contain terrace houses with Sydney wrought-iron "lace" in varying states of repair.

The once-grand residences of the 19th-century élite were mostly towards the harbour end of Glebe Point Road, with workers' cottages clustered nearer Parramatta Road. Glebe is still partly a gentrified member of the café society, although its proximity to the Broadway shopping mall and its popularity with students from the nearby University of Sydney have given it a more bustling atmosphere.

It is densely populated and lively, with many restaurants and cafés in all price ranges, traditional and trendy pubs, good bookshops, an art-house cinema and shops selling everything from antique clocks to New Age goods and chattels. Glebe Market, held every Saturday, sells an array of jewellery, secondhand clothing and bric-à-brac.

❺ Sydney Fish Market

Cnr Pyrmont Bridge Rd & Bank St, Pyrmont. **Map** 3 B2. **Tel** 9004 1100. 🚌 443, 501. 🚆 Fish Market. **Open** 7am–5pm daily. **Closed** 25 Dec. ♿ 🅿 6:40pm Mon & Wed–Fri. Booking essential; phone 9004 1143. 🅦 **sydneyfishmarket.com.au** *See Shops and Markets: p202.*

Every weekday, about 200 seafood retailers and dealers arrive at this market's private auction to bid for the previous day's catch. It is sold by Dutch auction, with prices starting high and decreasing. The volume and variety of the catch, including fish and seafood, makes this the most diverse fish market after Tokyo.

A fair amount of this catch ends up, later in the morning, in the fish market's six large retail outlets which, for the general public, are its main attraction. As well as fresh fish, these retailers sell smoked salmon and roe, sushi, marinated baby octopus and many other ready-to-eat delicacies. Visitors watch the experts as they tenderize octopus and squid in concrete mixers. As well as fishmongers, there are a number of fresh food shops, several restaurants and a seafood school – cost includes tuition, seafood and wine.

❻ Balmain

🚌 433, 434, 442. *See Shops and Markets p203 and Four Guided Walks pp144–5.*

Balmain was once one of Sydney's most staunchly working-class areas, with shipyards, a dry dock and repair yards, a coal mine, numerous rough-and-ready pubs and an intimidating criminal element. Its late 19th-century town hall, post office, court house and fire station in Darling Street reflect the civic pride of the suburb in the Victorian era.

The many stone and timber cottages of what had become a slum have transformed into a charming, bustling suburb that still retains its village character, with interesting shops, galleries, cafés, restaurants and pubs.

The proximity of the Balmain peninsula to the city and its bohemian ambience may explain why many prominent writers – including novelist Kate Grenville and playwright David Williamson – have lived and worked here.

The Saturday market, held at St Andrews Congregational Church in Darling Street, is one of Sydney's best. Antiques, estate jewellery and ingenious art and craft items are on sale.

Imposing entrance to Balmain court house on Darling Street

❼ Barangaroo

Map 1 A2–3. 🚌 Barangaroo.
🌐 **barangaroo.sydney**

Named after Barangaroo, a Cammeraygal woman who was a key figure in the early days of Colonial Sydney, this area stretches along the foreshore west of Hickson Road near Millers Point, and from The Rocks to King Street Wharf and Darling Harbour in the south. The massive redevelopment has transformed this former industrial site and shipping-container terminal into a stunning foreshore precinct comprising recreation, culture, retail and business offerings.

To the north, Barangaroo Reserve is a magnificent six-hectare (15-acre) harbourfront park (*see p46*). Filled with over 84 species of native plants, it offers walking paths, cycling trails and a welcome place to relax by the water. Signposts tell the story of the area's maritime and Aboriginal history, while there are tours for those wanting to explore in more detail.

The Wynyard Walk, a pedestrian tunnel, links Sydney's Central Business District to Barangaroo waterfront's dining and shopping precinct, which fills with office workers from the towers that have dramatically added to the skyline on the city's edge.

The final stage of the development, Barangaroo Central, will house a luxury hotel and controversial VIP-only casino. Once completed in 2024, the entire Barangaroo precinct will be connected by walking paths.

Ferris wheel at Luna Park, which is based on the Coney Island fair of the same name

❽ Luna Park

1 Olympic Drive, Milsons Point.
Tel 9922 6644. **Open** times vary, check website for details. 🚉 Milsons Point. 🚌 Milsons Point. ♿
🌐 **lunaparksydney.com**

Luna Park represents Sydney's collective childhood. It has been one of the most iconic destinations on the Sydney Harbour shoreline for both locals and visitors since its inception in 1935. The park's famous smiling face entrance has welcomed generations to experience its historic architecture and classic attractions, combined with modern rides. Inspired by New York's Coney Island, the predominant style here is Art Deco, with the two towers of the gateway face inspired by the Chrysler Building in New York City. Luna Park's heritage-listed Coney Island is the world's last

operating example of a true 1930s fun house, and the gentle Ferris Wheel ride is popular for its panoramic views of the harbour, especially as the sun sets.

Both an amusement and entertainment precinct, Luna Park includes the 2,000-seat Big Top entertainment and concert venue. While entry to the park is free, passes are required for the rides and entry into Coney Island.

❾ Kirribilli Point

Kirribilli Ave, Kirribilli. 🚌 Kirribilli North Sydney.

Best seen on the water from a ferry or harbour cruise, the two houses occupying this prominent headland, in their delightful garden settings, are typical of the magnificent homes in sprawling grounds that once ringed the harbour. Most have been demolished now and the land subdivided for apartment living. Kirribilli, meaning "place for fishing", is the most densely populated suburb in Australia.

The larger, more dominant of the two houses is Admiralty House, built as a single-storey residence in 1843. Between 1885 and 1913 it served as the residence of the commanding officer of Britain's Royal Navy Pacific Squadron, which was based in Sydney. Fortifications on the shoreline recall its military history. Now the official Sydney home of Australia's governor-general, it is said that even its shed could be considered the city's best address.

In 1855, the charming Gothic Kirribilli House, with its steep gables and decorative fretwork, was built in the grounds of Admiralty House. Today it is the official Sydney residence of Australia's prime minister.

❿ Nutcote

5 Wallaringa Ave, Neutral Bay. **Tel** 9953 4453. 🚌 Neutral Bay. **Open** 11am–3pm Wed–Sun. **Closed** some public hols. 🅿 ♿ 🌐 **nutcote.org**

One of the classics of Australian children's literature, *Snugglepot and Cuddlepie*, was published in

Walking paths in Barangaroo Reserve, a harbour foreshore park

Shop façades featuring decorative gables along Manly's Corso

1918. Since then, these two characters – known as the "gumnut" babies along with the cartoon characters Bib and Bub – have been loved by countless young Australians.

Nutcote was, for 44 years, the home of their creator, illustrator and author May Gibbs. Saved from demolition then restored and refurbished in the style of the 1930s, it opened in 1994 as an historic house museum. Visitors can view the author's painstakingly kept notebooks and other memorabilia (including the table at which she worked), as well as original editions of her books. There is a garden with views across the harbour and a shop that sells a range of May Gibbs' souvenirs.

⓫ Taronga Zoo

See pp136–7.

⓬ Manly

Manly. Manly SEA LIFE Sanctuary: West Esplanade. **Tel** 1800 614 069. **Open** 9:30am–5pm daily. **Closed** 25 Dec. *See Four Guided Walks: pp148–9.* **W** manlysealifesanctuary. com.au

Long after Australia's conversion to the metric system, the slogan "seven miles from Sydney and a thousand miles from care" is still current. It refers to Manly and the 7-mile (11-km) journey from Circular Quay by harbour ferry. If asked to suggest a single excursion to enjoy during

your time in the city, most Sydneysiders would nominate a ferry ride to Manly. This narrow stretch of land lying between the harbour and ocean was named by Governor Phillip, even before the township of Sydney got its name, for the impressive bearing of the Aboriginal men.

As the ferry pulls in to Manly Wharf you will notice on the right many shops, restaurants and bars and on the left, the tranquil harbourside beach known as Manly Cove.

At the far end of Manly Cove is Manly SEA LIFE Sanctuary, where visitors can see reptiles, sharks and giant stingrays in an underwater viewing tunnel. You can also dive with sharks, and details of Shark Dive Xtreme are on the sanctuary's website.

The Corso is a lively pedestrian thoroughfare of souvenir shops and fast-food outlets, with a market held there on Sundays. The Corso leads to Manly's ocean beach, with its promenade lined by towering

pines. Nearby is a monument to a local newspaper proprietor who, in 1902, defied bans on daytime bathing and was promptly arrested.

Every October Manly hosts a great jazz festival *(see p50)*.

⓭ North Head

Manly. Quarantine Station Ghost Tours: bookings essential (starting times vary). **Tel** 9466 1500. **W** qstation.com.au

The majestic cliffs of North Head afford the finest views in Sydney Harbour National Park, providing vistas along the coastline, across to Middle Harbour and towards the city. North Head is also the ideal place for observing the movements of harbour and seagoing craft and especially for seeing off the yachts at the start of the annual Sydney to Hobart race *(see p51)*.

The Quarantine Station nestles just above Spring Cove within the national park. Here, between 1832 and the 1960s, many ships, with their crews and their migrant passengers, were quarantined to protect Sydneysiders from the spread of epidemic diseases. More than 500 people died here, leading some to believe that the area is haunted.

Accommodation is available in Q Station's historic cottages, while the site, including its hospital, shower block and morgue, can be explored on a guided "ghost" tour. Countless migrants spent their first months in Australia in isolation here. Many of its internees left poignant messages carved in the sandstone.

First-class quarters at the Quarantine Station, North Head

⑪ Taronga Zoo

This harbourside zoo is home to more than 4,000 animals, including native wildlife and rare and endangered exotic species, living in environments closely resembling their natural habitat. A not-for-profit organization supporting wildlife conservation, Taronga Zoo offers a daily programme of shows, keeper talks, animal feedings and behind-the-scenes tours. Its elevated location provides one of the city's most spectacular vantage points – take the Sky Safari cable-car ride to the top entrance, then meander along the winding paths back to the bottom.

Australian Walkabout
Get a close look at kangaroos, wallabies, echidnas and native birds.

Learn about seals at the **Seal Show**. Be prepared to get splashed if seated near the front.

Lower entrance

The platypus is one of only three species of egg-laying mammals.

Key to Animal Enclosures
① Main entrance and Taronga Piazza
② Sky Safari
③ Australian Walkabout
④ Platypus
⑤ Australia's Nightlife
⑥ Blue Mountains Bushwalk
⑦ Red Kangaroo
⑧ Tasmanian Devils
⑨ Backyard to Bush
⑩ Wombat Burrow
⑪ Saltwater Crocodile
⑫ Cotton-top Tamarins
⑬ Penguins
⑭ Seal Show
⑮ Great Southern Oceans
⑯ Red Pandas
⑰ Rainforest Trail
⑱ Fishing Cat
⑲ Otters
⑳ Asian Elephants
㉑ QBE Free Flight Bird Show
㉒ Sun Bears
㉓ Sumatran Tiger Adventure
㉔ Meerkats
㉕ Giraffes
㉖ Chimpanzees
㉗ Reptile World
㉘ Koalas
㉙ Welcome to the Wild Theatre
㉚ Taronga Food Market
㉛ Gorillas
㉜ Lemur Forest Adventure

Athol Wharf Road
Bradleys Head Road
Athol Wharf R

Upper entrance

Sky Safari
The Sky Safari cable car gives visitors an aerial view of the zoo. It travels from the lower entrance near the ferry wharf, reached via a 12-minute ferry ride from the city, to the top entrance of the zoo's plaza.

Asian Elephants
Taronga has an extensive breeding and conservation programme for the endangered Asian elephants. The precinct features a rainforest habitat with pools, mud wallows and scratching posts.

VISITORS' CHECKLIST

Practical Information
Bradleys Head Rd, Mosman.
Tel 9969 2777. **Open** 9:30am–5pm daily (May–Aug & 31 Dec: to 4:30pm).

W taronga.org.au

Transport
238, 247, 250. Taronga Zoo.

Ferry to
Circular Quay

Taronga
Zoo

★ Sumatran Tiger Adventure
With just several hundred remaining in the wild, Sumatran tigers were added to the zoo in 2017 as part of conservation efforts to protect these endangered animals.

Meerkats
This southern African mongoose always forages in groups, with a guard standing alert for signs of danger.

The spectacular QBE Free Flight Bird Show
includes condors showing their talents in an amphitheatre overlooking the harbour.

Reptile World has amphibians, invertebrates and reptiles.

★ Koalas
Visitors can see the koalas in their eucalypt habitat at tree level, although they are most likely to be found resting – koalas can spend 18–20 hours sleeping each day.

0 metres 100
0 yards 100

Giraffes
The giraffes mark the start of the African Safari trail that includes bongos, meerkats and zebras.

For keys to symbols see back flap

Façade of Vaucluse House, with its garden and fountain

⑭ Vaucluse House

Wentworth Rd, Vaucluse. **Tel** 9388 7922. 🚌 325. **Open** 10am–4pm Wed–Sun (daily in Jan, NSW school hols & public hols). **Closed** Good Fri, 25 Dec. 🅿️ ♿ limited. 🚻 W **sydneyliving museums.com.au/vaucluse-house**

Tradition has it that the most riotous party colonial Sydney ever saw took place on the Vaucluse House lawns in 1831. W C Wentworth and 4,000 of his political cronies gathered there to celebrate the recall to England of Governor Ralph Darling, the arch-enemy.

W C Wentworth was a major figure in the colony, being one of the first three Europeans to cross the Blue Mountains *(see pp162–3)*. He was the son of a female convict and a physician forced to "volunteer" his services to the new colony in order to avoid conviction on a highway robbery charge.

The younger Wentworth became an author, barrister and statesman who stood for the Australian-born "currency" lads and lasses against the "sterling" English-born. He lived here with his family from 1829 to 1853, during which time he drafted the Constitution Bill, giving self-government to the state.

Vaucluse House was begun in 1803 by Sir Henry Browne Hayes, a knight of the realm transported for kidnapping a Quaker heiress. Sitting in 11 ha (27 acres) of parkland, natural bush and cultivated gardens, this Gothic Revival house, with its many idiosyncratic additions, resembles a West Indian plantation house. The interior and grounds

have been restored to 1840s style and the house contains furniture that belonged to the Wentworth family. A popular tea house is in the grounds.

Greycliffe House, in the tranquil grounds of Nielsen Park

⑮ Nielsen Park

🚌 325. **Open** Sunrise–10pm daily.

Part of the Sydney Harbour National Park, Nielsen Park, with its grassy expanses, sandy beach and netted swimming pool, is the perfect spot for a family picnic. Here visitors can savour

the unusual peace that descends on many harbour beaches on an endless sunny day. It is also an ideal vantage point from which to enjoy a spectacular summer sunset or simply to observe the coming and going of ferries and the meandering harbour traffic.

In the midst of this tranquil setting, enhancing its charm, stands Greycliffe House with its decorative gables and ornate chimney stacks. This Victorian Gothic mansion was completed in 1852 for W C Wentworth's daughter.

⑯ Watsons Bay

🚌 324, 325. 🚢 Watsons Bay. *See Four Guided Walks: pp150–51.*

As the base for the boats that take the pilots out to arriving ships, this pretty bay has been a vital part of the working harbour for many years. It is also the home of Doyle's famous waterfront seafood restaurant, long a magnet for Sydneysiders and visitors alike.

Just up the hill and almost opposite the bay on the ocean side is The Gap, a spectacular cliff with tragic associations. Many troubled people have taken a suicidal leap from this rugged cliff on to the wave-lashed rocks below.

It was here that the ill-fated ship *Dunbar* was wrecked in 1857, with the loss of all but one of its 122 passengers and crew. Treacherous conditions had led to miscalculation of the ship's distance from the Heads. All

View over Watsons Bay, looking southwest towards the city

The crescent-shaped Bondi Beach, Sydney's most famous beach, looking towards North Bondi

hands were ordered on deck as The Gap's rock walls loomed. The recovered anchor is now set into the cliff near the shipwreck site.

The 1883 Macquarie Lighthouse overlooking the Pacific Ocean

⓱ Macquarie Lighthouse

🚌 324, 325. ♿

This is the second lighthouse on this windswept site that is attributed to the convict architect Francis Greenway (see p116). He supervised the construction of the first tower, which was completed in 1818 and described by Governor Macquarie as a "noble magnificent edifice". The colony's first lighthouse, it replaced the previous system of bonfires lit up along the headland and earned Greenway a conditional pardon. When the sandstone eventually crumbled

away, the present lighthouse was built. Although designed by Colonial Architect James Barnet, it was based on Greenway's original and was illuminated for the first time in 1883.

⓲ Bondi Beach

🚌 333, 380, 381. See Four Guided Walks: pp146–7.

This long crescent of golden sand, so close to the city, has long been a mecca for the sun and surf set (see pp56–7). Throughout the year, surfing enthusiasts visit from far and

wide in search of the perfect wave, and inline skaters hone their skills on the promenade. Despite a growing awareness of the dangers of sun exposure (see p223) and an expansion of other cultural preoccupations, beach life still defines the lives of many Australians, who regard it as healthier than ever.

People seek out Bondi for its trendy seafront cafés and cosmopolitan milieu as much as for the beach. The pavilion, built in 1928 as changing rooms, has been a community centre since the 1970s. Note that Bondi Beach itself is an alcohol-free zone.

Bondi Surf Bathers' Life Saving Club

The founding of the surf lifesaving club at Bondi Beach in 1906 gave impetus to the formation of other local clubs, and ultimately to a global movement. An early club member demonstrated his new lifesaving reel, designed using hair pins and a cotton reel. Now updated, it is standard equipment on beaches worldwide. In 1938, Australia's largest surf rescue was mounted at Bondi, when up to 250 people were washed out to sea by freak waves. Five died, but lifesavers rescued or resuscitated more than 200, establishing their highly dependable reputation.

Bondi surf lifesaving team at the Bondi Surf Carnival, 1937

⑲ Captain Cook's Landing Place

Captain Cook Drive, Kamay Botany Bay National Park, Kurnell. **Tel** 9668 2000. 🚌 987. Toll Gate: **Open** 7am–7:30pm daily (to 5:30pm Jun & Jul). Visitor Centre: **Open** 9:30am–4:30pm daily. **Closed** 25 Dec. 🅿️ ♿ 🌐 nationalparks.nsw.gov.au

Although it is difficult to get to, visitors will find this place worth the effort. It is, after all, one of Australia's most important European historic sites. Here James Cook, botanists Daniel Solander and Joseph Banks and the crew of HMS *Endeavour* landed on 29 April 1770. Aboriginal peoples with spears were shot at. One, hit in the legs, returned with a shield to defend himself.

Nowadays people can cast a fishing line from the rock where the Europeans stepped ashore. Nearby are the site of a well where, Cook recorded, a shore party "found fresh water sufficient to water the ship" and a monument which marks the first recorded European burial in Australia.

There are also monuments to Solander, Banks and Cook, but it is the peaceful ambience that is most impressive. Now part of Kamay Botany Bay National Park, Captain Cook's Landing Place has lovely walks, some accessible to wheelchairs, where visitors may roam and observe the flora which led to the naming of Botany Bay.

The Visitor Centre in the park focuses on a number of themes: the bay's wetlands and the importance of their conservation; an interesting exhibition detailing Cook's exploration of the area; and an introduction to Aboriginal customs and culture.

Pampas grass and banana plants in the garden at Elizabeth Farm

⑳ Sydney Olympic Park

Homebush Bay. **Tel** 9714 7888. 🚈 Olympic Park. Visitor Centre (1 Showground Rd): **Open** 9am–5pm daily. **Closed** 1 Jan, Good Fri, 25 & 26 Dec. 📷 ♿ 🍴 🅿️ 🌐 sydneyolympicpark.com.au

Once host to the 27th Summer Olympic Games and Paralympic Games, Sydney Olympic Park is situated at Homebush Bay, 14 km (8.5 miles) west of the city centre. The interactive "ANZ Stadium Explore Tour" gives a taste of some of the stadium's best-loved sporting moments. For nature lovers, there is a tour of the five wetlands of the Bicentennial Park. You can buy tickets for tours at the Visitor Centre.

Other facilities at the park include the Aquatic Centre, with a kids' waterpark, and the Tennis Centre, where you can play in the footsteps of such greats as Lleyton Hewitt. There are picnic areas and cafés throughout the park that provide a welcome rest stop for those exploring the large precinct on its extensive bicycle paths. In summer, you can pack a picnic and enjoy Movies by the Boulevard, the Park's free programme of open-air cinema under the stars.

㉑ Elizabeth Farm

70 Alice St, Rosehill. **Tel** 9635 9488. 🚈 Parramatta. 🚈 Parramatta or Granville. **Open** 10am–4pm Wed–Sun (daily in Jan, NSW school hols & pub hols). **Closed** Good Fri, 25 Dec. 📷 📷 ♿ 🅿️ 🌐 sydneylivingmuseums.com.au

The discovery of fertile land at Parramatta, and the harvesting of its first successful grain crop in 1790, helped save the fledgling colony from starvation and led to the rapid development of the area.

This zone was the location of several of Australia's first Colonial land grants. In 1793, John Macarthur, who became a wealthy farmer and sheep breeder, was granted 40 ha (100 acres) of land at Parramatta. He named the property after his wife and this was to be Elizabeth's home for the rest of her life. Macarthur was often absent from the farm as the centre of his wool operations had moved to Camden.

Part of the house, a simple stone cottage built in 1793, still remains and it is the oldest

Cook's Obelisk, overlooking Botany Bay, Captain Cook's Landing Place

John Macarthur (1766–1834), architect of the house at Elizabeth Farm

European building in Australia. Over the next 50 years, it developed into a substantial home with many features of a typical Australian homestead. Simply furnished to the period of 1820–50, with reproductions of paintings and other possessions, it is now a museum that strongly evokes the original inhabitants' life and times.

The kitchen at Hambledon Cottage restored to how it was in the first half of the 1800s

㉒ Hambledon Cottage

Cnr of Hassall St & Gregory Place, Parramatta. **Tel** 9635 6924. ⓣ Parramatta. **Open** 11am–4pm Thu–Sun. **Closed** Good Fri, 25 & 26 Dec. 🅿️ ♿ 📷

This delightful cottage, with its walls of rendered and painted sandstock, was built in 1824 as the retirement home for Penelope Lucas, governess to the Macarthur daughters. It is set in a park containing trees brought to Australia from as early as 1817 by John Macarthur.

Visitors can see rooms restored to the period of 1820–50. An 1830 Broadwood piano is one of the furniture exhibits. The kitchen has walls of convict-made bricks and contains original appliances and utensils.

㉓ Experiment Farm Cottage

9 Ruse St, Parramatta. **Tel** 9635 5655. ⓣ Harris Park. **Open** 10:30am–3:30pm Wed–Sun. **Closed** Good Fri, 18–31 Dec. 🅿️ ♿ 📷 (groups must book in advance). 🌐 **nationaltrust.org.au/ places/experiment-farm-cottage**

When his sentence expired in 1789, convict farmer James Ruse was given 0.6 ha (1½ acres) of land at Parramatta on which to start a farm, along with a hut, grain for sowing, vital farming tools, two sows and six hens. He successfully planted and harvested a wheat crop with his wife Elizabeth's help. She was the first female convict to be emancipated in New South Wales. In 1791, they were rewarded with a grant of 12 ha (30 acres), the colony's first land grant. Arthur Phillip, governor of the day, called it Experiment Farm.

Medicine chest (c.1810), Experiment Farm

In 1793, Ruse sold this farm to surgeon John Harris for £40. The date of the cottage is not certain, but it is believed to be early 1830s. The woodwork is Australian red cedar and the cottage is furnished according to an 1838 inventory.

㉔ St John's Cemetery

O'Connell St, Parramatta. **Tel** 9891 0700. ⓣ Parramatta. ♿

This walled cemetery – the oldest European cemetery in Australia – houses the graves of many convicts and settlers who arrived on the First Fleet in 1788. The oldest grave that can be identified is the flat sandstone slab simply inscribed, "H.E. Dodd 1791". Henry Edward Dodd, known to be Governor Phillip's butler, was the tenth person buried in the cemetery, but the location of the other nine graves is unknown.

The first recorded burial was of a child on 31 January 1790. One prominent grave is that of churchman Samuel Marsden, who earned the title of the "flogging parson" during his time as magistrate general because of his harsh judgments. The merchant Robert Campbell (see p68) and the father of explorer William Charles Wentworth (see p138), D'Arcy Wentworth, are also buried here.

㉕ Old Government House

Parramatta Park (entry by Macquarie St gates), Parramatta. **Tel** 9635 8149. ⓣ Parramatta. **Open** 10am–4:30pm Tue–Fri, 10:30am–4pm Sat, Sun & most public hols. **Closed** Good Fri, 25 Dec. 🅿️ ♿ limited. 📷 🌐 **nationaltrust.org.au/places/ old-government-house**

The central block of Old Government House is the oldest intact public building in Australia. This elegant brick structure, plastered to resemble stone, was built by Governor Hunter in 1799 on the site of a cottage constructed in 1790 for Governor Phillip. Wings to the side and rear were added between 1812 and 1818. The Doric porch, added in 1816, has been attributed to Francis Greenway (see p116).

Australia's finest collection of early 19th-century furniture is now housed inside.

The drawing room of Old Government House, Parramatta

FOUR GUIDED WALKS

Sydney's temperate climate and natural beauty make it an ideal city for walking. The following walks have been chosen for their distinct character; they all capture a view of the essential Sydney. You can follow the paths that trace the headlands and inlets around Watsons Bay; enjoy an invigorating clifftop walk at Bondi; catch glimpses of the original landscape in Manly's unspoilt bushland; or explore the narrow streets of historic Balmain. Three of the walks incorporate ocean or harbourside beaches, so be prepared in warmer weather by packing a swimsuit, towel and hat and wearing good-quality sunscreen. In Sydney's national parks and bushland all the indigenous flora and fauna are protected. The best sign of appreciation is to leave the bush as you found it. The *Tips for Walkers* provide practical information about each walk, listing accessibility by bus, train or ferry and the estimated distance of the walk, along with scenic rest areas, picnic spots, cafés and restaurants en route. There are some useful websites, such as www.imfree. com.au and www.sydneywalks.com.au, that give details of accompanied walking tours available throughout Sydney.

Key

••• Walk route

③ Metroad route

0 kilometres 3

0 miles 2

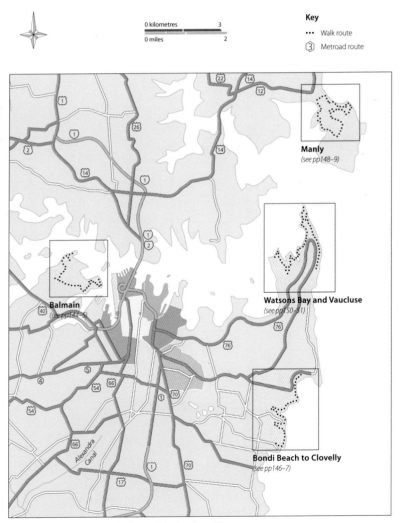

Manly
(see pp148–9)

Watsons Bay and Vaucluse
(see pp150–51)

Balmain
(see pp144–5)

Bondi Beach to Clovelly
(see pp146–7)

◀ The popular Bondi-to-Bronte coastal walk around Sydney's sandstone cliffs

A Two-Hour Walk Around Balmain

Historic Balmain village was named after William Balmain, a ship's surgeon on the First Fleet. In 1800, he was granted rights to 223 ha (550 acres) of the peninsula, which he later sold for a paltry 5 shillings in a dubious business transaction. From the mid-1800s, much of the land was subdivided for housing to support the then flourishing mining and maritime industries. Today, grand Colonial and Victorian buildings stand side by side with tiny workers' cottages, adding variety to every street.

③ The Waterman's Cottage, made of locally sourced sandstone

East Balmain

Begin from the Balmain East Wharf at the bottom of Darling Street ①. By the 1840s, when the ferry service began, shipyards dotted these foreshores. The sandstone building at No. 10 Darling Street ②, once the Dolphin Hotel then the Shipwright's Arms, was a watering hole for sailors and ferrymen. Opposite is The Waterman's Cottage (1841) ③, home to Henry McKenzie, whose boat ferried residents to and from Sydney Town.

Turn left into Weston Street and walk through the Illoura Reserve for views of the city and Darling Harbour. Leave the park via William and Johnston Streets, stopping in the latter to view Onkaparinga ④, the Colonial residence at No. 12. When building started in 1860, mussel shells from Aboriginal feasts stood in mounds upon the harbour foreshore beyond.

Turn left onto Darling Street then right into Duke Street. Gilchrist Place then leads down to Mort Bay Reserve ⑤. Ships' propellers stand as monuments to the area's working past. A path leads up to The Avenue's timber workers' cottages.

Back on Darling Street, turn left down Killeen Street. Take the path across Ewenton Park to Ewenton ⑥ (c.1854). Past the park, Hampton Villa ⑦ at 12B Grafton Street was home to state premier Henry Parkes.

Turn right into Ewenton Street and then left into Wallace Street, with its variety of early Australian architecture. The rough stone home at No. 1 is called the Railway Station as its narrow frontage makes it resemble one. The charming Clontarf ⑧ is at No. 4, while Maitland House ⑨ has a symmetry worth a second glance. Return to Darling Street.

Colourful flower cart on Darling Street, Balmain

The domestic grandeur of Louisa Road

Historic Links

Sydney's oldest extant lock-up, The Watch House (1854) ⑩ at No. 179 Darling Street, has been restored, and is open for visits on Saturday afternoons. Further along, enjoy a drink at The London Hotel (1870) ⑪, formerly a corner store and one of the oldest pubs in Sydney.

After the roundabout, visit St Andrew's Church ⑫ before losing yourself to the bookshops, cafés and delicatessens of Balmain. Every Saturday, Balmain Market fills the churchyard (see p203). At the shops' far end, the Victorian Post Office (1887) ⑬ and neighbouring Court House ⑭ reflect 1880s Sydney's prosperity. The Town Hall ⑮ dome was removed during World War II for fear of air raids. Across the street is the Fire Station ⑯ (1894). Set on the crest of a hill, its horse-drawn vehicles always travelled downhill on their outward journey.

The city and Sydney Harbour Bridge seen from Snails Bay

Balmain to Birchgrove

Retrace your steps to Rowntree Street. Turn left and wander down to Birchgrove (about 10 minutes' walk). From Birchgrove shops ⑰, take Cameron Street left and Grove Street right, to Birchgrove Park ⑱ and Snails Bay. Walk down Rose Street to Louisa Road. Two of the most notable homes are Nos. 12 and 14, Keba (1878) and Vidette (1876) ⑲, where deep verandas and iron-lace balconies hint at Colonial opulence. A poem in praise of the nearby park is inscribed on a plaque at Keba's entrance. Amid Vidette's formal greenery, a deep well is still fed by a natural spring. There is a wealth of interest in

Balmain War Memorial

the homes that follow: a tiny porch, Victorian entrance tiles, ornate iron lace – plus occasional glimpses of water frontage and private moorings. At the road's end, the reserve at Yurulbin Point ⑳ marks the mouth of Parramatta River. A fishing nook on its eastern corner is a perfect vantage point for taking in the city skyline and passing harbour traffic.

⑰ Shops nestled in the quiet Birchgrove village

Tips for Walkers

Starting point: Balmain East Wharf, end of Darling Street.
Length: 5.5 km (3¹/₂ miles).
Getting there: Ferries regularly leave Circular Quay for Darling Street's Balmain East Wharf. The 442 bus from the Queen Victoria Building stops in Darling Street. To return, there is a 15-minute ferry ride at hourly intervals from Birchgrove (pick up a schedule at Circular Quay). Alternatively, take Bus 441 from Grove Street (Snails Bay) back to the city (weekdays only).
Stopping-off points: Darling Street, in particular, has many good delicatessens, patisseries, restaurants and cafés. Places to picnic include Mort Bay Reserve, Gladstone Park, Birchgrove Park and Yurulbin Point.

0 metres 250
0 yards 250

Key
•••• Walk route

A Two-Hour Walk from Bondi Beach to Clovelly

This invigorating oceanside and clifftop walk explores the beautiful shoreline and surfing beaches of eastern Sydney. The local colour along this scenic trail is at its most vibrant at weekends, when people flock to the cafés and beaches. The Victorian cemetery at the walk's end bears witness to Sydney's multicultural heritage.

North Bondi Ocean Pool, one of two swimming pools on Bondi Beach

A Seaside Community
Walk north along Campbell Parade ①, passing a colourful array of hotels, beachwear shops and lively cafés that give the street a raffish atmosphere. Turn right into Hall Street for an indulgent treat at Gelato Messina. Back on Campbell Parade, keep walking until the Hotel Bondi ②, the parade's most significant building and easily spotted by its pretty clock tower. Opened as a first-class hotel in 1920, it initially stood alone by what was then a

Statue of lifesaver near Bondi Pavilion

bush-fringed beach. Turn right, crossing the road in front of the hotel, and walk down to Queen Elizabeth Drive to reach Sydney's most famous beach, Bondi.

Bondi's popularity dates back to the 1880s. Although daylight bathing was banned at the time, the beach was considered a fashionable place to stroll. Bondi trams came into use shortly after and, by the time bathing restrictions were lifted in 1902, the red and white trams were filled with beachgoers. Just ahead you will see Bondi Pavilion ③. Built in 1928, it was designed on a grand scale and originally housed a ballroom, gymnasium, restaurant, café, Turkish baths and open-air theatre. Although less glamorous today, the complex is still a thriving local community centre hosting cultural events. Photographs inside recall the romance of Bondi Beach in earlier times.

Next to the Pavilion is the home of arguably Australia's oldest surf lifesaving club, the Bondi Surf Bathers ④, which carried out Australia's largest mass rescue in 1938 on what became known as "Black Sunday" (see p139). Follow the sweep of the beach to its southern end.

Climb a flight of steps to continue on Notts Avenue, above Bondi Baths ⑤ and alongside the Bondi Icebergs clubhouse. Members of the Swimming Club swim every Sunday during the winter regardless of the weather.

Bronte's swimming baths, a safe alternative when the sea is rough

Bondi to Bronte
Veer left off Notts Avenue as the path drops down and skirts sharp rock formations, the result of years of erosion. Take the steep steps to Mackenzies Point lookout ⑥ on the headland. The magnificent view stretches for 180 degrees from Ben Buckler in the north to Malabar in the distant south.

Tips for Walkers

Starting point: Campbell Parade, southern end.
Length: 4 km (2¹⁄₂ miles).
Getting there: Take the train to Bondi Junction, then Bus 380 to Bondi Beach. Bus 339 runs from Clovelly Beach to Circular Quay. Waverley Cemetery is open from 8am to dusk every day.
Stopping-off points: Public toilets, showers and food and refreshments are available at Bondi, Tamarama and Bronte Beaches. Take-away cuisine can be bought along Bondi's Campbell Parade as the walk begins. Tamarama's beach café serves refreshing drinks. In warm weather, make the most of four of Sydney's best beaches by packing your swimming gear.

Tamarama Surf Life Saving Club, at the beach's northern end

Key

••• Walk route

Irish Memorial, Waverley Cemetery, a popular filming location

Bronte to Waverley

Continue down Bronte Road towards the southern end of Bronte Beach. After passing Bronte's cafés, walk through the car park and follow the road uphill, through a cutaway originally dug for trams. As the road winds through the cutting and veers right, take the steps through Calga Reserve. Walk down Trafalgar Street to the Waverley Cemetery ⑪.

In grand displays of Edwardian and Victorian monumental masonry, English, Italian and Irish residents have been laid to rest. Among notable Australians buried here are writers Henry Lawson and Dorothea Mackellar; Fanny Durack, the first woman to win an Olympic gold medal (in 1912), and do the Australian crawl swimming stroke; and aeronautical pioneer Lawrence Hargrave.

The Irish Memorial honours the 1798 Irish Rebellion and its leader Michael Dwyer, who was transported to Australia for his part in the uprising.

Leave the cemetery at the southern end. Walk through Burrows Park, hugging the coast, to Eastbourne Avenue, which leads to the walk's end at the narrow Clovelly Beach ⑫.

Resume your walk, passing through Marks Park into rocky Mackenzies Bay and over the next headland and down to Tamarama Bay ⑦. In 1906–11, this beach was the unlikely home of Wonderland City – a rowdy fun fair, boasting a roller coaster.

Across the beach and park, climb the steps to Tamarama Marine Drive. Follow the road around to the slopes of Bronte Park ⑧, once part of Bronte Estate. To explore Bronte Gully ⑨, and glimpse Bronte House ⑩, continue away from the beach. Take the track that follows the creek into a valley, passing under a canopy of fig and flame trees. The waterfall was once a natural feature of the ornamental gardens designed for Bronte Estate.

The steps on your left lead to Bronte Road and Bronte House. The mixture of Gothic and Swiss styling was the inspiration of the original owner, architect Mortimer Lewis *(see p123)*. Today it is owned by the municipal council and is leased as a private residence, with an annual open day.

⑥ Lookout at Mackenzies Point, a popular spot for watching surfers

For keys to symbols *see back flap*

A Three-Hour Walk Around Manly

This walk takes in the holiday atmosphere of downtown Manly and its splendid surf beach, before passing along quieter shorelines and clifftop streets, and through unspoilt bushland replete with native flora and fauna. It features marvellous views, the commanding architecture of the historic building that was formerly St Patrick's Seminary, and the charm of Collins Beach and Fairy Bower.

Houses rising above Fairy Bower

Brass band plays in The Corso that links the harbour cove to the ocean beach

From Harbour to Ocean

Start at Manly Wharf ①. This suburb was little more than a cosy fishing village until 1852, when entrepreneur Henry Gilbert Smith's vision of a resort similar to fashionable Brighton in his native England started to take shape. The ferry service began in 1855, operating from the same spot in use today.

Leaving Manly Cove, cross The Esplanade and walk down The Corso, a pedestrian mall. At the end of The Corso, to the left, stands the New Brighton Hotel ② in striking Egyptian Classical

Revival Style. In 1926, it replaced the original New Brighton, built in 1880 as the resort's first attraction.

Head towards the rolling surf and sweeping sands of Manly Beach ③ then continue south along the promenade. From the 1950s-style Surf Pavilion, follow Marine Parade walkway around to Cabbage Tree Bay. The pretty area around the rock pool was named Fairy Bower ④ for the delicate wildflowers and maidenhair ferns that once grew on the hillside. Beyond the rock pool, continue on the pathway around to Shelly Beach ⑤, a secluded scuba-diving and snorkelling spot, which is also an ideal swimming spot for children. The 1920s beach kiosk has been restored and converted into a smart restaurant.

Detail on the New Brighton Hotel

Shelly Beach to the former St Patrick's Seminary

Across the park, take the steps to your left to Shelly Beach Headland. A path further left loops around the headland. Viewing platforms ⑥ overlook the vast South Pacific Ocean.

Take the car park exit into Bower Street. Follow the road as it rounds high above Fairy

Bower, passing by homes of diverse architectural styles, from Spanish Mission to Neo-Georgian. Turn left into College Street, then right into Reddall Street, and left again into Addison Road. Opposite

Manly Wharf

Manly Cove

Little Manly Cove

MANLY POINT PEACE PARK

Little Manly Point

Tips for Walkers

Starting point: Manly Wharf
Length: 7.5 km (4½ miles).
Getting there: Regular ferry and Manly Fast Ferry services depart from Circular Quay.
Stopping-off points: The wide range of fresh food counters at Manly Wharf make it an ideal place to stock up on picnic fare. Restaurants and cafés line The Corso and Manly Beach Promenade. The Boathouse at Shelly Beach offers the choice of a smart restaurant, barbecue or snack bar. In warm weather, come prepared with a swimsuit, hat, towel and sunscreen.

⑤ The clear waters of sheltered Shelly Beach

the Victorian buildings at Nos. 97–99 and 95, a lane into Fairy Bower Road leads to views of the former St Patrick's Seminary, now the International College of Management, Sydney ⑦. Both Romanesque and Neo-Gothic architecture are in evidence in this 1885 edifice, built only after much deliberation by an essentially Protestant government. It was used as the Gatsby mansion in the making of the 2013 Baz Luhrmann-directed film, *The Great Gatsby*.

Leave Fairy Bower Road by Vivian Street to turn left into Darley Road and arrive at the seminary building.

⑦ The former St Patrick's Seminary, now the International College of Management, Sydney

North Head Reserve

At the top of Darley Road, turn right beneath the Parkhill Sandstone Arch ⑧ into North Head Reserve. Follow the right-hand fork (leading to the Institute of Police Management) onto Collins Beach Road down through bushland alive with bird calls and native lizards. Paper-barks, smooth-barked apple trees and banksias are some of the native flora found in abundance.

At the road's end, follow the track to your right across two footbridges, then down steps to Collins Beach ⑨. A stone cairn between the second foot-bridge and the beach marks where Governor Arthur Phillip was speared by the Aboriginal Wil-ee-ma-rin after a misunder-standing. The quiet waterfall and dense bushland make it possible to imagine this beach in pre-Colonial days.

Leave via a small set of stone steps at the right-hand end of the beach which lead to a foot-path, then out into Stuart Street.

Back to the Present

For memorable harbour views, follow the direction of Stuart Street through Little Manly Point Reserve, passing by the baths of Little Manly Cove ⑩. To continue this charming walk, turn left from Stuart Street and proceed to the end of Addison Road. Manly Point Peace Park offers a quiet place to take in a panorama of the distant city.

Return down Addison Road, making your way back to the wharf via Stuart Street and the East Esplanade. With its boat sheds and timber yacht clubs, the East Esplanade Park has a nautical atmosphere and is a relaxing place to meander. Continue ahead to Manly Wharf, which was your starting point, keeping an eye out for the little penguins that inhabit the water around the wharf.

Cabbage Tree Bay

BOWER STREET

SYDNEY HARBOUR NATIONAL PARK

DARLEY ROAD

SYDNEY HARBOUR NATIONAL PARK

COLLINS BEACH ROAD

Key

• • • Walk route

0 metres 500
0 yards 500

⑨ Collins Beach on the edge of Sydney Harbour National Park

For keys to symbols *see back flap*

A Three-Hour Walk in Watsons Bay and Vauclus

Tracing the perimeters of spectacular South Head, this walk touches on the area's Colonial connections and takes in a variety of ocean and harbourside terrain, from headlands with sweeping views and crashing waves, to secluded coves, white sandy beaches and the streets of one of Sydney's most desirable neighbourhoods.

weatherboard cottages on your left, follow the street to its end and onto Camp Cove Beach ⑥. It was here in 1788 that Captain Arthur Phillip first stepped ashore after leaving Botany Bay to explore the coastline.

Camp Cove to Watsons Bay

Take the wooden steps at the northern end of the cove to make the 40-minute return walk to South Head. Above the steps are signs of Colonial defences: a firing wall with rifle

② Signal Station built in 1848, looking out over Dunbar Head

Macquarie Lighthouse to Camp Cove

The start of this walk is majestic Macquarie Lighthouse (1883) ①. A copy of the country's first lighthouse built in 1818 *(see p139)*, it stands on the same site.

Take the walk northwards, passing by the Signal Station ② following Old South Head Road. Before the station was built in 1848, a flag was hoisted to warn the colony of ships entering the harbour.

Continue along the footpath, where a plaque marks the location of Australia's worst maritime disaster. It was here that the migrant ship *Dunbar* crashed onto the rocks in a gale in 1857 *(see pp138–9)*. The only survivor was hauled to safety up the treacherous cleft in the cliff face known as Jacob's Ladder ③. From here, follow the descending path, arriving at the jutting stony ledges of The Gap ④.

The *Dunbar's* anchor is set into concrete here, while salvaged personal effects are displayed at the Australian National Maritime Museum *(see pp96–7)*.

Taking the steps down from The Gap, bear right into the entrance of Sydney Harbour National Park. This single-lane roadway leads through natural bushland into HMAS *Watson* Military Reserve. Follow the road up to visit the Naval Memorial Chapel ⑤. A large clear window inside the chapel offers spectacular views of North Head and the Pacific Ocean. Resume your walk by taking the road out of the reserve, and then turn right into Cliff Street. Passing a row of

① Bust, Macquarie Lighthouse

Nudist Lady Bay beach, also known as Lady Jane beach

⑧ Doyle's well-known restaurant at Watsons Bay

Key

· · · Walk route

⑩ Suspension bridge across Parsley Bay

slots; a cannon lying further along. After passing Lady Bay Beach, you will reach Hornby Lighthouse ⑦, which marks the harbour's entrance. Retrace your steps to Camp Cove Beach. Climb the western-end stairs to Laings Point, a defence post in World War II. A net stretching across the harbour mouth was anchored here to prevent enemy ships entering.

Follow Pacific Street to Cove Street, then along to Marine Parade and Wharf Beach in Watsons Bay ⑧ *(see pp138–9)*. Named after Robert Watson of the First Fleet's *Sirius*, this was once first port of call for ships entering the harbour. Nearby, Doyle's restaurant offers seafood with a view. Follow the parade past the baths and tea rooms. Pilot boats ⑨ moored close by guide cruise and container ships into the harbour.

Watsons Bay to Vaucluse

Continue to secluded Gibsons Beach, taking the footpath left through native shrubbery, then right onto Hopetoun Avenue. Turn into The Crescent, tracing the curve of this exclusive street around to Parsley Bay Reserve. A short descent opens onto a suspension bridge hung across

the waters of tranquil Parsley Bay ⑩. Crossing the bridge, follow the pathway between two houses to arrive on Fitzwilliam Road. Continue right along Fitzwilliam Road, turning left into Wentworth Road to reach the extravagant Vaucluse House ⑪, surrounded by exotic gardens *(see p138)*.

To finish your walk, make your way along Coolong Road to Nielsen Park *(see p138)* and Shark Bay ⑫. Protected from its namesake by a netted enclosure, the natural setting and safe waters of this beach make it a favourite for picnics.

③ Dramatic rock cleft known as Jacob's Ladder near The Gap

Tips for Walkers

Starting point: Macquarie Lighthouse.
Length: 8 km (5 miles).
Getting there: Take Bus 324 from Circular Quay, or Bus 387 from Bondi Junction. Return by Bus 325 from Nielsen Park.
Stopping-off points: There are public toilets and showers at Camp Cove, Watsons Bay, Parsley Bay and Nielsen Park. Food and refreshments are available throughout the walk at Watsons Bay, Parsley Bay, Vaucluse and Nielsen Park. The tea rooms at Vaucluse House offer views of the gardens, and the café at Nielsen Park has an extensive menu. The walk covers several harbour beaches where you can swim safely. In warm weather, bring a swimsuit, towel, hat and sunscreen, and allow time for swimming, sunbathing and picnicking.

⑪ Children's bedroom, one of the exhibits at Vaucluse House

0 metres   500
0 yards   500

For keys to symbols *see back flap*

BEYOND SYDNEY

Exploring Beyond Sydney

To the east, Sydney is bounded by the Pacific Ocean; to the west, by the Great Dividing Range. To the north and south, within easy distance of the city, are superb beaches and stretches of coastal scenery, while inland, you will encounter waterfalls, deep valleys and fascinating flora and wildlife. On the Hawkesbury River, to the north and west of the city, are settlements of historical as well as scenic interest while, further north, the Hunter River meanders through sloping vineyards. The excursions on pages 156–67 offer the visitor the chance to sample the rich variety of Sydney landscapes from the exhilarating to the tranquil.

Three Sisters towering over the Jamison Valley

Façade of Hope Estate in the Hunter Valley

Sights at a Glance

❶ Pittwater and Ku-ring-gai Chase National Park
❷ Hawkesbury Tour
❸ Hunter Valley
❹ Blue Mountains
❺ Southern Highlands Tour
❻ Royal National Park

0 kilometres   50
0 miles   25

Getting Around

All the areas covered in these excursions can be easily reached by road from Sydney. Freeways and motorways take travellers part of the way to the Southern Highlands, Blue Mountains and Hunter Valley, while the other areas are accessible on sealed, well-signposted major roads. A number of tour operators offer guided one-day, or longer, tours to the Blue Mountains, Hunter Valley, Southern Highlands and South Coast, and parts of the Hawkesbury region. Sydney Trains and NSW TrainLink have regular train services to the Blue Mountains, Royal National Park and to parts of the area covered by the Southern Highlands Tour. Ferries offer access to some parts of the Hawkesbury River.

Grand old house in Kiama, near the Southern Highlands

◀ Three Sisters at sunset, Blue Mountains

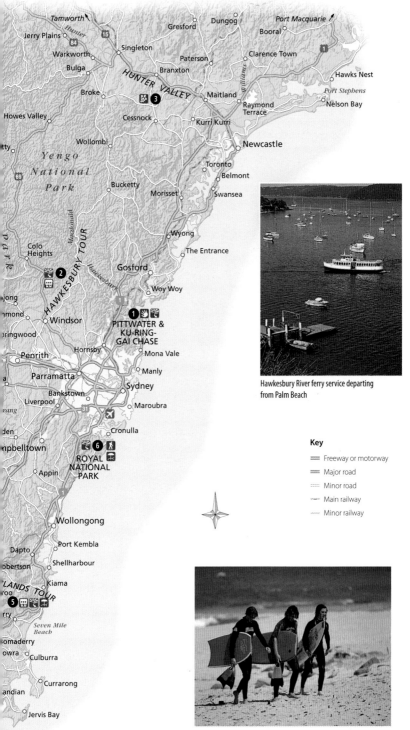

Tamworth

Jerry Plains

Warkworth

Bulga

Gresford

Dungog

Booral

Port Macquarie

Singleton

Paterson

Branxton

Broke

Maitland

Clarence Town

Hawks Nest

Port Stephens

Nelson Bay

Howes Valley

HUNTER VALLEY

Cessnock

Kurri Kurri

Raymond Terrace

Wollombi

Yengo National Park

Bucketty

Morisset

Newcastle

Toronto

Belmont

Swansea

Colo Heights

Wyong

The Entrance

Gosford

Woy Woy

Windsor

Hornsby

PITTWATER & KU-RING-GAI CHASE

Mona Vale

Penrith

Parramatta

Manly

Bankstown

Liverpool

Sydney

Maroubra

Cronulla

ROYAL NATIONAL PARK

Appin

Wollongong

Port Kembla

Dapto

Shellharbour

obertson

Kiama

Seven Mile Beach

omaderry

owra

Culburra

Currarong

Jervis Bay

HAWKESBURY TOUR

LANDS TOUR

Hawkesbury River ferry service departing from Palm Beach

Key

⚏ Freeway or motorway

▬ Major road

⋯ Minor road

⇥ Main railway

— Minor railway

Garie Beach, a popular surfing spot in Royal National Park

For keys to symbols *see back flap*

● Pittwater and Ku-ring-gai Chase

Pittwater and the adjacent Ku-ring-gai Chase National Park lie on Sydney's northernmost outskirts. They are bounded to the north by Broken Bay, at the mouth of the Hawkesbury River *(see pp158–9)*. Sparkling waterways and golden beaches are set against the unspoiled backdrop of the national park. Picnicking, bushwalking, surfing, boating, sailing and windsurfing are popular pastimes with visitors. The Hawkesbury River system curls around an ancient sandstone landscape rich in Aboriginal rock art, and flora and fauna.

Coal and Candle Creek
The pretty inlet is typical of eroded valleys formed during the last Ice Age. Water that melted from the ice caps flooded the valleys to form the bays and creeks of Broken Bay.

Akuna Bay
The isolated marina, general store and café serve the Hawkesbury River boating fraternity.

Aboriginal Art in Ku-ring-gai Chase

Ku-ring-gai Chase has literally hundreds of Aboriginal rock art sites, providing an insight into one of the world's oldest cultures. The most common are rock engravings, generally made in groups with as many as 100 individual figures. They include whales up to 8 m (26 ft) long, fish, sharks, wallabies, echidnas and Ancestral Spirits such as Daramulan, who created the land, its people and animals.

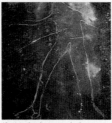

Aboriginal rock art near the Basin, Ku-ring-gai Chase

Brisbane National

Patonga

Fl St

Hawkesbury River

Juno Point

Gunyah Beach

Hungry Beach

Challenger Head

West Head Road

Refuge Bay

Cowan Creek

Cowan Point

Ku-ring-gai Ch National Park

Coal and Candle Creek

Cottage Point

Smiths Creek

Akuna Bay

General San Martin Drive

McCarrs Creek Road

Ryde, Chatswood

0 kilometres 2

0 miles 1

Key

▬ Major road

═ Secondary road

═ Minor road

▢ National Park

– – Ferry route

– – Walk route

Palm Beach Wharf

Palm Beach, a haven for sea birds such as pelicans, is popular with sun-seekers. It is also the base for the boats that visit and deliver supplies to the isolated communities on Pittwater and the Hawkesbury.

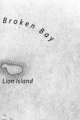

Pittwater

This graceful finger of water separates Palm Beach from Ku-ring-gai Chase. Pittwater boasts secluded beaches, picnic areas and several hamlets that can only be reached by water.

Broken Bay

Lion Island

Barrenjoey
Head

West
Head

Mackerel
Beach

Palm
Beach

Pittwater

Whale
Beach

Careel Bay

Longnose
Point

wlers Bay

Barrenjoey Road

Avalon
Beach

*Bilgola
plateau*

Scotland
Island

Bilgola
Beach

Church
Point

Newport
Beach

Bungan
Beach

Mona Vale Road

Pittwater Road

Mona Vale
Beach

*yde,
hatswood*

*Dee Why,
Manly ↓*

Whale Beach

Spectacular houses seem to hug the cliffs overlooking this fine surf beach. The Palm Beach Peninsula's beaches are often less congested than those closer to the city.

Tips for Travellers

Distance from Sydney: About 30 km (19 miles). **Duration of journey:** About 45 minutes to Mona Vale Beach. **Getting there:** Take Military Rd on the city's North Shore and cross the Spit Bridge. Follow Pittwater Rd to Mona Vale Beach. **When to go:** The Christmas holiday period is the peak season and beaches can be crowded. Ku-ring-gai Chase offers everything from shoreline to bushwalks and can be enjoyed year round. **Where to stay and eat:** Contact the visitors' information centre for full details of facilities. **Tourist information:** Bobbin Head Info Centre. **Tel** 9472 8949. **Open** 9am–4pm Mon–Fri. **Closed** Christmas Day. Ⓦ **nationalparks.nsw.gov.au**

Bilgola Beach

A small community of residents backs this patrolled surf beach set against a pretty rainforested valley. Wooden steps lead down from the ridge above through coastal heathland.

❷ Hawkesbury Tour

Australia's longest eastward-flowing river, the Hawkesbury-Nepean, forms Sydney's northern and western boundaries. It was at first thought to be two separate rivers until further exploration revealed that they were in fact one. The section known as the Hawkesbury runs from the Colo River Valley to Broken Bay in the north (see pp156–7).

Settled in 1794, by 1799 the Hawkesbury Valley's small farms produced three-quarters of the colony's grain. Its riverscape is little changed since then and much of the area remains a quiet backwater. It is an area rich in relics of the early Colonial period, including towns and villages established during the Macquarie era of 1810–19 (see p26). It is also a place of great scenic grandeur, with magnificent vistas of one of Australia's most beautiful rivers.

⑤ Tizzana Winery
A touch of Tuscany on the banks of the Hawkesbury, this sandstone winery was built in 1887 by Dr Thomas Fiaschi. It is open to visitors on weekends and public holidays.

④ Ebenezer Uniting Church
Built in 1809, the church and its 1817 schoolhouse have been superbly restored. The tree under which services were first held still stands.

⑥ Portland Reach
On the river, pleasure craft have replaced the grain barges of the past, but the area's farming community survives.

③ Colo River Drive
This pretty route travels along the Putty Road to Colo, then follows the river to Lower Portland.

Singleton

Colo River

Kurranjong heights

Ebenezer

Pitt Town

② Tebbutts Observatory
John Tebbutt (1834–1916), an early amateur astronomer, built this observatory in Windsor in 1854, where he studied the solar system and discovered a comet in 1861.

⑦ Sackville Ferry
It only takes a few minutes to cross the river by cable ferry.

Parramatta

① Windsor
Built in 1815, the Macquarie Arms Hotel is just one of Windsor's fine early Colonial buildings. Many others, including several by architect Francis Greenway (see p116), remain from the town laid out in 1810.

⑩ Settlers Arms Inn
Once an overnight stop for stage coaches to the Hunter Valley (see pp160–61), this atmospheric 1836 hotel is in the largely unchanged village of St Albans.

⑨ Webbs Creek Ferry
Opened in 1908, this cable ferry gives access to the western bank of the Hawkesbury for the drive beside the Macdonald River.

⑪ Old General Cemetery
A stark reminder of the hardships and tragedies of early settlement, this is the resting place of six First Fleeters (see p24).

⑧ Lower Portland Ferry
If taking the Colo River Drive, cross the river here by ferry for the River Road to Wisemans Ferry.

Macdonald River

Hawkesbury River

36 → Gosford

⑫ Old Great North Road
The convict-built road with its massive buttresses was completed in 1828. Part of it still remains.

36

Maroota

65

Cornelia

36

↓ Hornsby

⑬ Wisemans Ferry
This small village on a bend in the Hawkesbury River is where ex-convict Solomon Wiseman started his ferry service, Australia's oldest, in 1827.

Tips for Drivers

Distance from Sydney: 55 km (35 miles) to Windsor.

Duration of tour: About 3½ hours, excluding stops.

Getting there and back: Follow M4 to James Ruse Drive (53) just before Parramatta, then Windsor Road (40). To return from Wisemans Ferry, take the Old Northern Road (36) to Middle Dural, then Galston Road to Hornsby. From here, follow Pacific Highway south.

When to go: Peak season is from December to February. The river, national parks and small towns can be enjoyed year round.

Where to stay and eat: Cafés, restaurants and accommodation can be found at Windsor and Wisemans Ferry. The Settlers Arms Inn at St Albans has a few rooms, and a bar and restaurant.

Tourist information: Hawkesbury Information Centre. Tel 4560 4620. W hawkesbury tourism.com.au

Key

▬▬ Tour route

═ Scenic route

═ Other road

0 kilometres   5

0 miles   5

❸ Hunter Valley

Some of the earliest vineyards to be planted in Australia were on the fertile flats of the Hunter River in the 1830s, developing a thriving industry in fortified wine. Since the 1970s, it has evolved into a premium wine district *(see pp184–5)*. With some 150 wineries and cellar doors, the area is a great weekend trip from Sydney. Hot-air ballooning, golf and horse riding are other popular activities in the region. The Jazz in the Vines festival takes place in October, while some of the world's biggest acts have performed at Hope Estate, including Bruce Springsteen, Elton John and the Rolling Stones. Many wineries open daily but it is best to phone ahead and check.

Singleton, Upper Hunter

Sweetwater Creek

Terrace

Range

Old North Road

Hermitage Road

Rothbury Creek

🏠 Hunter Estate

Marsh Estate 🏠

Suthe

Deaseys Road

Rosemount Estate, Upper Hunter

Mary Anne's Creek

Broke Road

Brian 🏠 McGuig

Tyrrell's Wines 🏠

Brokenwood 🏠

Ta

Pokolbin ●

Debey

Hungerford 🏠 Hill

Draytons 🏠

Drayton Family Estate 🏠

McWilliam's 🏠

Petersons

Broken Back Range

Brokenwood

Under the ownership of Ian Riggs, this medium-sized winery has produced some of the region's finest Shiraz from the Graveyard vineyard, as well as an excellent Sémillon.

Lindemans

In 1842, Dr Henry John Lindeman resigned his naval commission to establish a vineyard in the Hunter Valley. His company has been a major producer in the Australian wine industry ever since.

Personalities of the Hunter Valley

The wine industry seems to attract or create larger-than-life characters. Among the legends was the great Len Evans, writer, wine judge, *bon vivant* and founder of the ambitious Hope Estate and Evans Family Wines, as well as Tower Estate. His contemporaries included Max Lake, a Sydney surgeon who started Lake's Folly as a weekend winery, and the late Murray Tyrrell, patriarch of a wine-making family that produced its first Hunter vintage in 1864 and proudly retains its independence.

Len Evans checking grape vines

Hope Estate

On the site of the late Len Evans' former winery, The Rothbury Estate, Hope Estate hosts dinners in the winery's cask hall, as well as open-air concerts.

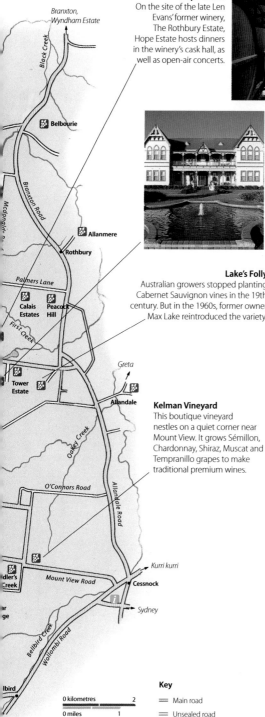

The Convent

A restored 1909 convent is now an elegantly appointed guest house, with the Pepper Tree vineyard and winery and Circa 1876 restaurant only a short walk away.

Lake's Folly

Australian growers stopped planting Cabernet Sauvignon vines in the 19th century. But in the 1960s, former owner Max Lake reintroduced the variety.

Kelman Vineyard

This boutique vineyard nestles on a quiet corner near Mount View. It grows Sémillon, Chardonnay, Shiraz, Muscat and Tempranillo grapes to make traditional premium wines.

Tips for Travellers

Distance from Sydney: 160 km (100 miles).

Duration of journey: About 2 hours from the centre of Sydney.

Getting there and back: Take the Sydney–Newcastle F3 freeway north of Sydney and follow the signs to Cessnock. Another route is through the picturesque Wollombi Valley. Allow about 3 hours as there are unsealed roads.

When to go: Year round. The best grapes are harvested between January and March.

Where to stay and eat: There is a wide variety of motels, guest-houses, self-catering cottages and cabins, cafés and restaurants.

Visitor information: Hunter Valley Wine Country Tourism, 455 Wine Country Drive, Pokolbin. **Tel** 4990 0900.

W winecountry.com.au

Further afield: The Upper Hunter vineyards are about 40 minutes by car northwest of Pokolbin.

Map labels

Branxton, Wyndham Estate

Black Creek

Belbourie

Branxton Road

Mcdonalds Rd

Allanmere

Rothbury

Palmers Lane

Calais Estates

Peacock Hill

First Creek

Greta

Tower Estate

Allandale

Oakey Creek

O'Connors Road

Allandale Road

...dler's Creek

Mount View Road

Kurri kurri

Cessnock

Sydney

Bellbird Creek

Wollombi Road

Ibird

Wollombi, ...dney

Key

| 0 kilometres | 2 |
| 0 miles | 1 |

═══ Main road
═══ Unsealed road

For keys to symbols *see back flap*

❹ Blue Mountains

The Blue Mountains, now a UNESCO World Heritage Site, prevented westward expansion of the European colony until 1813, when explorers Gregory Blaxland, William Lawson and William Charles Wentworth found a way across. The magnificent scenery, characterized by rugged cliffs and rock formations, ravines and waterfalls, is best appreciated on the bushwalks that wind along cliff tops and through valleys. The restaurants, cafés and antique shops in the centre of Katoomba will tempt the less energetic. The mountains are named for the blue haze, caused by light striking eucalyptus-oil particles in the air.

Zig Zag Railway
Steam trains travelled this railway until fire destroyed the historic carriages in 2013; services resumed in 2017.

KEY

① **Mount York**

② **Victoria Falls**

③ **The Grose River** flows between the two roads crossing the mountains.

④ **The Cathedral of Ferns** is a remnant of the temperate rainforest that once covered this area.

⑤ **Mount Banks**

⑥ **Kings Tableland**

⑦ **Jamison Valley**

⑧ **Leura village** is listed by the National Trust. Nearby are Leura Cascades, floodlit at night and one of the prettiest sights in the mountains.

Zig Zag railway ↑

Jenolan caves ➤

Grose Valley from Govetts Leap
Considered by many to be the most imposing view in the Blue Mountains, a great panorama with a series of ridges stretches into the far distance.

Three Sisters
This giant rock formation near Echo Point takes its name from an Aboriginal legend. The story tells of three sisters turned to stone by their witch-doctor father to keep them safe from an evil bunyip or monster.

Jenolan Caves

About 55 km (34 miles) south-west of Mount Victoria is a magical series of spectacular underground limestone caves with icy blue rivers and fleecy limestone formations. They are surrounded by an extensive wildlife reserve. People have been making the trek here since the caves were discovered in 1838, staying originally in the Grand Arch cave and later in the Edwardian splendour of Jenolan Caves House, which still operates today.

The vividly coloured Pool of Cerberus at Jenolan Caves

Key

━━ Major road

   Other road

• • Suggested walk

Mount Wilson
A picturesque village with cultivated gardens and exotic trees, it has been called a "little corner of the northern hemisphere". Some gardens are open to the public in spring and autumn.

Mount Tomah Botanic Gardens
This superbly landscaped garden, specializing in cool-climate plants, has sweeping views over the Grose Valley.

Richmond

Norman Lindsay Gallery and Museum
The stone cottage is home to a collection of works by artist and writer Norman Lindsay (1879–1967).

Tips for Travellers

Distance from Sydney: About 105 km (65 miles).

Duration of journey: About 90 minutes to Wentworth Falls.

Getting there and back: Follow Metroad route 4 and the Great Western Highway. Return by Bells Line of Road to Windsor. State Rail has regular services to the area. An Explorer Bus runs from Katoomba train station at 9:30am on weekends and public holidays.

When to go: Year round. Always be prepared for the cold, especially when hiking, as the weather can change rapidly in all seasons.

Where to stay and eat: Contact the Visitor Information Centre.

Tourist information: Blue Mountains Visitor Information Centre, Echo Point, Katoomba. **Tel** 1300 653 408. W visitblue mountains.com.au

0 kilometres   5

0 miles   3

Wentworth Falls
An impressive double waterfall is the starting point for the National Pass track, a challenging four-hour return walk to the next valley.

For keys to symbols see back flap

❺ Southern Highlands Tour

This easily accessible area to the south of Sydney is often said to resemble Great Britain more than Australia. It is actually a delightful combination of both: Australian high country and coastal hinterland with many European qualities. It is a land of sweeping hills and soaring valleys, dramatic waterfalls and peaceful streams; of quaint villages, cosy restaurants, antique shops and elegant places to stay. The tour takes in spectacular Seven Mile Beach and the pretty town of Berry before heading to picturesque Kangaroo Valley, sleepy Bundanoon and the antique shops and wineries of Berrima and Bowral. An exhilarating adjunct to the tour is nearby Minnamurra Falls with its boardwalk through rainforest.

⑧ Bowral
This highlands town holds a famous spring tulip festival every year and is home to cricket's Bradman Museum.

⑦ Berrima
By-passed by the railway in the 19th century, the only Georgian village in the highlands remains one of the most picturesque.

Wombeyan caves
Mittag
Bowral ⑧ ℹ
31
ℹ ⑦
Moss Vale
48
Sutton Forest
79
31
Goulburn
Bundanoon Creek
ℹ ⑥

⑥ Bundanoon
Romantic guesthouses and a glow-worm cave make this town a popular weekend destination.

Kangaroo R
Tallowa Dam

⑤ Fitzroy Falls
Part of Morton National Park, the falls plunge 80 m (262 ft) into the subtropical rainforest below. The falls lookout has access for the disabled and walking trails with stunning views.

Morton National Park
Shoal

0 kilometres   10
0 miles   5

Key

▬ Tour route
═ Scenic route (alternative)
═ Other roads

④ Kangaroo Valley
Hampden Bridge, a castellated suspension bridge, crosses the Kangaroo River at this small village. The river idyllic place for canoe

Berrima Gaol

Completed in 1839 by convict labour, this Georgian sandstone jail is featured in Rolf Boldrewood's classic 1888 bushranging novel, *Robbery Under Arms*. The fictitious character Captain Starlight, who escapes from Berrima, describes it as "the largest, most severe, the most dreaded of all prisons in New South Wales".

① Kiama
The historic town began life in the 1820s as a port for shipping cedar. Its blowhole can spurt water as high as 60 m (200 ft).

② Seven Mile Beach
Part of a national park and best seen from Gerroa's Black Head, the beach is flanked by dunes and hardy coastal vegetation, including forest and swamp. It is a great fishing, swimming and picnicking spot.

Tips for Drivers

Distance from Sydney: 120 km (75 miles).
Duration of tour: About 3½ hours, excluding stops.
Getting there and back: Take Metrod route 1, then follow the F3 freeway and Princes Hwy (1) to Kiama. Return via the F5 freeway (31) from Mittagong, then Metrod route 5 into the city.
When to go: Year round. The beaches are best in summer, and the gardens are at their peak in spring and autumn.
Where to stay and eat: Eating places, hotels and guesthouses are found all over the area.
Tourist information:
Kiama Visitor Centre, Blowhole Point, Kiama. **Tel** 4232 3322.
Ⓦ **kiama.com.au**
Southern Highlands Visitor Information Centre, 62–70 Main St, Mittagong. **Tel** 4871 2888.
Ⓦ **southern-highlands.com.au**

③ Berry
This town, surrounded by lush dairy country, is well known for its main street lined with shady trees, antique and craft shops, tea rooms and historic buildings. The Berry Museum, built in 1886, is in a former bank.

❻ Royal National Park

Designated as a national park in 1879, the "Royal" is the oldest national park in Australia. It covers 150 square km (58 sq miles) of landscape typical of the Sydney Basin sandstone. To the east, waves from the Pacific Ocean have undercut the sandstone and produced majestic coastal cliffs broken occasionally by small creeks and some spectacular beaches. Streams flowing north and east have incised deep river valleys. Heath vegetation on the plateaus merges with woodlands on the upper slopes. The park is ideal for bushwalking, picnicking, camping, swimming and birdwatching.

Hacking River
Boating, fishing and canoeing are common water sports.

Audley
A popular picnic area since the Edwardian era, it has a pavilion that was built in 1901. Look out for the 1920s dance hall also in the park.

Lady Carrington Drive
Named after a governor's wife and now closed to vehicles, the road is crossed by 15 creeks and is delightful to walk or cycle. It also leads to the track to Palona Cave.

KEY

① **Garie Beach** is a popular surf beach accessible by road.

② **Figure Eight Pool**

③ **Werrong Naturist Beach**

④ **The Forest Path** follows a circular route, passing through subtropical rainforest.

⑤ **Heathcote**

⑥ **Cronulla**

⑦ **Jibbon Lagoon**

⑧ **Little Marley Beach**

Key

— Main road

Walking track

Bundeena
Enclosed by national park on three sides, the small settlement at the mouth of the Hacking River may be reached by ferry from Cronulla or by road through the national park.

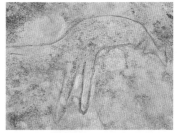

Jibbon Head
Guided tours of the Jibbon Head Aboriginal rock engravings site may be arranged.

Deer Pool
One of many fresh-water pools in the park, this sheltered spot is on the track from Bundeena Drive to Marley and Little Marley.

Wattamolla Lagoon
This pretty picnic spot has a lagoon with a waterfall at its edge and a protected ocean beach.

0 kilometres   4
0 miles   2

Curracurrang
This rock formation is about a 1-hour hike from Wattamolla Lagoon. Sea eagles and terns nest in caves at the base of this rocky cove, which also has a secluded swimming hole and waterfall.

Tips for Travellers

Distance from Sydney: 34 km (21 miles).

Duration of journey: About 1 hour from the centre of Sydney.

Getting there: Follow Metroad route 1 south to Sutherland, then the signs to Heathcote and Wollongong. The turn-off to Farnell Avenue and the park entrance is shortly after Sutherland. There is an entrance fee for vehicles.

When to go: Year round, but conditions for walking in summer can be hot so allow for this. If bushwalking, carry fresh water at all times and check on the fire danger at the Visitors' Centre.

Where to stay and eat: There are kiosks at Audley, Garie Beach and Wattamolla. Camping details can be obtained at the Visitors' Centre.

Tourist information: Royal National Park Visitors' Centre, Farnell Ave, Audley. Tel 9542 0648. **W nationalparks.nsw. gov.au**

Guided Walks, Adventure Tours and Kayak Hire: Tel 9544 5294. W bundeenakayaks.com.au

For keys to symbols *see back flap*

TRAVELLERS' NEEDS

WHERE TO STAY

Australia's emergence as a major tourist destination in the 1980s, coupled with a building boom before the 2000 Olympic Games in Sydney, resulted in a large pool of quality and good-value accommodation choices. Many of those hotels have undergone extensive refurbishments in the intervening years to meet the modern needs of a thriving visitor market. In addition to hotels, Sydney has an impressive array of self-catering apartments, numerous well-located backpacker hostels for those on a budget, and homestay accommodation, generally outside the main city areas. History buffs can find a range of accommodation in buildings with interesting post-European-settlement heritage, particularly from Colonial times to the early 1900s, in The Rocks, the finger wharves at Walsh Bay and Woolloomooloo. The hotels listed on pages 174–9 are among the best in Sydney and cater to a variety of different budgets and requirements.

Where to Look

It is easily possible to find accommodation within most price ranges throughout Sydney, although a sought-after central city location with or without harbour views comes with the heftiest price tag.

Cheaper accommodation can be found in the Kings Cross and Darlinghurst area. Choices here range from backpacker hostels to small boutique and budget chain hotels. Many of the older low-rise buildings may be three storeys but do not have lifts owing to heritage regulations. If mobility is an issue, ask about stairs and ground-floor rooms.

In The Rocks area, you can opt for a bed-and-breakfast in a converted Colonial-era building, a youth hostel with views from the rooftop deck or the opulence of a five-star luxury hotel.

The hotels around Chinatown and Surry Hills offer good value for shoppers and foodies and are also within easy reach of the city centre, while Darling Harbour hotels tend to the grander end of the scale, with Sydney's largest luxury hotel, the Sofitel. The adjoining reinvigorated Pyrmont area is a good choice for accommodation, blending contemporary fit-outs inside heritage buildings.

Quaint Paddington has limited offerings, with one low-rise hotel and a scattering of bed-and-breakfasts.

Just beyond the city fringe, imaginative urban planning has brought contemporary accommodation to the creative hub of Chippendale, while the

Eating alfresco at the Admiral Collingwood Lodge *(see p177)*

vibrant and bohemian inner west suburbs of Newtown, Enmore and Glebe are home to numerous affordable accommodation choices, while still being close to the city.

The popular beachside suburbs of Bondi, Coogee and Manly are a little way out of the centre of Sydney but are accessible by public transport and provide the opportunity to enjoy beach life during the warmer months.

Many pubs provide basic accommodation, usually on the floor above the ground-floor bar areas. Bear in mind it can be noisy at night, especially at weekends and if live music is playing. Check closing times and entertainment before booking if you are a light sleeper.

How to Book

It is advisable to book well in advance, especially for December and January, the Sydney Gay and Lesbian Mardi Gras in February to early March, Easter, the school holidays and when major sporting events are held.

Bookings can be made online, by phone or email, or through a travel agent. A credit card number is generally required to secure your booking. Check cancellation requirements. Many operators charge no cancellation fees as long as minimum notice periods are met, which could be anything from 24 hours to two weeks or more.

The **Sydney Visitor Centre** books certain hotels and has a

The stunning Full Harbour View junior suite at the Four Seasons Hotel Sydney *(see p177)*

◄ Detail of hand-painted didgeridoos

wealth of options on its website. **Australian Accommodation Services** ("Ausacom") arranges bookings for all styles of accommodation. If you belong to a motoring association, ask about discounts through hotels affiliated with the NRMA (National Roads and Motorists' Association). **NSW TrainLink** travel centres at major railway stations offer a comprehensive service, and AFTA travel agencies will book most major hotels. Tourist information centres can also offer valuable advice about where to stay in Sydney.

The opulence and understated elegance of The Langham *(see p179)*

Discount Rates

The best way to secure discount rates is by booking directly on the accommodation providers' website. Virtually all accommodation styles, from hostels to luxury, offer online booking. Most will show their best online flexible rate – a sensible choice if there is a chance you may need to cancel or change the booking. The best rates are usually for those with "no cancellation" clauses attached, so beware if your plans may change. It is always worth asking for the corporate rate at which hotels give discounts for group or company bookings.

At the weekend there are fewer business clients in the city centre, so this is the time when prices are frequently cheaper in the top hotels. Smaller operators

The stunning 1850s sandstone façade of the Radisson Blu Plaza Hotel *(see p178)*

often reduce the daily rate for bookings of five and seven days or longer. Asking for a room without a harbour or ocean view is another good way of reducing the costs. (You may still be able to secure an upgrade at check-in if the hotel isn't full.)

The booking service at the **Sydney Coach Terminal** can often arrange discounts off the price of regular hotel accommodation rates for those who book in person on the day a room is required (this does not normally apply to budget hotels).

Hidden Extras

Breakfast is usually charged on top of the room rate in the more expensive hotels. It is best to avoid consuming any of the contents of the mini-bar as alcohol and snacks are usually much more expensive here than in shops. Some B&Bs only provide breakfast provisions or cooking facilities and charge extra for providing a cooked breakfast. Free Wi-Fi is widely available, although in-room fixed broadband connections may incur extra charges. Also, be wary of telephone charges. There will almost certainly be a considerable mark-up on any calls you make from your room. In general, tipping is not widespread, but it is expected in the more expensive hotels. Make a note of the check-out time when you arrive, or negotiate a late check-out, since a surcharge may be incurred if you stay later.

Special Offers

Hotels promote special deals heavily on their own websites, so check regularly before your trip for any deals. They also often cooperate with airlines, theatres and entertainment and sporting event promoters to provide package deals that include discounted accommodation. Combined special event and accommodation packages can be a good way to snare a ticket to an otherwise sold-out event.

Disabled Travellers

Most new hotels now provide wheelchair access and toilets for the disabled, but many older establishments will have more limited facilities.

Spinal Cord Injuries Australia's website provides information regarding getting around (such as public transport, driving and car hire) and where there are public toilets. Its online publication *RollAwayz* opens in Google Earth to show the location of wheelchair-accessible accommodation across Australia.

Sydney-based **Time Flys Travel** focuses on planning travel, including hotels and specialized transport for the disabled.

Travelling with Children

Many of the larger hotels offer deals that allow children (usually aged up to 12, sometimes 14) to stay for free when

Bet's B&B, a self-contained studio in the suburb of Annandale *(see p175)*

sharing a room with parents, though there may be a charge for extra bedding.

Self-Catering Apartments

Accommodation including full kitchen and laundry facilities offers the traveller greater independence. In addition to comfort, they also provide good value because the living space is larger than standard hotel rooms and the prices are competitive.

All the "apartment" hotels in the listings on pages 174–9 offer self-catering facilities. Many of these rival the big hotels for location and features. Most are professionally managed by developers, with many properties to choose from *(see p173)*.

Homestays

European-style bed-and-breakfast accommodation in a private home can be an ideal way to experience a city. There are limited options close to the city centre, especially Surry Hills, the inner west and beachside suburbs. Most, but not all, bed-and-breakfast-type accommo-dation includes breakfast, so it is wise to check when booking.

People from all walks of life offer rooms in a variety of house styles and locations. Agencies such as **Bed and Breakfast NSW** and the **Homestay Network** make it easy to search for suitable accommodation from centralized listings. **Airbnb** options are plentiful, though it is best to check reviews carefully.

Budget Accommodation

As a favoured destination for many young travellers, Sydney has a large number of hostels that cater specifically to their needs. Standards vary widely, but, at their best, hostels offer excellent value.

It is best to book in advance or call hotels ahead of arriving to make sure a room or bed is available. Kings Cross and the southern end of the city near Central Station have the largest concentration of cheap accommodation.

Summer House and **Original Backpackers** are smaller hostels offering good facilities in restored buildings close to Kings Cross. Original Backpackers also offers inexpensive secure parking.

Blue Parrot Backpackers is situated in a converted mansion in the quieter end of Potts Point, with a sunny garden courtyard and large, cosy common room complete with fireplace.

YHA Australia is a useful source of information when planning your trip, offering advice about travel deals, as well as helping you decide on your itinerary and find places to stay. Two other useful online sources that provide lists of budget hostels in Sydney are **hostels. com** and **hostelworld.com**.

Halls of Residence are another good option for travellers on a budget. Student rooms with shared bathroom facilities are available at the **University of Sydney** over the summer break from late November to mid-February. The university is conveniently close to the city

and to public transport, and the moderate price usually includes breakfast.

Gay and Lesbian Accommodation

Lesbian and gay visitors are welcome in all of Sydney's hotels. In fact, quite a number of places cater primarily to same-sex couples, particularly in small hotels in the inner-city areas of Darlinghurst, Paddington, Newtown and Surry Hills.

At the **IGLTA** (International Gay and Lesbian Travel Association) and the **Gay and Lesbian Tourism Australia** websites, you can search for gay or gay-friendly travel-related businesses, including hotels, guesthouses and tours. **Planet Dwellers** arranges accommodation as well as "gaybourhood" walking tours.

Camping

Although not an option in the city itself (other than on the harbour at Cockatoo Island, *see p108*), camping is available in several national parks close by.

The Royal National Park *(see pp166–7)* has a camp site with facilities at Bonnie Vale, just outside Bundeena. Free bush or "walk-in" camping is allowed in many other places, but call the park in advance to obtain the necessary camping permit. At The Basin camp site in **Ku-ring-gai Chase National Park** *(see pp156–7)*, there are toilets, cold showers, barbecue facilities and a phone. There are basic camp sites near Glenbrook, Woodford, Blackheath and Wentworth Falls in the **Blue Mountains National Park** *(see pp162–3)*. **Jenolan Caravan Park** in Oberon has cabins and caravans for hire, as well as camping pitches with and without electric hook-ups. You will need to book if you want to camp at the Euroka Clearing near Glenbrook, but this is not necessary for the other sites. Bush camping is also permitted in the park, but there are some restrictions. The **NSW National Parks and Wildlife Service** website lists camp-grounds and their facilities.

Recommended Hotels

The accommodation options featured in this guide have been selected for their excellent facilities and unique appeal. They have been divided into a number of categories to help you make the best choices for your trip.

There are a wide range of apartments available to rent for short stays in Sydney. Some are privately owned and others are maintained by bigger companies. All have been furnished to a high standard and offer independent living in the centre of the city.

B&Bs are dotted throughout the city and can range from no-frills digs to luxurious rooms in heritage buildings, though not all include breakfast in their rates.

The cosiness of a roaring fire at The Lord Nelson Brewery Hotel *(see p178)*

Basic hotels, hostels and chain hotels may lack character, but those listed in this guide offer great value for money, with good-quality rooms and excellent service.

Boutique hotels place an emphasis on chic design. They generally offer the same facilities and services as larger hotels, but in a more intimate setting.

There are a number of historic hotels to choose from in Sydney. These are situated in places with a unique history and are often decked out with period features.

Luxury hotels provide five-star facilities, most with stunning views and beautifully decorated rooms.

Outstanding hotels are highlighted as a DK Choice. These hotels offer something really special, be it excellent service, opulent decor, a huge range of amenities, or something entirely unique.

DIRECTORY

Useful Booking Addresses

Australian Accommodation Services
Tel 9974 4884.
w tourist.net

NSW TrainLink
Central Railway Station.
Map 4 E5. Tel 132 829.
w nswtrainlink.info

Sydney Visitor Centre
Cnr Argyle & Playfair Sts,
The Rocks, NSW 2000.
Map 1 A2.
Tel 8273 0000.
w sydney.com

Discount Agencies

Sydney Coach Terminal
Eddy Ave, NSW 2000.
Map 4 E5.
Tel 9281 9366.

Disabled Assistance

Spinal Cord Injuries Australia
1 Jennifer St, Little Bay,
NSW 2036.
Tel 9661 8855 or
1800 819 775.
Postal address:
PO Box 397, Matraville,
NSW 2036.
w scia.org.au

Time Flys Travel
577 Sydney Rd, Seaforth,
NSW 2092.
Tel 9949 5099.
w timeflystravel.
com.au

Self-Catering Apartments

Medina
359 Crown St, Surry Hills,
NSW 2010. Map 5 A3.
Tel 1300 633 462.
w medina
apartments.com.au
Also nine other locations.

Pacific International Hotels
Sydney, Chatswood and
Parramatta.
Tel 1300 987 604.
w pacificinthotels.com

Homestay Agencies

Airbnb
w airbnb.com.au

Bed and Breakfast NSW
Tel 1300 888 862.
w bbfaccommodation.
com.au

Homestay Network
PO Box 270, Beecroft,
NSW 2119.
Tel 9412 3100. w
homestaynetwork.
com.au

Budget Accommodation

Base Backpackers
477 Kent St, NSW 2000.
Tel 9262 7277.
w stayatbase.com

Blue Parrot Backpackers
87 Macleay St, Potts Point,
NSW 2011. Tel 9356 4888.
w blueparrot.com.au

Original Backpackers
160 Victoria St, Kings
Cross, NSW 2011.
Map 5 B1. Tel 9356 3232.
w originalbackpackers.
com.au

Summer House
153 Forbes St,
Woolloomooloo, NSW
2011. Map 5 B1.
Tel 9358 4327.

University of Sydney
International House
Tel 9950 9800.
St John's College.
Tel 9394 5200.
Sancta Sophia.
Tel 9577 2100.
Wesley College.
Tel 9565 3333.
Women's College.
Tel 9517 5000.

YHA Australia
Level 3/9, Castlereagh St,
NSW 2000. Map 1 B4.
Tel 9261 1111.
w yha.com.au

Gay and Lesbian Accommodation

Gay and Lesbian Tourism Australia
w galta.com.au

IGLTA
PO Box 20891, World
Square, NSW. Tel 9575
4869. w iglta.org

Planet Dwellers
Tel 0419 230 670.
w planetdwellers.
com.au

Camping

Blue Mountains National Park
Tel 4787 8877.

Jenolan Caravan Park
Tel 6336 0344.

Ku-ring-gai Chase National Park
Tel 9472 8949.

NSW National Parks and Wildlife Service
w nationalparks.nsw.
gov.au

Royal National Park
Tel 9542 0648.
w royalnationalpark.
com.au/royal-national-
park-camping

Where to Stay

Apartments

The Rocks and Circular Quay

Rendezvous Hotel Sydney $$$
75 Harrington St, The Rocks
Tel *9251 6711*   **Map** 1 B2
Ⓦ tfehotels.com/brands/
rendezvous-hotels/rendezvous-
hotel-sydney-the-rocks
Good-sized apartments with
kitchenettes in an excellent
location. Some rooms come with
harbour views. There is also a
lovely outdoor pool with a café.

The York Apartment $$$
5 York St
Tel *9210 5000*   **Map** 1 A3
Ⓦ theyorkapartments.com.au
Sizable apartments, from studio
to two-bedroom, are well
appointed. Standard studios have
older-style decor, while deluxe
apartments have contemporary
furnishings. It can be noisy on
the lower floors.

City Centre

Fraser Suites Sydney $$
488 Kent St
Tel *8823 8888*   **Map** 4 E3
Ⓦ sydney.frasershospitality.com/en
These serviced apartments come
with all mod cons in an edgy
42-storey tower with a striking
glass façade designed by architect
Sir Norman Foster, complete with
indoor pool, sauna and gym.

Meriton Pitt Street $$
329 Pitt St
Tel *9277 1111*   **Map** 4 E3
Ⓦ meritonapartments.com.au/
sydney/pitt-street
Immaculate and well-managed
modern apartments in the heart
of the city. There is an on-site
pool, spa, sauna and gym. A large
supermarket is just a block away.

Darling Harbour and Surry Hills

**Adina Apartment Hotel
Crown Street** $$
359 Crown St, Surry Hills
Tel *8302 1000*   **Map** 5 A3
Ⓦ adinahotels.com
Functional and clean, the
accommodation here is
comfortable, if lacking a little in
natural light. There is a lovely
palm-fringed pool and room
service from the wonderful Bill's
restaurant next door.

**Meriton Serviced Apartments
Campbell Street** $$
6 Campbell St
Tel *8318 8888*   **Map** 4 F4
Ⓦ meritonapartments.com.au/
sydney/campbell-street
Spacious and modern apartments
have free Wi-Fi, a washer/dryer, an
indoor pool and friendly staff.

DK Choice

**Adge Boutique Apartment
Hotel** $$$
222 Riley St, Surry Hills
Tel *8093 9888*   **Map** 4 F4
Ⓦ adgehotel.com.au
With a daring design and
colourful, bold styling, including
pink fridges and gaudy striped
carpets, these two-bedroom
urban apartments sit in the
heart of the inner city's best
café and dining area. Quality
amenities and extras include a
complimentary welcome drink.

Meriton World Tower $$$
95 Liverpool St
Tel *8263 7500*   **Map** 4 E3
Ⓦ meritonapartments.com.au/
sydney/world-tower-sydney
Outstanding modern apartments
in Sydney's tallest residential
tower. Floor-to-ceiling windows
offer stunning views.

**Zara Tower Serviced
Apartments** $$$
61–65 Wentworth Ave
Tel *8228 7659*   **Map** 4 F4
Ⓦ zaratower.com.au
Spacious apartments on the city
fringe, with gourmet kitchen
appliances and a choice of pillows.
Although this is a convenient
location, it is not especially pretty.

The entrance to Meriton Serviced
Apartments Campbell Street

Price Guide
Prices are based on one night's stay in
high season for a standard double room,
inclusive of service charges and taxes.

$	up to A$150
$$	A$150 to A$350
$$$	over A$350

Kings Cross and Darlinghurst

Regent's Court Apartments $$
18 Springfield Ave, Potts Point
Tel *9331 2099*   **Map** 2 E5
Ⓦ regentscourtsydney.com.au
A character Art Deco building with
warmth and charm in a pretty,
tree-lined street. There are 25 self-
contained studios, all with access
to a gorgeous rooftop garden.

**Woolloomooloo Waters
Apartment Hotel** $$
88 Dowling St, Woolloomooloo
Tel *8837 8000*   **Map** 2 E5
Ⓦ woolloomooloo-waldorf-
apartments.com.au
Not on the waterfront despite
the name, this aparthotel is a
block back from the bay and offers
basic, no-frills apartments with a
good, light breakfast included.
There is a small indoor pool.

Further Afield

**Adina Apartment Hotel
Bondi Beach** $$
69–73 Hall St, Bondi
Tel *9300 4800*
Ⓦ tfehotels.com/brands/adina-
apartment-hotels/adina-apartment-
hotel-bondi-beach
These small, modern but pricey
apartments with a beachhouse
feel are in the hip Hall St strip
that runs down to the beach.

Meriton Bondi Junction $$
97 Grafton St, Bondi Junction
Tel *8305 7600*
Ⓦ meritonapartments.com.au/
sydney/bondi-junction
Halfway between the city and
Bondi Beach, and surrounded by
shopping choices, from luxury
boutiques to street markets. Suites
are clean, spacious, and well-
equipped, with great views.

QT Bondi Beach $$
180 Campbell Parade, Bondi Beach
Tel *1800 991 928*
Ⓦ pacificbondibeach.com.au
Opposite Australia's most iconic
stretch of sand, this place boasts
chic beachside glamour. There is
an eclectic art-filled entrance area
and white-walled designer fit-outs
in the studios and apartments.

B&Bs

The Rocks and Circular Quay

Sydney Harbour B&B $$
140–142 Cumberland St, The Rocks
Tel *9247 1130*   **Map** 1 B2
🅦 bbsydneyharbour.com.au
A restored historic mansion with a communal lounge, garden and nine comfortable rooms, some with views of the Opera House. The handcrafted, pretty Colonial-style furniture is in keeping with the location.

Darling Harbour and Surry Hills

Brickfield Hill $$
403 Riley St, Surry Hills
Tel *9211 4886*   **Map** 4 F5
🅦 brickfieldhill.com.au
Four rooms (only one with a private bathroom) in a vibrant neighbourhood. Breakfast incurs an extra cost. Some of Sydney's best cafés can be found nearby.

Kings Cross and Darlinghurst

Simpsons of Potts Point $$
8 Challis Ave, Potts Point
Tel *9356 2199*   **Map** 2 E4
🅦 simpsonshotel.com
A peaceful and elegant Victorian mansion with an old-world charm. Relax in the character-filled drawing room with a fireplace and books over a glass of sherry or port. Breakfast is served in the charming conservatory.

Paddington

Five Ways B&B of Paddington $$
34 Goodhope St, Paddington
Tel *9360 4084*   **Map** 6 D2
🅦 babs.com.au/fiveways
Plenty of returning customers enjoy the quiet and airy first-floor room, the well-equipped private bathroom, and the small balcony overlooking a charming street. Located near cafés, galleries, shopping and transport.

Hart's Home Stay $$
91 Stewart St, Paddington
Tel *9380 5516*   **Map** 6 D4
🅦 bbbook.com.au
In a 19th-century, Gothic-style cottage with a central courtyard in a quiet residential street, Hart's Home Stay is just a short stroll away from the cafés and shops of Oxford Street.

Bright, colourful interiors at Adge Boutique Apartment Hotel

Further Afield

Dadirri Studio Apartment $
68 Lennox, Newtown
Tel *0430 883 067*
🅦 dadirri.com.au
A basic but clean first-floor option opposite a lovely historic park. No breakfast, but there is a kitchenette for making your own.

101 Addison Rd B&B $$
101 Addison Rd, Manly
Tel *9977 6216*
🅦 bb-manly.com
Character-filled property in a quiet street close to the beach. Warm host, Jill, shares local knowledge and serves a great breakfast in your private living room.

Australia Street Cottage $$
227 Australia St, Newtown
🅦 australiastreetcottage.com
A large sandstone house with an open plan and contemporary fit-out. No breakfast, but there is a full kitchen, and it's just a short walk to King St cafés.

Bundeena Beach B&B $$
75 Bundeena Drive, Bundeena
Tel *9527 9977*
🅦 beachbedandbreakfast.com.au
Step off the front lawn and on to the beach at this self-contained luxury accommodation with

breakfast. Explore the nearby Royal National Park, or relax in the double spa bath and open shower.

Cecil Street B&B $$
18 Cecil St, Manly
Tel *9977 8036*
🅦 cecilstreetbb.com.au
Two spacious and airy bedrooms with a shared bathroom, located in a quiet area. Breakfast is served in the cosy sitting room.

Forsyth B&B $$
3 Forsyth St, Glebe
Tel *9552 2110*   **Map** 3 A3
🅦 forsythbnb.com
Outstanding hospitality and breakfast, just a minute's walk from Blackwattle Bay. The hosts do airport pick-up and drop-off for a very reasonable charge.

Manly Beach View Bed & Breakfast $$
37 Kangaroo St, Manly
Tel *9977 7520*
🅦 manlybeachviewbedand breakfast.com.au
Enjoy views over Manly from your private balcony on Kangaroo Hill, a few blocks back from the beach. Warm hospitality makes this a home away from home.

Newtown Darlington Suites $$
30 Golden Grove St, cnr Abercrombie St, Darlington
Tel *8003 7333*
🅦 bedbreakfastsydney.com.au
Two large, self-contained apart-ments with a full kitchen between the city fringe and vibrant Newtown. Art installations feature in the old shopfront window.

Tara Guesthouse $$
13 Edgeware Rd, Enmore
Tel *9519 4809*
🅦 taraguesthouse.com.au
This is a gracious place to stay in a busy area that is full of bohemian character. Free airport transfers.

For more information on types of hotels *see pages 172–3*

Basic Hotels

The Rocks and Circular Quay

The Mercantile Hotel $$
25 George St, The Rocks
Tel 9247 3570   **Map** 1 B2
W themercantilehotel.com.au
Spacious rooms (some with Jacuzzi baths), with period fittings and marble fireplaces. A continental breakfast is included. Basic-rate rooms share a bathroom.

City Centre

Song Hotel Hyde Park $$
5–11 Wentworth Ave
Tel 9264 2451   **Map** 4 F3
W yhotels.com.au/y-hotel-hyde-park
Excellent-value accommodation in a prime spot in the city, with basic continental breakfast and clean, functional rooms. Opt for a courtyard-facing room, as street-facing rooms can be noisy.

Travelodge Wynyard $$
7–9 York St
Tel 9274 1222   **Map** 1 A4
W tfehotels.com/brands/travelodge-hotels
No fancy extras, just good, clean rooms and a central location that is ideal for exploring the city. Rooms near the old lifts tend to be noisiest.

Darling Harbour and Surry Hills

The Ultimo $$
37 Ultimo Rd, Haymarket
Tel 9281 5555   **Map** 4 D4
W aaronssydney.com.au
No bells and whistles here – just good-value, well-kept digs in an ideal location for exploring the southern end of the city. It is also very close to transport links for exploring the rest.

DK Choice

Vibe Sydney $$
111 Goulburn St
Tel 8272 3300   **Map** 4 E4
W tfehotels.com/brands/vibe-hotels
Neat and clean, simple yet comfortable, this hotel has almost 200 rooms and is located in the heart of the city. It is within easy walking distance of most major attractions. Facilities include a bar and café, and there are also a small but attractive pool on the roof.

Kings Cross and Darlinghurst

The Bayswater $
17 Bayswater Rd, Kings Cross
Tel 8070 0100   **Map** 5 B1
W sydneylodges.com/lodges/the-bayswater-sydney/
Great-value rooms in a convenient spot for transport, shops and restaurants. There's a nice guest lounge area with kitchenette.

Hotel 59 $
59 Bayswater Rd, Rushcutters Bay
Tel 9360 5900   **Map** 5 C1
W hotel59.com.au
Great-value, family-run place with just nine rooms. Complimentary breakfast is served in the property's street-front café.

Mariners Court $$
44–50 McElhone St, Woolloomooloo
Tel 9320 3800   **Map** 2 E5
W marinerscourt.com.au
Clean, comfortable rooms in a great location. The place is reasonably quiet for a busy area, and there are plenty of good dining choices nearby.

O'Malley's Hotel $
228 William St, Kings Cross
Tel 9357 2211   **Map** 5 B1
W omalleyshotel.com.au
This conveniently located, characterful hotel has 15 ensuite rooms. It is situated above a pub on a busy corner, so expect noise.

Paddington

Arts Hotel $$
21 Oxford St, Paddington
Tel 9361 0211   **Map** 5 B3
W artshotel.com.au
Friendly, family-run hotel with small basic rooms. Quieter garden rooms face a central courtyard with a small pool. Bicycles are available for free hire.

Further Afield

Alishan Guesthouse $
100 Glebe Point Rd, Glebe
Tel 9566 4048   **Map** 3 A5
W alishan.com.au
Functional, no-frills accommodation with a communal kitchen for preparing meals. Convenient location on Glebe's main street.

The Merton Hotel $$
38 Victoria Rd, Rozelle
Tel 8065 9577
W themertonhotel.com.au
A pub on a main road with clean rooms and breakfast included. It also has a good bistro and offers live music in the evenings. Some rooms can be a little noisy.

Central courtyard and pool at the friendly, family-run Arts Hotel

Boutique Hotels

The Rocks and Circular Quay

Harbour Rocks Hotel $$$
34 Harrington St, The Rocks
Tel 8220 9999   **Map** 1 B2
W harbourrocks.com.au
This hotel offers very small, basic rooms in a heritage building located in a desirable central location. The staff are friendly.

City Centre

Park8 $$
185 Castlereagh St
Tel 9283 2488   **Map** 1 B5
W park8.com.au
Rooms tend to be small, stylish and somewhat dark. There is a 24-hour, guests-only espresso bar.

DK Choice

QT Sydney $$$
49 Market St
Tel 8262 0000   **Map** 1 B5
W qtsydney.com.au
Kooky, cutting edge and a little over the top, this designer hotel, set within the Art Deco historical State Theatre and Gowings building, is one of a kind. It has an in-house "design and art curator", and customer-service staff wear red wigs.

Darling Harbour and Surry Hills

Ovolo 1888 Darling Harbour $$$
139 Murray St, Pyrmont
Tel 8586 1888   **Map** 3 C2
W ovolohotels.com.au
This is a vibrant, stylish converted wool store that has been meticulously restored with recycled wooden beams.

Pensione Hotel $$$
631–635 George St
Tel *9265 8888* **Map** 4 E4
W pensione.com.au
Convenient hotel in a busy area.
The corridors are a bit of a maze,
but the rooms are modern and
generally well maintained.

Botanic Garden and The Domain

Sir Stamford at Circular Quay $$$
93 Macquarie St
Tel *9252 4600* **Map** 1 C3
W stamford.com.au/sscq
This historic hotel has character
and charm and offers gracious,
old-fashioned service and good
modern amenities.

Kings Cross and Darlinghurst

Larmont Sydney $$
2–14 Kings Cross Rd, Kings Cross
Tel *9295 8888* **Map** 5 B1
W lancemore.com.au/larmont
Modern, stylish rooms close to
lots of eateries and transport.
Lovely staff, and there is free
Wi-Fi and iPads for guests' use.

Medusa $$
267 Darlinghurst Rd, Darlinghurst
Tel *9331 1000* **Map** 5 B1
W medusa.com.au
A labyrinth of 18 rooms, styled to
maximize comfort and privacy.
There is also a pretty courtyard
with a reflection pool.

Old Clare Hotel $$$
1 Kensington St, Chippendale
Tel *8277 8277* **Map** 4 D5
W theoldclarehotel.com.au
Retaining the best features of the
pub and brewery that once
occupied this site, this aesthetic
gem has a lobby bar, a rooftop
pool and bar and four restaurants.

Further Afield

Admiral Collingwood Lodge $$
5 Collingwood St, Drummoyne
Tel *9181 3881*
W admiralcollingwoodlodge.com.au
A lovely 1880s Italianate mansion
with well-kept rooms near waterfront parklands. There are regular
buses and ferries to the city.

Hotel Ravesi's $$$
118 Campbell Parade, Bondi
Tel *9365 4422*
W hotelravesis.com.au
Stay in beachside glamour in one
of 12 chic, individually styled
rooms. The iconic beach is
right across the road.

Chain Hotels

The Rocks and Circular Quay

Four Seasons Hotel Sydney $$$
199 George St
Tel *9250 3100* **Map** 1 B3
W fourseasons.com/sydney/
Harbour views, a handy location
and top-notch facilities for
business and leisure travellers.
The service is excellent.

Holiday Inn Old Sydney $$$
55 George St, The Rocks
Tel *9252 0524* **Map** 1 B2
W ihg.com/holidayinn/hotels/
us/en/sydney/sydgs/hoteldetail
Step back to Colonial Sydney.
Old-world charm is comple-
mented by modern facilities.

City Centre

Hilton Sydney $$$
488 George St
Tel *9266 2000* **Map** 1 B5
W hiltonsydney.com.au
There are no waterfront views
here, but it is right in the pulsing
city centre. Pop into the historic
Marble Bar downstairs.

Swissotel Sydney $$$
68 Market St
Tel *9238 8888* **Map** 4 E2
W swissotel.com/hotels/sydney
Comfortable rooms with contem-
porary styling. The colourful kids'
rooms – stocked with toys and
facilities – are great for families.

Darling Harbour and Surry Hills

Travelodge Wentworth Ave $$
27–33 Wentworth Ave
Tel *8267 1700* **Map** 4 F4
W tfehotels.com/brands/
travelodge-hotels
Rooms are basic and simple.
Surprisingly quiet despite its size
and central location, this is a
handy base from which to explore.

Novotel Sydney on Darling Harbour $$$
100 Murray St, Pyrmont
Tel *9934 0000* **Map** 3 C2
W novoteldarlingharbour.com.au
Opt for a room with a view of
Darling Harbour. Rooms are
spacious and there is an outdoor
pool, gym, tennis court,
restaurant, bar and café.

Rydges World Square $$$
389 Pitt St
Tel *8268 1888* **Map** 4 E3
W rydges.com
Good hospitality and service
complement a terrific central
location, and neat and tidy
rooms. The furnishings may be
are a little uninspiring but the
beds are very comfortable.

Kings Cross and Darlinghurst

Ibis Budget Sydney East $
191–201 William Street,
Kings Cross
Tel *9326 0300* **Map** 5 B1
W accorhotels.com.au
Living up to low-cost expectations,
rooms are very basic. Street-
facing rooms can be noisy due to
traffic and nightlife. Cheerful staff.

Further Afield

Novotel Manly Pacific $$
55 N Styne, Manly
Tel *9977 7666*
W novotelmanlypacific.com.au
This hotel opposite the beach
has plenty of on-site dining and
entertainment options, as
well as a lovely rooftop pool.

Quest Bondi Junction $$
28 Spring St, Bondi Junction
Tel *9078 1700*
W questapartments.com.au
Three train stops from the city, a
short bus ride to the beach and
shopping of every kind at your
doorstep. Quest Bondi Junction
offers pleasant, modern well-
appointed rooms and facilities.

Bright and spacious room at the Admiral Collingwood Lodge

For more information on types of hotels *see pages 172–3*

Historic Hotels

The Rocks and Circular Quay

The Lord Nelson Brewery Hotel   **$$**
19 Kent St, The Rocks
Tel *9251 4044*   **Map** 1 A2
W lordnelsonbrewery.com
Brimming with history and personality, the top floor of this celebrated pub brewery, Australia's oldest pub brewery, offers cosy rooms with stone walls and rustic decor.

Pier One Sydney Harbour   **$$**
11 Hickson Rd, Walsh Bay
Tel *8298 9999*   **Map** 1 A2
W pieronesydneyharbour.com.au
The 1912 Pier One wharf played a role in Sydney's early shipping and cargo history. This beautiful hotel has revived and preserved this historic landmark.

The Russell Hotel   **$$**
143a George St, The Rocks
Tel *9241 3543*   **Map** 1 B2
W therussell.com.au
The site of the colony's "movable hospital" in 1790, this charming hotel sits above the historic Fortune of War pub. It has a quaint sitting room, a well-stocked library, a rooftop garden and lovely staff.

City Centre

The Grace   **$$$**
77 York St
Tel *9272 6888*   **Map** 1 A4
W gracehotel.com.au
Built by Grace Bros in the 1920s as a showpiece department store, this place is a fine example of Neo-Gothic architecture with a contrasting Art Deco interior.

Radisson Blu Plaza Hotel   **$$$**
27 O'Connell St
Tel *8214 0000*   **Map** 1 B4
W radissonblu.com/en/plaza hotel-sydney
With its stunning 1850s sandstone façade, this was once home to John Fairfax & Sons' newspaper empire and the Bank of NSW. Today, you'll find exceptional comfort and service.

Paddington

The Hughenden   **$$**
14 Queen St, Woollahra
Tel *9363 4863*   **Map** 6 E4
W thehughenden.com.au
A restored grand mansion with a colourful history, The Hughenden has formerly been a masonic hall, a nurses' home and a dance hall.

Further Afield

DK Choice

Cockatoo Island   **$$**
Cockatoo Island
Tel *8969 2111*
W cockatooisland.gov.au
Why stay by the harbour when you can stay on it? This is the only harbour island where you can stay overnight, just a short ferry ride from the city. Embrace your sense of adventure and explore its convict and shipbuilding history, then relax on the balcony or deck of a self-contained apartment.

Q-Station   **$$**
North Head Scenic Drive, Manly
Tel *9466 1500*
W qstation.com.au
Stay in Sydney Harbour National Park and take history or ghost tours of the 1830s North Head Quarantine Station (*see p135*).

Beyond Sydney

The Carrington   **$$**
15–47 Katoomba St, Katoomba
Tel *4782 1111*
W thecarrington.com.au
This 1883 grand old lady was a magnet for Sydney's elite, and the southern hemisphere's most popular retreat in the early 1900s. Bags of old-world charm.

The Hydro Majestic   **$$$**
Great Western Highway, Medlow Bath
Tel *4782 6885*
W hydromajestic.com.au
Stretching 1.1 km (0.7 miles) along the escarpment overlooking the Megalong Valley, this magnificent property's Art Deco-styled 54 guest rooms reflect its rich heritage and the glitz and glamour of yesteryear.

Modern fittings and a stunning view at Pier One Sydney Harbour

Hostels

The Rocks and Circular Quay

DK Choice

Sydney Harbour YHA   **$$**
110 Cumberland St, The Rocks
Tel *8272 0900*   **Map** 1 B2
W yha.com.au
Private rooms with harbour views here cost slightly more than standard hostels, but are worth it. There are double, family and dormitory rooms, and it's just a short walk to major attractions and transport. The relaxing, large rooftop deck offers incredible views of the Opera House.

Darling Harbour and Surry Hills

Big Hostel   **$**
212 Elizabeth St
Tel *9281 6030*   **Map** 4 E4
W bighostel.com
This place attracts less of the party crowd than other hostels. There is a complimentary basic breakfast – toast, cereal, coffee, tea. Common areas have Wi-Fi.

Railway Square YHA   **$**
8 Lee St
Tel *2981 9666*   **Map** 4 D5
W yha.com.au
Next to Central Station, this hostel has private rooms in the historic 1904 main building and shared rooms in a funky railway carriage.

Wake Up!   **$**
509 Pitt St
Tel *9288 7888*   **Map** 4 E5
W wakeup.com.au
Fun, modern backpacker accommodation in a convenient location with shared and private rooms. Activities include barbecues, pool competitions and guided city orientation tours. Good on-site café and bar.

Kings Cross and Darlinghurst

Eva's Backpackers   **$**
6 Orwell St, Potts Point
Tel *9358 2185*   **Map** 2 E5
W evasbackpackers.com.au
Small, clean rooms and friendly staff. Facilities include a large kitchen, a common room with a fireplace and hot chocolate, and a rooftop terrace for barbecues.

Luxury Hotels

The Rocks and Circular Quay

The Langham $$$
89–113 Kent St, Millers Point
Tel *9256 2222*   **Map** 1 A2
Ⓦ sydney.langhamhotels.com.au
This is a charming, bright, impossibly pretty hotel that strikes a wonderful balance between opulence and understated elegance. It also has a magnificent indoor pool, with a sky-dappled star ceiling.

Guests sunning themselves on the terrace at Big Hostel

DK Choice

Park Hyatt $$$
7 Hickson Rd, The Rocks
Tel *9256 1234*   **Map** 1 B1
Ⓦ sydney.park.hyatt.com
In the the best harbourfront location, with views straight across the water to the Opera House, this intimate, low-rise hotel has been outfitted with impeccable attention to detail. The 155 spacious contemporary guest rooms and suites have floor-to-ceiling glass doors that open to private balconies. The rooftop pool area is lovely, too.

Pullman Quay Grand Sydney Harbour $$$
61 Macquarie St
Tel *9256 4000*   **Map** 1 C3
Ⓦ pullmanquaygrandsydney harbour.com
Get a room with a spectacular view at this spacious, upscale, all-suite property on the edge of Circular Quay, with the Opera House as your next-door neighbour.

Quay West Suites $$$
98 Gloucester St, The Rocks
Tel *9240 6000*   **Map** 1 A3
Ⓦ quaywestsuitessydney.com.au
Enjoy a swim with a view of the Harbour Bridge in the stunning, sunken, Roman-style heated pool on level 24 of this truly opulent apartment hotel.

City Centre

Establishment Hotel $$$
5 Bridge Lane
Tel *9240 3100*   **Map** 1 B3
Ⓦ merivale.com.au/accommodation/ establishmenthotel/
The effortlessly cool Establishment is tucked away in a hidden lane. It has beautifully appointed rooms, access to a private gym, and a handful of Sydney's best restaurants, bars and clubs all under one roof.

Sheraton on the Park $$$
161 Elizabeth St
Tel *9286 6000*   **Map** 1 B5
Ⓦ sheratonontheparksydney.com
Grand columns and a sweeping staircase welcome guests to this hotel, which is set in an idyllic spot opposite Hyde Park. There is also a lovely indoor rooftop pool.

Westin $$$
1 Martin Place
Tel *9223 1111*   **Map** 4 E1
Ⓦ westinsydney.com
Soaring above the historic GPO building at 1 Martin Place, this property mixes old-fashioned service with modern comforts.

Darling Harbour and Surry Hills

The Darling $$$
80 Pyrmont St, Pyrmont
Tel *9777 9000*   **Map** 3 B1
Ⓦ thedarling.com.au
Rooms with floor-to-ceiling windows give stunning views of Sydney from this opulent property, part of The Star complex. It has a luxury spa and outdoor pool.

Botanic Garden and The Domain

Hotel InterContinental $$$
117 Macquarie St
Tel *9253 9000*   **Map** 1 C3
Ⓦ sydney.intercontinental.com
A real meeting of style and history, from the grand sandstone exterior beauty of the restored former 1851 Treasury Building, to the rooftop view from Club Continental.

Ovolo Woolloomooloo $$$
6 Cowper Wharf Roadway, Woolloomooloo
Tel *9331 9000*   **Map** 2 D4
Ⓦ ovolohotels.com
This relaxed, waterfront hotel is in a restored, century-old wool warehouse on a historic wharf. The superb on-site restaurant-bar, Lo Lounge, is open all day.

Further Afield

InterContinental Sydney Double Bay $$$
33 Cross St, Double Bay
Tel *8388 8388*
Ⓦ ihg.com/intercontinental/hotels/ gb/en/sydney/sydic/hoteldetail
This is an exclusive sanctuary, the lavish jewel in the crown of picturesque Double Bay village. The whole place is pure luxury – from the Italian marble floors in the foyer, to the swanky rooftop pool bar.

Jonah's $$$
69 Bynya Rd, Palm Beach
Tel *9974 5599*
Ⓦ jonahs.com.au
A sumptuous and discreet ocean retreat on Sydney's northern beaches, just a 50-minute drive from the city or scenic 20-minute flight by seaplane.

Beyond Sydney

Lilianfels $$$
5–19 Lilianfels Ave, Katoomba
Tel *4780 1200*
Ⓦ lilianfels.com.au
A short walk from the iconic Three Sisters at Echo Point in the Blue Mountains, this graceful and elegant resort is a throwback to yesteryear.

One & Only Wolgan Valley Resort & Spa $$$
2600 Wolgan Rd, Wolgan Valley
Tel *9308 0550*
Ⓦ wolganvalley.com
Luxury and seclusion abound at this exclusive, conservation-based retreat with stunning views of the valley and the rugged sandstone escarpments in the Greater Blue Mountains.

For more information on types of hotels *see pages 172–3*

WHERE TO EAT AND DRINK

Sydney is home to a diverse dining scene, the result of multiple cultural and culinary influences. Australia's largest city has been populated by successive waves of migrants who have added to the communal table. These influences have inspired contemporary adaptations of a variety of international cuisines, often called "Modern Australian", drawing on flavours from around the world.

A Japanese take on traditional French cooking using native Australian produce would not be out of place on a Sydney menu.

A detailed guide to the best restaurants in the city can be found on pages 186–97. These cover a variety of different types of restaurant across all price brackets, ranging from some of the world's best fine-dining establishments to inexpensive casual cafés.

Where to Eat

The city centre, Darlinghurst, Potts Point, Surry Hills and Paddington are the areas where you will find the best and widest choice of places to eat. Many restaurants at Darling Harbour, Cockle Bay, Barangaroo and King Street Wharf also have outside tables, so diners can enjoy the atmosphere of the lights, the water and the boats. At Barangaroo, Wulugul Walk boasts an array of eateries, from cafés and food-hall providers to restaurants and bars.

Just outside the city centre, and not covered in depth in these listings, are the inner-city "eat streets" of Glebe Point Road, Glebe *(see p133)*, and King Street, Newtown and Enmore, as well as relatively new dining destinations, Pyrmont and the up-and-coming creative hub around Kensington Street, Chippendale.

On the lower North Shore, you will find the food hub of Willoughby Road, Crows Nest, while the beach suburbs of Bondi, Coogee and Manly are awash with dining choices.

Keep an eye out for the growing number of gourmet food trucks and pop-up restaurants, often offshoots of well-known restaurants, which temporarily appear in popular locations (www.sydneyfoodtrucks.com.au).

How Much to Pay

The sheer number of dining options in Sydney means there are a variety of great options at a range of prices. While a fine-dining experience at an award-winning restaurant can cost more than A$200, many delicious meals can be had for a fraction of the cost in less grand settings. The cost can be reduced further if you choose a BYO (bring your own) restaurant, where you can avoid paying the heavily marked-up price of restaurant wine by taking your own wine, and sometimes beer. However, there will usually be a corkage cost per drinker or per bottle. Check that a restaurant is BYO before you arrive.

Opening Times

Sydney does not have a late-night dining culture. Most restaurants serve lunch from noon to 3pm and dinner from 6pm to about 10:30pm, though last orders are often at 10pm. Outside the city centre, restaurants may close one day a week, usually Monday. Many restaurants close on public holidays *(see p53)*, and those that open usually add a 10 per cent surcharge to the bill.

Reservations

Booking is recommended for most restaurants. However, if you want to secure a table in a top-end or very popular restaurant, it is advisable to make a reservation at least one week, or even up to one month, in advance. Many restaurants offer online bookings via their websites. Some restaurants require credit card details to secure a booking, particularly for groups of four or more, which may incur a charge in the event of a "no show". Many casual brasseries and bistros are open throughout the day and do not take bookings. You may have to wait for a table at busy times, particularly weekend breakfast and brunch.

Licensing and Smoking Laws

When a restaurant is described as licensed, this usually refers to its licence to sell alcohol. BYO restaurants are not licensed to sell liquor, and you will need to buy it beforehand if you want to drink alcohol with your meal.

Paddington's reputed Four in Hand by Guillaume pub, which offers great food *(see p194)*

Non-smoking legislation is in place for indoor dining areas of all restaurants, pubs and clubs. However, venues can provide a separate, designated outdoor area for smokers.

How to Pay

Most restaurants accept a range of credit cards as well as debit cards linked to an international card network (such as Cirrus or Maestro). Only the smallest restaurants and some cafés are cash-only. Others require a minimum spend (usually A$10) for credit or debit cards.

Authentic Indian food at Maya, in Surry Hills *(see p196)*

Tax and Tipping

A 10 per cent goods and services tax (GST) is inclusive in prices. While tipping is not compulsory, most customers leave 10 to 15 per cent of the total bill as a reward for good service in restaurants. Cafés often have a tip jar at the counter.

Dress Codes

Dress standards in Sydney restaurants are quite relaxed, even in the upmarket establishments.
   Smart-casual dress is the safest option. Jackets and ties are uncommon unless the wearer has come straight from the office or is conducting a business meeting over a meal.

Eating with Children

Children are welcome in restaurants, although fine-dining establishments do not generally offer separate children's menus. Affordable and convenient options for families include any of the numerous cafés, Chinese, Thai or noodle bar restaurants, or the cheap pasta eateries like Bill and Toni's *(see p192)* in East Sydney, where children are always welcome. Harry's Café de Wheels *(see p193)* next to the Finger Wharf is a cheerful roadside pie cart. Many restaurants offer good-value children's menus, usually featuring burgers, fish and chips, and pasta, a drink and ice cream.
   Many shopping centres have inexpensive food halls, including The Galeries on George St *(see pp198–9)* or Market City food court in Haymarket, Darling Harbour. They offer a variety of casual eating places featuring a range of cuisines in one complex, with a central seating area. Casual pub bistros offer menus with plenty of choices for children and also serve alcohol for the adults.

Vegetarians

Almost all restaurants and cafés in Sydney have several vegetarian options on the menu. There are also a number of specialist vegetarian and vegetarian-only restaurants, including the highly regarded Yellow *(see p194)* and Govinda's *(see p193)*. You will find vegan cafés, especially in the Glebe and Newtown areas, as well as in the city centre, such as Bodhi in the Park *(see p187)*, while many eateries also list gluten-free options.

Wheelchair Access

Most restaurants in Sydney provide wheelchair access and toilet facilities for the disabled. However, it is always best to check the facilities available in advance.

Recommended Restaurants

The restaurants listed in this guide are among the best in Sydney. They have been selected for their reliably good food, location, service, value or a combination of these. The listings cover a variety of cuisines and eateries, from pubs, bistros and cafés to top, award-winning restaurants.
   Establishments labelled DK Choice have been selected because they are outstanding in some way. They may offer superb cuisine, a stunning setting, great value or a combination of these.

Decorative saucers on the walls at Lucio's Italian restaurant, in Paddington *(see p195)*

The Flavours of Sydney

Sydney is a paradise for food-obsessed visitors, with its countless bars, restaurants and cafés. The cutting-edge food scene is often categorized with New York, London and Paris. Successive waves of immigration from different parts of the world have established a multicultural culinary experience, and local chefs blend diverse influences to create new takes on traditional cuisines. Many of the world's top chefs have set up shop here, bringing their versions of internationally renowned dishes to the city, while using locally sourced ingredients. Numerous food festivals and markets are held throughout the year.

Wattleseed, pepperberry and lemon myrtle

Fresh seafood dishes at one of the city's many upmarket restaurants

Native Ingredients

There are many native foods in Australia that have been used by Aborigines for thousands of years, and which are now becoming popular as ingredients in mainstream cooking. Fruits and vegetables with distinctive colours, flavours and textures include quandong, munthari, bush tomato, wild limes, warrigal greens and rosellas. All of them

are still wild-harvested by Aboriginal communities, as well as commercially grown to meet increased demand. Native herbs and spices, such as lemon myrtle, wattleseed, mountain pepperleaf, pepperberry, forest berry and akudjura are used as seasoning. Native meats such as kangaroo and emu are also being used more frequently, for instance as pizza toppings, although don't expect to see witchity grubs on many

menus. Restaurants still favour the vast and impressive array of beef, lamb and, of course, seafood that has sustained Australian diners for decades. Fish native to Australia include barramundi, trevalla and blue eye trevalla. The popular native shellfish, yabbies and moreton bay bugs are similar to, but smaller than, lobster. Delicious honeys with distinct fragrances are produced out of native Australian forests.

Samphire Snapper Lobster Red mullet Oyster
Scallop

Selection of seafood available in Sydney's restaurants and food shops

Local Dishes and Specialities

There's nowhere better in the world to enjoy fish and chips than sitting on a Sydney beach. As well as the standard choice of hake fillets, you may find other popular local fish on offer, such as shark, barramundi, John Dory or flathead.

Sausage rolls (pork mince wrapped in pastry) and meat pies, especially popular at football games and carnivals, are ubiquitous; most bakeries sell a variety of fillings. Anzac biscuits made with crunchy rolled oats were sent to soldiers during World War I and remain a favourite snack even today. Vegemite, the iconic, salty yeast-based spread, is best enjoyed on toast or bread.

For those keen on cooking, steaks and sausages of fresh kangaroo, and to a lesser extent crocodile, can be found in large supermarkets.

Anzac biscuits

Kangaroo pizza This Italian classic is given a modern Australian spin with the addition of seared lean fillet.

Diners enjoying an outdoor meal on the harbour at Circular Quay

The World on a Plate

With a climate that favours a wide range of fruit, vegetables, grains, livestock and seafood, great flavours and fresh, seasonal produce are a given in Sydney. A large part of the food supply is grown in market gardens within two hours of the city centre, before finding its way to restaurants, supermarkets, and, increasingly, growers markets dotted throughout the city.

Farming plays a major role in Australia, the world's largest producer of beef. The lush pastures on the coast are particularly good for farming, and milk-fed lamb from New South Wales is wonderful. King Island, off the coast of Victoria, is dedicated to dairy produce, selling amazing cheeses and creams. Other well-established industries include wine, olive oil and balsamic vinegar production.

Australia has one of the most diverse marine faunas in the world, due to its range of habitats, from the warm tropical northern waters to the sub-Antarctic Tasman sea. A total of 600 marine and freshwater species are caught in Australian

Fresh fruit on sale at Paddy's Markets in Chinatown

waters, providing chefs with plenty of inspiration (see p202). Restaurants and sellers often specify the origin of their produce, in keeping with the emphasis on freshly caught, sustainable seafood.

Every kind of fruit and vegetable is grown in Australia. Pineapples and mangoes are widely grown in Queensland, apples in Victoria, strawberries in New South Wales, rambutans in the Northern Territory and the native macadamia nut in the warmer regions. Exotic and notoriously hard to farm, truffles are cultivated in several areas, including Tasmania, highlighting the versatility of Australia's land.

FOOD ON THE RUN

Sushi The city is dotted with tiny counters offering fresh sushi to grab on the go.

Juice bars These serve delicious, cool blends of fruits and vegetables, with optional extras such as protein balls.

Vietnamese rolls A tasty yet inexpensive option, *bánh mì* is a meat (or tuna) and salad roll, with a dash of fish sauce, pâté, coriander and chili.

Food carts Mobile food trucks cater to the lunch or dinner rush, as well as popular events.

Pies An Aussie institution, pies and pastry-wrapped sausage rolls are sold in bakeries.

Grilled barramundi Served on ginger and bok choy risotto, this is a great mix of local seafood and Asian flavours.

Pavlova This dessert made from meringue and topped with tropical fruit and fresh cream is a summer favourite.

Lamingtons These little Victoria sponge cakes are coated in chocolate icing and shredded coconut.

What to Drink in Sydney

Australia has no shortage of choice when it comes to drinks, be it beer, wine, juice, coffee, tea or water. There are wines to suit all tastes and budgets, with many of the bargain-priced wines rating well in blind tastings. Niche craft beers produced on a smaller scale by micro-breweries enjoy a cult status, while major domestic and international brands are also widely available. Sydneysiders love their morning coffee, too, being particular not just about the style of coffee but, at cafés with in-house coffee roasters, the bean as well. When it comes to bottled water, a mini-industry has grown around labels, with the novelty name, colourful label and quirky description on the outside sometimes as popular as what lies inside the bottle. Juice bars cater to the health-conscious, offering superfood blends, exotic ingredients and extras such as protein powders.

Sparkling Wine

Australia is justly famous for its sparkling wines, from Yalumba's Angas Brut to Seppelts Salinger. Tasmania has showed considerable promise in producing some high-quality sparkling wines, particularly Pirie from Pipers Brook. However, the real hidden gems are the sparkling red wines – the best are made using the French *méthode champenoise*, matured over a number of years and helped by a small drop of vintage port. The best producers of red sparkling wines are Rockford and Seppelts. These sparkling wines are available throughout Sydney from "bottle shops", which sell alcohol.

Domaine Chandon in the Yarra Valley produces high-quality sparkling wines

Angas Brut premium

White Wine

The revolution in winemaking in the 1970s firmly established dry wines made from international grape varieties on the Australian table. Chardonnay, Sauvignon Blanc, and more recently Viognier and Pinot Gris or Pinot Grigio are all popular. However, there has also been a renaissance and growing appreciation for Riesling, Sauvignon Blanc and Sémillon, which age very gracefully. Australia's other great wines are their fortified and dessert wines. Australian winemakers use *Botrytis cinerea*, or noble rot, to make luscious dessert wines such as De Bortoli's "Noble One".

Australian Riesling

Botrytis Sémillon

Some of the vines in Australia are the oldest in the world

Grape Type	State	Best Regions	Best Producers
Chardonnay	VIC	Geelong, Beechworth	Bannockburn, Giaconda, Stoniers
	NSW	Hunter Valley	Lakes Folly, Rosemount, Tyrrell's
	WA	Margaret River	Leeuwin Estate, Pierro, Cullen
	SA	Barossa Valley, Eden Valley	Penfolds, Mountadam
Sémillon	NSW	Hunter Valley	Brokenwood, McWilliams, Tyrrell
	SA	Barossa Valley	Peter Lehmann, Willows, Penfolds
	WA	Margaret River	Moss Wood, Voyager, Evans & Tate
Riesling	SA	Clare Valley and Adelaide Hills	Grosset, Pikes, Petaluma, Mitchells
	SA	Barossa Valley	Richmond Grove, Leo Buring, Yalumba
	TAS	Tasmania	Piper's Brook
Marsanne	VIC	Goulburn Valley	Chateau Tahbilk, Mitchelton

Red Wine

Australia's benchmark red is Grange Hermitage, the creation of the late vintner Max Schubert in the 1950s and 1960s. Due to his work, Shiraz has established itself as Australia's premium red variety. However, there is also plenty of diversity with the acknowledged quality of Cabernet Sauvignon produced in the Coonawarra. Recently, there has also been a reappraisal of traditional "old vine" Grenache and Mourvedre varieties in the Barossa Valley and McLaren Vale.

Vineyards of Leeuwin Estate, Margaret River

Shiraz   Pinot Noir

Grape Type	State	Best Regions	Best Producers
Shiraz	NSW	Hunter Valley	Brokenwood, Lindmans, Tyrrells
	VIC	Great Western, Sunbury	Bests, Seppelts, Craiglee
	SA	Barossa Valley	Henschke, Penfolds, Rockford, Torbreck
	SA	McLaren Vale	Hardys, Coriole, Chapel Hill
	WA	Margaret River, Great Southern	Cape Mentelle, Plantagenet
Cabernet Sauvignon	WA	Margaret River	Cape Mentelle, Cullen, Moss Wood
	SA	Coonawarra	Wynns, Lindemans, Bowen Estate
	SA	Barossa, Adelaide Hills	Penfolds, Henschke, Petaluma
	VIC	Yarra Valley, Great Western	Yarra Yering, Yerinberg, Bests
Merlot	VIC	Yarra Valley, Great Western	Bests, Yara Yering
	SA	Adelaide Hills, Clare Valley	Petaluma, Pikes
Pinot Noir	VIC	Yarra Valley	Coldstream Hills, Tarrawarra
	VIC	Gippsland, Geelong	Bass Philip, Bannockburn, Shadowfax

Beer

Most Australian beer is vat-fermented, or lager, and consumed chilled. Full-strength beer has an alcohol content of about 4.8 per cent, mid-strength beers have around 3.5 per cent, while "light" beers have less than 3 per cent. Traditionally heat-sterilized, cold filtration is now popular. Fans of real ale should seek out one of the city's pub breweries. Beer is ordered by glass size and brand: a schooner is a 426 ml (15 fl oz) glass and a middy is 284 ml (10 fl oz). It is also available in bottles, cans and "on tap", through a hose connected to a keg and poured straight into glasses at pubs and restaurants. While mainstream brands produced by big breweries wane in popularity, craft beers produced by microbreweries and bearing names reflecting their place of origin, such as Young Henrys Newtowner, have attracted a loyal following, mainly among young professionals and hipsters.

Middy   Schooner

Juices

Pear and kiwi frappé   Banana smoothie   Strawberry juice

While a wide array of fruit-based drinks such as juices, frappés and smoothies are easily available, premium juice products (at premium prices) are gradually making their mark. Gourmet and health-focused ranges using exotic fruits and superfood ingredients such as kale and beetroot can be found at supermarkets and convenience stores, as well as at juice bars offering creative concoctions on their extensive menus.

Young Henrys Newtowner   Cascade Premium Lager

Coffee and Tea

Sydney's coffee culture had its beginnings in the 1980s. Now a sophisticated and thriving industry, many cafés feature in-house roasted blends and promote the origins of the coffee beans they serve. Campos, Toby's Estate and Single Origin are all popular local blends. More recently, a culture around tea has emerged, with speciality tea store T2 and the Rabbit Hole Organic Tea Bar café (see p196) leading the way.

Other Drinks

Tap water in Sydney is fresh and clean, but local and imported bottled waters are fashionable, especially those with quirky names, creative bottle designs and innovative labelling.

Spring water

Where to Eat and Drink

The Rocks and Circular Quay

Cabrito Coffee Traders $
Café **Map** 1 B3
10–14 Bulletin Place, Circular Quay
Tel 8065 8895 **Closed** *Sat, Sun*
Tucked away in a tiny alley, this friendly place is favoured by city workers looking for a takeaway caffeine fix. Once the morning rush hour has passed, sit in and enjoy the aroma of in-house roasted beans with a toasted sandwich or lamington.

Ground Control Café $
Café **Map** 1 B3
Shop W4, Alfred St, Circular Quay
Tel 9247 4330
Located under Circular Quay railway station, this spot has limited seating and is therefore primarily a grab-and-go destination. The coffee is excellent, and there is a small selection of delicious cakes, pastries, wraps and sandwiches.

Vintage Café $
Mediterranean **Map** 1 B2
3 Nurses Walk, The Rocks
Tel 9252 2055
Set in a cobblestoned courtyard, this hidden gem is a great pit stop for refuelling while out exploring by day. In the evening, it's an excellent place to enjoy a romantic dinner for two, accompanied by live jazz several nights a week.

The Australian Heritage Hotel $$
Pub **Map** 1 B2
100 Cumberland St, The Rocks
Tel 9247 2229
Pizza features heavily at this classic Australian watering hole, with toppings given a local twist – try the kangaroo, emu or saltwater crocodile. Other options on the menu include Aussie beef-and-beer pies, and burgers. An interesting range of suggested beers complements the menu.

Café Nice $$
French **Map** 1 C3
Level 3, 2 Phillip St, Circular Quay
Tel 8248 9600
A charming, bright and airy space featuring honest, rustic Provençal-style cooking and with views to the Harbour Bridge. This is a great place to enjoy a meal before a show at the Opera House. Service can be slow during busy periods, so let your waiter know if you are in a hurry.

El Camino Cantina $$
Mexican **Map** 1 A2
18 Argyle St, The Rocks
Tel 9259 5668
Come to this bright, character-filled space for tequila, sangria and authentic Tex Mex shared plates, served to the beat of a rock "n" roll soundtrack.

The East Chinese Restaurant $$
Chinese **Map** 1 C2
Shop 8, 1 Macquarie St, East Circular Quay
Tel 9252 6868
Subtle, pungent, hot, mild – there is something for every palate here. Contrasting tastes, colours and textures appeal to the eye and the taste buds. Dishes include stir-fried kangaroo and crocodile tail fillet.

The Glenmore $$
Pub **Map** 1 B2
96 Cumberland St, The Rocks
Tel 9247 4794
Head up the steep stairs to the rooftop to enjoy drinks and food with superb views of Sydney Harbour at this casual, buzzing spot. Don't let poor weather put you off – there is a retractable roof. It's a popular spot with young city workers.

Heritage Belgian Beer Café $$
Belgian **Map** 1 A3
135 Harrington St, The Rocks
Tel 8488 2460
This atmospheric restaurant is set in a historic building. The Belgian mussels are a must-try. Enjoy them cooked one of eight ways, or try Flemish beef stew, Belgian sausages or other specialities, washed down with an array of artisan beers.

The bright and airy Café Nice, ideal for a pre-show meal

Lotus Dumpling Bar $$
Chinese **Map** 1 A1
16 Hickson Rd, Dawes Point
Tel 9251 8328
Dumplings are served almost as quickly as they are made, making this a great fast-food choice. The menu also has entrées and mains.

DK Choice

MCA Café $$
Café **Map** 1 B2
Level 4, 140 George St, The Rocks
Tel 9250 8443
It's all about the beautiful harbour views from the open sculpture terrace on the fourth floor of the Museum of Contemporary Art. Enjoy a cup of coffee or glass of wine with a light bite on the expansive deck that overlooks the Harbour Bridge and Opera House.

The Morrison Bar & Oyster Room $$
Seafood **Map** 1 B3
225 George St, The Rocks
Tel 9247 6744
There is a setting for every occasion here – from the quiet of the conservatory to the communal dining area and the party atmosphere of the Oyster Room. Enjoy breakfast, bar snacks, a diverse mains menu or oysters "shucked to order".

Nelson's Brasserie $$
Pub **Map** 1 A2
19 Kent St, The Rocks
Tel 9251 4044 **Closed** *Sun, Mon*
This eatery is on the first floor above the Lord Nelson Brewery Hotel. Enjoy a drink downstairs, then head up for innovative food in a historic 18th-century sandstone-walled building.

Neptune Palace $$
Chinese and Malaysian **Map** 1 B3
Level 1, Gateway Building, cnr of Pitt & Alfred Sts, Circular Quay
Tel 9241 3338
Popular with the business crowd for more than two decades, Neptune Palace serves award-winning fare including salt-and-pepper king prawns, wasabi beef, and Kapitan chicken.

Opera Bar $$
Modern Australian **Map** 1 C2
Lower Concourse, Sydney Opera House, Bennelong Point
Tel 9247 1666
This is a great place to stop on the way to the Opera House – or to just settle in, relax and watch the ferries over a drink and choice of bar food, light meals and sharing plates. There is live music most evenings.

Pei Modern $$
Modern Australian **Map** 1 B3
199 George St, The Rocks
Tel 9250 3160
Superb gourmet dishes are served in this relaxed bistro-style setting in the Four Seasons Hotel. Pre-theatre and bar menus are available for diners who are not after the full dining experience.

Saké Restaurant & Bar $$
Japanese **Map** 1 B2
12 Argyle St, The Rocks
Tel 9259 5656
Set within an impressive designer space featuring dark wood, low light and loud music, Saké Restaurant & Bar has a resident sushi master who serves up an authentic mix of delicious new and classic sushi dishes.

Tapavino $$
Spanish Tapas **Map** 1 B3
6 Bulletin Place, Circular Quay
Tel 9247 3221 **Closed** Sun
It's like Barcelona by the harbour at this wine and sherry bar with an extensive menu of more than 300 Spanish wines, 80 sherries and a long list of tapas. There is a strong "sip a little bit of this and eat a little bit of that" philosophy.

Ventuno $$
Italian **Map** 1 A2
21 Hickson Rd, Walsh Bay
Tel 9247 4444
This is a chic modern Italian eatery where you can savour antipasti, pizza or pasta al fresco while enjoying the lovely water views across Walsh Bay. It is located a short stroll away from the theatres.

Young Alfred $$
Italian **Map** 1 B3
31 Alfred St, Circular Quay
Tel 9251 5192 **Closed** Sun
From the former owners of one of Sydney's all-time favourite pizza places comes modern Italian fare with flair. Enjoy pasta and fabulously named pizzas dished up in the historic Georgian Customs House building near the harbour.

Nelson's Brasserie, with its original 18th-century sandstone walls

Altitude $$$
Modern Australian **Map** 1 A3
Level 36, Shangri-La Hotel, 176 Cumberland St, The Rocks
Tel 9250 6123 **Closed** Sun
Floor-to-ceiling windows maximize the dramatic harbour views, especially at night. Service can be slow, but at least that gives you more time to enjoy the stunning panorama.

ARIA $$$
Modern Australian **Map** 1 C2
1 Macquarie St, East Circular Quay
Tel 9252 2555
An intimate, elegant dining experience on the edge of the harbour with stunning views, with a choice of set-price menus from one to four courses, a seasonal tasting menu and pre- and post-theatre dining. There is an exceptional wine list and very helpful sommeliers on hand.

DK Choice
Bennelong $$$
Modern Australian **Map** 1 C2
Sydney Opera House
Tel 9240 8000
Renowned chef Peter Gilmore serves art and innovation on a plate in a modern, cathedral-like space befitting this premiere location under the Opera House sails. The sophisticated menu reinvents Australian classics, with bush meats, superb seafood and lamington and pavlova.

The Bridge Room $$$
Modern Australian **Map** 1 B3
44 Bridge St, Circular Quay
Tel 9247 7000 **Closed** Sun
Come here for a unique take on Asian and European dishes, some cooked over a charcoal grill and slow-smoked in the Japanese *robata* style. With just 66 seats, the service is as flawless as the food.

Café Sydney $$$
Modern Australian **Map** 1 B3
Level 5, Customs House, 31 Alfred St, Circular Quay
Tel 9251 8683
Enjoy picture-postcard harbour views from the covered terrace of this prime rooftop location above Circular Quay. Service is warm and friendly. The ever-changing menu has consistently excellent dishes.

The Cut Bar & Grill $$$
Steak **Map** 1 A2
16 Argyle St, The Rocks
Tel 9259 5695
Meat-lovers rejoice! The four-hour slow-roast Wagyu standing rib is served straight from the carving trolley. There's also sustainable seafood for those wanting something lighter, as well as an extensive wine list and original cocktails.

Quay $$$
Modern Australian **Map** 1 B2
Upper level, Overseas Passenger Terminal, West Circular Quay
Tel 9251 5600
A spectacular view with food to match. Star chef Peter Gilmore makes magic out of the best and freshest produce, combining ingredients in surprising ways, by reworking old favourites and creating new dishes each season.

City Centre

Bodhi in the Park $
Vegetarian **Map** 1 C5
Cook & Phillip Park, 2–4 College St
Tel 9360 2523
In a peaceful park location, this is a wonderful place for alfresco lunch or dinner. The menu features delicious pan-Asian cuisine in the *yum cha* (tea with dim sum) tradition.

For more information on types of restaurants see pages 180–81

Double Barrel Coffee Merchants
Café   **$**
        Map 4 E2
33 York St
Tel *0419 832 949*   **Closed** *Sat, Sun*
City office workers get their morning coffee fix here as they pour out of Wynyard Station. Great for a hearty breakfast, or lunch on the go.

GPO Pizza by Wood
Italian   **$**
        Map 1 B4
Lower ground floor, GPO,
1 Martin Place
Tel *9229 7722*   **Closed** *Sun*
This pizzeria brings a tasty slice of Italy to the heart of Sydney. The light and crispy traditional thin-crust pizzas feature delicately balanced toppings and are cooked in wood-fired ovens.

Madame Nhu
Vietnamese   **$**
        Map 4 E2
Shop 5, Lower ground floor,
The Galeries, 500 George St
Tel *9283 3355*
The simple and delicious modern Vietnamese street food is just as it should be – fresh and fuss-free. This place is ideal for a fast, filling, flavoursome lunch at food-court prices. The pho noodle soup and stir fries are highlights.

Mother Chu's Vegetarian Kitchen
Asian Vegetarian   **$**
        Map 4 E3
367 Pitt St
Tel *9283 2828*
Overlook the very simple decor and join the regulars enjoying big helpings of hearty food blending the flavours of Taiwan, China and Japan – all served with warm hospitality. There are plenty of vegan options and a great-value takeaway menu, too.

Pablo & Rusty's
Café   **$**
        Map 4 E2
161 Castlereagh St
Tel *9807 6293*   **Closed** *Sun*
Warm service in an inviting, buzzy, industrial space, but it's the coffee, tea and food menu that shines here at breakfast and lunch. The service is helpful and friendly, but there can be a wait for a table at peak times.

Sushi Hotara
Japanese   **$**
        Map 4 E2
Level 1, The Galeries, 500 George St
Tel *9264 9917*
In a bustling setting with Japanese-inspired interiors, Sushi Hotara offers a fresh, authentic, reasonably priced sushi conveyer belt – which explains why there's often a queue at the door.

Workshop Espresso
Café   **$**
        Map 4 E2
The Galeries, 500 George St
Tel *9264 8836*
It would be easy to miss this hole-in-the-wall spot were it not for the regulars lining up for their coffee fix. Great for a simple, tasty breakfast or lunch on the go.

York Lane
Café   **$**
        Map 1 A4
56 York Lane, Wynyard
Tel *9299 1676*   **Closed** *Sat, Sun*
Stop by for tasty quick meals, sandwiches, breakfasts, cakes and coffee by day. By night, the place becomes a bar and restaurant with split-level seating and a backing track of vinyl records.

Bambini Trust
European   **$$**
        Map 4 F2
Ground floor, 185 Elizabeth St
Tel *9283 7098*   **Closed** *Sun*
A sophisticated spot. The elegant wood-panelled interiors, crisp white linen and excellent service complement the well-executed menu. This is a great place for a stylish breakfast, working lunch or leisurely dinner.

Barrafina
Spanish Tapas   **$$**
        Map 1 B4
2 Bligh St
Tel *9231 2551*   **Closed** *Sat, Sun*
A wide selection of sharing plates and grazing boards here include produce from the restaurant gardens, Spanish cheeses and artisan cured meats. A genuine taste of Spain, from light starters to more substantial offerings.

Bistrode CBD
Modern bistro   **$$**
        Map 4 E1
Level 1, Hotel CBD, 52 King St
Tel *9240 3000*   **Closed** *Sat, Sun*
Modern British cuisine with a focus on local produce from English expat chef Jeremy Strode. Wide-arched windows give the first-floor location an elegance that matches the food.

Chophouse
Steak   **$$**
        Map 1 B4
25 Bligh St
Tel *1300 246 748*   **Closed** *Sun*
Reminiscent of the fine steak-houses of old New York, here you can settle into the leather and dark wood booths and tuck into a steak with home sauces, or opt for lighter salad and seafood options.

Danjee
Korean   **$$**
        Map 4 E3
1–7 Albion Place
Tel *8084 9041*
Taking Korean BBQ into the fine-dining arena, the quality and

Madame Nhu – the place to go for reasonably priced Vietnamese street food

presentation of the food at this spot attracts a cool crowd eager to try new tastes. The lunch-box specials are great value.

Diethnes
Greek   **$$**
        Map 1 B5
336 Pitt St
Tel *9267 8956*   **Closed** *Sun*
A Sydney institution, Diethnes has been in the same basement location since 1952. The decor might show its age, but the hearty Greek fare still satisfies.

Felix
French Bistro   **$$**
        Map 1 B4
2 Ash St
Tel *9240 3000*
Designed as a romantic homage to the quintessential French brasserie, Felix offers classic fare and an extensive wine list in an elegant room, with white-tiled walls, mounted bread baskets and red table lamps.

Fix Wine Bar + Restaurant
Modern Australian   **$$**
        Map 4 F2
111 Elizabeth St
Tel *9232 2767*   **Closed** *Sat, Sun*
Wash down tasty bar snacks or rustic modern dishes with a wine from the extensive list of over 200, sourced from all over the world. The menu focuses on fresh seasonal produce.

Gowings Bar & Grill
Modern European   **$$**
        Map 4 E2
QT Hotel, 49 Market St
Tel *8262 0062*
The interior is in the style of a European brasserie with an edgy contemporary design feauring exposed bricks. The menu takes its cues from around the world and across generations, but the grill is the star. Save room for the decadent retro desserts.

Machiavelli $$
Italian **Map** 1 A4
123 Clarence St
Tel *9299 3748* **Closed** *Sat, Sun*
A Sydney institution, this is where politicians, lawyers and business leaders come to eat and be seen, doing deals over hearty Italian food. The decor is rustic, with air-dried meats hanging from the ceiling.

Mr Wong $$
Chinese **Map** 1 B3
3 Bridge Lane
Tel *9240 3000*
Sprawled over two stylish levels, Mr Wong pays tribute to classic Chinese influences with a Cantonese-based menu. A choice of more than 60 dishes is listed on one of the best dim sum menus in town.

No. 1 Bent St $$
Modern Australian **Map** 1 B2
1 Bent St
Tel *9252 5550* **Closed** *Sun*
This place offers a memorable dining experience, serving delicious, uncomplicated food, cooked in an open kitchen with a wood-burning oven and accompanied by fine wines. Even the bread is homemade. Half of the seating is at communal tables.

Rockpool Bar & Grill $$
Steak **Map** 1 B4
66 Hunter St
Tel *8078 1900*
Drawing a crowd from the big business end of town, this place has a grand Art Deco interior that would not be out of place in Manhattan. Steak is the main attraction, but there's much more to enjoy here, including an extensive wine and cocktail list.

Sushi e $$
Japanese **Map** 1 B3
Level 4, Establishment, 252 George St
Tel *9240 3000* **Closed** *Sun*
Exceptionally fresh fish is served up in stunning surroundings. A good way to experience a range of delicious tastes is by ordering a selection of small pieces from the sashimi menu or a mix of items from the sushi nigiri menu. Excellent service.

Eleven Bridge $$$
Modern Australian **Map** 1 B3
11 Bridge St
Tel *9252 1888* **Closed** *Sun*
The exceptional, innovative menu from celebrated chef Neil Perry features fine sustainable produce. This elegant, grand dining room is located in a sandstone heritage building.

DK Choice

est. $$$
Modern Australian **Map** 1 B3
*Level 1, Establishment,
252 George St*
Tel *9240 3000* **Closed** *Sun*
The head chef at this restaurant, Peter Doyle, is widely regarded as a founding father of "Modern Australian" cuisine. Attention to detail reigns here: every dish is prepared to perfection and exquisitely presented. The menu features French fusion fare with a unique Antipodean twist, complemented by exceptional service and a superb wine list.

Glass Brasserie $$$
Modern Australian **Map** 1 B5
Level 2, Hilton Sydney, 488 George St
Tel *9265 6068*
Celebrity chef Luke Mangan's bright space with floor-to-ceiling windows gets diners arguing over what are better – dishes from the grill, or desserts. The best way to settle the score is to try both.

Spice Temple $$$
Chinese **Map** 4 F1
10 Bligh St
Tel *8078 1888*
A modern Chinese marvel. Chillies are the star – fresh, dried, salted, pickled, brined and fermented – served in a dark, moody basement with Chinese lanterns and red table lamps.

Tetsuya's $$$
Japanese-French **Map** 4 E3
529 Kent St
Tel *9267 2900* **Closed** *Sun, Mon*
Internationally acclaimed, this serene restaurant features a set degustation menu that fuses Japanese flavours with French technique. A vegetarian version is available on request.

Darling Harbour and Surry Hills

BBQ King $
Chinese **Map** 4 E4
76–78 Liverpool St
Tel *9267 2586*
A Chinatown institution since 1983, this is still the go-to destination for many of the city's night owls in search of a late meal of barbecued duck, pork and Chinese beer. Great vegetable dishes and sides, too.

Boon $
Thai **Map** 4 E4
1/425 Pitt St, Haymarket
Tel *9281 2114*
With a different take on Thai cuisine, this café combines the best of Thai street food with Sydney coffee culture. There are spicy curries, tasty sandwiches and superb salads. The on-site fruit and vegetable store sells fresh produce to take home.

Cafe Rumah $
Café **Map** 4 F4
71–73 Campbell St, Surry Hills
Tel *9280 2289*
A Malaysian-inspired place serving familiar café favourites and South-east Asian staples such as buttermilk pancakes, pork belly rice bowl, and congee. Try the fresh baked Madeleine biscuits with *kaya* (Malaysian coconut jam).

Caysorn Thai $
Thai **Map** 4 D4
Level 1, 8 Quay St, Haymarket
Tel *9211 5749*
Challenge your taste buds' heat tolerance here, where the speciality is Southern Thai food – known as the spiciest in Thailand. The chicken *larb* is highly recommended. The food is hot, but the service is warm and gracious.

Diners enjoying the excellent Chinese food at Mr Wong

For more information on types of restaurants *see pages 180–81*

Chat Thai $
Thai   **Map** 4 E4
20 Campbell St, Haymarket
Tel *9211 1808*
A standout among a sea of Chinese restaurants, with an interesting menu featuring daily specials. Food is prepared in the shop-front window, which helps entertain those who are waiting in line for a table.

Devon $
Café
76 Devonshire St, Surry Hills
Tel *9211 8777*
One of Sydney's best breakfast spots, with only seasonal produce used – much of it picked from the café's own walled garden. If you're lucky, you'll be there when truffle-infused eggs are on the menu.

Din Tai Fung $
Chinese   **Map** 4 E3
World Square, 644 George St
Tel *9264 6010*
A haven for dumplings and pork-bun aficionados. Locals can't get enough of the steamed *xiao long bao* – soupy pork dumplings that ooze flavour. The pork and vegetable buns are fabulous, too.

Mamak $
Malaysian   **Map** 4 D4
15 Goulburn St, Haymarket
Tel *9211 1668*
Be prepared to wait outside for a table, where you can watch the chefs at work. Once inside, enjoy the buzz of the crowd and staff as you tuck into tasty street food.

Paramount Coffee Project $
Café   **Map** 4 F4
80 Commonwealth St, Surry Hills
Tel *9211 1122*
A speciality coffee destination in the historic Paramount House building. Filling sweet and savoury dishes such as waffles and breakfast burritos accompany your caffeine fix.

Pasteur $
Vietnamese   **Map** 4 E4
709 George St, Haymarket
Tel *9212 5622*
The service is fast in this no-frills setting. Locals and students come for great-value authentic tastes rather than the ambience. Try a hearty bowl of *pho bo* (beef and rice noodle soup).

Reuben Hills $
Café   **Map** 4 F5
61 Albion St, Surry Hills
Tel *9211 5556*
There's hot coffee, warm service and a cool atmosphere in this industrial-style warehouse

conversion. The wait for a table for breakfast at weekends is worthwhile. The salted-caramel milkshake is a hit.

Taste Baguette on Sussex Lane $
Vietnamese   **Map** 4 D1
275 Kent St
Tel *9211 5556*   **Closed** *Sat, Sun*
You can really smell the freshly baked bread here. Don't miss the signature baguettes, baked on-site and stuffed with your choice of fillings – from traditional Vietnamese lemongrass beef to Portuguese chicken.

Berta $$
Italian   **Map** 4 F4
17–19 Alberta St
Tel *9264 6133*   **Closed** *Sun, Mon*
The menu changes daily to deliver simple, seasonal fare, including dishes designed for sharing, with a sustainable philosophy of using the whole animal. There is a big focus on imported Italian wines.

Bodega $$
Tapas
216 Commonwealth St, Surry Hills
Tel *9212 7766*   **Closed** *Sun, Mon*
The dishes celebrate Spanish and South American cuisine. Savour the flavours with a giant mural of a matador and large bull looking down at you. There's an excellent selection of matching wines, too.

The Dolphin Hotel Dining Room $$
Pub   **Map** 5 A3
412 Crown St, Surry Hills
Tel *9331 4800*
The bright dining room with beautiful installation art is worthy of an art gallery. The menu consists of a modern take on Italian favourites, including thin-base Roman-style pizza.

Sepia, a multi-award-winning fine-dining restaurant set in a New York-style diner

Encasa $$
Spanish   **Map** 4 E4
423 Pitt St
Tel *9211 4257*
This casual Spanish restaurant offers great authentic tapas, paella and sangria. There are also Spanish-themed pizzas and dishes from the pot, such as *romesco de peix*, a Catalan seafood stew with a traditional hazelnut and tomato sauce.

Home Café & Thai Restaurant $$
Thai   **Map** 4 D3
1/299 Sussex St
Tel *9261 5058*
There are often queues to get into this place, and no wonder as it offers fantastic food, great value and very fast service. Portions are big, too, so if you order too much, ask for a takeaway container to enjoy later.

King Street Brewhouse $$
Pub   **Map** 4 D1
22 The Promenade, King St Wharf
Tel *8270 7901*
The diverse menu at this micro-brewery and restaurant features all the pub favourites – burgers, wings, grilled steaks, steamed mussels and seafood platters. Wash the food down with a delicious cold beer.

El Loco at Slip Inn $$
Pub   **Map** 1 A4
111 Sussex St
Tel *8295 9999*   **Closed** *Sun*
Tuck into tacos, Mexican-style pork or grilled fish burgers, or try one of the weekly specials in the colourful surroundings of this pub. If you're after a change, there's a good Thai menu on the ground floor, too.

Longrain $$
Asian   **Map** 4 F4
85 Commonwealth St, Surry Hills
Tel *9280 2888*
Top Asian fare is served in a big space that fills quickly. The menu includes large portions of Southeast Asian dishes designed for sharing. A long communal table is the centrepiece of the hip industrial-chic setting.

Mahjong Room $$
Chinese   **Map** 5 A2
312 Crown St, Surry Hills
Tel *9361 3985*
The food does the talking at this low-profile restaurant. A creative spin on Chinese cuisine attracts a young crowd, with dishes served at mahjong tables in a series of small rooms. There are mahjong lessons on Fridays and Saturdays.

The Malaya
$$
Malaysian **Map** 4 D1
39 Lime St, King Street Wharf
Tel *9279 1170*
A Sydney institution since 1963, this restaurant was originally in George Street but is now by the water. It's noisy, but the cooking packs a punch, with a feisty, flavour-filled range of dishes covering all the favourites, as well as some surprises.

Marigold
$$
Chinese **Map** 4 E4
Level 4 & 5, Citymark Building, 683–689 George St
Tel *9281 3388*
An enormous restaurant, spread over two floors above a shopping arcade, Marigold is home to one of Sydney's best *yum cha* offerings. Banquet menus make ordering easy when you can't decide what to choose.

Mohr Fish
$$
Seafood
202 Devonshire St, Surry Hills
Tel *9318 1326*
A humble, classy, small fish-and-chip shop, where you can enjoy your order fresh, steamed, grilled or fried. You can wait for a table or eat your takeaway order in the pub next door.

Nick's Bar & Grill
$$
Seafood and Steak
The Promenade, Cockle Bay Wharf
Tel *9279 0122*
A delicious menu and a fabulous spot to enjoy the sunshine or night lights on the water. Keep little ones happy with a value kids' meal of pasta, fish, calamari or chicken, with salad, chips and dessert.

Steersons Steakhouse
$$
Steakhouse **Map** 4 D1
17 Lime St, King Street Wharf
Tel *9295 5060*
A huge choice of succulent steaks are served in a surprisingly swish dining room, with menus that carry over the theme – they are bound in cow hide. There are lighter chicken, seafood and vegetarian dishes on offer, too.

Zaafran
$$
Indian **Map** 3 C2
Level 2, 345 Harbourside Shopping Centre, Darling Harbour
Tel *9211 8900*
This is the pick of the eateries on this side of the Darling Harbour tourist strip, with good-value set menus and a range of delicious dishes to satisfy vegetarians and meat-lovers alike.

Diners at the long communal table at Longrain

Golden Century
$$$
Chinese **Map** 4 E4
393–399 Sussex St
Tel *9281 1598*
The menu is huge, the staff friendly and the selection of live seafood enormous at this award-winning restaurant. With the kitchen open until 4am, it's not at all unusual to find it full of chefs from other restaurants relaxing after work.

Kobe Jones
$$$
Japanese **Map** 4 D1
29 Lime St, King Street Wharf, Darling Harbour
Tel *9299 5290*
Stylishly decorated in black and red, this restaurant puts a Californian twist on traditional Japanese and teppanyaki. Helpful staff will guide you through the extensive and tantalizing offerings to suit all palates.

LuMi Bar & Dining
$$$
Italian-Japanese **Map** 4 D2
56 Pirrama Rd, Pyrmont
Tel *9571 1999*
Enjoy a casual fine-dining experience at this restaurant in a waterfront location and winner of two Chefs Hat awards, where modern Italian dishes are fused with Japanese flavours. Leave the decisions to the chef with the five- or eight-course tasting menu. Vegetarian versions of all dishes are available.

Momofuku Seiobo
$$$
Japanese **Map** 3 B1
The Star, 80 Pyrmont St, Pyrmont
Tel *9777 9000* **Closed** *Sun*
This first off-shoot of the renowned New York original has a set-price tasting menu, or you can arrive early for one of the five bar seats for walk-ins and try the limited bar menu.

DK Choice

Sepia
$$$
Modern Japanese Fusion **Map** 4 D2
201 Sussex St
Tel *9283 1990* **Closed** *Sun, Mon*
Lauded with titles including NSW Restaurant of the Year 2016, Sepia offers a unique take on Japanese flavours, artfully done, set in an upscale, uptown New York-style bar and diner. There is a choice of four set menus or a degustation menu, while a separate bar offering includes a selection of Japanese charcoal-grill dishes. First-class service from the waiting staff and sommelier.

Botanic Garden and The Domain

Botanic Garden Café
$
Café **Map** 2 D4
Royal Botanic Garden, Mrs Macquaries Rd
Tel *9241 2419*
Set in the lush gardens overlooking the duck pond, this place serves gourmet sandwiches, salads, baked goods and coffee. There's also the option to pre-order a picnic basket to enjoy at leisure as you explore the Garden.

Café at the Gallery
$
Café **Map** 2 D4
The Art Gallery of NSW, Art Gallery Rd, The Domain
Tel *9225 1744*
Head to the Gallery's lower level 1 for a casual dining experience in a relaxed environment, with freshly prepared light snacks, sandwiches, salads and baked goods. It stays open till late on Wednesday for Art After Hours.

For more information on types of restaurants *see pages 180–81*

Charlie's $
Café   **Map** 2 D5
7–41 Cowper Wharf Roadway,
Woolloomooloo
Tel 9358 4443
A no-fuss, long-established café
serving up a big selection of hot
and fresh fast food, including
burgers, sandwiches, rolls,
barbecue chicken, hot chips
and salads. This is the perfect
way to fuel the troops on a
family outing.

Courtyard Café da Capo $
Café   **Map** 1 C4
8 Macquarie St
Tel 9382 7359
Tucked away in Sydney Hospital's
courtyard off Macquarie Street,
this is a quiet and pleasant place
to refuel with a coffee, snacks, a
light meal or more substantial
offerings. There is both open-air
and indoor seating.

The Pavillion Kiosk $
Café   **Map** 2 D4
1 Art Gallery Rd, The Domain
Tel 9232 1322
Order light refreshments at this
café in The Domain across from
the Art Gallery. The menu has
sandwiches, soup and freshly
baked pastries and muffins. Find
a spot on the green to enjoy lunch.

Poolside Café $
Café   **Map** 2 E3
Andrew (Boy) Charlton Pool,
1C Mrs Macquaries Rd, The Domain
Tel 8354 1044   **Closed** June, July
Perched above the Olympic-sized
Andrew (Boy) Charlton swimming
pool, this café has views across
Woolloomooloo Bay. Enjoy a
swim and a snack – from healthy
salads, to fish-and-chips and ice-
cream sandwiches.

Aki's $$
Indian   **Map** 2 D4
6 Cowper Wharf Roadway,
Woolloomooloo
Tel 9332 4600
Masterful modern Indian food
offers a combination of tandoori
flavours from the north, classics
from the chef's native Chennai
and seafood dishes from Goa. Sit
at an outside table and dine
during sunset, or enjoy the cool,
split-mezzanine interior.

Botanic Garden Restaurant $$
Modern Australian   **Map** 1 C3
Royal Botanic Garden,
Mrs Macquaries Rd
Tel 9241 2419
An enchanting venue in the
middle of the picturesque
Botanic Garden, featuring the
original 19th-century façade and

offering beautiful leafy views.
Enjoy an open-air lunch any day
or a lazy breakfast at weekends.

Chiswick at the Gallery $$
Modern Australian   **Map** 2 D4
The Art Gallery of NSW,
Art Gallery Rd, The Domain
Tel 9225 1819
Head to the contemporary
dining room and grab a bite to
eat at the large communal table,
or have a drink in the casual bar
area before or after enjoying
the exhibitions.

Kingsleys Sydney $$
Steak and Crab   **Map** 2 D4
10/6 Cowper Wharf Roadway,
Woolloomooloo
Tel 1300 546 475
No need to decide between
steak or seafood; enjoy both
with surf and turf options –
from Wagyu rib-eye scotch fillet,
to yellow-fin tuna sashimi and
Singapore chilli crab.

The Pavilion Restaurant $$
Modern Australian   **Map** 2 D4
1 Art Gallery Rd, The Domain
Tel 9232 1322
In The Domain, just across the
road from the Art Gallery, this
elegant restaurant's uniquely
shaped curved building serves
up breakfast and lunch with
beautiful garden views from
the terrace and deck.

Sienna Marina $$
Italian   **Map** 2 D5
6/7–41 Cowper Wharf Roadway,
Woolloomooloo
Tel 9358 6299
Choose from the breakfast, lunch,
dinner, pizza or kids' menus –
there's something for every time
of day. The leather loungers in
front of the fireplace are perfect
for relaxing.

China Doll $$$
Modern Asian   **Map** 2 D4
4/6 Cowper Wharf Roadway,
Woolloomooloo
Tel 9380 6744
A favourite with celebrities, this
wharf eatery with spectacular
views is a real gem. It offers
modern versions of traditional
dishes from China, Japan, Hong
Kong and Southeast Asia and a
well-priced banquet menu.

Manta $$$
Seafood   **Map** 2 D4
6 Cowper Wharf Roadway,
Woolloomooloo
Tel 9332 3822
This destination is best enjoyed
from a prime position outside,
with fish so fresh they could have

Classic salad with a stylish twist at Italian
Otto Ristorante

jumped from the harbour waters
below straight onto the plate.
Good-quality house wine.

DK Choice

Otto Ristorante $$$
Italian   **Map** 2 D4
Area 8, 6 Cowper Wharf Roadway,
Woolloomooloo
Tel 9368 7488
The Finger Wharf is great for
people-watching and celebrity-
spotting, but Otto is the real
star among stars on this
waterfront, reinventing the
flavours of Italy in stylish
new forms, with dishes that
delight and superb service.
The food somehow tastes even
better if you can get a seat on
the alfresco terrace.

Kings Cross and Darlinghurst

Bar Coluzzi $
Café   **Map** 5 B1
322 Victoria St, Darlinghurst
Tel 0412 253 782
Established in 1957, this small
old-school original has stood
the test of time. Locals, from
politicians to art students, get
their morning coffee fix sitting on
the little stools on the footpath.

Bill and Toni's $
Italian   **Map** 5 A1
74 Stanley St, East Sydney
Tel 9360 4702
A stalwart loved for its great-
value, no-frills Italian food,
strong coffee, free cordial and
old-fashioned red tablecloths.
Enjoy simple but tasty and filling
pasta dishes upstairs, then head
downstairs for *gelato.*

Bills
Café   **$**
     Map 5 B2
433 Liverpool St, Darlinghurst
Tel *9360 9631*
Regulars would be up in arms if owner-chef Bill Granger's famous ricotta hotcakes were ever taken off the menu here. Breakfast or brunch is the best time to visit.

Flour and Stone
Café   **$**
     Map 5 A1
53 Riley St, Woolloomooloo
Tel *8068 8818*   **Closed** *Sun*
There are savoury offerings such as gourmet tarts, pies and sandwiches, but it's the sweet treats here that get customers salivating. Delights range from lamingtons and lemon drizzle cake, to more healthy bran muffins.

Fratelli Paradiso
Italian   **$**
     Map 2 E4
12–16 Challis Ave, Potts Point
Tel *9357 1744*
This spot morphs from breakfast and lunch café to sassy wine bar and restaurant. No bookings, so arrive early. Go for the fabulous breakfasts or, later, for the pasta, tiramisu and Italian cheeses.

Govinda's
Vegetarian Buffet   **$**
     Map 5 B1
112 Darlinghurst Rd, Darlinghurst
Tel *9380 5155*   **Closed** *Mon, Tue*
Pile up a plate of curries, breads and salads from the opulent buffet. For a little extra, lie on cushions or couches and watch a movie at the boutique cinema upstairs.

Harry's Café de Wheels
Pie Cart   **$**
     Map 2 E4
Cnr Cowper Wharf Roadway & Brougham Rd, Woolloomooloo
Tel *8346 4100*
Now at several locations, this branch is the original and best, serving meat pies topped with mashed potato, peas and gravy to sailors, taxi drivers, celebrities, tourists and locals since the Great Depression in 1938.

Phamish
Vietnamese   **$**
     Map 5 B2
50 Burton St, Darlinghurst
Tel *9357 2688*   **Closed** *Mon*
A small place with moody red-and-black interiors. It can get very crowded, but service is swift. Seating is on small stools, so don't come expecting to recline after a flavoursome and filling meal.

A Tavola
Italian   **$$**
348 Victoria St, Darlinghurst
Tel *9331 7871*   **Closed** *Sun*
Join fellow diners at the long pink-marble table, the centrepiece of this stylish trattoria's narrow dining room. The menu changes weekly and is determined by the fresh seasonal produce that is available. Delicious, authentic Italian cuisine.

Bar Brosé
Contemporary   **$$**
     Map 5 B1
231A Victoria St, Darlinghurst
Tel *0450 307 117*   **Closed** *Mon*
This long, narrow wine bar and foodie haven buzzes with atmosphere. Enjoy delicious sharing plates, the famous Late Night Sandwich filled with pineapple-glazed leg ham and an extensive list of fine wines.

Billy Kwong
Chinese-Australian   **$$**
     Map 2 E5
Shop 1, 28 Macleay St, Potts Point
Tel *9332 3300*
Celebrity chef Kylie Kwong puts her unique spin on Chinese food, featuring locally grown, organic and biodynamic produce, with a strong focus on Australian native bush foods. The steamed mini pork buns and saltbush cakes are highlights.

Casoni
Italian   **$$**
     Map 5 A2
371–373 Bourke St (cnr Foley St), Darlinghurst
Tel *0449 516 798*   **Closed** *Mon*
Be surprised, as the chefs create a new pasta dish daily, which is on the menu until sold out. There are plenty of other Italian choices, too, at a place that puts an emphasis on shared dishes, fun times and fresh food.

The Fish Shop
Seafood   **$$**
     Map 2 E4
22 Challis Ave, Potts Point
Tel *9326 9000*
A little piece of The Hamptons in Potts Point, with its white-washed walls and fun East Coast American seaside feel. Grab a stool and enjoy fresh, locally caught fish and delicious seafood dishes.

Fu Manchu
Asian   **$$**
     Map 5 B1
229 Darlinghurst Rd, Darlinghurst
Tel *9360 9424*
A smart dining room with carved timber screens and silk cushions on the chairs. Portions are small but delicious. Finish with a cocktail at the adjoining Eau de Vie.

Lucio Pizzeria
Italian   **$$**
     Map 5 A2
248 Palmer St, Darlinghurst
Tel *9332 3766*   **Closed** *Tue*
A superb slice of Naples in the corner of a piazza, with relaxed indoor or outdoor dining in the pretty courtyard. There's a good menu of antipasti to start and indulgent desserts – but it's really all about perfect pizza.

Ms G's
Modern Asian   **$$**
     Map 2 E5
155 Victoria St, Potts Point
Tel *8313 1000*
Four levels of fabulous fun. This place is styled like no other: there's a pink neon-bathed entrance, graffiti wall, rows of jars on the ceiling and veggie garden courtyard. And the food? Mouthwateringly excellent. Don't miss the spicy squid ink *nasi goreng* (Indonesian stir-fried rice).

Red Lantern on Riley
Vietnamese   **$$**
     Map 5 A1
60 Riley St, Darlinghurst
Tel *9698 4355*   **Closed** *Mon*
Go on a flavour journey to old Saigon with a focus on shared dishes from celebrity chef Luke Nguyen and his team, in a designer setting that evokes French-Colonial Vietnam.

Poolside Café, a relaxing dining venue with superb views

For more information on types of restaurants *see pages 180–81*

Riley Street Garage $$
Modern Australian **Map** 5 A1
55 Riley St, Woolloomooloo
Tel 9326 9055 **Closed** *Sun*
This former 1930s car depot,
garage and machine shop pays
homage to its heritage with a
stylish fit-out and food "for all your
gastronomic service and repairs".
Dishes are designed for sharing.

Tilbury Hotel $$
Pub **Map** 2 D5
12–18 Nicholson St, Woolloomooloo
Tel 9368 1955 **Closed** *Mon*
(restaurant; café open daily)
Try breakfast or a light bite from
the small but tasty selection in the
café, or enjoy a more substantial
meal in the restaurant dining
room looking out on a courtyard.

Trunk Road $$
Indian **Map** 5 A1
163 Crown St, Darlinghurst
Tel 8354 1096
Get your fill of delectable Indian
fare without emptying your
wallet. Try the curry chips and
the curry of the day. The house
speciality, Roadies, a nod to
Kolkata street food, has spicy
fillings wrapped in *paratha* bread.

DK Choice

Yellow $$
Vegetarian **Map** 2 E4
57 Macleay St, Potts Point
Tel 9332 2344
Reinvented as a vegetarian
restaurant, Yellow takes meat-
free cooking to new heights
with delicious, beautiful-looking
dishes that even meat-lovers
will enjoy. The building's artistic
history brought bohemia to
Potts Point, first as an art gallery,
then as home to contemporary
illustrator Martin Sharp and his
Yellow House artist collective.

Beppi's $$$
Italian **Map** 4 F3
21 Yurong St, East Sydney
Tel 9360 4558 **Closed** *Sun*
This restaurant has been delivering
Italian hospitality and fine food
that's all about taste not trends
since 1956. Ask for a table in the
magnificent cellar room.

Macleay Street Bistro $$$
Modern French **Map** 2 E5
73A Macleay St, Potts Point
Tel 9358 4891
The small seasonal menu and
weekly specials board of artfully
prepared dishes, raise the bar
above typical bistro fare. This is a
touch of France in an area known
as the Paris end of Potts Point.

Paddington

Ampersand Café & Bookstore $
Café **Map** 5 B3
78 Oxford St, Paddington
Tel 9380 6617
Soak up the tranquillity at
this charming café in a quaint
second-hand bookstore.
There's a lovely selection
of breakfast items, baked
goods, sandwiches, pastas
and salads – and more than
30,000 books over three levels.

Crème Café $
Café **Map** 6 E4
101–103 Queen St, Woollahra
Tel 9327 6543
Stroll one of the prettiest streets
in Paddington, then enjoy
breakfast, lunch or a sweet treat
at the outdoor tables on the
footpath, shaded by giant
trees. Dine alfresco Friday and
Saturday evenings – if the
weather permits.

Tiger Mottle $
Café **Map** 6 D2
248 Glenmore Rd, Paddington
Tel 0402 520 516
In a restored terrace house, Tiger
Mottle is a good place for
relaxing over a great coffee and
delicious brunch or burgers
against a backdrop of vinyl
records playing on the turntable.

10 William Street $$
Italian **Map** 6 D4
10 William St, Paddington
Tel 9360 3310 **Closed** *Sun*
A great vibe at this small wine
bar and restaurant that oozes
style. Servings are small, so don't
come hungry. Order tapas-style
dishes, and enjoy a matching
drink recommended by the
helpful bar staff.

The minimalist interiors of Saint Peter, a
seafood restaurant in Paddington

Bellevue Dining $$
Pub **Map** 6 E3
159 Hargrave St, Paddington
Tel 9363 2293
A Chefs Hat Award-winning
restaurant tucked away at the
back of a pub. There are more
upmarket offerings than in most
pubs, with European dishes taking
pride of place on the menu.

Big Mama's $$
Italian **Map** 6 E4
51 Moncur St, Woollahra
Tel 9328 7629 **Closed** *Mon*
A long-established, old-style
trattoria with a large menu
for lengthy, relaxed dinners.
The generous portions of
uncomplicated but delicious
food and friendly service mean
you'll feel like one of the family.

Bistro Moncur $$
French **Map** 6 E4
*The Woollahra Hotel, 116 Queen St,
Woollahra*
Tel 9327 9713
This stylish spot is more Paris
bistro than pub, delivering
a consistently good menu
of classic dishes, complemented
by daily specials made from
the best available Australian
seasonal produce.

Brigade Dining $$
Modern Australian **Map** 6 D4
2A Oxford St, Woollahra
Tel 9357 0815 **Closed** *Sun*
A contemporary restaurant
located above the Light
Bridge Hotel. Start with a
drink downstairs, then head
upstairs for dinner, where
generous servings of flavourful
food come jam-packed with
interesting ingredients.

Buzo $$
Modern European **Map** 6 D4
3 Jersey Rd, Woollahra
Tel 9328 1600 **Closed** *Mon*
Diners will be spoilt for choice
at this cosy restaurant that offers
a lighter take on traditional
European food and some classic
Australian dishes. There is a
seasonal à-la-carte menu, a bar
menu, a fantastic tasing menu
and an extensive wine list.

Four in Hand by Guillaume $$
Pub **Map** 6 E3
105 Sutherland St, Paddington
Tel 9326 2254
Savour sophisticated cuisine by
master French chef Guillaume
Brahimi in an intimate, casual
dining space. The same quality
food, but with some more
affordable options, is available
on the bar menu.

Fred's $$
Modern Australian   Map 6 D4
380 Oxford St, Woollahra
Tel *9240 3000*   **Closed** *Mon*
There's a commitment to ethically produced, sustainable local produce here, so you can feel good about your meal cooked on free-standing Tuscan grills and a custom-made hearth.

Hotel Centennial $$
Pub   Map 6 E5
88 Oxford St, Woollahra
Tel *9362 3838*
On a road overlooking Centennial Park, the relaxed dining area here is beautifully fitted out for dining in style. The menu offers a modern take on comfort food, using fresh, seasonal produce.

The London Hotel $$
Pub   Map 6 D3
85 Underwood St (cnr William St), Paddington
Tel *9331 3200*
You will not go hungry at this historic pub nestled in the winding back streets. There's an array of classics available here – pasta, steaks and fish – as well as a separate pizza menu. Warm, friendly service.

The Paddington $$
Modern Australian   Map 6 D4
384 Oxford St, Paddington
Tel *9240 3000*
Part relaxed pub, part cocktail bar, The Paddington serves up hearty rotisserie meats, fish, vegetables, and lighter meals to share. A late-night menu is available after 10:30pm.

Paddington Inn $$
Pub   Map 6 D4
338 Oxford St, Paddington
Tel *9380 5913*
A perennially popular pub. The front bar serves handmade burgers, whereas the contemporary dining room with white-washed brick walls has a modern menu.

DK Choice

Saint Peter $$
Seafood   Map 6 D4
362 Oxford St, Paddington
Tel *8937 2530*   **Closed** *Mon, Tue*
Exceptional sustainably sourced seafood is served with impeccable attention to detail in a minimalist setting. The menu changes daily and all parts of the fish are used innovatively to deliver taste without waste. There is a custom-designed cool room for dry-aged fish, as well as a dedicated pastry chef.

Beppi's, serving fine Italian classic dishes

Vino e Cucina $$
Italian   Map 5 C3
211 Glenmore Rd, Paddington
Tel *9331 7389*
Pasta, pizza and traditional dishes are made with fresh produce to create simple flavours. The service is friendly, but it can get loud and raucous during busy periods. The seats out the back are quieter. There's a good Italian wine list, too.

Wine Library $$
European   Map 6 D4
18 Oxford St, Woollahra
Tel *9360 5686*
An array of small dishes is offered to share here from a menu that spans charcuterie, items "from the sea", meats, salads, cheeses and desserts. There's also a 29-page wine list, in what must be Sydney's loudest library.

Buon Ricardo $$$
Italian   Map 5 C2
108 Boundary St, Paddington
Tel *9360 6729*   **Closed** *Sun, Mon*
Owner-chef Armando Percuoco has been serving up the fine flavours of Italy since 1987. The delicious food focuses on dishes from his native Naples, and is made to order; the truffled-egg fettuccine is tossed at the table.

Lucio's $$$
Italian   Map 6 D3
47 Windsor St, Paddington
Tel *9380 5996*   **Closed** *Sun, Mon*
An art gallery in a fine-dining restaurant – the walls are adorned with works by Australian artist Tim Storrier, and the menu covers are designed by another Australian artist, John Olsen. The artistry also extends to the food, which focuses on Northern Italian dishes; the pesto is even freshly ground at the table.

Further Afield

Badde Manors $
Café
37 Glebe Point Rd, Glebe
Tel *9660 3797*
Keeping the locals happy and nourished since 1992, the café fare here is simple and reliable. From the twin angels on the awning outside, to the retro fittings inside, the decor is quirky.

Il Baretto $
Italian   Map 5 A4
496 Bourke St, Surry Hills
Tel *9361 6163*   **Closed** *Sun, Mon*
Simple Italian cooking with home-made pasta is served in a crowded space that can mean queues for a table. The signature pappardelle duck *ragù* is a menu stalwart.

Belle's Hot Chicken $
Café   Map 4 D1
33 Barangaroo Ave, Barangaroo
Tel *8355 7879*
Spicy southern fried chicken is the speciality at this waterfront café, offering a variety of fast food, from chicken wings to chicken and waffles, and organic wines.

Bean Drinking $
Café
1/13 Ernest Place, Crows Nest
Tel *9436 1678*
This speciality coffee and espresso bar has a grass area out the front for the kids to run around on while grown-ups choose from the mostly organic all-day menu.

Brewtown $
Café
6–8 O'Connell St, Newtown
Tel *9519 2920*
This micro roaster and brew bar takes its coffee seriously. The breakfast and lunch menus feature seasonal, organic and pasture-fed produce.

For more information on types of restaurants *see pages 180–81*

Café Mint $
Middle Eastern
579 Crown St, Surry Hills
Tel *9319 0848*   **Closed** *Mon*
If the small cosy space doesn't warm your heart, the quality of the food will. Mediterranean and Lebanese classics pack a flavour punch – from hot breakfasts to lunch meze plates, with salad, dips and bread. Be sure to try the hummus and lamb mince.

The Crabbe Hole $
Café
1 Knotts Ave, Bondi Beach
Tel *0450 272 223*
A tiny spot but big on views and value. Perched above the Bondi Icebergs ocean pool, here you can grab a coffee, breakfast roll, sandwich or ice cream after swimming and see the beach life unfold. Great for people-watching.

Fika Swedish Kitchen $
Café
5B Market Lane
Tel *9976 5099*
A bright space with splashes of blue and yellow. Enjoy traditional Swedish breakfast offerings like Kalles cod roe on crispbread, washed down with Scandinavian hot chocolate or, later in the day, Swedish beer.

Kensington Street Social $
Contemporary
3 Kensington St, Chippenale
Tel *8277 8533*
A very modern and polished take on snacks, bread bases and drinks, including a Vegemite-infused cocktail, plus more substantial dishes, are served in a wonderful industrial heritage interior.

Maya $
Indian Vegetarian
470 Cleveland St, Surry Hills
Tel *9699 8663*
Join the diverse crowd of students, taxi drivers and foodies at this humble purveyor of authentic treats. Try *thali* plates of assorted curries and breads and the famous *masala dosa*. Finish with Indian fudge. A simple setting offering fabulous food.

Rabbit Hole Organic Tea Bar $
Café   **Map** 4 D1
Shop 1, 23 Barangaroo Ave, Barangaroo
Tel *9045 3756*
Tea lovers rejoice – here you will find everything from tea lattes to tea sodas on tap, with more than 120 original tea blends. The menu also features a delicious range of tea-inspired sweet and savoury foods.

Stunning view of the Sydney Harbour Bridge and Opera House at Aqua Dining

Shenkin Kitchen $
Middle Eastern Café
129 Enmore Rd, Enmore
Tel *9519 7463*
Awarded Sydney's best breakfast. It's worth the wait for the *shakshuka*, served in a copper pan with a thick, rich tomato sauce and soft-boiled eggs, with wads of bread to soak it up.

Sonoma $
Café
215A Glebe Point Rd, Glebe
Tel *9660 2116*
This place may be small in space but it is big on flavour – from the must-try breakfast rolls, which will keep you fuelled for hours, to the wonderful artisan breads.

Tom Yum Tum Gang $
Thai
249 Glebe Point Rd, Glebe
Tel *8065 0859*
It's always busy here, but the prompt, courteous service means you won't wait long to taste the home-style Thai that keeps locals coming back for more.

X74 Café $
Café
10 Bream St, Coogee
Tel *9665 2222*
This eatery draws a crowd away from the beach with classic breakfast choices on its all-day menu, and some filling dinner options in the evening.

3 Weeds Restaurant $$
Modern Australian
197 Evans St, Rozelle
Tel *9818 2788*   **Closed** *Sun, Mon*
Start with a drink at the bar at this pub-restaurant off Balmain and Rozelle's main drag, where the vibe is casual and comfortable. The food served in the stylish dining room is top-notch.

Aqua Dining $$
Italian
Cnr Paul & Northcliff Sts, Milson's Point
Tel *9964 9998*
This restaurant is perched above the North Sydney Olympic Pool, with a sweeping view across the harbour to the Bridge and Opera House. The food is good, if pricey, but it's mostly about the view.

Automata $$
Contemporary
5 Kensington St, Chippendale
Tel *5277 8555*   **Closed** *Mon*
In a warehouse-style interior, Automata offers a superb five-course set menu that changes regularly. Drinks range from wine, and beer to sake.

Barzura $$
Modern Australian
62 Carr St, Coogee
Tel *9665 5546*
A café, restaurant and bar, so come for breakfast, lunch, dinner or a drink, with spectacular views over Coogee Beach. There's even a healthy menu for the kids.

Mouthwatering Indian *thali*, as served at Maya, in Surry Hills

Bondi Trattoria $$
Italian
34 Campbell Parade, Bondi
Tel *9365 4303*
A long-time favourite on the strip opposite the beach, with some of the best pizza and *gelato* in the city. Get the day off to a great start with a filling "Bondi Trat" breakfast.

Chiswick $$
Modern Australian   **Map** 6 F3
65 Ocean St, Woollahra
Tel *8388 8688*
A delightful white, bright, cheerful casual dining venue in a small park with fresh produce from the kitchen garden. The menu includes a range of dishes for sharing – or just indulge yourself.

Continental Deli Bar & Bistro $$
Bistro
210 Australia St, Newtown
Tel *8624 3131*
Serving cured meats, fine cheeses, canned goods and all-things delicatessen, this is a good place for sophisticated bar snacks, and a quality wine list.

Coogee Pavillion $$
Modern Australian
169 Dolphin St, Coogee
Tel *9664 2900*
Family-friendly and fun, there's something for everyone in this multi-level, beachfront pavilion, from breakfast to oysters, burgers, grills and wood-fired pizza. There's even a nostalgic games area, barbershop and flower stand.

Garfish $$
Seafood
2/21 Broughton St, Kirribilli (off Burton St)
Tel *9922 4322*
The menu promises the best seafood from each season – you choose how you'd like it prepared. Try the locals' favourite, snapper pie, or go early for a breakfast of smoked salmon and eggs.

Glebe Point Diner $$
Modern Australian   **Map** 3 A4
407 Glebe Point Rd, Glebe
Tel *9660 2646*
Come here for wholesome hearty food from a seasonal menu, with the bread, butter and pasta all made from scratch and served in a relaxed space. A "local" feel, with friendly staff.

Hugo's Manly $$
Italian
Manly Wharf, East Esplanade, Manly
Tel *8116 8555*
Hip Sydney at its lazy, waterfront best. Contemporary Italian,

signature pizzas and decadent desserts are served at lunch or dinner, or try the Afternoon Deck menu (3–6pm) for light snacks, more pizza and sweet treats.

Icebergs Bistro $$
Bistro
Bondi Icebergs, 1 Notts Ave, Bondi
Tel *9130 3120*
An old-school club bistro: find a table, order hearty pub-style meals at the counter, and choose from a wide selection of drinks at the bar. Enjoy the same view as the very expensive restaurant upstairs. The place is packed at weekends, so come early to secure your spot.

Manly Wharf Hotel $$
Pub
Manly Wharf, 21 East Esplanade, Manly
Tel *9977 1266*
Steaks, burgers, chicken, salads, pizza, seafood and a kids' menu to keep the little ones happy – it's all on offer at this relaxed spot with harbour views that are worth the price alone. A friendly place with excellent staff.

**The Boathouse on
Blackwattle Bay** $$$
Modern Australian   **Map** 3 A3
End of Ferry Rd, Glebe
Tel *9518 9011*   **Closed** *Mon*
On the upper level of a boat shed, with views across the working harbour, here you will find a changing menu, but seafood dominates – which is not surprising, with the fish markets across the water. There's also an extensive oyster menu.

Catalina $$$
Modern Australian
1 Sunderland Ave, Lyne Park, Rose Bay
Tel *9371 0555*
Seafood is the speciality here, befitting the harbourside

location of this gastronomic icon. If you don't have the time – or wallet – for a long lunch or dinner, a bar menu provides a casual, affordable alternative.

Pilu at Freshwater $$$
Italian
End of Moore Rd, Freshwater
Tel *9938 3331*   **Closed** *Mon*
You will wish you could move into this gorgeous cottage by the beautiful Freshwater Beach. There are whitewashed walls, crisp white linen, attentive staff and food that will leave you very satisfied.

Sean's Panorama $$$
Modern Australian
270 Campbell Parade, Bondi
Tel *9365 4924*   **Closed** *Mon, Tue*
The tiny dining room here makes for an intimate experience – and means booking is essential. Sean's Panorama has been serving artful meals cooked with care since 1993, and the iconic handmade nougat is still the best.

Beyond Sydney

True to the Bean $
Café
123 Katoomba St, Katoomba
Tel *4782 6926*
Coffee and waffles are the dynamic duo here. Come for enough caffeine and sugar to fuel a day exploring the mountains or for a post-adventure afternoon tea break.

Ashcrofts $$$
European
18 Govetts Leap Rd, Blackheath
Tel *4787 8297*   **Closed** *Mon–Wed*
A cosy mountain hideaway with warm lighting, village hospitality and personal touches that whet the appetite for the meal ahead.

Manly Wharf Hotel – a beautiful setting for a friendly dining experience

For more information on types of restaurants *see pages 180–81*

SHOPS AND MARKETS

The range of goods on offer in Sydney is enormous. The city centre has numerous elegant arcades, shopping malls and boutiques, with plenty of nooks and crannies to explore. Major international labels, including luxury brands and high-street chains, sit alongside the best local talent in many fields, notably jewellery, fashion and indigenous arts and crafts. Markets sell everything from fresh produce to clothes. The most interesting shopping does not stop at the city centre; there are several "satellite" alternatives. Some of the best shopping areas are highlighted on pages 200–201.

A typical junk-shop-cum-café in Balmain (see p133)

Shopping Hours

Most shops are open from 10am to 5:30pm each day of the week, though some may close early on Sundays. On Thursdays, most shops stay open until 9pm. Most shops in Chinatown are open late every evening.

How to Pay

Major credit and debit cards are accepted almost everywhere. Department stores will exchange goods or refund your money if you are not satisfied, provided you have the receipt. Other stores will only refund if an item is faulty.

Prices include a 10 per cent Goods and Services Tax (GST).

Sales

Many shops conduct sales all year round. The big department stores of **David Jones** and **Myer** have two gigantic clearance sales each year. The post-Christmas sales start on 26 December, lasting into January. The other major sale time is during June, in the lead up to the end of the financial year.

Tax-Free Sales

Duty-free shops are found in the city centre as well as at Kingsford Smith Airport (see p228). You can save 10 per cent on goods such as perfume, jewellery and watches and perhaps up to 30 per cent on alcohol, but you must show your passport and onward ticket. Some stores will also deliver your goods to the airport to be picked up on departure. Duty-free items must be kept in their sealed bags until you leave the city.

You can claim back the GST paid on most goods, purchased for A$300 or more, at the airport (see p219).

Chifley Tower, with the Chifley Plaza shopping arcade at its base

Arcades and Malls

The **Queen Victoria Building** (see p84) is Sydney's most palatial shopping space. Four levels contain more than 200 shops. The top level, Victoria Walk, is devoted to merchandise such as silver, antiques, designer knitwear and high-quality souvenirs. The **Strand Arcade** (see p86) was originally built in 1892. Jewellery, designer wear, chocolates, coffee shops and tea rooms are its stock in trade.

Pitt Street Mall shopping precinct contains several shopping centres, including **Mid City Centre**, which has local and global brands popular with a young crowd and **Westfield Sydney**, featuring numerous local and international designer brand stores, including Zara, Leona Edmiston, Gucci and Gap.

Next door to the Hilton, **The Galeries** houses the fantastic Kinokuniya bookstore, which sells both Australian and American imprints as well as Chinese and Japanese language, anime art books and stationery. The Monsterthreads mixes folk and street art with

Inside Gleebooks, popular with students and locals in Glebe (see p133)

Greengrocer's display of fresh fruit and vegetables

contemporary graphic design on clothing, accessories, homeware, stationery, bags and jewellery lines and also sells brands like Loqi and MOMOT paper toys.

Further down George Street, **World Square** houses more than 90 speciality stores, from electronics to Australian menswear label Jack London.

The **MLC Centre**, which faces onto Castlereagh Street, and **Chifley Plaza** also cater to the prestige shopper. Cartier, Tiffany & Co., MaxMara and Kenzo are among the shops here.

The **Harbourside Shopping Centre** has dozens of shops, as well as waterfront restaurants. The atmosphere is festive and the merchandise includes fine arts, jewellery, duty-free shopping, beachwear and Australiana.

Department Stores

The **David Jones** and **Myer** chains compete fiercely, each snaring exclusive rights to stock

Part of the spring floral display, David Jones department store

local design talents and international labels. David Jones, or DJs, is legendary for its spring floral displays, luxurious perfumery and cosmetics. The magnificent store spreads out in two buildings, across the road from each other on Market and Elizabeth streets, while there is a smaller store in Barangaroo.

Both Myers and David Jones sell women's clothing, lingerie, menswear, baby goods, children's clothes, cosmetics, toys, stationery, electronical goods, kitchenware, furniture, china, crystal and silver.

Shopping Further Afield

Good shopping areas outside central Sydney are Balmain, for village-style shopping, and Double Bay, with its chic, though pricey, boutiques. Just south of the city fringe, in Chippendale and Broadway, are the small but stylish **Central Park Mall** and the bigger **Broadway Sydney**. For quirky gifts, head to Central Park Mall's Pigeonhole store. Shop for local and international brands, including Sephora and H&M at Broadway Sydney.

The enormous mega-mall **Westfield Bondi Junction** is only a short train journey from central Sydney, while the inner-west suburbs of Newtown and Glebe have Left Bank-style student haunts.

Bargains can be found at the factory outlets in the suburb of Redfern, at **Market City** and at **Birkenhead Point**, while **DFO**, near Sydney Olympic Park, has outlet stores selling luxury and popular brands.

Sydney's Best: Shopping Streets and Markets

Sydney's best shopping areas range from galleries, arcades and department stores selling expensive gifts and jewellery *(see pp198–9)*, to boutiques of extroverted cutting-edge fashion. The range of styles is impressive, encompassing both international couture brands and acclaimed local designer labels *(pp204–5)*. The city's hip fringe areas, such as Glebe and Surry Hills, are alive with street fashion and accessories.

Colourful markets are a delight for collectors and bargain-hunters alike *(p203)*. Those who seek out quirky and one-off items are well catered for, as are those looking to take home quality craft and Indigenous art as mementos of their visit. Specialist browsers will find a tempting selection of book and music shops *(pp206–7)*.

The Rocks Market
At weekends, the stalls offer affordable arts and crafts and jewellery. *(See p203.)*

THE ROC
AND
CIRCULA
QUAY

Darling Harbour
Quality Australiana, surf and beach wear, souvenir ideas, children's clothes, colourful knits and art and craft shops abound.

Queen Victoria Building
This elegant shopping gallery offers four floors of designer wear, gifts and speciality stores amid cafés.

CITY
CENT

0 metres   500
0 yards   500

DARLING
HARBOUR
AND
SURRY HILLS

Newtown
Trawl the stores along the suburb's main King Street for the best in original new, second-hand, offbeat and eclectic designer clothing, accessories, books and homewares.

Chinatown
This is the place to find watches, gold jewellery, opals and fabrics. There are also Chinese butchers shops, herbalists and supermarket Market City show cases emerging Asian trends and designers. *(See p2*

City Centre
Dazzling shopping arcades and smart malls are dotted throughout the city centre, notably Pitt Street Mall, Strand Arcade and Westfield Sydney.

Castlereagh Street
The city's designer row is home to Chanel, Gucci, Hermès and others. The most exclusive names cluster near the King Street intersection.

Darlinghurst and Surry Hills
These suburbs are the youth culture barometer: young designers, leather à la mode, gay fashion, hot music and gifts for those who love quirky collectables.

BOTANIC GARDEN AND THE DOMAIN

KINGS CROSS AND DARLINGHURST

PADDINGTON

Paddington Markets
Considered by many to be Sydney's best market and a showcase for up-and-coming fashions and designers, it is held every Saturday. (See p203.)

Paddington and Woollahra
Upmarket clothing, shoes, homeware and gourmet food are on show here, while cafés and galleries add to the allure. Queen Street, Woollahra, is the antique-shop strip.

Sydney Fish Market

Sydney is synonymous with fish and the Sydney Fish Market *(see p133)* is the ideal place to see the wide variety on offer. It is the largest fish market in the southern hemisphere and the world's third largest by range. Visitors can see the market's fishing fleet regularly docking and unloading, or watch displays of oyster-shucking in the shops, complete with sloshy floors and the distinct smell of uncooked seafood in the air.

For early risers, the behind-the-scenes tour gives a fascinating insight into the journey from ocean to plate, including a chance to watch the unusually quiet auction from a viewing gallery. Every day, 55 tonnes (tons) of fresh fish and other seafood is sold at the Fish Market's Dutch Clock auction. Prices start high, and gradually decrease on a digital display until a buyer makes a bid. The first bid is accepted, and the deal done.

For those who prefer a later start, the Sydney Seafood School operates above the market and offers lessons in preparing a range of delicious seafood dishes, which you get to enjoy after cooking. The market's retailers sell both fresh and cooked seafood on-site. There are also cafés, a sushi bar, bakery, gourmet deli and wine shop.

The low-rise Sydney Fish Market occupies a prime waterfront location at Pyrmont. The lively waterfront cafés are a great place to enjoy fresh seafood from the market.

Big-eye ocean perch, found off the coast of New South Wales, is one of the many types of fish available at the Sydney Fish Market. It can grow up to 40 cm (16½ in) in length and weigh up to 1.5 kg (3.3 lb). Its white flesh has a delicate flavour.

Selecting your Fish

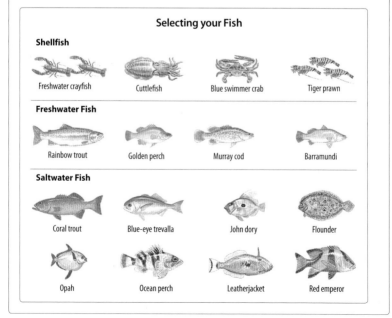

Shellfish

Freshwater crayfish   Cuttlefish   Blue swimmer crab   Tiger prawn

Freshwater Fish

Rainbow trout   Golden perch   Murray cod   Barramundi

Saltwater Fish

Coral trout   Blue-eye trevalla   John dory   Flounder

Opah   Ocean perch   Leatherjacket   Red emperor

Markets

Scouring markets for the cheap, the cheerful and the chic has become a popular weekend pastime in Sydney. Weekly or monthly markets that suit both the bargain-hunter and the serious shopper have sprung up all over the suburbs. Food-related markets are hugely popular, ranging from weekly fresh food and growers' markets in the suburbs to night markets in Chinatown and the popular Night Noodle Markets during the Good Food Month festival in October *(see p50)*.

Balmain Market

Cnr Darling St & Curtis Rd, Balmain. 🚌 *442, 434.* **Open** *8:30am–4pm Sat.*

Held in the grounds of St Andrew's Congregational Church in the shade of a fig tree said to be more than 150 years old, this compact market attracts both locals and tourists. Fees from stallholders contribute to the ongoing restoration of the church, which was built in 1853. As well as stalls selling children's wear, second-hand books, contemporary and antique jewellery, stained-glass mobiles and Chinese healing balls, there is a food hall where you can find fresh and aromatic Japanese, Thai, Indian and specialist vegetarian dishes in the making.

Bondi Beach Market

Bondi Beach Public School, Campbell Parade, North Bondi. 🚌 *333, 380.* **Open** *10am–5pm Sun in summer; 4pm in winter.*

Many Sydney fashion labels start off here, as did current darlings **Sass & Bide** *(see p204).* There are also lots of second-hand clothing buys; funky 1970s gear is particularly popular. Arrive early as some of the stalls are all set up by 9am. The best bargain clothes are near the back of the market. Expect to see the odd actor or rock star among the browsers.

The Entertainment Quarter

Lang Rd, Moore Park. **Map** *5 C5.* 🚌 *Oxford St or Anzac Pde routes.* **Open** *10am–3:30pm Wed, Sat, 10am–4pm Sun. (See p128.)*

There is plenty of fresh produce and gourmet delicacies to sample at the EQ Village Markets every Wednesday and Saturday, located next to the working Fox Studios, where films such as Mission: Impossible II and the Star Wars prequels were shot. There is a Merchandise Market on Sunday.

Glebe Market

Glebe Public School, Glebe Point Rd, Glebe. **Map** *3 B5.* 🚌 *431, 433.* **Open** *10am–4pm Sat.*

A treasure trove for the junk-shop enthusiast and canny scavenger, this market is popular with the inner-city grunge set. Best buys are bric-à-brac and crafts made from recycled wood, metal and glass. Arrive early for bargain porcelain and, perhaps, the odd undervalued lithograph. A few fashion students also sell their work. You will also find handmade bags, hats and jewellery. Second-hand clothes are a good buy here, as are rings and pendants, books, CDs and records.

Orange Grove Farmers' Markets

Cnr Balmain Rd & Perry St, Leichhardt. 🚌 *470.* 🚈 *Lilyfield.* **Open** *8am–1pm Sat.*

Arrive early for the best fresh organic produce, including fruit, vegetables and herbs straight from market gardens, homemade jams, spreads and dips, as well as fresh seafood and meat direct from producers. Stalls offer fresh cooked food such as pies, Turkish *gözleme* (stuffed flatbreads), dumplings, French pastries and artisan breads. There is also great handcrafted clothing and jewellery. For the kids, there is a small playground and a large grass area, as well as pony rides.

Paddington Markets

(See p128.)

From nouveau to novelties, there is always something tempting here, and it is unlikely you will come away empty-handed. Silver jewellery is abundant, so prices are very competitive; there are also children's clothes, leather goods, unusual buckles, belts and accessories, stationery, candles, and oddities such as babies' baseball caps and rubbery novelty masks.

Paddy's Markets

(See p101.)

In the 19th century, Paddy's in the Haymarket was the city's fringe market and also the location of fairgrounds and circuses. Today, it has between 500 and 1,000 stalls under one roof. Early birds will get the best flowers, fruit, vegetables and seafood. There are also good buys in caneware, luggage, leather goods, tools, homewares, ornaments, souvenirs and toys.

The Rocks Market

George St, The Rocks. **Map** *1 B2.* 🚌 *431, 432, 433, 434.* **Open** *10am–5pm Sat & Sun.*

At weekends, rain or shine, a sail-like canopy is erected at the top end of George Street, transforming the area into an atmospheric marketplace. Get there early to beat the afternoon crowds. There are about 140 stalls, whose wares are unique rather than inexpensive. Quality is a priority here. Look out for wind chimes, pewter picture frames, pub poster prints, oils, leather goods, wooden toys, gold-plated bush leaves, and jewellery made from wood, shell, silver or crystal. Every Friday in November The Rocks Market hosts "Markets by Moonlight", a combination of night markets, live music and outdoor bars and food stalls.

Chinatown Markets

Dixon St Plaza. **Map** *4 D4.* 🚈 *Central.* 🚈 *Paddy's Markets.* **Open** *4–11pm Fri. (See pp100–101.)*

This bustling late-night market on Fridays showcases local designers, Asian street food and an array of products. It consists of more than 50 stalls operated by students, young designers and local artists with Asian heritage or whose designs draw on Asian culture. The "Little Eat Street" food stalls offer cuisines from Hong Kong to Hanoi, including *yum cha*, teppanyaki, sushi and the popular Vietnamese noodle soup, *pho*.

Carriageworks Farmers Markets

245 Wilson St, Eveleigh. 🚌 *352, 370, 423, 426, 442.* **Open** *8am–1pm Sat.*

These farmers' and artisans' markets, with a focus on fresh local produce and creative arts and crafts, are held in a historic railway workshop a short walk from Redfern train station.

Clothes and Accessories

Australian style was once an oxymoron. Sydney now offers a plethora of chic shops as long as you know where to look. Top boutiques sell both men's and women's clothing, as well as accessories. The city's "smart-casual" ethos, particularly in summer, means there are plenty of luxe but informal clothes available.

Australian Fashion

A number of Sydney's fashion designers have attained a global profile, including **Akira Isogawa**. Japanese-born Isogawa makes artistic clothing for women and men. Some of the most interesting fashion is from young emerging designers like **Kaliver**, who began designing at age 12.

Young jeans label **Sass & Bide** (women only) has also shot to fame, with celebrities wearing their denims. **Scanlan & Theodore** is another stalwart of the Australian fashion scene, as is **Country Road**, known for its stylish office- and weekend-wear.

For retro women's and children's clothes head to **Dragstar**. **Jack London** stocks upscale, trendy menswear; their suits are particularly popular. The **Tigerlily** swimwear brand offers comfortable dresses perfect for summer, while **Zimmermann** stocks women's and girls' clothes and is famous for its swimwear. **Camilla** is known for its flamboyant, colourful print kaftans and dresses. Head to **Farage Women** for classic tailored suits and shirts.

High-street clothing can be found in and around Pitt Street Mall and Bondi Junction. Here you will find both international and homegrown fashion outlets. **Sportsgirl** sells funky clothes that appeal to both teens and adult women. The **Witchery** stores are a favourite among women for their stylish designs. **Just Jeans** doesn't just sell jeans; it stocks the latest trends for men and women.

General Pants has funky street labels like One Teaspoon and Just Ask Amanda. Surry Hills is the place for discount and vintage clothing; check out **Zoo Emporium**. New designers try out their wares in Bondi, Glebe and Paddington markets.

International Labels

Many Sydney stores sell designer imports. For the best ranges, visit **Belinda** – a men's and women's boutique – as well as others in Double Bay, and the MLC Centre. For shoe addicts, **Cosmopolitan Shoes** stocks the latest designs straight from the runway of labels such as Dolce & Gabbana, Sonia Rykiel and Dior. **Jimmy Choo**'s cutting-edge designer footwear and luxury accessories can be found in the MLC Centre. **Hype DC** offers all the latest youth ranges. For classic tailored suits and shoes, head to the King Street store of German fashion house, **Hugo Boss**.

Luxury Brands

You'll find international labels such as **Louis Vuitton** in Castlereagh Street, along with **Chanel**. The Queen Victoria Building is home to **Bally**, and Martin Place has resident A-listers such as **Prada** and **Giorgio Armani**. **Girls With Gems** has Australian designer fashions and is further afield in Double Bay.

Surf Shops

For the latest surf gear, look no further than Bondi where the streets are lined with shops selling clothing, swimwear and boards of all sizes to buy and hire. Serious surfers and novices should check out **Between the Flags** and **Bondi Surf Co**. Besides stocking its own beachwear label, **Rip Curl** also sells Australian brands such as Tigerlily (see above) and Billabong. **Surfection** and **Surf Dive 'n' Ski** are hugely popular surf- and skatewear shops packed with the latest fashion and performance brands and accessories.

Clothes for Children

Department stores, **David Jones** and **Myer** (see pp199), are one-stop shops for children's clothes, from newborn to teenage. **Bardot Junior** and **Pavement** have a fashionable range of well-made clothing for youngsters, with stores at most major

Size Chart

Women's clothes

Australian	6	8	10	12	14	16	18	20
American	4	6	8	10	12	14	16	18
British	6	8	10	12	14	16	18	20
Continental	38	40	42	44	46	48	50	52

Women's shoes

Australian	6–6½	7	7½–8	8½	9–9½	10	10½–11	
American	5	6	7	8	9	10	11	
British	3	4	5	6	7	8	9	
Continental	36	37	38	39	40	41	42	

Men's suits

Australian	44	46	48	50	52	54	56	58
American	34	36	38	40	42	44	46	48
British	34	36	38	40	42	44	46	48
Continental	44	46	48	50	52	54	56	58

Men's shirts

Australian	36	38	39	41	42	43	44	45
American	14	15	15½	16	16½	17	17½	18
British	14	15	15½	16	16½	17	17½	18
Continental	36	38	39	41	42	43	44	45

Men's shoes

Australian	7	7½	8	8½	9	10	11	12
American	7	7½	8	8½	9½	10½	11	11½
British	6	7	7½	8	9	10	11	12
Continental	39	40	41	42	43	44	45	46

shopping centres. The popular **Seed Heritage** store at the Broadway Shopping Centre caters for children and babies.

Accessories

The team behind **Dinosaur Designs** are some of Australia's most celebrated designers. They craft chunky bangles, necklaces and rings, and also bowls, plates and vases, from jewel-coloured resin. **Chilli Coral** sells home decor and gifts, including Australian-made Samantha Ronson bowls, Bison tableware, vintage bottles and handmade jewellery. At trendy **Family Jewels**, unique silver creations feature Australian pearls, nautilus shell and crystals. They also showcase international designers. In her plush store, **Jan Logan** sells exquisite jewellery, using precious and semi-precious stones. Australian hat designer **Helen Kaminski** uses fabrics, raffia, straw, felt and leather to make hats and bags. In a different style, **Crumpler** uses high-tech fabrics to make bags that will last a century. And in a street of designer names, **Andrew McDonald**'s little studio shop doesn't cry for attention, but he does sell handcrafted shoes for men and women.

DIRECTORY

Australian Fashion

Akira Isogawa
12A Queen St, Woollahra. **Map** 6 E4. **Tel** 9361 5221.
Level 2, Strand Arcade. **Map** 1 B4. **Tel** 9232 1078.

Camilla
132A Warners Ave, Bondi. **Tel** 9130 1430.

Country Road
Ground level, Queen Victoria Building. **Map** 1 B5. **Tel** 9261 2009.

Dragstar
535A King St, Newtown. **Tel** 9550 1243.

Farage Women
Shop 79, Level 1, Strand Arcade. **Map** 1 B5. **Tel** 9233 1272.

General Pants
Ground level, Westfield Sydney, Pitt St Mall. **Map** 1 B5. **Tel** 8275 5160.

Jack London
World Square Shopping Centre, 680 George St. **Map** 4 E3. **Tel** 9261 2012.

Just Jeans
Shop 56, Mid City Centre, Pitt St Mall. **Map** 4 E2. **Tel** 9223 1696.

Kaliver
428 Oxford St, Paddington. **Map** 6 D4. **Tel** 8283 8542.

Sass & Bide
132 Oxford St, Paddington. **Map** 5 B3. **Tel** 9360 3900.

Scanlan & Theodore
122 Oxford St, Paddington. **Map** 5 B3. **Tel** 9380 9388.

Sportsgirl
Street level, Westfield Sydney, Pitt St Mall. **Map** 1 B5. **Tel** 9223 8255.

Tigerlily
Westfield Sydney, Pitt St Mall. **Map** 1 B5. **Tel** 9221 1665.

Witchery
Shop 3, Met Centre, 273 George St. **Map** 1 B4. **Tel** 9252 8450.

Zimmermann
Shop 2, 2–16 Glenmore Rd, Paddington. **Map** 5 B3. **Tel** 9357 4700.

Zoo Emporium
180B Campbell St, Surry Hills. **Map** 5 A2. **Tel** 9380 5990.

International Labels

Belinda
8 Transvaal Ave, Double Bay. **Tel** 9328 6288.

Cosmopolitan Shoes
Shop 1, 5 Knox St, Double Bay. **Tel** 9362 0510.

Hugo Boss
97 King St. **Map** 1 B5. **Tel** 9223 9211.

Hype DC
Shop 50, Queen Victoria Building, 455 George St. **Map** 1 B5. **Tel** 9262 7444.

Jimmy Choo
MLC Centre, 41 Castlereagh St. **Map** 1 B4. **Tel** 8666 0606.

Luxury Brands

Bally
Ground floor, Queen Victoria Building, 455 George St. **Map** 1 B5. **Tel** 9267 3887.

Chanel
70 Castlereagh St. **Map** 1 B5. **Tel** 1300 242 635.

Giorgio Armani
4 Martin Place. **Map** 1 B4. **Tel** 8233 5888.

Girls With Gems
Shop 15, 28–34 Cross St, Double Bay. **Tel** 9328 3056.

Louis Vuitton
365 George St. **Map** 1 B4. **Tel** 1300 883 880.

Prada
Level 5, Westfield Sydney, Castlereagh St.
Map 1 B5. **Tel** 9231 3929.

Surf Shops

Between the Flags
152–158 Campbell Parade, Bondi Beach. **Tel** 9365 5611.

Bondi Surf Co.
80 Campbell Parade, Bondi Beach. **Tel** 9365 0870.

Rip Curl
82 Campbell Parade, Bondi Beach. **Tel** 9130 2660.

Surf Dive 'n' Ski
Westfield Bondi Junction, 500 Oxford St. **Tel** 9387 6170.

Surfection
31 Hall St, Bondi Beach. **Tel** 9130 1051.

Clothes For Children

Bardot Junior
Westfield Bondi Junction, 500 Oxford St. **Map** 4 F3. **Tel** 9387 7057.

David Jones
See pp198–9.

Myer
See pp198–9.

Pavement
Westfield Bondi Junction, 500 Oxford St. **Map** 4 F3. **Tel** 9387 2899.

Seed Heritage
Broadway Shopping Centre, 1 Bay St. **Map** 3 C5. **Tel** 9211 9066.

Accessories

Andrew McDonald
Second floor, Strand Arcade. **Map** 1 B5. **Tel** 8084 2595.

Chilli Coral
401 Crown St, Surry Hills. **Map** 5 A3. **Tel** 8021 7869.

Crumpler
The Strand Arcade. **Map** 1 B5. **Tel** 9222 1300.

Dinosaur Designs
See pp206–7.

Family Jewels
48 Oxford St, Paddington. **Map** 6 E4. **Tel** 9331 6647.

Helen Kaminski
Shop 3, Four Seasons Hotel, 199 George St. **Map** 1 B3. **Tel** 9251 9850.

Jan Logan
36 Cross St, Double Bay. **Tel** 9363 2529.

Specialist Shops and Souvenirs

Sydney offers an extensive range of gift and souvenir ideas, from unset opals and jewellery to Aboriginal art and hand-crafted souvenirs. Museum shops, such as at the Museum of Sydney *(see p87)* and the Art Gallery of NSW *(see pp110–13)*, often have specially commissioned items that make great presents or reminders of your visit.

One-Offs

Specialist shops abound in Sydney – some practical, some eccentric, others simply indulgent. **R M Williams**' stock-man's gear includes its signature cowboy-style boots, belts, clothes and accessories. You can find unique, stylish leather goods such as wallets, handbags and sandles at **Leo Monk**, while **Yoshi Jones** features unique Australian designs with a Japanese aesthetic. Vintage silk kimonos are unpicked, cut by hand and transformed into innovative styles.

Wheels & Doll Baby is a powder-room, with 1950s chic, a mix of rock'n'roll and Hollywood glamour. **The Hour Glass** stocks traditional-style watches, while milliner **Rosie Boylan** creates bespoke lifestyle headwear in her Newtown studio.

Australiana

Australiana has become more than just a souvenir genre; it is now an art form in itself.

Artist Ken Done's distinctive prints feature on posters, scarves, books and more, are available at his small **Ken Done Gallery**. The shop at the **Art Gallery of New South Wales** stocks art books, posters, prints and gifts. The **Australia the Gift** store sells products ranging from clothing to quirky tea bag holders. The Queen Victoria Building's Victoria Walk *(see p84)* is dominated by Australiana: souvenirs, silver, antiques, art and crafts.

The **Australian Museum** *(see pp90–91)* has a shop that sells unusual gift items such as native flower presses, bark paintings and Australian animal puppets and puzzles, as well as Sydney designers Corban & Blair's upcycled sets of boxed plates.

Books

The large **Dymocks** store has a good range of guidebooks and maps on Sydney, as well as stationery and art supplies. For more eclectic browsing, try **Abbey's Bookshop**, **Ariel** and **Gleebooks**. **Berkelouw Books** has three floors of new, second-hand and rare books. **The Book-shop Darlinghurst** specializes in gay and lesbian fiction and non-fiction. The **State Library of NSW** *(see p114)* bookshop has a good choice of Australian books, particularly on history. **Kinokuniya** regularly hosts book-related events *(see p198)*.

Music

Several specialist music shops of international repute can be found in Sydney. Sydney's largest inde-pendent music retailer, **Red Eye Records**, is for the streetwise, with its stock of collectables, rarities and alternative music. **Suzie Q Coffee + Records** has an eclectic mix of LPs and offers a good caffeine hit. **Mojo Record Bar** has a great selection of rock, blues, country and psychedelia. **The Record Store** offers music from jazz to electronica and also sells turntables, needles, and other accessories for vinyl-lovers, while **Utopia Records** has an impressively comprehensive stock of hard rock and heavy metal. **Fish Fine Music** specializes in classical music and jazz.

Aboriginal Art

Traditional paintings, fabric, jewellery, boomerangs, cards and carvings can be bought at the **Aboriginal and Pacific Art**. You can find tribal artifacts from Aboriginal Australia at several shops in the Harbourside Shopping Centre, Darling Harbour. The **Coo-ee Aboriginal Art Gallery** boasts a large selection of limited edition prints, hand-printed fabrics, books and Aboriginal music. The **Kate Owen Gallery & Studio** in Rozelle features a wide range of contemporary Aboriginal art displayed over three floors. With works by numerous indigenous artists, it has been voted one of Sydney's best Aboriginal art galleries. Works and accessories by urban indigenous artists are found at the **Boomalli Aboriginal Artists' Cooperative**.

Opals

Sydney offers a variety of opals in myriad settings. **Opal Minded**, an Australian family-owned business, uses opals sourced from its own mines in Queensland. At **Opal Fields** you can view a museum collection of opalised fossils, before buying from the wide range of gems. **Giulian's** has unset opals, including blacks from Lightning Ridge, whites from Coober Pedy and boulder opals from Quilpie.

Jewellery

Long-established Sydney jewellers with 24-carat reputations include **Fairfax & Roberts**, **Hardy Brothers** and **Percy Marks**. World-class pearls are found in the waters off the northwestern coast of Australia. Rare and beautiful examples can be found at **Paspaley Pearls**.

Bill Hicks Jewellery's award-winning owner can create unique one-off pieces according to your designs. Alternatively, browse their ready-made collection. **Dinosaur Designs** made its name with colourful, chunky resin jewellery, while at **Love & Hatred**, jewelled wrist cuffs, rings and crosses recall lush medieval treasures. **Jan Logan** is a leading Australian jewellery designer, with stores in Melbourne, Hong Kong and London. Choose from beautiful and unusual contemporary pieces of the highest quality; the shop also carries antiques.

DIRECTORY

One-Offs

The Hour Glass
142 King St.
Map 1 B5.
Tel 9221 2288.

Leo Monk
417 King St.
Map 1 B5.
Tel 9557 5728.

R M Williams
Level 4, Westfield
Sydney, Pitt St.
Map 4 E2.
Tel 9223 7978.

Rosie Boylan
273 Australia St,
Newtown.
Tel 9557 1378.

Wheels & Doll Baby
259 Crown St,
Darlinghurst.
Map 5 A2.
Tel 9361 3286.

Yoshi Jones
Level 1, 249 King St,
Newtown.
Map 4 E2.
Tel 9550 1663.

Australiana

**Art Gallery of New
South Wales Shop**
Art Gallery Rd.
Map 2 D4.
Tel 9225 1700.

Australia the Gift
312 George St.
Map 1 B4.
Tel 9223 4066.

**Australian Museum
Shop**
6 College St.
Map 4 F3.
Tel 9320 6150.

Ken Done Gallery
1 Hickson Rd, The Rocks.
Map 1 B1.
Tel 8274 4599.
w kendone.com.au

Books

Abbey's Bookshop
131 York St.
Map 1 A5.
Tel 9264 3111.

Ariel
42 Oxford St,
Paddington.
Map 5 B3.
Tel 9332 4581.

Berkelouw Books
19 Oxford St, Paddington.
Map 5 B3. **Tel** 9360 3200.
Also at: 70 Norton St,
Leichhardt. **Tel** 9560 3200.
w berkelouw.com.au

**The Bookshop
Darlinghurst**
207 Oxford St,
Darlinghurst.
Map 5 A2.
Tel 9331 1103.

Dymocks
424 George St.
Map 1 B5.
Tel 9235 0155.
One of many branches.

Gleebooks
49 Glebe Point Rd,
Glebe. **Map** 3 B5.
Tel 9660 2333.

Kinokuniya
Level 2, The Galeries,
500 George St.
Map 1 B5.
Tel 9262 7996.

**State Library of NSW
Shop**
Macquarie St.
Map 1 C4.
Tel 9273 1611.

Music

Fish Fine Music
Shop 40, Level 2, Queen
Victoria Building.
Map 1 B5.
Tel 9264 6458

Mojo Record Bar
Basement level,
73 York St. **Map** 1 A4.
Tel 9262 4999.

The Record Store
255 Crown St,
Darlinghurst. **Map** 5 A4.
Tel 9380 8223.

Red Eye Records
143 York St,.
Map 1 A5.
Tel 9267 7440.

**Suzie Q Coffee +
Records**
1/18 Hutchinson St,
Surry Hills.
Map 5 A3.
Tel 9332 2739.

Utopia Records
Lower Ground floor, 511
Kent St (entrance on
Bathurst St).
Map 4 D3.
Tel 9571 6662.

Aboriginal Art

**Aboriginal and
Pacific Art**
2 Danks St, Waterloo.
Tel 9699 2211.

**Boomalli Aboriginal
Artists' Cooperative**
55–59 Flood St,
Leichhardt. **Tel** 9560 2541.

**Coo-ee Aboriginal
Art Gallery**
31 Lamrock Ave, Bondi
Beach. **Tel** 9300 9233.

**Kate Owen Gallery &
Studio**
680 Darling St, Rozelle.
Tel 9555 5283.

Opals

Giulian's
Level 3, Four Seasons
Hotel, 199 George St.
Map 1 B3.
Tel 9247 5630.
Also at: 98 Harrington St,
The Rocks. **Tel** 9252 2051.

Opal Fields
Queen Victoria Building,
George St, The Rocks.
Map 1 B5.
Tel 9264 6660.
One of two branches.

Opal Minded
55 George Street,
The Rocks.
Map 1 B2.
Tel 9247 9885.

Jewellery

Bill Hicks Jewellery
Suite 1005/155 King St.
Map 4 E1.
Tel 9231 0994.

Dinosaur Designs
Strand Arcade.
Map 1 B5.
Tel 9223 2953.
One of two branches.

Fairfax & Roberts
19 Castlereagh St.
Map 1 B5.
Tel 9232 8511.

Hardy Brothers
60 Castlereagh St.
Map 1 B5.
Tel 8262 3100.

Jan Logan
36 Cross St, Double Bay.
Tel 9363 2529.

Love & Hatred
Strand Arcade.
Map 1 B5. **Tel** 9233 3441.

Paspaley Pearls
2 Martin Place.
Map 1 A4. **Tel** 9232 7633.

Percy Marks
70 Castlereagh St.
Map 1 B5.
Tel 1800 651 825.

ENTERTAINMENT IN SYDNEY

Sydney has the standard of entertainment and nightlife you would expect from a cosmopolitan city. Everything from opera and ballet at Sydney Opera House to open-air productions in the Botanic Garden is on offer. The multi-theatre ICC Sydney at Darling Harbour *(see p100)* and large venues in the suburb of Homebush host major concerts. The Capitol, Sydney Lyric and Theatre Royal stage the latest musicals, while Sydney's many smaller theatres host interesting fringe events, modern dance and rock and pop concerts. Pub rock thrives in the inner city. Movie buffs are well catered for with film festivals, art-house films and foreign titles, as well as the latest Hollywood blockbusters. Comedy shows take place at small venues most nights of the week, and the Sydney Comedy Festival is a highlight of the spring calendar *(see p211)*. Free outdoor entertainment is a feature of the summer.

Modern dance at the Roslyn Packer Theatre *(see p210)*

Information

For details of events in the city, you should check the online listings calendars provided by the **City of Sydney**, **Tourism NSW** and major news websites. The printed versions of the daily newspapers also carry cinema, and often arts and theatre, listings and advertisements. The most comprehensive listings appear in the *Sydney Morning Herald*'s "Spectrum" section on Saturdays. The *Daily Telegraph* has good entertainment coverage on most days.

Tourism NSW has information kiosks at Circular Quay and Chinatown, which have free guides and the quarterly *What's on*, while the City of Sydney's One-Stop Shop at Town Hall *(see p221)* provides information services, too. *Where Magazine* is available at the airport and the **Sydney Visitor Centre** at The Rocks. Hotels offer free guides, or try the **True Local** website.

Music fans are well served by the free weekly guide *The Music*, found at video and music shops, pubs and clubs, or online at www.themusic.com.au.

Buying Tickets

Some of the most popular operas, shows, plays and ballets in Sydney are sold out months in advance. While it is better to book ahead, some theatres set aside tickets to be sold at the door on the night.

The easiest way to buy tickets is online, either through the major ticket agencies or the venue's official website, although you may be placed in "electronic queues" if it is a major event. You can also buy tickets from the box office or by telephone. Some orchestral performances do not admit children under seven, so check before buying. If you make a phone booking using a credit card, the tickets can be mailed to you. Alternatively, tickets can be collected from the box office an hour before the show. The major agencies will take overseas bookings by phone if you have a valid credit card.

Buying tickets from touts is not advisable. Unscrupulous sellers have been known to sell electronically delivered "e-tickets" and their PDF attachments multiple times. In such a case, the ticket's barcode will only allow entry to the first person to enter the venue. It is legal to sell on a ticket, but not for more than the original cost.

Choosing Seats

Whether booking in person at either the venue or the agency or booking online, you will be able to look at a seating plan by price category and date availability, and choose your own seat. Check seating plans carefully, as many venues have unusual lettering: Row A may not always be the front row.

In Sydney, there is not much difference in price between seats in the side and to the rear of the stalls and the dress

The annual Sydney Gay and Lesbian Mardi Gras Festival's Dog Show *(see p51)*

circle, but prime seats located towards the front and in the centre do command a premium.

If booking by phone, you will only be able to get a rough idea of where your seats are. The computer will select the "best available" tickets.

Booking Agencies

Sydney has two main ticket agencies: **Ticketek** and **Ticketmaster**. Between them, they represent all the major entertainment and sporting events. Although both agencies operate manned ticketing outlets (check the websites for locations and opening hours), booking online is quickest and easiest. When booking online, electronic tickets can be delivered via email or to a mobile phone.

A booking fee applies to all bookings, whether made online, by phone or in person, plus a postage and handling charge if tickets are mailed out via registered post. There are generally no refunds (unless a show is cancelled) or exchanges. Ticket insurance can be bought for protection against lost tickets or for inability to attend a performance

Discount Tickets and Free Entertainment

Tuesday is budget-price day at most cinemas. Some independent cinemas have special prices throughout the week. The Sydney Symphony Orchestra and Opera Australia (see p212) offer a special Student Rush price to full-time students under 28 but only if surplus tickets are available. These can be bought on the day of the performance, from the box office at the venue.

The Belvoir and Ensemble theatres (see pp210–11) offer discounted tickets for students for most shows.

Outdoor events are especially popular in Sydney, and many are free (see pp50–53). Sydney Harbour is a splendid setting for the fabulous New Year's Eve fireworks, with a display at

The Spanish firedancers Els Comediants at the Sydney Festival

9pm for families, as well as the midnight display.

The Sydney Festival in January is a huge extravaganza of performance and visual art. Various outdoor venues in The Rocks, Darling Harbour and in front of the Opera House feature events to suit every taste, including musical productions, drama, dance, exhibitions and circuses. The most popular free events are the symphony and jazz concerts held in The Domain. Also popular is the spectacular Vivid Sydney festival that runs for more than three weeks from late May to June (see p52).

Disabled Visitors

Many older venues were not designed with the disabled visitor in mind, but this has been redressed in most newer

The highly respected Australian Chamber Orchestra (see p212)

buildings, with designated seats available for those requiring special assistance. It is best to phone the box office before buying your tickets to request special seating and other requirements, or call **Ideas Inc**'s free information service for a list of Sydney's most wheelchair-friendly venues. The **Sydney Opera House** has disabled parking, wheelchair access and a loop system in the Concert Hall for the hearing impaired. A brochure, *Services for the Disabled*, is also available.

DIRECTORY

Useful Information

City of Sydney
🅆 whatson.cityofsydney.nsw.gov.au

Ideas Inc
Tel 1800 029 904.

Sydney Opera House
Information Desk: Tel 9250 7111.
Bookings & Disabled Information: Tel 9250 7175.

Sydney Visitor Centre
Tel 8273 0000 or 9281 2244.
🅆 sydney.com

Tourism NSW
🅆 visitnsw.com.au
🅆 bestof.com.au/nsw/

True Local
🅆 truelocal.com.au

Ticket Agencies

Ticketek
Tel 132 849. 🅆 ticketek.com.au
🅆 premier.ticketek.com.au

Ticketmaster
Tel 136 100.
🅆 ticketmaster.com.au

Theatre and Film

Sydney's theatrical venues are well known for their atmosphere and quality. There is a stimulating range of productions, from musicals, classic plays and Shakespeare to contemporary, fringe and experimental theatre. Comedy also has a strong foothold, with celebrated performers as well as upcoming artists performing on small stages and at major festivals. Prominent playwrights include David Williamson, Debra Oswald, Brendan Cowell, Stephen Sewell, Louis Nowra and Andrew Upton.

Australian film-making also has an excellent international reputation. A rich variety of both local and foreign films is screened throughout the year.

Theatre

Sydney's large musical productions are staged at the **Theatre Royal**, the **Sydney Lyric** theatre at The Star, the opulent **State Theatre** (see p84) and the **Capitol Theatre** (see p101).

Smaller venues also offer a range of interesting plays and performances. These include the **Seymour Theatre Centre**, which has three theatres; the **Belvoir**, which has two; the **Ensemble Theatre**, a theatre-in-the-round by the water; and the **Footbridge Theatre**. The **Griffin Theatre** specializes in works by new Australian playwrights, while the **Old Fitz Theatre**, located in the back lanes of the historic Woolloomooloo area, is a 60-seat venue that stages classic and contemporary theatre. **Carriageworks** presents an ambitious and risk-taking artistic programme reflecting social and cultural diversity. The **Parade Theatre** at the National Institute of Dramatic Arts (NIDA) showcases work by NIDA's acting, directing and production

students throughout the year. The well-respected **Sydney Theatre Company** (STC) stages some of the most acclaimed productions, often featuring big-name performers. Most STC productions are at **The Wharf** or the **Roslyn Packer Theatre** at Walsh Bay, though some are staged in the Drama Theatre of the Sydney Opera House (see pp76–9).

The **Bell Shakespeare Company** interprets the Bard with an innovative slant without tampering with the original text. Its productions are ideal for young or wary theatre-goers.

Street performances and open-air theatre are popular during the summer months when life in Sydney moves outdoors. **Shakespeare Australia** puts on open-air productions in the Botanic Garden in January.

For the adventurous, the **Sydney Festival** (see p51) offers a celebration of original, often quirky, Australian theatre, dance, music and visual arts. Once considered somewhat frivolous, it has developed the reputation of having serious artistic depth.

Children's Theatre

Sydney thrives on spectacles that delight children, and their parents. You will often find jugglers, mime artists, buskers and magic shows at Circular Quay and around Darling Harbour (see p93). The Sydney Opera House regularly has performances for children.

In the suburb of Killara, the **Marian St Theatre for Young People** stages the occasional theatrical production. With luck, you may even be able to see a performance by the incredibly athletic **Flying Fruit Fly Circus**. This troupe of boys and girls, aged from eight to 18, excels in aerial gymnastics and has an annual residence at the Sydney Opera House.

Film

The city's largest cinema complex, the **Event Cinemas** multiplex is in George Street, just one block south of Town Hall, and screens the most recent film releases. Similar multiplexes, such as **Hoyts at Broadway**, can be found at the Broadway Shopping Centre, in the Entertainment Quarter on Driver Avenue, and in Bondi Junction in the Westfield Shopping Centre.

Cinephiles flock to the **Palace Norton St Cinema** at Norton Street, and to the **Dendy Cinemas** at Newtown and Opera Quays. **Cinema Paris** shows arthouse and indie films, and often screens Bollywood movies as well. The **Chauvel Cinema** at Paddington Town Hall screens the best of independent and world movies in a lovely space with proscenium-arched stage.

For a movie and a meal, **Govinda's** (see p193), which is also an Indian restaurant, screens films that have just finished their run at the cinemas. The admission price includes a tasty vegetarian buffet dinner.

The latest screenings are usually at 9:30pm, although most major cinema complexes run shows up to as late as midnight. Commercial cinema houses offer reduced-price tickets on Tuesday, while Palace and Dendy do so on Monday.

Film Festivals

The **Sydney Film Festival** is a highlight of the city's calendar (see p53), screening some 200 new features, shorts and

Film Censorship Ratings

G For general exhibition
PG Parental guidance recommended for those under 15 years
M 15+ Recommended for mature audiences aged 15 and over
MA 15+ Restricted to people 15 years and over
R 18+ Restricted to adults 18 years and over

documentaries from all over the globe. The main venue is the State Theatre but other venues hold satellite screenings.

The **Flickerfest International Short Film Festival** (see p51) is held at the Bondi Pavilion Amphitheatre at Bondi Beach in early January. It screens shorts and animation films from around the world. In February, **Tropfest** (see p51) holds open-air screenings of the best short films for its annual competition.

Run by Queer Screen, the **Mardi Gras Film Festival** (see p51), starts mid-February and continues for 15 days. Films dealing with issues relevant to the lesbian, gay and transgender community are shown at various inner-city venues.

Comedy

Sydney's most established comedy venue, the **Comedy Store** is known for performances by the best of the touring comedians. Monday is comedy night at **The Old Manly Boatshed**, where both local and visiting comics perform. The **Harold Park Hotel** also hosts regular comedy nights every week. From late April until late May, the annual **Sydney Comedy Festival** features top acts by seasoned professionals and newcomers alike, with events taking place at dozens of venues across the city (see p52).

DIRECTORY

Theatre

Bell Shakespeare Company
Tel 8298 9000.
w bellshakespeare. com.au

Belvoir
25 Belvoir St, Surry Hills.
Tel 9699 3444.
w belvoir.com.au

Capitol Theatre
13 Campbell St, Haymarket. **Map** 4 E4.
Tel 9320 5000.
Box Office: **Tel** 1300 558 878. w capitoltheatre. com.au

Carriageworks
245 Wilson St, Eveleigh.
Tel 8571 9099.
w carriageworks. com.au

Ensemble Theatre
78 McDougall St, Kirribilli.
Tel 9929 8877.
Box Office: **Tel** 9929 0644.
w ensemble.com.au

Footbridge Theatre
University of Sydney, Parramatta Rd, Glebe.
Map 3 A5. **Tel** 9351 2222.

Griffin Theatre
10 Nimrod St, Kings Cross.
Map 5 B1. **Tel** 9361 3817.
w griffintheatre. com.au

Old Fitz Theatre
129 Dowling St, Woolloomooloo.
Map 2 D5. **Tel** 9356 3848.
w oldfitztheatre.com

Parade Theatre
215 Anzac Parade, Kensington. **Map** 5 B4.

Tel 9697 7613.
w nida.edu.au

Roslyn Packer Theatre
22 Hickson Rd, Walsh Bay.
Map 1 A2. **Tel** 9250 1999.
w roslynpacker theatre.com.au

Seymour Theatre Centre
Cnr Cleveland St and City Rd, Chippendale.
Tel 9351 7940.
w seymourcentre.com

Shakespeare Australia
Tel 1300 122 344.
w shakespeare australia.com.au

State Theatre
49 Market St. **Map** 1 B5.
Tel 9373 6852.
w statetheatre.com.au

Sydney Festival
Tel 8248 6500.
w sydneyfestival. org.au

Sydney Lyric
Pirrama Road, Pyrmont.
Map 3 C1.
Tel 9509 3600.
Box Office:
Tel 1300 795 267.
w sydneylyric.com.au
w star.com.au

Sydney Theatre Company
Tel 9250 1777.
w sydneytheatre. com.au

Theatre Royal
MLC Centre, King St.
Map 1 B5.
Tel 1300 723 038.
w theatreroyal.net.au

The Wharf
Pier 4, Hickson Rd, Walsh Bay. **Map** 1 A1.
Tel 9250 1777.

Children's Theatre

Flying Fruit Fly Circus
Tel 6043 0777.
w fruitflycircus.com.au

Marian St Theatre for Young People
2 Marian St, Killara.
Tel 9411 1800.
w mstyp.org.au

Film

Chauvel Cinema
Paddington Town Hall, 249 Oxford St. **Map** 5 C3.
Tel 9361 5398. w palace cinemas.com.au

Cinema Paris
Entertainment Quarter, Driver Ave, Moore Park.
Map 5 C5. **Tel** 9003 3870.
w hoyts.com.au

Dendy Cinemas
Newtown
261–263 King St, Newtown. **Tel** 9550 5699.
Opera Quays
Shop 9/2, East Circular Quay. **Tel** 9247 3800.
w dendy.com.au

Event Cinemas
505–525 George St.
Map 4 E3. **Tel** 9273 7300.
w eventcinemas.com

Govinda's
112 Darlinghurst Rd.
Map 5 A2. **Tel** 9380 5155.
w govindas.com.au

Hoyts at Broadway
Broadway Shopping Centre, 3 Bay St.

Map 3 C5. **Tel** 9003 3820.
w hoyts.com.au

Palace Norton St Cinema
99 Norton St, Leichhardt.
Tel 9550 0122.
w palacecinemas. com.au

Film Festivals

Flickerfest International Short Film Festival
Tel 9365 6888.
w flickerfest.com.au

Mardi Gras Film Festival
Tel 9280 1533.
w queerscreen.org.au

Sydney Film Festival
Tel 9318 0999.
w sff.org.au

Tropfest
w tropfest.com

Comedy

Comedy Store
Entertainment Quarter, Driver Ave, Moore Park.
Map 5 C5. **Tel** 9357 1419.
w comedystore. com.au

Harold Park Hotel
70A Ross St, Forest Lodge, Glebe. **Tel** 9660 4745.
w haroldparkhotel. com.au

The Old Manly Boatshed
40 The Corso, Manly.
Tel 9977 4443.

Sydney Comedy Festival
Tel 9519 9231.
w sydneycomedy festival.com.au

Opera, Classical Music and Dance

Music buffs cannot possibly visit Sydney without seeing an opera or hearing the city's premier orchestra perform in the Sydney Opera House. And that is just the start. The wide range of music on offer in Sydney includes influences from Asia, Europe and the Pacific, as well as local compositions. For the visitor, there is a wealth of orchestral, choral, chamber, contemporary and traditional Aboriginal music to choose from.

Opera

Australia has produced a number of world-class opera singers, including Joan Sutherland, and eminent conductors such as Sir Charles Mackerras, Simone Young and Stuart Challender. The first recorded performance of an opera in Sydney was in 1834. For 120 years, most opera was performed by visiting international companies.

In 1956, the Australian Opera (now called **Opera Australia**) was formed. It presented four Mozart operas in its first year. But it was the opening of the **Sydney Opera House** (see pp76–9) in 1973 that heralded a new interest in the art form. Each season usually includes one accessible opera in English as well as more challenging shows. Looking to push the boundaries of performance, the company has staged productions of *Turandot* and *Carmen* on Sydney Harbour for an audience seated at the water's edge. Every year at the hugely popular Opera in The Domain (see p51), members of Opera Australia put on a free, open-air performance as part of the Sydney Festival.

Orchestral Music

Much of Sydney's orchestral music and recitals are the work of the famous **Sydney Symphony Orchestra** (SSO). Numerous concerts are given, mostly in the Opera House Concert Hall, the **City Recital Hall** and the **Sydney Town Hall** (see p89). A Tea and Symphony series is held mid-year on Friday mornings at the Sydney Opera House.

The renovated Conservatorium of Music (see p108), set in the Royal Botanic Garden, provides a wonderful atmosphere and location. It holds a number of concerts, where you can enjoy symphony and chamber orchestras, or jazz big bands.

Formed in 1973, the **Sydney Youth Orchestra**, is praised for its talent, enthusiasm and impressive young soloists. With a loyal following, it stages several performances in major concert venues throughout the year. Aficionados of Baroque and classical music should try to catch a performance by the **Australian Brandenburg Orchestra**. Australia's first period instrument orchestra, this popular group appears regularly in Sydney's major concert halls.

Contemporary Music

The first concert held by **Musica Viva** was in 1945, at the NSW Conservatorium of Music. Originally specializing in chamber music, it now also presents string quartets, jazz, piano groups, percussionists, soloists and international avant-garde artists. Concerts take place at the Opera House and the City Recital Hall.

Synergy is one of Australia's foremost percussion quartets. The group commissions works from all over the world and gives its own concert series at the Sydney Opera House and at Sydney Town Hall. It also collaborates with dance and theatre groups.

Eastside Arts, held, like Paddington Markets (see p128), in the Uniting Church, hosts Café Carnivale every Friday night, showcasing some of the best world music, including rembetika, Indian, African, percussion, gypsy, salsa and tango music.

Fourplay is a group of classically trained musicians who play electric string quartet versions of popular music at various venues.

Chamber Music

Under director Richard Tognetti, the **Australian Chamber Orchestra** has won acclaim for its creativity and interesting choice of venues, including museums, churches and even wineries. Its main concerts are held at the Opera House and the City Recital Hall, Angel Place.

The **Australia Ensemble** is the resident chamber music group at the University of New South Wales. It performs six times a year at the Sir John Clancy Auditorium and also appears for Musica Viva. Many choral groups and ensembles like to book **St James' Church** because of its atmosphere and acoustics.

Free Concerts

Throughout the year, festivals (see pp50–53) provide free live music. These are mostly held outdoors, to take advantage of Sydney's warm climate. During the Sydney Festival the city's favourite outdoor concerts take place, including Opera and Symphony performances staged under the stars in The Domain (see p109), while regular shows and events are held in the Sydney Opera House forecourt.

The Conservatorium of Music holds a weekly series of inexpensive concerts in their Verbrugghen Hall (see p108) at 1:10pm each Wednesday during the university semester; entry is by gold coin (A\$1 or A\$2) donation. Staff and students present classical, modern and jazz music in ensemble, soloist and chamber performances. Each January the renowned choir of St James' (see p117 and p213) presents two orchestral masses to the congregation, and entry to these events is free.

Choral Music

Comprised of four choirs, the 300-member Festival Chorus, the 100-member Symphony Chorus, the 32-member Chamber Singers and the 25-member Vox, the **Sydney Philharmonia Choirs** are the city's finest. They perform at the Opera House. December is the focal point of Sydney's choral scene, with regular massed choir performances of Handel's *Messiah*.

The **Australian Youth Choir** is booked for many private functions, but if you are lucky, you may catch one of their major annual performances.

One of Sydney's most impressive vocal groups is the **Café of the Gate of Salvation**, described as an "Aussie blend of a capella and gospel."

The choir of St James' Church is an excellent choral group. The orchestral masses performed in January, such as those by Mozart, Haydn and Schubert, usually fill the church to capacity, so arrive early. Former choir members who are now professional soloists also occasionally perform.

Dance

There is an eclectic variety of dance on offer in Sydney. The **Australian Ballet** has two seven-week Sydney seasons at the Opera House: one in March/April, the other in November/December. The company's repertoire spans traditional through to modern, although it is perhaps most noted for classical ballets such as *Swan Lake* and *Giselle*.

Sydney Dance Company is the city's leading modern dance group, often combining its vigorous productions with innovative musical scores. The company has performed in Italy, New York, London and China. Productions are mostly staged at the Sydney Opera House, but are, on occasion, held at The Wharf or the Roslyn Packer Theatre *(see pp210–11)*. Rafaela Bonachela was appointed artistic director in 2009.

The **Performance Space**, which is now located at the Carriageworks, is very popular for its experimental dance and movement theatre. Artists with backgrounds in dance, mime, circus work, Butoh or performance art are likely to appear here.

Bangarra Dance Theatre uses traditional Aboriginal and Torres Strait Islander dance and music as its inspiration, infused with contemporary elements. It makes outback interstate and international tours, but is based in Sydney.

The startling and original **Legs on the Wall** are a physical theatre group who work all over the world, combining circus and aerial techniques with dance and narrative to form a heady mix. Their spectacular performances take place in intimate theatres or use dramatic settings, such as skyscrapers, from which the performers are suspended.

Golden Oldies

Seniors are treated to concerts by well-known Australian performers, including tenor David Hobson, several times a year through **The Good Old Days** series. There are morning and afternoon performances at the Sydney Town Hall.

DIRECTORY

Opera

Opera Australia
Tel 9318 8200.
W opera.org.au

Sydney Opera House
Bennelong Point.
Map 1 C2. **Tel** 9250 7111.
W sydneyopera
house. com

Sydney Town Hall
483 George Street.
Map 4 E2. **Tel** 9265 9333.
W sydneytownhall.
com.au

Orchestral Music

Australian Brandenburg Orchestra
Tel 9328 7581. W brand
enburg.com.au

City Recital Hall
Angel Place. **Map** 1 B4.
Tel 8256 2222.
W cityrecithall.com

Sydney Symphony Orchestra
Tel 8215 4600.
W sydneysymphony.
com

Sydney Youth Orchestra
Tel 9251 2422.
W syo.com.au

Contemporary Music

Eastside Arts
395 Oxford St, Paddington.
Tel 93312646.
W paddingtonuca.
org.au

Fourplay
W fourplay.com.au

Musica Viva
Tel 8394 6666.
W mva.org.au

Synergy
Tel 9663 5532.
W synergypercussion.
com

Chamber Music

Australian Chamber Orchestra
Tel 8274 3888.
W aco.com.au

Australia Ensemble
Tel 9385 4874.
W ae.unsw.edu.au

St James' Church
173 King St. **Map** 1 B5.
Tel 8227 1300. W sjks.
org.au

Choral Music

Australian Youth Choir
Tel 1300 761 039.
W niypaa.com.au

Café of the Gate of Salvation
W cafeofthegateof
salvation.com.au

Sydney Philharmonia Choirs
Tel 8274 6200. W sydney
philharmonia.com.au

Dance

Australian Ballet
Tel 1300 369 741.
W australianballet.
com.au

Bangarra Dance Theatre
Tel 9251 5333.
W bangarra.com.au

Legs on the Wall
Tel 9560 9479. W legs
onthewall.com.au

Performance Space
245 Wilson St, Everleigh.
Tel 8571 9111.
W performancespace.
com.au

Sydney Dance Company
W sydneydance
company.com

Golden Oldies

The Good Old Days
W goodolddays
concerts.com.au

Music Venues and Nightclubs

Sydney attracts some of the biggest names in modern music all year round. Venues range from the ICC Sydney showpiece in Darling Harbour to small and noisy back rooms in pubs. Visiting international DJs frequently play sets at Sydney clubs. Some venues cater for a variety of music tastes – rock and pop one night, jazz, blues or folk the next. There are free online gig guides, including www.themusic.com.au, www.thebrag.com.au and www.inthemix.com.au, where you can find out what is on.

Getting In

Tickets for major shows are available through booking agencies such as Ticketek and Ticketmaster (see p209). Prices vary considerably, depending on the type of show. You may pay from A$30 to A$70 for a gig at the Metro, with tickets for concerts by major international artists ranging from A$100 to A$350, depending on the seats. **Moshtix** also sells tickets for smaller venues across Sydney and their website gives a good idea of the line-up at various venues. Buying online also saves you from having to queue early for tickets on the door.

You can pay at the door on the night at most places, unless the show is already sold out. Nightclubs often have a cover charge, but some venues will admit you free before a certain time in the evening or on weeknights.

Most venues serve alcohol, so shows are restricted to those at least 18 years of age. This is the usual case unless a gig is specified "all ages". It is advisable that people under 30 years old carry photo identification because entry to some venues is very strict. You are also not allowed to carry any kind of bottle into or from most nightclubs or other venues. Similarly, any professional cameras and recording devices are usually banned.

Dress codes vary, though flip-flops are generally not welcome and are considered a safety hazard. Wear thin layers that you can remove when you get hot. Many venues provide a cloakroom, but sometimes this incurs a cost.

Rock, Pop and Hip Hop

Pop's big names and famous rock groups perform at the **Qudos Bank Arena**, **Hordern Pavilion** and sports grounds such as the ANZ Stadium at **Sydney Olympic Park** (see p140) in Homebush Bay. More intimate locations include the **State Theatre** (see pp210–11), **Enmore Theatre** and Sydney's best venue, **The Metro Theatre**. Hip hop acts usually play in rock venues rather than in nightclubs. You are almost as likely to find a crew rapping as a band strumming and drumming at the Metro, **The Gaelic Club**, **The Bridge Hotel** and **The Merton** in Rozelle, while up-and-coming acts from rock to punk can be found at the inner west's grungy **The Bald Faced Stag**. A little further west, **The Factory Theatre** in Marrickville hosts live performances by both established and emerging artists, as well as dance and small cabaret shows.

Pub rock is a constantly changing scene in Sydney. Check the websites of the venues or the printed or online version of the free local publication, The Music (see p208). Music stores are also full of flyers. Many pubs host live music only on Friday and Saturday nights. Note that gigs by international acts and popular Australian bands, on every week at the Metro Theatre and Gaelic Club, usually sell out.

Jazz, Folk and Blues

For many years, the first port of call for any jazz, funk, groove or folk enthusiast has been **The Basement**. Visiting luminaries play some nights, talented but struggling local musicians

others, and the line-ups now also include increasingly popular world music and hip hop bands. **Slide**, in a converted Art Deco bank building on Oxford Street, is a combination of a Parisian-style nightclub and a New York-style lounge bar. It plays host to both local and international performers. Experimental jazz is offered on Fridays and Saturdays at the **Seymour Theatre Centre** (see pp210–11). **Leadbelly** also offers dinner and show deals, as well as show-only tickets, and has been drawing an excellent roster of jazz, blues and roots talent. The **Fitzroy Hotel** in Windsor, north-west of Sydney, holds a blues festival in October, and the **Cat & Fiddle Hotel** in Balmain offers acoustic music and folk at weekends.

House, Breakbeats and Techno

Darling Harbour's super club, **Home Sydney** in Cockle Bay, features three levels and a gargantuan sound system. Friday night is the time to go, as the DJs present house, trance, drum and bass, and breakbeats. In the city centre, the multi-venue Ivy Complex at **Pacha** features live music, DJs and special international artists every Saturday. A mainstream crowd flocks to the nearby **Bungalow 8** with its fresh seafood dishes and great views of the Harbour. Once the sun has set, house DJs turn the place into a club. **The Marquee**, at The Star, hosts international DJs in the venue's three distinct spaces, while **Cargo Bar** showcases a diverse mix of performers in its mainstream house club.

For something a little more hip, try the underground **Candy's Apartment** with its bunker-style bar on Bayswater Road, or the buzzy **World Bar** on the same street. Based in a converted Victorian terrace, World Bar is known for serving its cocktails in teapots designed for sharing. Or try the low-ceilinged **Chinese Laundry** on Sussex Street, tucked under the gentrified pub, Slip Inn (see El Loco, p190).

Gay and Lesbian Pubs and Clubs

Sunday night is the big night for many of Sydney's gay community, although there is plenty of action throughout the week. A number of venues have a gay or lesbian night on one night of the week and attract a mainstream crowd on the other nights. Waywards at the **Bank Hotel** in Newtown hosts free live band performances from 8pm onwards every Thursday to Saturday.

ARQ on Flinders Street is the largest of the gay clubs, with pounding commercial house music. This is a world-class venue with great facilities, from the cutting-edge sound systems to the state-of-the-art lighting shows. **Oxford Art Factory** attracts a diverse crowd to its live music performances, held in a stunning space inspired by Andy Warhol's New York Factory of the 1960s. **Midnight Shift** on Oxford Street has both the Shift Bar and the Shift Club, and **Stonewall** is a lively gay bar which offers nightly entertainment over three

levels, including DJs, dancers and drag shows.

The **Colombian** is the best and one of the most popular of the Oxford Street bars. It has a mock-Central American jungle decor, self-styled as "South American chic", and large windows that open out to the street. The **Oxford Hotel** and its upper-level cocktail bars are popular, too. Some of Sydney's most entertaining drag shows can be found at the **Imperial Hotel** where shows are staged most nights of the week.

DIRECTORY

Getting In

Moshtix
Tel 1300 438 849.
W moshtix.com.au

Rock, Pop and Hip Hop

The Bald Faced Stag
345 Parramatta Rd, Leichhardt. Tel 9560 7188.
W baldfacedstag.com.au

Bridge Hotel
119 Victoria Rd, Rozelle.
Tel 9810 1260.

Enmore Theatre
130 Enmore Rd, Newtown.
Tel 9550 3666. W enmore theatre.com.au

The Factory Theatre
105 Victoria Rd, Marrickville. Tel 9550 3666. W factorytheatre.com.au

Gaelic Club
64 Devonshire St, Surry Hills. Tel 9211 1586.
W gaelicclubsydney.com

Hordern Pavilion
Driver Ave, Moore Park.
Map 5 C5. Tel 9921 5333. W playbill venues.com

The Merton
38 Victoria Rd, Rozelle.
Tel 8065 9577.

The Metro Theatre
624 George St. Map 4 E3.
Tel 9550 3666.
W metro theatre.com.au

Qudos Bank Arena
Edwin Flack Ave, Sydney Olympic Park.
Tel 8765 4321.

State Theatre
49 Market St. Map 1 B5.
Tel 9373 6852.
W statetheatre.com.au

Sydney Olympic Park
Homebush Bay.
Tel 9714 7888.
W sydneyolympicpark.com.au

Jazz, Folk and Blues

The Basement
29 Reiby Place. Map 1 B3.
Tel 9251 2797.
W thebasement.com.au

Cat & Fiddle Hotel
456 Darling St, Balmain.
Tel 9810 7931.
W catandfiddle.com.au

Fitzroy Hotel
161 George St, Windsor.
Tel 4577 3396.

Leadbelly
42 King St, Newtown.
Tel 9557 7992.
W theleadbelly.com.au

Seymour Theatre Centre
Cnr Cleveland St & City Rd, Chippendale.
Tel 9351 7940.
W seymourcentre.com

Slide
41 Oxford St, Darlinghurst.
Map 4 F4. Tel 8915 1899.
W slide.com.au

House, Breakbeats and Techno

Bungalow 8
The Promenade, King St Wharf. Tel 9299 4660.
W kingstreetwharf.com.au

Candy's Apartment
22 Bayswater Rd, Kings Cross. Map 5 B1. Tel 9380 5600. W candys.com.au

Cargo Bar
52–60 The Promenade, King St Wharf, Darling Harbour. Tel 8070 2424.
W thekeystonegroup.com.au

Chinese Laundry
Slip Inn, 111 Sussex St.
Map 1 A3. Tel 8295 9999.
W chineselaundryclub.com.au

Home Sydney
Wheat Rd, Cockle Bay, Darling Harbour.
Map 4 D2. Tel 9266 0600.
W homesydney.com

The Marquee
The Star, Pyrmont.
Map 3 C1. Tel 9777 9000.
W marqueesydney.com

Pacha
330 George St. Map 1 B3.
Tel 9240 3000. W pacha sydney.com

World Bar
24 Bayswater Rd, Kings Cross. Map 5 C1.
Tel 9357 7700.
W theworldbar.com

Gay and Lesbian Pubs and Clubs

ARQ
16 Flinders St, Taylor Square. Map 5 A2.
Tel 9380 8700.
W arqsydney.com.au

Bank Hotel
324 King St, Newtown.
Tel 8568 1900.
W bankhotel.com.au

Colombian
Cnr Oxford & Crown Sts, Surry Hills. Map 5 A2.
Tel 9360 2151.
W colombian.com.au

Imperial Hotel
35 Erskineville Rd, Erskineville.
Tel 9516 1766.

Midnight Shift
85 Oxford St, Darlinghurst. Map 5 A2.
Tel 9358 3848.
W themidnight shift.com.au

Oxford Art Factory
36 Oxford St, Darlinghurst. Map 4 F4.
Tel 9332 3711.
W oxfordartfactory.com

Oxford Hotel
134 Oxford St, Darlinghurst. Map 5 A2.
Tel 9331 3467.
W theoxfordhotel.com.au

Stonewall
175 Oxford St, Darlinghurst. Map 5 A2.
Tel 9360 1963.
W stonewallhotel.com

SURVIVAL GUIDE

LEGUARD

PRACTICAL INFORMATION

As a modern, global city that welcomes over 30 million visitors to its shores each year, Sydney has all the services expected of a major destination, including reliable and inexpensive public transport, plenty of cash dispensers and bureaux de change, good communications networks and a comprehensive range of comfortable accommodation, making it easy for visitors to enjoy Sydney's thriving dining scene, shopping, arts and culture, sporting activities, entertainment, exciting nightlife and natural beauty. A multi-billion dollar upgrade of the city's public transport facilities, including new Light Rail and Metro trains, will provide more efficient and better connections for getting around, and are set to transform major thoroughfares into pedestrian-friendly zones with more public open spaces by 2019 *(see p230)*. Visitors will find Sydney a safe, clean and welcoming city. They should encounter few practical problems as long as they follow a few commonsense guidelines about personal security *(see pp222–3)*.

When to Go

The best times to travel are during autumn (March–May) and spring (September–November), when the weather is warm to mild. The summer months tend to be hot and humid, particularly in February. However, if you can stand the heat then some of the best deals often occur during this period when children are back at school. Winter (June–August) is rarely very cold, and temperatures can be as high as 20° C (68° F).

Visas and Passports

All visitors to Australia must hold a valid passport and, with the exception of New Zealand, must either have an Electronic Travel Authority (ETA) or a tourist visa (depending on your country of origin). Citizens of the UK, the USA, France, Spain, Ireland, Germany, Denmark and several other countries qualify for an ETA, which allows entry to Australia for up to three months. The ETA can be applied for online or through a travel agent, airline or an Australian Visa Office, and has a service fee of A$20. Visitors who are not eligible for an ETA, who want to stay longer or enter on a working holiday, should check the requirements through the **Department of Immigration and Citizenship**. All visitors must also have an onward ticket and proof that they have sufficient funds for their visit.

Travel Safety Advice

Visitors can get up-to-date travel safety information from the **Foreign and Commonwealth Office** in the UK, the **State Department** in the US and the **Department of Foreign Affairs and Trade** in Australia.

Customs Information

The customs allowance per person over 18 entering Australia is up to the value of A$900 plus 2.25 litres (3.75 pints) of alcohol and a carton of 250 cigarettes or 250 grams (0.5 pounds) of cigars/tobacco.

Australia's quarantine regulations are strict and all people entering the country at Sydney Airport will be given a customs form to fill in on the plane. Visitors must declare all foods – it is illegal to bring in fruit, vegetables, seeds, live plants and plant products, and any endangered species or animal products. Packaged food such as biscuits and chocolates are usually allowed but must still be declared. There are severe penalties for bringing in illegal drugs. Because of these restrictions, personal luggage and hand luggage may be X-rayed before you can leave the baggage reclaim area and often customs officers with sniffer dogs will check luggage both near the baggage carousel and along the queues of exiting passengers from the airport.

Australia levies a departure tax on all passengers aged 12 or over. This is included in the cost of your airline ticket.

Tourist Information

To obtain information about Sydney and the rest of Australia before leaving home, travellers should look at the **Destination NSW** website.

In Australia, Sydney's principal tourist information points are the **The Rocks and Darling Harbour Sydney Visitor Centres**. Both centres can book tours as well as recommend accommodation at certain listed hotels. Information booths can also be found in **Chinatown** and at **Circular Quay** and **Town Hall**, as well as at Sydney's major attractions. These booths have free maps, brochures and flyers promoting activities and tours *(see p208)*.

For visitors arriving by air, there are free Sydney visitor

An information sign at the Museum of Contemporary Art at Circular Quay

◄ Surfers and beachgoers on Bondi Beach

booklets available on stands just before the duty-free shops and customs area and in the arrivals hall of Sydney Airport (see p229). If you have any questions or need directions, volunteer Airport Ambassadors offer assistance. They are identifiable by their bright-blue jackets (Mandarin-speaking ambassadors wear red jackets) and can be found throughout the international departures and arrivals terminals, the domestic arrivals terminal, and at the information desks. There is a Commissionaire Desk in the domestic departures terminal for passengers requiring wheelchair assistance.

Public toilets with brightly painted murals

The striking sandstone entrance to the Art Gallery of New South Wales

Admission Prices

Most of Sydney's museums, galleries and historic houses charge a reasonable admission fee, usually A$8–12. The Art Gallery of New South Wales (see pp110–13) is free but charges for special exhibitions. Family attractions such as zoos and wildlife parks are more expensive, often A$20–60. However, cheaper family passes are usually available on the company's website. A multi-attraction pass offers big savings for those planning to visit SEA LIFE Sydney Aquarium (see p98), WILD LIFE Sydney Zoo (see p99), Sydney Tower Eye (see p85) and other **Merlin Entertainment Group** venues. Buy tickets in advance online for further discounts.

Student and senior concessions are available at many attractions on presentation of an official international ID card.

The **Sydney Living Museums** Pass, valid for one month, allows one-time entry to the 12 member museums and historic houses.

Opening Hours

Although opening hours vary, the majority of museums and galleries are open from 10am to 5pm daily, except on Good Friday and Christmas Day. Smaller galleries are usually closed on Mondays. The Art Gallery of New South Wales is open until 10pm every Wednesday and the Museum of Contemporary Art (see p75) stays open until 9pm on Thursdays. Museums, galleries and other attractions are often at their busiest at weekends.

Etiquette and Smoking

While Sydney society is generally laid back, there are a few rules to follow. Eating and drinking is prohibited on public transport. There are no real dress codes – casual and smart-casual are the most common approaches. Topless bathing is accepted on many beaches, but not at public swimming pools.

Smoking is banned in all public venues, including beaches, playgrounds, restaurants, pubs and bars, but many clubs have designated covered outdoor areas (often accessed via corridors) where smoking is allowed.

Accessibility to Public Conveniences

Free public toilets can be found in Sydney's galleries and museums, department stores and all bus and railway stations. They are generally well serviced and clean. A national public toilets map at www.toiletmap.gov.au is a useful way to locate the nearest convenience. The City of Sydney also operates self-cleaning automatic public toilets with visits capped at 20 minutes in busy areas. Check www.cityofsydney.nsw.gov.au/explore/facilities/public-toilets for details. Baby changing facilities are also quite common, particularly in department stores and major museums and galleries.

Clean drinking fountains can be found throughout the city.

Taxes and Tipping

Australia has a 10 per cent Goods and Services Tax (GST), included in the listed price. If travellers spend more than A$300 in one store (even across multiple transactions), they can claim back the GST when they leave Australia – this is known as the Tourist Refund Scheme (TRS). Refunds are available at the airport and at cruise-line terminals. All goods must either be carried as hand luggage or worn (unless they are liquids, which must be unopened and packed in your checked baggage). It is advisable to allow extra time at the airport or port to make your claim, although you can use the mobile app or website to make the process faster. For more information, check the **Australian Customs and Border Protection** website.

Although tipping is optional, it is the custom to leave about 10 per cent for good service in restaurants (see p181) and to leave any small change for bartenders and taxi drivers. Most small cafés have a tip jar on the counter for gratuities.

Travellers with Special Needs

Sydney infrastructure largely caters to the needs of the disabled. The public transport network has been developed to accommodate people with mobility disabilities, with specially adapted buses, trains and ferries. Accessible buses run on most routes, with the body of the bus lowered to allow people in wheelchairs access to the vehicle. There is also priority seating for those with a disability, and bus handrails and steps are marked with bright-yellow paint to assist the visually impaired. All Light Rail stations are also wheelchair accessible, as are many train stations and ferry wharves. The Transport Infoline (see p233) has details on disabled access at each station and bus stop.

For the visually impaired, push buttons at traffic lights emit a series of beeps to indicate when the pedestrian light has turned green and it is safe to cross.

Museums, many hotels and some major sights cater to the less mobile, including those in wheelchairs, as well as people with other disabilities. It is still advisable to phone all sights in advance to check on facilities.

For detailed information on accessible services and venues, Access Sydney is available from Spinal Cord Injuries Australia (see p173). A map and directory for those with limited mobility can be obtained from the **City of Sydney One-Stop Shop** behind Sydney Town Hall.

Sydney Time

Sydney is in the Australian Eastern Standard Time zone (AEST). Daylight saving in New South Wales starts on the last Sunday in October and finishes on the last Sunday in March. The Northern Territory, Queensland and Western Australia do not observe daylight saving, so check time differences when you are there.

City and Country	Hours + or − AEST
Adelaide (Australia)	−½
Brisbane (Australia)	same
Canberra (Australia)	same
Darwin (Australia)	−½
Hobart (Australia)	same
Melbourne (Australia)	same
Perth (Australia)	−2
London (UK)	−9
Los Angeles (USA)	−17
Singapore	−2
Toronto (Canada)	−14

Travelling with Children

Sydney is an easy city to explore with children. There are many beaches, several wildlife parks (two either in or very near the city centre) and plenty of fun attractions to keep families entertained, plus parks and gardens such as the Darling Quarter Kids Playground (see pp94–5). Public transport and most attractions offer cheaper tickets for children and many offer discount family tickets. Several free festivals and events are held in the city and tourist areas, like Sydney Festival (see p51) and Sculpture by the Sea (see p50), that appeal to families. Details can be found at the **Sydney Visitor Centre** and are often publicised in the free monthly publication, Sydney's Child (www.childmags.com.au).

Student Travellers

Student travellers carrying the **International Student Identity Card (ISIC)** are eligible for discounts in many museums, theatres and cinemas, as well as discounted air fares and 15 per cent off interstate coach travel.

Overseas visitors who are full-time students can buy an ISIC card (which comes with a guide book) for A$25 from Sydney branches of **STA Travel**.

Non-students aged 30 or under can take advantage of the same discounts with an **International Youth Travel Card (IYTC)** through the same provider.

Gay and Lesbian Travellers

Sydney is an ultra gay-friendly city with many gay bars and nightclubs. It also hosts the annual Sydney Gay and Lesbian Mardi Gras, which attracts thousands of international visitors and a vast TV audience. The hub of Sydney's gay community is Oxford Street, Darlinghurst (on the city's eastern fringe, see pp118–23). There are several gay newspapers including the Sydney Star Observer and Lesbians on the Loose, with online editions found at www.starobserver.com.au and www.LOTL.com. **Pride Centre** is a not-for-profit organization supporting the

Entrance gates with wheelchair access at Circular Quay railway station

Gay pride event, Sydney harbour

gay and lesbian community. A well-known gay travel agency is **Out Travel** in Elizabeth Bay.

Electricity

Australia's electrical current is 240–250 volts AC. Electrical plugs can have either two or three pins. Most good hotels will provide 110-volt shaver sockets and hair dryers, but a flat, two- or three-pin adaptor will be necessary for other appliances. These can be bought from electrical stores, department stores, some convenience stores and airports.

Conversion Table

Imperial to Metric
1 inch = 2.54 centimetres
1 foot = 30 centimetres
1 mile = 1.6 kilometres
1 ounce = 28 grams
1 pound = 454 grams
1 pint = 0.6 litres
1 gallon = 4.6 litres

Metric to Imperial
1 centimetre = 0.4 inches
1 metre = 3 feet, 3 inches
1 kilometre = 0.6 miles
1 gram = 0.04 ounces
1 kilogram = 2.2 pounds
1 litre = 1.8 pints

Responsible Tourism

Most Sydney hotels have adopted power-saving and green-energy practices, and recycling initiatives are the norm. Many hotels have been bench-marked by the **EarthCheck** organization for their efficient energy plans. The purpose-built Sydney Harbour YHA (youth hostel) also has a strong eco focus (see p178).

Increasing numbers of restaurants are making a point of using produce from local growers or their own farms and choosing suppliers of sustainably grown and ethically farmed produce, particularly wild-caught seafood. **Farmers' Markets** have sprung up in the city and main tourist areas, including Carriageworks, Eveleigh (near Redfern railway station) and Orange Grove (see p203). These offer an opportunity to buy fresh, organic produce for a delicious meal.

DIRECTORY

Embassies and Consulates

Canada
Level 5, 111 Harrington St.
Map 1 B3. **Tel** 9364 3000.
W canada
international.gc.ca

New Zealand
Level 10, 55 Hunter St.
Map 1 B4.
Tel 1300 559535.
W nzembassy.
com/australia

Republic of Ireland
Level 26, 1 Market St.
Map 4 E2. **Tel** 9264 9635.
W irishconsulate
sydney.net

United Kingdom
Level 16, Gateway
Building, 1 Macquarie
Place. **Map** 1 B3.
Tel 9247 7521.
W gov.uk/government/
world/australia

USA
Level 10, MLC Centre,
19–29 Martin Place.
Map 1 B4. **Tel** 9373 9200.
W sydney.usconsulate.
gov

Visas and Passports

**Department of
Immigration and
Citizenship**
W border.gov.au

Travel Safety Advice

Australia
W dfat.gov.au
W smartraveller.gov.au

United Kingdom
W gov.uk/foreign-
travel-advice

United States
W travel.state.gov

Tourist Information

Chinatown
Cnr of Dixon & Goulburn
Sts. **Map** 4 D5.
Open 11am–5pm daily.

Circular Quay
Cnr of Pitt & Alfred Sts,
Circular Quay. **Map** 1 B3.
Open 9am–5pm daily.

**Darling Harbour
Sydney Visitor Centre**
Darling Harbour.
Map 3 C2. **Tel** 9281 2244.

Open 9:30am–
5:30pm daily.
W visitnsw.com

Destination NSW
W sydney.com

**The Rocks Sydney
Visitor Centre**
Cnr Argyle & Playfair Sts,
The Rocks. **Map** 1 B2.
Tel 8273 0000.
Open 9:30am–5:30pm
daily. W sydney.com

Town Hall
George St.
Map 4 E2. **Open** 9am–
5pm daily.

Admission Prices

**Merlin Entertainment
Group**
W merlinattractions.
com.au

**Sydney Living
Museums**
W sydneyliving
museums.com.au

Taxes and Tipping

**Australian Customs &
Border Protection**
W customs.gov.au

Travellers with Special Needs

**City of Sydney
One-Stop Shop**
Town Hall House, Sydney
Square. **Map** 4 E3.
Tel 9265 9333. W cityof
sydney.nsw.gov.au

Student Travellers

ISIC
Tel 1800 819 775.
W isiccard.com.au

STA Travel/IYTC
W statravel.com.au

Gay and Lesbian Travellers

Out Travel
47 Elizabeth Bay Rd.
Map 2 F5. **Tel** 8667 3336.
W out-travel.com.au

Pride Centre
W pridecentre.com.au

Responsible Tourism

EarthCheck
W earthcheck.org

Farmers' Markets
W farmersmarkets.
org.au

Personal Security and Health

Street crime in Sydney is less prevalent than in many other large cities, but it does exist, particularly late at night in some popular entertainment areas. You can minimize any risks by exercising reasonable caution and following the advice given below. Members of Sydney's police patrol the city's streets and public transport system, on foot, bicycle and motorbike, in cars, and even on horseback during major events. A police presence is usually visible at crowded tourist areas and during public events. Nature presents other safety considerations, at surf beaches and in the bushland. The following information offers some practical advice for coping with environmental hazards.

Police officers patrolling the streets of Sydney on motorbikes

Police

Sydney has a strong police force with hundreds of officers stationed in the city centre, The Rocks and Kings Cross. To report emergencies, major crimes and fires call 000 from any phone. Victims of non-life-threatening crimes such as personal theft, car theft, breaking and entering, and malicious damage should call the Police Assistance Line on 131 444. There are 24-hour police stations at **The Rocks**, **Kings Cross** and **Day Street**, Sydney.

What to Be Aware of

Leave valuables and important documents in your hotel safe, and don't carry large sums of cash. Try to avoid carrying all of your credit and debit cards with you. Leave one of your cards in the hotel safe as a backup if your wallet is stolen. It is also worth photocopying vital documents in case of loss or theft.

Be on guard against purse snatchers and pickpockets in big crowds. Prime places for theft are tourist areas, shopping centres,

beaches, markets, sporting venues and on public transport.

Never carry your wallet in an outside pocket and do wear shoulder bags and cameras with the strap across your body and the bag or camera in front. Park cars in well-lit, reasonably busy streets, and don't leave any valuables visible inside the car. Leaving your vehicle unlocked is an offence.

Sydney has no definite off-limit areas during the day, but try to avoid the more unsavoury side streets and lanes of areas such as Kings Cross. At night, stay clear of deserted, poorly lit streets and toilets in parks.

When travelling by train at night, travel in the carriage near the guard's compartment, which is marked with a blue light. Nightsafe buses run from major train stations to the suburbs when trains stop running from midnight to dawn.

Taxis are probably the safest means of travel at night, especially for shorter journeys or for women on their own. Secure, signposted taxi ranks in the city centre are manned by security guards on Friday and Saturday nights.

See www.transport nsw.info for late-night bus routes and departure points.

In an Emergency

For all emergencies – **police**, **fire** and **ambulance** – call 000. If you witness suspicious activity, report it to the National Security Hot Line on 1800 123400.

Lost and Stolen Property

If you lose anything on public transport or in a taxi you should report it immediately, providing the transport route you were travelling on. **NSW Trains** and **Sydney Trains** have one number. **Sydney Ferries** has a separate number, while bus passengers should call the individual **Sydney Buses** depots. For anything left in a taxi, call the taxi company.

If your passport is stolen, report it to your embassy or consulate (see p221). Lost or stolen credit or debit cards should also be reported to the card provider so that the account can be blocked.

Hospitals and Pharmacies

Sydney has excellent medical services. If you are in need of urgent medical attention, dial 000 for an ambulance or go to the emergency department of the nearest main public

Police car

Fire engine

Intensive care ambulance

Surf lifesaving sign indicating a dangerous undertow or "rip"

hospital. **Sydney Hospital**, **Royal Prince Alfred Hospital** and **St Vincent's Hospital** have emergency departments. For less urgent treatment, look under "Medical Centres" in the Yellow Pages of the Sydney telephone directory or at www.yellowpages.com.au.

The **King's Cross Clinic** and the **International Travel Vaccinations Centre** offer treatment for travel-related illnesses and vaccinations.

Dentists are listed in the Yellow Pages. For urgent cases, call 000 or go to the emergency department of a hospital.

Pharmacies, generally known as "chemists", can be found throughout the city and suburbs. They sell a wide range of drugs and medical supplies over the counter. A handful of city, Kings Cross and Bondi Beach chemists, such as **Blakes Pharmacy**, stay open until around 9pm.

Travel and Health Insurance

It is a good idea to buy travel insurance before arriving in Australia. Most overseas visitors are not covered by Australia's "Medicare" government health scheme, and medical, dental and ambulance costs are expensive.

British and New Zealand passport-holders (and nationals from eight other European countries) are entitled to free basic emergency medical and hospital treatment.

The **Department of Human Services** provides details on health cover for visitors under the "Migrants, Refugees and Visitors"

section of its website. The Department of Foreign Affairs and Trade's **Smart Traveller** website has information on health and safety.

Environmental Hazards

When swimming at an ocean beach, check that there are life-savers on patrol and swim within the "flagged" areas. In their red and yellow caps, volunteer surf lifesavers keep an eye out for changing surf conditions, people in difficulty and surfers close to areas set aside for swimmers only. Lifeguards from district councils have blue uniforms (see p56). Look out for beach signs indicating that it is dangerous to swim.

If you plan to bushwalk, do not hike alone. Always tell someone where you are going and when you will be back. Take a map, a basic first-aid kit, food and water, and warm, waterproof clothing. It is unlikely that you will run into any poisonous snakes or spiders, but do wear substantial footwear, keep a close eye on where you step, and check around logs and rocks before sitting on them.

Protecting Your Skin

Australia has the world's highest rates of skin cancer, caused by the harmful effects of ultraviolet rays. The risk of skin damage is high, even on cloudy days, and particularly between 10am and 2pm (11am and 3pm in daylight saving). Always wear a good SPF 50+ sunscreen and cover up with protective clothing, hat and sunglasses. The **Cancer Council** has more information.

Banking and Local Currency

Sydney is Australia's financial capital. In the Central Business District (CBD) are the imposing headquarters of several of the country's leading banks, as well as the Australian head offices of major foreign banks. Visitors will find local, state and national bank branches dotted at convenient intervals throughout the city and suburbs.

There is no limit to the amount of personal funds that visitors can bring into Australia, but they must declare amounts over A$10,000 on their entry form. Most currencies can be exchanged on arrival at the airport. Money can be changed at banks, bureaux de change (these generally offer the best exchange rates) and also at hotels.

High street bank logos of four major
Australian banks

Banks and Bureaux de Change

Bank trading hours are usually 9:30am–4pm Monday to Thursday, and 9:30am–5pm on Fridays. Some branches are also open to midday on Saturdays. Major city banks open 8:30am–5pm on weekdays.

Most bureaux de change are open Monday to Saturday, 9am–5:30pm, and some are open Sundays. Many state they don't charge commissions or fees, but their exchange rates are generally lower than at banks. The current exchange rates, which can vary considerably day to day, are shown in the windows or foyers of banks and bureaux de change.

Pre-paid travel cards or money cards, loaded with Australian dollars before you travel, are an easy and secure way to access your money through ATMs and make purchases while avoiding excess transaction fees and fluctuating exchange rates.

ATMs

ATMs can be found in most bank lobbies or on an external wall near the bank's entrance, on main streets and in shopping areas throughout the city. Ask your home bank or credit card provider which Australian banks and cash dispensers will accept your debit and credit cards, and what the transaction charges per use will be. To avoid multiple charges, it is preferable to make a larger cash withdrawal rather than several smaller ones when using an ATM not associated with your card account.

Credit and Debit Cards

All well-known international credit cards are widely accepted in Australia, as well as debit cards issued by major foreign banks. Visa and MasterCard (Access) are the most widely accepted cards, while American Express is also taken by most retailers and travel providers. Some smaller establishments such as cafés, newsagents and convenience stores do not accept card payments. If your card is linked to a savings account, you can use it as a debit card to both pay for goods and withdraw cash from your account in the same transaction, minimizing ATM fees.

Most retailers have "tap-and-go" terminals that use chip readers for card transactions up to A$100, eliminating the need to enter a PIN code.

Carry the phone number of your credit card issuer in case your card is lost or stolen.

Wiring Money

Money can only be transferred to a person travelling in Australia if that person has set up a bank account in Australia. Transfer fees, which may average around £10, are charged by UK banks and the Australian bank may also charge a fee. The **ANZ Bank** has a branch in London where travellers can set up an Australian account before they leave home. It can take

DIRECTORY

Banks and Bureaux de Change

American Express
12 Shelley St, King St Wharf.
Map 4 D1.
45 Sussex St. **Map** 4 D1.
181 Castlereagh St (inside Australia Post). **Map** 4 E2.
Tel 1300 736 659 or 1300 139 060.

ANZ Bank
20 Martin Place. **Map** 4 E1.
Tel 131 314.

The Change Group
Jetty 6, Circular Quay. **Map** 1 B3.
Tel 9247 2082. **Open** 9am–7pm daily.
222 Pitt St (Piccadilly Arcade).
Map 4 E3. **Tel** 9266 0644.
W changegroup.com

Citibank
2 Park St. **Map** 4 E2.
55–57 Pitt St. **Map** 1 B3.
695 George St. **Map** 4 E4.
Tel 9978 2871.

Commonwealth Bank
48 Martin Place. **Map** 1 B4.
Tel 132 221.

National Australia Bank
343 George St. **Map** 1 B4.
Tel 132 265.

Travelex
330 George St. **Map** 1 B4.
570 George St. **Map** 1 B5.
Tel 9978 2871.

Westpac Bank
341 George St. **Map** 1 B4.
Tel 132 032.

Wiring Money

ANZ Bank UK
40 Bank St, Canary Wharf,
London, E14 5EJ, UK.
Tel 0203 229 2121.

Western Union
W westernunion.co.uk

up to five days for the money to arrive. A quicker way is via **Western Union** and other similar operators.

Currency

The Australian currency is the Australian dollar ($ or A$), which breaks down into 100 cents (c).

Single cents may still be used for some prices, but as the Australian 1c and 2c coins are no longer in circulation, the total amount to be paid will be rounded up or down to the nearest five cent amount.

It can be difficult to get A$100 notes changed, so avoid using them in smaller shops and cafés and, more particularly, when

paying for taxi fares. If you do not have smaller notes, it is always wise to tell the taxi driver before you start your journey. Taxis accept credit cards, but impose a hefty surcharge for their use.

To improve security, as well as increase their circulation life, all Australian bank notes have now been plasticized.

Bank Notes

Australian bank notes are produced in denominations of A$5, A$10, A$20, A$50 and A$100. All bank notes are made of plastic. Paper notes have been phased out and are no longer legal tender.

A$100 note

A$50 note

A$20 note

A$10 note

A$5 note

5 cents (5c)

10 cents (10c)

20 cents (20c)

50 cents (50c)

1 dollar (A$1)

2 dollars (A$2)

Coins

Coins currently in use are 5c, 10c, 20c, 50c, A$1 and A$2 (shown here actual size). There are several 20c, 50c and $1 coins in circulation; all are the same shape, but have different commemorative images.

Media and Communications

Australia has efficient mobile and data services networks, with major telecommunications operators providing good coverage across the Sydney region, though mobile signals can be patchy in some rural areas. Free Wi-Fi is widely available in Sydney and near popular attractions. Australia has one of the world's highest rates of mobile phone use, with more than 31 million active mobile phone accounts in a population of 23 million. In spite of this, the national carrier Telstra maintains a network of public payphones. Daily newspapers are still published, but news is largely accessed online and via mobiles. Six main television networks and numerous radio stations cover a range of interests and entertainment needs.

People using free Wi-Fi on their laptops at a café in the Kings Cross area of Sydney

International and Local Phone Calls

Local calls (those with the 02 area code) are untimed and cost 50 cents. Credit card public phones have a minimum charge of A$1.20, making them uneconomical for local calls. A cheaper option is to buy an international calling card for the country you will be calling. These are available at newsagents and convenience stores.

Online phone directories are available at www.whitepages. com.au, or on the free Sensis White Pages smartphone app.

Mobile Phones

Mobile phones are ubiquitous in Australia. You can rent one from **Vodafone** at their shop in the airport international arrivals hall (open 6am–10pm).

A popular option is to buy an Australian SIM card to use in your mobile phone – the call and data rates are much cheaper than roaming charges using your own service plan. SIM cards

offering a range of plans are available from **Optus**, **Telstra**, **Virgin** and Vodafone, and online companies such as **Telestial**. You will get a nine-digit local mobile number. You must have an unlocked compatible international phone; if in doubt, check with your service provider.

Public Telephones

Telstra-operated public payphones are found all over the city. Payment options include coins, pre-paid phonecards (available at newsagents, convenience stores and some chemists), and the more expensive operator-assisted calls. Most payphones accept coins and phonecards, although some operate solely with phonecards and credit cards.

Newer smart payphones include SMS text messaging services and a hearing aid coupler to assist the hard of hearing. The phone booths display instructions and numbers to call for assistance.

Internet and Wi-Fi

Numerous free Wi-Fi hotspots are available throughout the city. Most hotels, cafés, libraries, shopping centres, transport hubs and tourist attractions provide free access – some require a password, while others just invite you to join the network. A list of free Wi-Fi hotspots is available at www.freewifi.com.au.

As Wi-Fi has become more widely available and smartphones provide easy access to mobile data and online services, there are fewer Internet cafés in the city. A popular one, however, is **Legend Café**, which offers high-speed access to a range of pre-installed games at an hourly rate. The State Library provides free access to Internet-enabled computers for up to an hour at a time in the Governor Marie Bashir Reading Room, and for 30 minutes on express computers in the Verandah and Special Collections area.

Postal Services

All domestic mail is first class and usually arrives within one to four days, depending on distance. Be sure to include the postcode in the address to avoid delays in delivery.

Express Post, for which you need to buy one of the special yellow envelopes sold in post offices, guarantees next-day delivery in designated areas of Australia. International airmail takes up to 10 days to reach most countries, longer at busy times such as Christmas.

Telstra public telephone booths

Reaching the Right Number

- To ring Sydney from the UK, dial 0061 2, then the local number.
- To ring Sydney from the USA and Canada, dial 011 61 2, then the local number.
- For long-distance direct-dial calls outside your local area code, but within Australia (STD calls), dial the appropriate area code, then the number, e.g. for Melbourne dial 03 first.
- For international direct-dial calls (IDD calls): dial 0011, followed by the country code (USA and Canada: 1; UK: 44; New Zealand: 64), then the city or area code (omit initial 0) and then the local number.
- International directory enquiries: dial 1225.
- Local directory enquiries: dial 1223.
- Call Connect: dial 12455 (call connection charges apply).
- International operator assistance: dial 1225.
- For reverse-charge calls to national and mobile numbers, dial 1800 662 274.
- Numbers beginning with 1800 and six-digit numbers beginning with 13 are charged at local call rates from fixed lines and at higher rates from mobiles.
- Ten-digit numbers beginning with 04 are mobile phones.
- See also Emergency Numbers, *p223*.

International postage for post-cards and standard-sized cards is fixed and based on the region it is being sent to. Sending anything bigger or heavier, including parcels, is very expensive.

There are two types of international express mail. Express Courier International is the fastest service and will reach nearly all overseas destinations within two to four days, with its delivery tracked from door-to-door. Items sent via Express Post International will reach most destinations in three to seven days.

If you want to ensure the addressee receives the letter or parcel, use Registered Post

Red standard postboxes (for normal post) and yellow postboxes (for Express Post)

International where the recipient signs for the item on delivery.

Sydney has red and yellow postboxes. The red boxes are for the standard postal service; the yellow boxes are for Express Post within Australia.

Post offices are open 9am–5pm weekdays, with some outlets also open on Saturdays. Almost all post offices offer a wide range of services, including money orders and money transfer, as well as selling stamps, envelopes, packaging, stationery and postcards. Stamps can also be bought from hotels and shops where postcards are sold, and from some newsagents.

Address **Poste Restante** letters to c/- Poste Restante, GPO Sydney, NSW 2000, but collect them from 310 George St, Hunter Connection Building, opposite Wynyard Station. You will need to show proof of identity.

Newspapers and Magazines

Sydney's chief daily morning newspaper is the *Sydney Morning Herald*. It includes a comprehensive listing of local entertainment on Saturdays. The other Sydney daily is the *Daily Telegraph*.

The *Australian* is the country's only daily national general paper with the most comprehensive coverage of overseas news; the *Australian Financial Review* largely reports on business and finance. Some newspapers require a subscription for access to online editions. Others, including www.news.com.au, www.thenewdaily.com.au and national broadcaster www.abc.net.au, are free. A wide range of magazines is available at newsagents and supermarkets.

Television and Radio

Australia has two state-run television networks, ABC (Channel 2) and SBS. There are also commercial networks: Channels 7, 9 and 10. Each network operates multiple digital channels, and their online sites give access to view missed programmes. Foxtel is the subscription-based Pay TV provider offered by most hotels as part of in-room entertainment. ABC provides news and current affairs coverage, children's programmes and local and international dramas. The Special Broadcasting Service (SBS) caters to Australia's many cultures with foreign-language programmes. Commercial channels offer a variety of entertainment from sport and news to soap operas.

Sydney has several AM and FM radio stations and numerous digital stations. ABC stations cater for various musical tastes, as well as providing news and magazine-style programmes.

DIRECTORY

Mobile Phones

Optus
w optus.com.au

Telestial
w telestial.com

Telstra
w telstra.com

Virgin
w virginmobile.com.au

Vodafone
w vodafone.com.au

Internet and Wi-Fi

Legend Café
505 George St. **Map** 4 E5.
Tel 8034 3201.
w legendinternetcafe.com.au

Postal Services

General Post Office (GPO)
1 Martin Place. **Map** 4 E1. **Tel** 131 318. **Open** 8:30am–5:30pm Mon–Fri, 10am–2pm Sat.

Poste Restante: 310 George St, Level 2A, Hunter Connection Building. **Map** 4 E1. **Tel** 9244 3732. **Open** 9am–5:30pm Mon–Fri.

TRAVEL INFORMATION

International travel to Sydney can mean a long and tiring flight. Long-haul flights from Europe require at least one stop for refuelling. Most visitors from Europe fly via Dubai, Hong Kong or Singapore. Direct flights from the US west coast and Dallas take about 15 hours; some visitors break the journey in Hawaii. A break can mean the difference between arriving in Sydney jet-lagged or stepping off the plane refreshed and ready to take in the sights. Sydney is the major gateway to other state capitals, with many interstate flights daily. Relatively less expensive though more time-consuming options are the efficient rail and coach connections, some taking scenic routes with stopovers offered by some coach companies, and a well-maintained highway and freeway network for long-distance car travel, again with options for scenic detours.

Arriving by Air

The main gateway to the city is **Sydney Airport** (Kingsford Smith), which has three terminals. T1, the international terminal, is 3 km (2 miles) from the two domestic terminals, T2 and the Qantas-only T3. The international and domestic terminals are connected by a shuttle bus (fare A$5.50) and train line (fare A$5). Taxis and Über pick-ups are also available.

T1 can get busy at peak times (usually early morning), which can sometimes result in delays in immigration and baggage collection. There is a large duty-free shop for arriving passengers and a stand with free Sydney guidebooks. The arrivals lounge has Airport Ambassadors and a help desk to answer questions *(see p219)*. T1 also has a bureau de change, Internet facilities, shops, ATMs and several car hire desks.

Australia's major international and domestic carriers, **Qantas Airways**, **Jetstar** and **Virgin Australia**, link Sydney with other cities and tourist destinations in Australia from T2 and T3. Regional carriers, including QantasLink and **REX**, which connects Sydney to New South Wales, also use T2.

Tickets and Fares

International flights to Sydney are often heavily booked, especially from December to February. December is the most expensive time to fly. Tickets can be cheaper from February to mid-April. Airfares purchased in advance are often the best priced, though these and other discounted fares usually come with strict no-change and no-cancellation rules. Round-the-world fares can offer good value, as can flight-comparison web-sites such as www.webjet.com.au and www.skyscanner.com.

On Arrival

International airline passengers are issued with an Incoming Passenger Card to be filled in before passport control. This card, along with your passport, is presented to immigration and customs officials, who will mark and return it. Keep the card safe, because you must hand it to another customs officer once you have collected your luggage and are exiting the customs area. Packaged food, plant materials and other goods deemed to be a risk must be declared *(see p218)*.

Taxis lining up to take passengers at Sydney Airport

Getting into the City

Sydney airport is about 9 km (5 miles) from the Central Business District. **Sydney Airport Pick-Up** lists the designated pick-up zones for various transport providers. The **Airport Link** rail line (a private line that links with Sydney Trains), takes 13 minutes to get into the city and costs A$18.50 from T1. Shuttle bus companies, such as **KST Sydney Airporter**, **Airport Connect** and **AirBus Sydney**, run from the airport to hotels in the city, Darling Harbour and Kings Cross. Tickets cost from A$16 one way; booking online is cheaper than buying tickets on the bus.

Catch buses and taxis from outside the terminals or take the train from the underground station at each terminal. A State Transit bus (Metro route 400) stops at the airport. It travels to Bondi Junction and the western suburb of Burwood (but not the city; connections to the city are available along the route). A taxi from the airport to the city costs A$40–45.

Qantas flight arriving at Sydney Airport

A passenger ship berthed at Circular Quay

Arriving by Sea

The most delightful way to arrive in Sydney is by ship. Passenger ships berth at terminals at **Circular Quay** and **White Bay** at Rozelle. The Circular Quay site (known as the Overseas Passenger Terminal) is in The Rocks, with the information booths, volunteer greeters, tour booking centres, buses, trains, ferries, taxis and water taxis all close at hand. White Bay caters predominantly to the domestic cruise market, since most international cruise ships are too tall to cross under the Sydney Harbour Bridge to reach the terminal. The terminal is a 10–15-minute taxi trip across Anzac Bridge to or from the city, although at peak hours it may take longer. There are ATM facilities, short-term parking and a taxi rank at the terminal, and it is wheelchair accessible.

Arriving by Train

All interstate and regional trains arrive at **Central Railway Station**. Australia's nationwide rail network is known by a different name in each state, but it still operates cohesively. **NSW TrainLink** is the New South Wales regional rail network. Its reservations line answers queries and takes bookings (6:30am–10pm daily) for train services throughout Australia.

The city train operator, **Sydney Trains** (see p232), also has slower but cheaper services to some country areas such as Newcastle and Wollongong, but seats cannot be booked in advance.

The Transport Infoline (see p233) has details about NSW Trains' services beyond Greater Sydney.

Arriving by Coach

Most long-distance bus or coach services arrive at the **Sydney Coach Terminal** at Central Railway Station. The terminal has left-luggage facilities but will not store anything overnight. Competition between the coach companies is fierce, so shop around to get the best price.

Arriving by Car

The four major routes into Sydney are the Pacific Highway from the north; the Great Western Highway from the west; the Princes Highway, following the coast from Melbourne; and the Hume Highway, which runs inland from Melbourne.

As these routes approach Sydney, they feed into freeways or tolled motorways, which either link to other motorways or lead towards the city centre. Some include tunnels, such as the Sydney Harbour Tunnel, an alternative to the Sydney Harbour Bridge. All exits are clearly marked with green and white signs, as are connecting roads.

DIRECTORY

Arriving by Air

Airport Information – Sydney Airport (Kingsford Smith)
Tel 9667 9111.
W sydneyairport.com.au

Air Canada
Tel 1300 655 767.
W aircanada.com

Air New Zealand
Tel 132 476.
W airnewzealand.com

British Airways
Tel 1300 767 177.
W britishairways.com

Emirates
Tel 1300 303 777.
W emirates.com

Japan Airlines
Tel 1800 802 228.
W jal.com

Jetstar
Tel 131 538.
W jetstar.com

Qantas Airways and QantasLink
Tel 131 313.
W qantas.com

REX – Regional Express Airlines
Tel 131 713.
W rex.com.au

Singapore Airlines
Tel 131 011.
W singaporeaircom.

Thai Airways
Tel 1300 651 960 or 9844 0936.
W thaiairways.com

United Airlines
Tel 131 777.
W united. com

Virgin Australia
Tel 136 789.
W virginaustralia.com

Getting into the City

AirBus Sydney
W airbussydney.com.au

Airport Connect
Tel 9557 7615.
W airport connect.com.au

Airport Link (Train)
Tel 131 500.
W airportlink.com.au

KST Sydney Airporter
Tel 9666 9988.
W kst.com.au

Sydney Airport Pick-up
W pickup.sydney airport.com.au

Arriving by Sea

Circular Quay
West Circular Quay, Sydney. **Map** 1 B3.

White Bay Cruise Terminal
off James Craig Rd, Rozelle.

Arriving by Train

Central Railway Station
Tel 9379 1777.

NSW TrainLink
Tel 132 232.

Arriving by Coach

Sydney Coach Terminal
Cnr of Eddy Ave & Pitt St.
Map 4 E5. **Tel** 9281 9366.

Getting Around Sydney

In general, the best way to see Sydney's many sights and attractions is on foot, coupled with use of the public transport system, made easy by the integrated Opal ticketing system. Buses, trains and the Sydney Light Rail system (modern trams) will take visitors to within easy walking distance of anywhere in the inner city. They also serve the suburbs and outlying areas. A new Light Rail line to the eastern suburbs will open in 2019. Buses have been removed from the major thoroughfare of George Street and routes changed to accommodate its construction. An excellent trip planner that will show you all options and travel times to get to any destination by public transport is available on the Transport NSW website.

Traffic crossing Johnstons Bay on Sydney's Anzac Bridge

Finding Your Way Around Sydney

Sydney is a sprawling metropolis, however, the Central Business District (CBD) is quite small. The city centre lies on the south side of the harbour; the Sydney Harbour Bridge connects it with the north. The main shopping area is an easy walk south from the harbour's edge. Darling Harbour is on the city's western edge; the closest beaches, including Bondi, are about 9 km (6 miles) to the east of the city and Manly is 11 km (7 miles) northeast (and over the Bridge).

Circular colour-coded signs show the locations of major bus (blue with a capital B), train (orange with a capital T), Light Rail (red with a capital L) and ferry (green with a capital F) stops, stations and wharves.

The **Transport NSW** website gives the latest information on all forms of transport. The TripView app has maps, routes, timetables and live data for buses, trains and ferries. The Lite version is free.

Walking

Take care when walking around the city. Vehicles are driven on the left and often move quickly. It is wise to use pedestrian crossings; there are two types. Push-button crossings are found at traffic lights. Wait for the green man signal and do not cross at lights if the red warning sign is on or flashing. Zebra crossings are marked by yellow-and-black signs and white striped road markings. Police occasionally issue on-the-spot fines for jaywalking.

Guided Tours

Tours and excursions range from bus tours for food-lovers to jaunts on the back of a Harley Davidson, guided nature or history walks, cruises on replica tall ships, guided bicycle tours and aerial adventures by hot-air balloon, seaplane or helicopter.

A good introduction to Sydney's attractions is the hop-on-hop-off tour in an open-top double decker bus run by **Sydney and Bondi Explorer**. Visitors can use commuter ferries *(see pp234–5)* as a less costly alternative to commercial harbour cruises, of which there are many.

Tickets and Travel Passes

Passengers wanting to use multiple public transport options across Sydney's integrated network should obtain a pre-paid chip-based **Opal** card. Opal cards are available from airport train stations, airport terminal retailers, the Circular Quay Transport Information Centre, post offices, newsagents and convenience stores. Alternatively, Opal single-trip tickets can be bought from the ticket machines at selected stations and wharves. Opal single-trip bus tickets can be purchased on-board from the driver except on PrePay bus services, which includes all city centre buses.

Opal cards are a convenient way to use all public transport options – bus, train, Light Rail and ferry, including Sydney Trains services to the Blue Mountains, Newcastle and Southern Highlands. Opal cannot be used for NSW TrainLink and regional coaches, and for private and Fast Ferry services (such as those offering sightseeing, tours and travel to Fort Denison).

Customers pre-load value onto an Opal card, with a starting balance of A$10 for adults and A$5 for children. There is no charge for the card itself. You can register your Opal card online to check the balance, top up, and block its use in the event that it is lost or stolen. Top-ups can also be made wherever the cards are sold or at machines at stations and wharves.

To use an Opal card, riders "tap on" by placing the card on the Opal touchpad as they board, and "tap off" in the same way when they disembark. The fare is calculated based on distance travelled. The touchpad will also show the remaining balance on the card. After eight journeys in a week, the remaining journeys for the week are at half-price. Daily and weekly fare caps are in place (A$15 and A$60 for adults and A$7.50 and A$30 for children, respectively); once the cap is reached, travel is free for the rest of the day or the week. There is a A$2.50 fare cap on Sundays, after which travel is free.

Driving in Sydney

If you are planning to use a car to drive around Greater Sydney, you will need an in-car Global Positioning System (GPS), which is usually offered as an option when you hire a car.

Kerbside Traffic Signs

Always pay strict attention to Sydney's parking and traffic signs, as fines for infringements can be very expensive.

It is best to avoid the peak-hour traffic periods (about 7:30–9:30am and 4–7:30pm), if possible. Regular traffic update reports are broadcast on many radio stations. Live updates are also available via Transport NSW's **Live Traffic NSW** website and smartphone app, and at Live Traffic Sydney (@LiveTrafficSyd) on Twitter.

Petrol is a little more expensive than in North America, but about half the price of petrol in Europe. Most petrol stations are self-service; a small number require pre-payment via a credit card.

Overseas visitors can use their usual driver's licence to drive in New South Wales, but must have proof that they are only visiting. Make sure you keep your licence on you at all times when driving.

Australians drive on the left-hand side of the road and over-take on the right. Speed limits vary and are well-signposted, as are bus lanes and T2 and T3 lanes for cars carrying two, three or more passengers. The 0.05 per cent maximum blood alcohol level for drivers is enforced by random breath tests and mobile drug testing on busy and suburban roads. A driver found to be over the legal limit will incur a heavy fine, loss of licence and even a prison sentence.

Parking

Parking in Sydney is strictly regulated with fines for any infringements. In certain areas, particularly along clearways (indicated by signposts),

vehicles are towed away if parked illegally. Contact the **Transport Management Centre** if this happens.

Car parks in the city area charge fees from A$4 to A$25 an hour on weekdays. Look out for the blue-and-white "P" signs. On-street parking meters vary in price, depending on the time and area. Shopping centres tend to offer two to three hours of free parking before charges apply.

Taxis

Taxis are plentiful in Sydney in the city and inner suburbs, although they can be scarce "between shifts" at 2:30–3:15pm. There are taxi ranks at many city locations and taxis are often found outside large hotels. Meters indicate the fare plus any extras, such as booking fees and waiting time. Fares and extra charges are regulated and are more expensive after 10pm. **Über** is available and **GoCatch** is another taxi booking platform via a mobile app.

Taxis designed to accommodate disabled passengers can be booked through any of the major companies.

Cycling

Visitors should restrict their cycling to designated bicycle tracks, or to areas where motor traffic is likely to be light. They should also remember that wearing a helmet is compulsory. Centennial Park (*see p55*) is a popular biking spot. For more

Cycling, an eco-friendly way to explore the city

information, including maps, routes, bike stores and hire, visit www.sydneycycleways.net.
Bonza Bike Tours and **Manly Bike Tours** offer entertaining guided cycling tours.

DIRECTORY
Guided Tours

Sydney and Bondi Explorer
theaustralianexplorer.com.au

Tickets and Passes

Opal
opal.com.au

Transport NSW
Tel 131 500.
transportnsw.info

Driving in Sydney

NSW Live Traffic
m.livetraffic.rta.nsw.gov.au

Parking

Transport Management Centre
Tel 132 701 (24-hour service).
rms.nsw.gov.au

Car Hire Companies

Avis
avis.com.au

Budget
budget.com.au

Hertz
hertz.com.au

Thrifty
thrifty.com.au

Taxis

GoCatch
gocatch.com

Legion Cabs
Tel 131 451.

Premier Cabs
Tel 131 017.

Silver Service Taxis
Tel 133 100.

Taxi Complaints
Tel 1800 648 478.

Über
uber.com

Cycling

Bonza Bike Tours
Tel 9247 8800.

Manly Bike Tours
Tel 8005 7368.

Travelling by Sydney Trains and Light Rail

Sydney's railway network (operated by Sydney Trains) connects the suburbs with the city and serves a large part of the Central Business District. Sydney Trains also operates services to the Blue Mountains, Central Coast and Southern Highlands. The Light Rail (tram) line is a convenient alternative for exploring Darling Harbour, as well as Chinatown, The Star casino and some inner west suburbs. A new Light Rail line connecting the city to the east is due to open in 2019, while a new underground Metro network, including stops in the city and Barangaroo, is also under construction, due to open in 2024.

Sydney Trains train at a platform, Central Railway Station

Travelling by Sydney Trains

The **Sydney Trains** network covers a vast area and is the quickest way to get into the city from most suburbs, as well as to and from the airport. The City Circle loop runs through the city centre stopping at Central, Town Hall, Wynyard, Circular Quay, St James and Museum stations.

All suburban lines connect with the City Circle at **Central Railway Station**. The western, northern and southern suburbs are well covered by the network, but it does not extend to the eastern or northern beaches (note: Bondi Junction is covered by the eastern suburb trains but not Bondi Beach, for which there is a bus connection).

Trains run from 4:30am to about midnight. After midnight, NightSafe buses travel along rail routes, and all routes pick up from George Street and Town Hall, providing long-haul services to many suburban areas.

Using the Sydney Light Rail Trams

The **Sydney Light Rail** is both a tourist and commuter service. The environmentally friendly trams offer a quicker and quieter way of visiting places of interest between Glebe and Darling Harbour.

Sydney Light Rail stop sign

The trams travel from Central Railway Station to the inner western suburb of Dulwich Hill on a disused goods line, calling at several stations, including stops at The Star casino, the Sydney Fish Market and Jubilee Park.

Buy single-trip Opal tickets on board from the conductor or use a pre-paid Opal card. The Light Rail is a good sightseeing option for those who want to venture out of the main city areas. The Jubilee Park stop is in a beautiful park with wetlands, bridges and a delightful walking path around Rozelle Bay, with

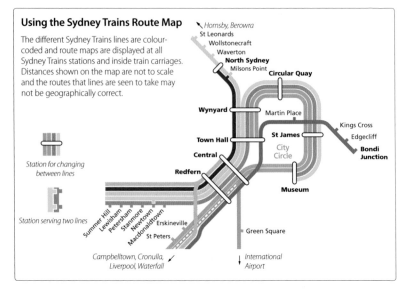

Using the Sydney Trains Route Map

The different Sydney Trains lines are colour-coded and route maps are displayed at all Sydney Trains stations and inside train carriages. Distances shown on the map are not to scale and the routes that lines are seen to take may not be geographically correct.

Station for changing between lines

Station serving two lines

Hornsby, Berowra
St Leonards
Wollstonecraft
Waverton
North Sydney
Milsons Point
Circular Quay

Wynyard
Martin Place

Town Hall
St James
Kings Cross
Edgecliff

Central
City Circle
Bondi Junction

Redfern
Museum

Summer Hill
Lewisham
Petersham
Stanmore
Newtown
Macdonaldtown
Erskineville
St Peters

Green Square

Campbelltown, Cronulla, Liverpool, Waterfall

International Airport

A tram on the Light Rail network leaving Central Railway Station

plaques pointing out some of the area's history. The path leads around to the Sydney Fish Market, where there is another Light Rail stop, from which you can head back to the city.

Another pleasant excursion from Jubilee Park station is a stroll through the park to the food providers at the restored Tramsheds (www.tramsheds haroldpark.com.au), followed by a walk back through the park to Glebe Point Road, a long stretch filled with bookshops, and antiques and second-hand stores.

Late-night gamblers can take advantage of the Central–The Star–Central trams that run along this limited-stop route 24 hours a day. The all-stops service between Central and Dulwich Hill operates 6am–11pm daily (until midnight on Fridays and Saturdays). The daily service runs every 10–15 minutes at peak times, and every 30 minutes between midnight and 6am.

DIRECTORY

Useful Information

Central Railway Station
Eddy Avenue, Haymarket.
Map 4 E5. **Tel** 9379 1777.

Circular Quay Railway Station
Alfred Street. **Map** 1 B3.
Tel 9224 3553.

Sydney Light Rail
Tel 131 500.
W transportnsw.info

Sydney Trains
Tel 131 500.
W sydneytrains.info

Transport Infoline
Tel 131 500.
W transportnsw.info

Making a Journey by Sydney Trains

1 Plan your trip online at www. transportnsw.info or study the Sydney Trains route map. Route lines are distinguished by colour, so simply trace the line from where you are to your destination, noting where you need to change and make connections.

Sydney Trains sign

2 If you don't already have a pre-paid Opal card, purchase a single-use Opal ticket from the ticket-dispensing Opal machines at the station. Return tickets are not available.

3 To pass through the ticket barrier, tap your pre-paid or single-use Opal card on the display pad at the front of the barrier machines.

4 To find the right platform, follow the signs with the same colour code as the line you need and the name of the line's final station.

5 On the platform, display signs show all the stations the line travels through. Stations at which the next train will stop are lit up and are announced as the train arrives at the station.

6 Tap off using your Opal card or ticket at the end of your journey.

Travelling by Ferry and Water Taxi

Travelling by ferry is a great way to commute between the harbour suburbs. State-owned, privately managed Sydney Ferries provides the majority of services, but it competes with Fast Ferry, managed by a second private operator on the Manly run. Water taxis are a convenient but expensive alternative, and there are numerous sightseeing cruises offering a wide range of tours, from showcasing landmarks within the harbour to travelling to the open ocean on whale-watching expeditions.

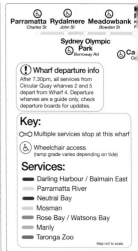

Parramatta (Ⓖ Charles St)   Rydalmere (Ⓖ John St)   Meadowbank (Ⓖ Bowden St)

Sydney Olympic Park (Ⓖ Burroway Rd)   Ⓖ Ca

⚠ Wharf departure info
After 7.30pm, all services from Circular Quay wharves 2 and 5 depart from Wharf 4. Departure wharves are a guide only, check departure boards for updates.

Key:
C○○ Multiple services stop at this wharf

Ⓖ Wheelchair access
(ramp grade varies depending on tide)

Services:
━━ Darling Harbour / Balmain East
━━ Parramatta River
━━ Neutral Bay
━━ Mosman
━━ Rose Bay / Watsons Bay
━━ Manly
━━ Taronga Zoo

Map not to scale.

Captain Cook ferry approaching the Sydney Opera House

Using Sydney's Ferries

There is a constant procession of **Sydney Ferries** traversing the harbour between 6am and midnight daily. The boats cover most of Sydney Harbour and stops along the Parramatta River. Frequent services run to and from Manly, Darling Harbour, Balmain, Parramatta, Taronga Zoo, Neutral Bay, Pyrmont Bay, Balmain/Woolwich, Mosman, Rose Bay and Watsons Bay, with stops en route. Sydney Buses (see p236) provide convenient connections at most wharves.

The Transport NSW website provides complete information, including timetables, stops and fares. You can also call the **Sydney Ferries Infoline** for details. Contact ferry operator **Harbour City Ferries** about lost property.

Making a Journey by Ferry

Most ferry journeys start and end at the Circular Quay Ferry Terminal, but you can board and disembark at any stop along the route. Electronic destination boards at the entrance to each wharf indicate the wharf from which your ferry will leave, and also give departure times and all stops made en route.

If you don't have a pre-paid Opal Card (see p230), you can buy a single-trip ferry ticket from the Opal machines at the wharf. To board the ferry, tap your Opal ticket or card on the Opal pad on the barrier machine. You need to tap off at the end of your journey, too.

Manly's ferry terminal is serviced by regular ferries and the faster, privately run **Manly Fast Ferry**. The trip takes 17 minutes, compared to 30 minutes by traditional ferry. This service operates every 10 minutes during peak times in the morning and afternoon, and twice an hour outside peak times. Tickets can be bought from the Manly Fast Ferry booth at the wharf or on board the vessel.

Types of Vessel

Sydney Ferries operates six types of vessel: the SuperCats serving Watsons Bay, the

RiverCats that travel upriver to Parramatta, the HarbourCats, the First Fleet Class for short inner suburb routes, the Lady Class and the large and elegant Freshwaters that pass by the North and South Heads on their way to Manly. A new-style ferry for the Parramatta River is under development.

A Sydney Ferries SuperCat

The Freshwater *Collaroy* en route to Manly

A Sydney Ferries RiverCat

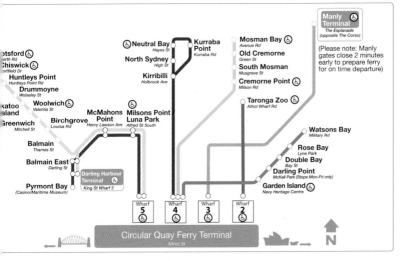

Wharf 5 &

Wharf 4 &

Wharf 3 &

Wharf 2 &

Circular Quay Ferry Terminal
Alfred St

N

Sightseeing by Ferry and Commercial Operators

Catching a commuter ferry is a relaxing and picturesque way to discover the harbour, and no visit to Sydney is complete without seeing the skyline from the water. Close-up views of the Opera House and Fort Denison can be had from any of the North Shore commuter routes, while the Balmain/Woolwich ferry and the RiverCat ferry stop at Cockatoo Island *(see p108)*. As well as providing a fascinating glimpse of Sydney's convict history, this island offers perhaps the best vantage point for views of Harbour Bridge and the city skyline and waterfront mansions, including those at Kirribilli Point *(see p134)*.

Sydney Ferry stop sign

Other harbour islands can also be visited: the **National Parks and Wildlife Service** runs tours of Fort Denison and Goat Island, while **Captain Cook Cruises** operates the hop-on hop-off Harbour Explorer, which is a 24-hour cruise pass that allows visits to seven harbour sights including Fort Denison *(see p109)* and Shark Island. Numerous commercial sight-seeing cruises cover all budgets, themes and time constraints. Whale-watching cruises ranging from two to four hours travel

outside the Heads to the open water during whale migration season. Many of these leave from Wharf 6 (Circular Quay). **Whale Watching Sydney** has a modern fleet and a range of tours. Most sightseeing operators also pick up and drop off passengers at Darling Harbour.

Water Taxis

Small, fast taxi boats, such as **H2O Taxis** and **Water Taxis Combined**, go to any number of destinations on the harbour, including harbour islands. You can flag them down like normal cabs – try Circular Quay near the Overseas Passenger Terminal or King Street Wharf. You can also telephone or book online. They will pick up and drop off at any navigable pier. Rates vary, but expect to pay a charge of around A\$90–110 for a 10-minute ride from Darling Harbour to the Opera House for up to 10 people. Confirm the cost and number of passengers in advance..

A water taxi on Sydney Harbour – a convenient but pricey ride

DIRECTORY

Using Sydney's Ferries

Harbour City Ferries
Tel 8113 3002.
W beyondthewharf.com.au

Manly Fast Ferry
Tel 9583 1199.
W manlyfastferry.com.au

Sydney Ferries Infoline
Tel 131 500.
W transportnsw.info

Sightseeing by Ferry

Captain Cook Cruises
Tel 1800 804843.
W captaincook.com.au

National Parks and Wildlife Service
Tel 1300 072 757.
W nationalparks.nsw.gov.au

Whale Watching Sydney
Tel 9583 1199.
W whalewatchingsydney.com.au

Water Taxis

H2O Taxis
Tel 1300 420 829.
W h2owatertaxis.com.au

Water Taxis Combined
Tel 9555 8888.
W watertaxis.com.au

Travelling by Bus

Sydney Buses provides a punctual service that links up conveniently with the city's rail and ferry systems. As well as covering city and suburban areas, there are regular routes that serve the airport (see p228) and privately owned hop-on hop-off sightseeing buses. The Transport NSW Infoline and website (see p233) give the routes, fares and journey times. The construction of a new Light Rail line, due to open in 2019, means buses no longer travel down the main city thoroughfare of George Street, but they do cover other parts of the city centre.

An Opal card and ticket reader on a bus for tapping on and off

Using Sydney Buses

Sydney Buses operates an extensive network covering more than 300 routes throughout the city and suburbs. The removal of buses from the city's main north-south thoroughfare to accommo-date the introduction of a new Light Rail line means most city buses travel along Elizabeth Street, north to Circular Quay. Buses heading south generally travel to the city's eastern and southern suburbs, while those going to Central, Broadway and the inner west, including Glebe, Balmain and Newtown, travel south along Castlereagh Street.

To take a bus, you need a pre-paid Opal card (see p230) or a single-trip Opal ticket that you can buy from the driver on board, except for PrePay services, which are cashless and require an Opal card. All buses within the Central Business District are PrePay only from 7am to 7pm on weekdays.

Most buses are blue and white. Red Metro buses travel on longer routes between major suburban hubs, often via the city. An X in front of a bus number means it is an express bus that travels longer distances

with fewer stops; an L means it makes limited stops.

Front seats on buses have fold-up seats for wheelchairs and prams and are designated for the elderly, disabled and parents with prams. Eating, drinking or smoking is prohibited on buses. To signal that you wish to alight, press one of the stop buttons, which are mounted on the vertical handrails, well before the bus reaches your stop.

B

Sydney Bus stop sign

Bus Stops

Main bus stations and inter-changes are indicated by large, circular wayfinding signs, with a capital B on a blue background. Bus stops along a route are indicated by yellow-and-black signs displaying a profile of a bus and a boarding passenger. The route numbers of the buses travelling along the route are listed below this symbol.

Timetables are usually found on the bus stop sign or in the nearby shelter. The Sunday timetable also applies to public

holidays. Timetables are also available at the Sydney Buses booth at Railway Square, while the Sydney Buses and Transport NSW website and mobile app provides comprehensive timetables, routes and maps, which you can download.

Sightseeing by Bus

The brightly coloured Sydney Explorer buses (see p230) operate a daily hop-on hop-off service that visits 26 Sydney sights in a loop from Circular Quay. The whole journey takes 90 minutes if you don't get off. Stops include Kings Cross, the Botanic Garden and Darling Harbour.

The same company runs the Bondi & Bays Explorer that departs from Central Railway Station and calls at 10 stops, including Bondi Beach, Double Bay, Rose Bay and Paddington. Buses run from 8:30am until 7:30pm, with buses departing every 15–20 minutes. A combined ticket for both the city and Bondi tours is A$45 for 24 hours, or A$65 for 48 hours.

Sydney Buses travel to most of the same destinations at a lower cost, including Route 333 to Bondi Beach and Watsons Bay, but with less frequency. The advantage of the Explorer services is that you can get on and off as often as you wish. To make the most of your journey choose the sights you want to see and plan a basic itinerary.

Tickets can be bought on the buses at any stop or booked online in advance.

Hop-on hop-off Sydney Explorer bus in front of the Opera House

Travelling Beyond Sydney

Sydney is close to several areas of scenic beauty and an excellent wine region. The best way to explore the nearby regions of the Blue Mountains, Hunter Valley and the Southern Highways, or national parks on the edge of Sydney is by car and train. The far north-coast New South Wales beach towns and outback and regional centres of western New South Wales are between 1 and 1½ hours away by plane.

Blue Mountains National Park

Domestic Flights

Qantas and its subsidiary QantasLink, Jetstar and Virgin Australia are the main domestic airlines. Regional carriers REX – Regional Express Airlines – and QantasLink operate from T2 in Sydney Airport *(see pp228–9)*.

Fares can be quite low on competitive routes, and the cheapest rates can often be found online. Domestic flights depart from Sydney Airport's terminals 2 and 3; the latter is used exclusively by Qantas.

Country and Inter-Urban Trains

Sydney Trains *(see p232)* include InterCity trains that travel beyond Greater Sydney to the Blue Mountains, the South Coast (via five stations near the Royal National Park), the Southern Highlands and Newcastle, and the Central Coast. All depart from Central Railway Station *(see p229)*.

While the network also includes the Hunter regional line, this does not service the popular wineries near the town of Pokolbin. Passengers wanting to visit the wineries should take the train to Morrisett (on the Newcastle and Central Coast line), then a Rover Coach to Pokolbin.

The NSW TrainLink network *(see p229)* covers more than 360 regional destinations in New South Wales, along with connections to Brisbane and Melbourne. On its way out west, the train travels through the Blue Mountains, and trains to Melbourne stop at some Southern Highlands towns.

Tickets are available at Central Railway Station *(see p233)* and suburban stations in Sydney, or over the phone or online. Using a pre-paid Opal card is less expensive. Trains depart from the main concourse of Central Railway Station, upstairs from the suburban train platforms.

Long-Distance Bus Travel

Long-distance bus travel can be cost effective, but many journeys are long: for example, a coach to Coffs Harbour (considered the mid-way stop between Sydney and Brisbane) takes over 7 hours. **Greyhound Australia** covers the nation, while other operators, such as **Firefly Express** and **Murrays Coaches**, run services on certain routes.

Fares on the Sydney–Melbourne route are around A$110 one-way and discounts are often available, but it is a long 12- to 14-hour trip. Coaches leave from Central Railway Station. Greyhound's Volvo fleet, operating between Cairns and Melbourne (via Sydney), has leather seats that recline slightly.

Road Travel

Highways in Sydney and New South Wales are improving all the time. The biggest challenge is knowing which route to take out of the city, so hire a car with a GPS system. Many areas of scenic beauty are within 2 hours' drive of Sydney. Ensure that your hire car comes with road-side breakdown assistance. For more on driving, *see pp230–31*.

Car Hire

The rates of major agencies *(see p231)* range from about A$35 a day for a small car to A$100 a day for a larger vehicle, plus extra fees and taxes. These rates become cheaper over a week's rental and usually include insurance. Be sure to read the fine print on hire agreements. **Bayswater Car Rental** has among the best rates in Sydney, but check comparison sites such as www.skyscanner.com, www.carhire.com.au and www.vroomvroomvroom.com.au. Some companies only rent cars to those over 21 years of age. If you do not have a credit card, you will need to leave a deposit.

DIRECTORY

Using Sydney Buses

Sydney Buses
Tel 131 500.
w sydneybuses.info
w transportnsw.info

Long-Distance Bus Travel

Firefly Express
Tel 1300 730 740 or (03) 8318 0318. w fireflyexpress.com.au

Greyhound Australia
Tel 1300 473 946.
w greyhound.com.au

Murrays Coaches
Tel 132 251.
w murrays.com.au

Car Hire

Bayswater Car Rental
Tel 02 9360 3622.
w bayswatercarrental.com.au

SYDNEY STREET FINDER

The page grid superimposed on the *Area by Area* map below shows which parts of Sydney are covered in this *Street Finder*. Map references given for all sights, hotels, restaurants, shopping and entertainment venues described in this guide refer to the maps in this section. All the major sights are clearly marked so they are easy to locate.

A complete index of the street names and places of interest follows on pages 246–9. The key, set out below, indicates the scale of the maps and shows what other features are marked on them, including railway stations, bus terminals, ferry boarding points, emergency services, post offices and tourist information centres.

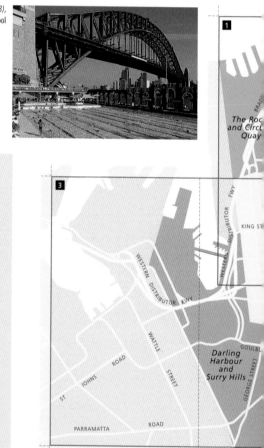

Sydney Harbour Bridge *(see pp72–3)*, viewed from North Sydney Olympic Pool

Key

▪	Major sight
▪	Place of interest
▫	Other building
🚆	Sydney Trains station
🚉	Central Railway station
🚈	Sydney Light Rail station
🚌	Bus terminus or coach station
⛴	Ferry boarding point
ℹ	Tourist information office
✚	Hospital with casualty unit
▣	Police station
✝	Church
✡	Synagogue
☪	Mosque
══	Freeway
─ ─	Railway line
─	Ferry route
	Pedestrianized street

0 metres   250
0 yards   250

0 metres   500
0 yards   500

Sundial in the Royal Botanic Garden *(see pp106–7)*

Statues on the Art Deco Anzac Memorial in Hyde Park *(see p88)*

Enjoying coffee outside Bar Coluzzi in Darlinghurst *(see p192)*

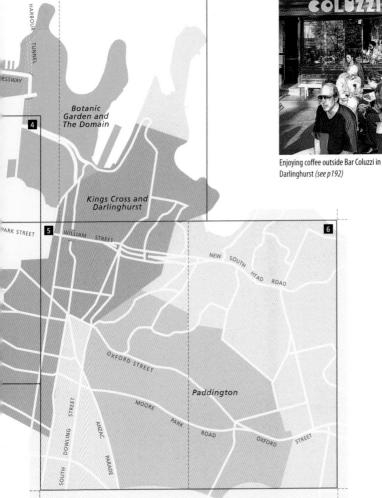

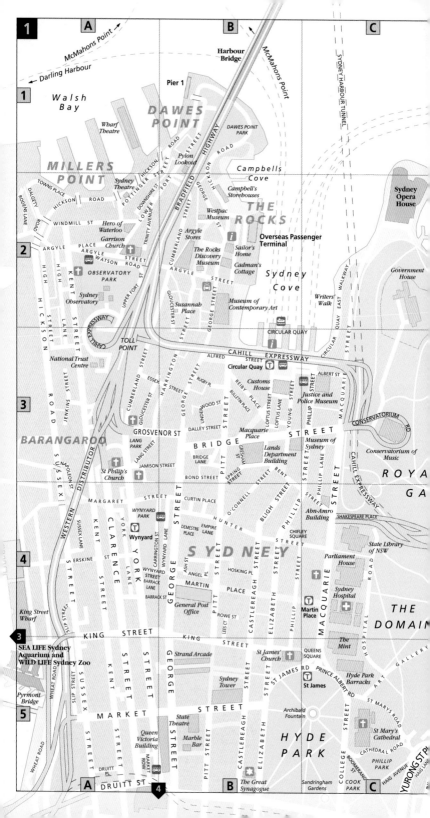

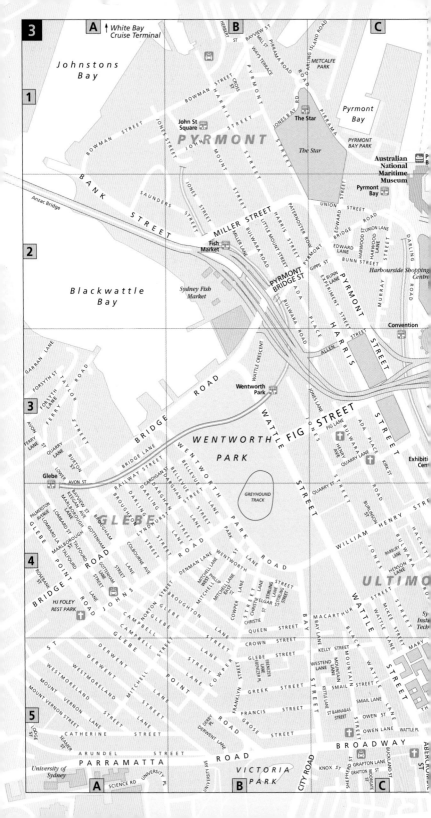

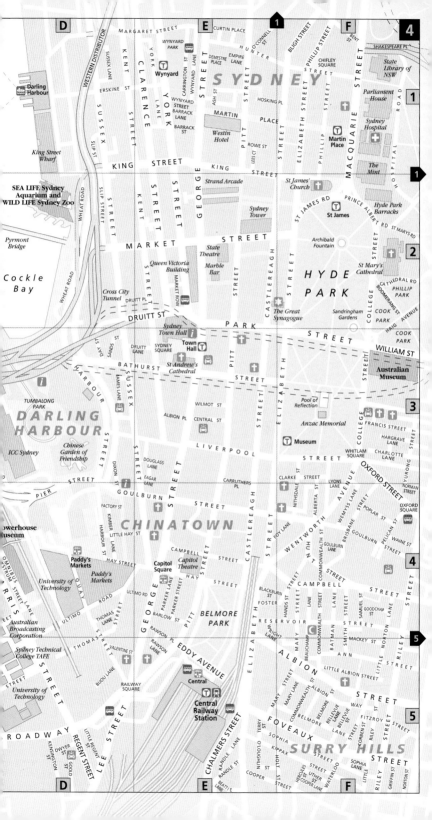

Street Finder Index

General Index

Acknowledgments

Dorling Kindersley would like to thank the following people whose help and assistance contributed to the preparation of this book.

Main Contributors

Ken Brass grew up on Sydney's Bondi Beach. He began his career in journalism with the *Sydney Morning Herald* and later worked as a London correspondent before becoming a staff writer on national daily newspapers in the United Kingdom. Returning home, he worked on the *Australian Women's Weekly, Weekend Australian* newspaper and *Australian Geographic* magazine. His photographs appear regularly in Australian magazines.

Kirsty McKenzie grew up on a sheep station in outback Queensland. She entered journalism after completing an arts degree. After making Sydney her home in 1980, she worked on a number of lifestyle and travel publications. Since becoming a freelance writer in 1987, she has regularly contributed to food, interior design and travel magazines.

Additional Text and Research

Angus Cameron, Leith Hillard, Kim Kitson, Siobhán O'Connor, Rupert Dean.

Additional Photography

Claire Edwards, Leanne Hogbin, Esther Labi, Siobhán O'Connor, Ian O'Leary, Carol Wiley.

Additional Illustrations

Leslye Cole, Stephen Conlin, Jon Gittoes, Steve Graham, Ray Grinaway, Helen Halliday, David Kirshner, Alex Lavroff, Iain McKellar, Chris Orr, Oliver Rennert.

Additional Cartography

Land Information Centre, Sydney.
Dorling Kindersley Cartography, Sydway.

Editorial and Design

Deputy Editorial Director Douglas Amrine
Deputy Art Directors Gillian Allan, Gaye Allen
Map Co-ordinators Michael Ellis, David Pugh
Production David Proffit
Picture Research Wendy Canning
DTP Designer Leanne Hogbin
Maps Gary Bowes, Fiona Casey, Casper Morris, Anna Nilsson, Christine Purcell, Richard Toomey (Era-Maptec Ltd)
Revisions Team: Emma Anacootee, Charis Atlas, Vandana Bhagra, Jenny Cattell, Louise Cleghorn, Sherry Collins, Stephanie Driver, Mariana Evmolpidou, Joy Fitzsimmons, Clare Forte, Anna Freiberger, Caroline Gladstone, Emily Green, Vinod Harish, Julia Harris-Voss, Gail Jones, Sumita Khatwani, Lisa Kosky, Priyanka Kumar, Esther Labi, Phoebe Lowndes, Jim Marks, Sam Merrell, Rebecca Milner, Sonal Modha, Kylie Mulquin, Rachel Neustein, Scarlett O'Hara, Louise Parsons, Helen Partington, Alok Pathak, Susie Peachey, Marianne Petrou, Clare Pierotti, Pure Content, Rada Radojicic, Ruth Reisenberger, Marisa Renzullo, Ellen Root, Sands Publishing Solutions, Ankita Sharma, Azeem Siddiqui, Susana Smith, Deborah Soden, Rachel Symons, Tracey Timpson, Richa Verma, Ros Walford, Dora Whitaker, Carol Wiley, Sophie Wright.

Index Hilary Bird

Special Assistance

Art Gallery of New South Wales, in particular Sherrie Joseph; Australian Museum, in particular Liz Wilson; Ann-Marie Bulat; the staff of Elizabeth Bay House; Historic Houses Trust; Lara Hookham; Info Direct, in particular Frank Tortora; Professor Max Kelly; Lou MacDonald; Adam Moore; Museum of Sydney, in particular Michelle Andringa; National Maritime Museum, in particular Jeffrey Mellefont and Bill Richards; National Trust of Australia (NSW), in particular Stewart Watters; Bridget O'Regan; Royal Botanic Garden Sydney, in particular Anna Hallett and Ed Wilson; State Transit Authority; Sydney Opera House, in particular David Brown and Valerie Tring; Diane Wallis.

Photography Permissions

Dorling Kindersley would like to thank all those who gave permission to photograph at various cathedrals, churches, museums, restaurants, hotels, shops, galleries and other sights too numerous to thank individually.

Picture Credits

a-above; b-below/bottom; c-centre; f-far; l-left; r-right; t-top.

Works of art have been reproduced with the permission of the following copyright holders:
© **Museum of Sydney** 1996: *Edge of the Trees* Janet Laurence and Fiona Foley, on the site of **First Government House**: 36tr, 87b.

The publisher would like to thank the following individuals, companies and picture libraries for their kind permission to reproduce their photographs:

ACP: 31cb, 32bc; **Adge Boutique Apartment Hotel**: 175tr; **Admiral Collingwood Lodge**: David Young 170c, 177br; **Alamy Stock Photo**: martin berry 101br; John Buxton 222br; byvalet 118; Maurice Crooks 235bc; CulturalEyes-AusGS 232cla; Chad Ehlers 34; frank'n'focus 228cra; Jeff Greenberg 218bc; Daniel Hewlett 222cr; *Aboriginal art painted on urban brick wall* by Danny and Jamie Eastwood Suzanne Long 8-9; Network Photographers 182cl; Debbie and Nigel Picknell 13clb; picturelibrary 98cl; sammy 200bl; Alan Smithers 219cla; richard sowersby 226br; Diane Stoney 197br; Travel-shots 183tl; Mike V 216-7; David Wall 183c; Rob Walls 124; Wildlight Photo Agency/Rob Cleary 219tr; Worldwide Picture Library 10br; **Andrew (Boy) Charlton Poolside Cafe**: 59tl, 193br; **ANZ National Bank Ltd**: 224cla; **Art Gallery of New South Wales**: *Portrait of Arthur Streeton* (date unknown) Grace Joel oil on canvas on hardboard, 55.6 x 40.7 cm, gift of Miss Joel 1925: 29cb; © Bundanon Trust 1996 *The Expulsion* 1947–48 Arthur Boyd (1920–99), oil on hardboard 99.5 x 119.6 cm: 35c; © Ms Stephenson-Meere 1996 *Australian Beach Pattern* 1940 Charles Meere (1890–1961) oil on canvas 91.5 x 122 cm: 37tl; © estate of the artist, courtesy Andindilkawa Land Council *Dugong Hunt* (1948) Jabarrgwa (Kneepad) Wurrabadalumba natural pigments on bark 46 x 95cm, gift of the Commonwealth Government 1956: 38b; *Bridge Pattern* Harold Cazneaux (1878–1953), gelatin silver photograph 29.6 x 21.4 cm, gift of the Cazneaux family 1975: 60bc(d); © AGNSW 1996 *Sofala* 1947 Russell Drysdale (1912–81), oil on canvas on hardboard 71.7 x 93.1 cm 110bl; *Mars and the Vestal Virgin* 1638 Jacques Blanchard 110cl; Margaret Preston *Wheelflower* (circa 1929) © Margaret Rose Preston Estate 113bl; © Tiwi Design Executive 1996 *Pukumani Grave Posts, Melville Island* 1958 various artists, natural pigments on wood 165.1 x 29.2 cm, gift of Dr Stuart Scougall 1959: 111tc; *The Golden Fleece* (1894) Tom Roberts (1856–1931), oil on canvas, 104 x 158.7 cm: 111br; *Natives on the Ouse River, Van Diemen's Land* 1838 John Glover, 111crb; *The Curve of the Bridge* 1928-9 Grace Cossington Smith 112cla; Brett Whiteley The balcony 2 1975 112tr; © Wendy Whitely 112bl, 113tr; **Arts Hotel Sydney**: 176tr; **Australian Museum**: C. Bento 22tl, 22clb,

22cb, 23tl, 23c, 23crb; 37bl, 90cr, 90crb, 91cra, 91crb; **Australian National Maritime Museum:** 96cl, 97tl; **AWL Images:** Walter Bibikow 119; Andrew Watson 62–3, 104. **Greg Barrett:** 209bc; **Bartel Photo Library:** 162bc; **Beppi's Restaurant:** 195tr; **Bet's B&B:** Peter Koudounas 172tl; **Big Hostel:** 179tr; **Mervyn G Bishop:** 24crb; Courtesy of **Bluetongue Brewery:** 185cl; **Bonza Bike Tours:** 230cla; **Botanic Gardens Trust, Sydney:** 106bc, Jaime Plaza 50bl; **BridgeClimb Sydney:** 70br, 73tl; **Bula'bula Arts:** Tony Dhanyula *Nyoka* (Mud Crabs), circa 1984, ochres and synthetic polymer on bark, J.W. Power Bequest, purchased 1984 by the Museum of Contemporary Art, Sydney 36clb; **Bridgeman Art Library:** private collection *Ned Kelly, Outlaw* (1946), oil on panel, Sir Sidney Nolan (1917–92) 33ca; **Botanical Gardens Trust, Sydney:** 106cla, 106bc.
Café Nice: 186bc; **Captain Cook Cruises:** 234cla; courtesy **City sightseeing:** 236br; **Corbis:** Richard Cummins 88tl; E. O. Hoppé 67cra; Reuters/Mick Tsikas 231tl; David Jones (Australia) P/l: 27crb(d).
Rupert Dean: 184cl, 184crb; **Dixson Galleries, State Library of New South Wales:** 22tr, 24blb(d), 28cla, 72tr, 140br; **Destination NSW-Tourism:** Hamilton Lund 221tl, 237cla; Phase IX 154tr; **Dreamstime.com:** Andrew Chambers 12br; Dcdigitalphoto 33tl, Esmehelit 32-33c, Sadequl Hussain 12tc; Jackmalipan 13tr; Kjuuurs 64; Lev Kropotov 95tc; Chaiwat Leelakojonkij 134bl, Chee-onn Leong 152–3; Pominoz 46clb, 233tl, Mark Ward 2-3; David May 130; Gordon Tipene 80; Volodymyr Vyshnivetskyy 47br; **Max Dupain:** 79br.
Fairfax Photo Library: 30bl; 54cra; 73br; 116cl(d); 79tc; ASCUI 53br; Dallen 33cra; Gerrit Fokkema 32br; Ken James 209tr; McNeil 122bl; White 45clb.
Fire and Rescue NSW (FRNSW): 222crb; **The Four in Hand Dining Room:** 180bl; **Four Seasons Hotel Sydney:** Elbow Room Productions 170br.
Getty images: Paco Alcantara 154tr; Image from Scott Gibbons 46tr; Pacific Press 32clb; Oliver Strewe 142; Stringer/ Brendon Thorne 45trl Stringer/Cole Bennetts 208cl; **Global Gossip Group:** 226br; **Government Printing Office Collection, State of New South Wales:** 28clb, 30clb, 78bl; **Guillaume Brahimi/The Cru - Media + Communications:** 194bc.
C Moore Hardy: 208br; **Hood Collection, State Library of New South Wales:** 73bl, 139br (d); **Hotel London, Paddington, Australia:** 126bc.
iStockphoto.com: Onfokus 100tr; sasimoto 92; ToolX95bl.
Lake's Folly Vineyards:161cr; **The Langham, Sydney:** 171tr; **Leura Gardens Festival Inc:** 50cr; **Liberty Wines:** 160cla; **Lonley Planet Images:** Juliet Coombe 11tr; **The Lord Nelson Brewery Hotel:** 172br, 187tr; **Lucio's Italian Restaurant:** 181bl; Courtesy **Luna Park Trust:** 134cl, 134tc.
Madame Nhu: 188tr; **Maya Restaurant:** 181tr, 196br; **The Mercantile Hotel:** Martin Brady 173tc; **Meriton Serviced Apartments:** 174bc; **Mitchell Library, State Library of New South Wales:** 23br, 23bcb, 24br(d), 24–5, 25tl, 25ca(d), 25cb, 26clb(d), 26cb(d), 26bl, 27tl, 27ca(d), 27bl(d), 28cr, 28bc, 28br, 29tl, 29br, 31ca(d), 31blb, 33cb, 73cra, 114tl; **David Moore:** 32cla; **Mount Franklin:** 185br; **Multiplex Property Services:**

100c; **Museum of Contemporary Art, Sydney:** 36cl, 66bl; Alex Davies 75tl.
National Library of Australia, Canberra: 26cla, 27brb(d), 29bc; **National Maritime Museum:** 24cl, 97cra; **Nature Focus:** Kevin Diletti 49br(d); John Fields 46bl; Pavel German 49tr; **Norman Lindsay Gallery:** Photo courtesy National Trust of Australia 163cr; **NSW Police Force:** 222cla.
Otto Ristorante/BLACK Communications: 192tr.
Pablo and Rusty's: 189br; **Parliament House:** The Hon Max Willis, RFD, ED, LLB, MLC, President, Legislative Council, Parliament of New South Wales. The Hon J Murray, MP, Speaker, Legislative Assembly, Parliament of New South Wales. Artist's original sketch of the historical painting in oils by Algernon Talmage, RA, *The Founding of Australia*. Kindly loaned to the Parliament of New South Wales by Mr Arthur Chard of Adelaide: 75bl; **Parramatta City Council:** S. Thomas 44tr; **Pier One Sydney Harbour:** 178bc; **Photolibrary.com:** David Messent 11bl, 229tl; images reproduced courtesy of **Powerhouse Museum:** 25br, 26bcb, 30cla, 30cb, 30bc, 31crb, 31bc, 36br; 103crb; 102–3; all, John-Francois Lanzarone 102cla; Tyrrell Collection 108tc.
Radisson Blu Plaza Hotel: Gerry O'Leary 171bl; **The Rocks Discovery Museum:** 67tl.
Sepia Restaurant: 190bc; **Simon Johnson Purveyor of Quality Foods:** 221bl; **Southcorp Wines Europe:** 185tr; **State Library of Tasmania:** 24clb; **Stopmotion:** 162tr; **Suzie Thomas Publishing:** Thomas O'Flynn 76bc, © DACS, London 2011, 78clb; **Superstock:** Digital Vision 10cl; **Sydney Film Festival:** 53cb; **Sydney Fish Market:** 202cl, 202cr. **Sydney Freelance:** J Boland 51cl; **Sydney Jewish Museum:** 37br; **Sydney Opera House Trust:** 76tr, 76cla, 77tc, 77br, 77bl, 78br, 79cla, 79ca, 79cra, 79c; Lisa Tomasetti 78cl; Willi Ulmer Collection 79bc; **Sydney Restaurant Group:** 196tr; **Sydney Tower Eye:** 85br; **Sydney Wilderness Tours:** 154tr.
Taronga Zoo: 136br, 137cra, 137bl; Paul Fahy 136tr, 137cla, 137cr. **Tebutt's VII Restaurant and Function Centre:**158clb.
University of Technology, Sydney/uts.edu.au: Coptercam 132br.**Transport for NSW:** 233crb; © Transport for NSW 2015 233cra, © Transport for NSW 2016 233cr, 233br, 235c, 236cl, 236c.
Vintage Estates: 161ca.
Westfield Sydney: 83crb; **WILD LIFE Sydney Zoo:** courtesy of Merlin Entertainments Group 99 all.
Yalumba Wines: 184cra.
Young Henrys Brewing & Distilling: 185cr.

Front Endpaper: **Alamy Images:** Rob Walls Rcr; sasimoto Lbc; **AWL Images:** Walter Bibikow Rcra; Andrew Watson Rtc; **Dreamstime.com:** Kjuuurs Lcl; Gordon Tipene Lclb; **iStockphoto.com:** byvalet Rtc.

Map cover: Getty / Guy Vanderelst
Cover – Front and spine: Getty / Guy Vanderelst';
Back: Dreamstime.com: Gordon Bell

All other images © Dorling Kindersley.
For further information see: www.dkimages.com